C. Curtis.

PELICAN BOOKS

The Puritans in Africa:
A History of Afrikanerdom

Willem de Klerk was born in Marquard, South Africa, in 1917, but was mainly brought up in the Cape. He graduated from Grey College, University of Stellenbosch, in law and practised at the Cape Bar from 1941 to 1946, when he left to devote his time to writing novels and plays in Afrikaans. His works have been widely read and performed in South Africa and he has broadcast both at home and abroad.

Since the 1940s he has been involved with other writers in questioning the dominant political and social tendencies in South Africa; notably with Marthinus Versfeld, with whom he has collaborated in several publications. He was a direct influence on younger writers who later developed the Sestiger (Sixties) renewal-movement in Afrikaans literature. A member of the South African Academy of Arts and Sciences, he has won most of the South African literary awards for Afrikaans writing, including the Grey College Centenary Medal in 1956. He has toured widely in Germany and the U.S.A. and written in English on the white wines of the Cape. Among his most important works are *The Thirstland* (*Die Laer*, a novel) and *Beyond the Framework* (*Buite die Raamwerk*, a literary-philosophical essay on the Tyranny of the Idea). Willem de Klerk now lives and farms at Saffier in Klein-Drakenstein.

W. A. de Klerk

The Puritans in Africa:
A History of Afrikanerdom

Penguin Books
In association with Rex Collings Ltd

Penguin Books Ltd,
Harmondsworth, Middlesex, England
Penguin Books,
625 Madison Avenue, New York, New York 10022, U.S.A.
Penguin Books Australia Ltd,
Ringwood, Victoria, Australia
Penguin Books Canada Ltd,
41 Steelcase Road West, Markham, Ontario, Canada
Penguin Books (N.Z.) Ltd,
182–190 Wairau Road, Auckland 10, New Zealand

First published by Rex Collings Ltd 1975
Published in Pelican Books 1976

Copyright © W. A. de Klerk, 1975

Made and printed in Great Britain by
C. Nicholls & Company Ltd,
The Philips Park Press, Manchester
Set in Monotype Plantin

Contents

Acknowledgements

My sincere thanks go to various people who in some or other way, at some or other stage, were concerned with the writing of this book. These include the late Mr Les Webb, Prof. J. J. Degenaar, Prof. Monica Wilson and Senator Denis Worrall. More than anybody else, however, Dr Francis Wilson contributed by way of intelligent criticism and discussion. For example, the opening up of a key theme in the book, the true nature of the Reformed heritage, was a direct result of this. To him I express a very special word of appreciation. My thanks must also extend to Mrs Rolien Smith for her valiant typing and retyping of the script.

Last but not least, my debt is towards my own people, in whose communal life, in whose tradition, I must fully share, for good or ill, for better or for worse. With them I have conducted a life-long dialogue on their particular human existence here in the far south of a vast continent.

Because, in so many ways, he represented the best in their heritage, this writing is dedicated to the memory of A. M. Hugo. He died, aged 45, on 24th January, 1975.

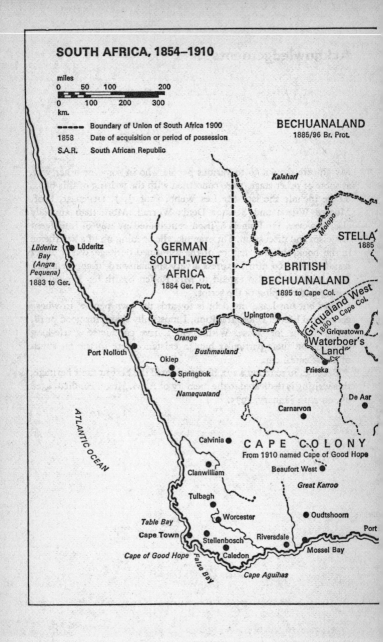

SOUTH AFRICA, 1854–1910

miles
0   50   100   200
0   100   200   300
km.

- - - - - Boundary of Union of South Africa 1900
1858   Date of acquisition or period of possession
S.A.R.   South African Republic

BECHUANALAND
1885/96 Br. Prot.

Kalahari

Lüderitz Bay (Angra Pequena)
1883 to Ger.

● Lüderitz

GERMAN SOUTH-WEST AFRICA
1884 Ger. Prot.

Molopo

STELLA
1885

BRITISH BECHUANALAND
1895 to Cape Col.

Griqualand West
1880 to Cape Col.

● Upington

Orange

● Griquatown
Waterboer's Land

● Port Nolloth

Bushmauland

Okiep
●- Springbok

Namaqualand

● Prieska

ATLANTIC OCEAN

● Carnarvon

● De Aar

● Calvinia

CAPE COLONY
From 1910 named Cape of Good Hope

● Clanwilliam

● Beaufort West

Great Karroo

● Tulbagh

● Oudtshoorn

● Worcester

Table Bay
Cape Town ●
● Stellenbosch
● Caledon

● Riversdale

Port

Cape of Good Hope   *False Bay*

● Mossel Bay

Cape Aguihas

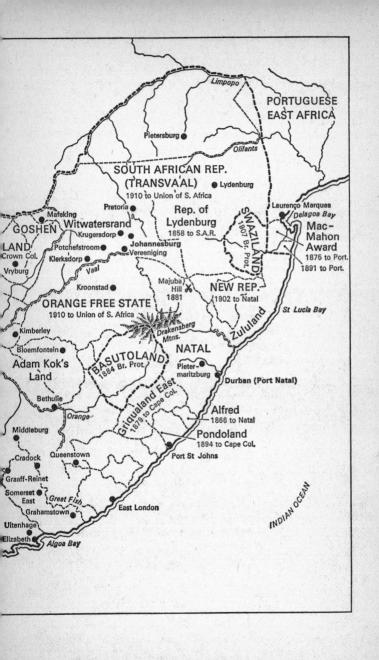

Limpopo

PORTUGUESE
EAST AFRICA

Pietersburg

Olifants

SOUTH AFRICAN REP.
(TRANSVAAL)
1910 to Union of S. Africa

Lydenburg

Pretoria

Rep. of
Lydenburg
1858 to S.A.R.

SWAZILAND
1907 Br. Prot.

Laurenço Marques
Delagoa Bay

Mac–
Mahon
Award
1875 to Port.
1891 to Port.

Mafeking

GOSHEN

Witwatersrand

Krugersdorp

LAND

Crown Col.

Potchefstroom

Johannesburg
Vereeniging

Klerksdorp

Vryburg

Vaal

Kroonstad

Majuba
Hill
1881

NEW REP.
1902 to Natal

ORANGE FREE STATE
1910 to Union of S. Africa

Zululand

St Lucia Bay

Kimberley

Drakensberg
Mtns.

Bloemfontein

Adam Kok's
Land

BASUTOLAND
1884 Br. Prot.

NATAL

Pieter-
maritzburg

Durban (Port Natal)

Bethulie

Orange

Griqualand East
1879 to Cape Col.

Alfred
1866 to Natal

Middleburg

Pondoland
1894 to Cape Col.

Cradock

Queenstown

Port St Johns

Graaff-Reinet

Somerset
East

Great Fish

East London

Grahamstown

Uitenhage

Elizabeth

Algoa Bay

INDIAN OCEAN

To be immersed in the human situation is to assume without illusion, in the mood of playful irony, all that life requires from us. It means accepting, with the prospect of humour, conflict, struggle, disaster, death, never surrendering to depression or guilt, but rather to the knowledge of human frailty; to meet the world as it comes, knowing that life can and should be a shining experience.

Introduction: A Human Study

This is a book about the attempt by a small people, totalling no more than the population of an average-sized American or European city, to remake their particular world to the concept of a rational plan from the radical Right. In no other way can the modern Afrikaners be understood.

South Africa, more particularly the Afrikaners – for it is their political philosophy which has generated the considerable postwar attention from distant shores – has been described as 'a very strange society'. This is true enough, but not so much in the sense of their having conceived a revolutionary political idea or of their having implemented it in a variety of singular ways. Rather, the situation in which they find themselves is unusually relentless, intricate and dismaying. Whether history has seen anything at all similar remains an open question. The piece of social reconstruction which has become known to the world as 'apartheid', but which Afrikaners themselves generally in a more positivist mood have preferred to call 'separate development', is an attempt to deal with the situation in fundamental concepts, formulating it anew in terms of what is intensely believed to be freedom.

'Apartheid' is an attempt to remake a society in the total vision of a socio-political ideal. As such it is yet another of the many secular manifestations with their roots in the protestant ethic of a particular order, which the past two centuries have known. It is radical because it is the politics of redemption trying to reach down to man's existential roots. It is rational because it is an extensive human exercise of the mind, endeavouring to formulate a moral justification for what is basically the will to power.

Nothing bespeaks the 'human condition' so eloquently as the cry from the heart that we are the instruments of Providence: or of History, which may well be the substitute for Providence.

The abstractions of freedom are always, beyond our recognition, the fruit of our despair. Safety in power is what we are after; but naked power for Western Christian man, especially those in the Calvinist–Puritan tradition, is not in order. What is done should also be morally justifiable. Hence the cry from the heart, affirming the rightness of what we do, passionately denying our despair.

The cry is grandiloquent, strident, defiant, sentimental, sober or solemn, according to the particular life-style of which it forms a part. It might be the absolute individual at the top of a hierarchy seeing himself as God's special instrument. It may be the collective passion of a class, people, nation, institution, church, or the state.

It has been the claim of kings, emperors, prime ministers, dictators: James I of England, Napoleon Bonaparte, the Führer of the Third Reich, Hendrik Verwoerd, Idi Amin and a host of others. It has consistently been the claim of puritan radicals for some centuries now, who believed that they had been called not only to govern, but also to remake society from the roots upwards. The very pursuit of the ideal, however, guarantees a conclusion which is its substantive denial.

The messianic style of the post-Second World War Afrikaners finds no substantial antecedents in those countries from which they predominantly originated: the Netherlands, Germany, France. Strangely, as will appear, their spiritual kin are rather to be discovered in the Anglo-Saxon world, particularly New England.

The key to the Afrikaners is Calvinism. But the primitive or original Calvin will be insufficient to explain the modern Afrikaners. It is especially the subtle mutations which Calvinism underwent in the Puritan mind of the Anglo-Saxon world which become relevant. Finally, it is the phenomenon of political idealism, engendered in the same *milieu*, which provides a fuller perspective.

All this means that a proper study of the Afrikaners needs attention also to the thought, motivations and actions of the

Puritans, in both Old and New England. The strangest thing about the Afrikaners will then be seen to be the fact that they are so like the very people who have probably looked more critically at them than any other. In a sense, it is a family quarrel.

The discovery of a variety of parallels between the Afrikaners of our time, pursuing their vision of redemption, and the Anglo-Saxon Puritans, establishing their Holy Commonwealths and finally constituting the Rights of Man, is no attempt to justify historicism. The case-history of the Afrikaners is not offered as further proof of the ineluctability of human existence. It is rather another demonstration of the vast potential for, and the realities of, human error. If tragi-comedy were not a necessary part of man's free intelligence, there would be neither great literature nor great art.

Shakespeare might well have sensed the fibre of the developing age, when England was gathering her spiritual forces for the coming struggle. Hamlet is the model of all who are seized with a tremendous but fatal urge to mend the rottenness around them:

> . . . to take arms against a sea of troubles
> And by opposing end them . . .

The world with its oppressors' wrongs, the law's delay, the ubiquitous insolence of office, must be set aright. The future, for time and eternity, must be secured now, whatever the cost.

If only everybody knew that what he was opposing with such righteous passion now, he would in time be defending.

This is whatever as absolute pretends to be our own, rational and radical, solution to life. These are the Anglo-Saxon revolutionaries in Old and New England, working, talking, fighting for their Commonwealths. These are the Jacobins, washing away the sins of the world in the blood of the guillotine. These are the Marxist-Leninist Communists, burningly devoted to the cause of alienated man. These are the capitalist philanthropists of the twentieth century declaring themselves to be, at last, collaborators with God. These are the Afrikaners of our time, utterly concerned with the re-structuring of their own society, with a view to lasting racial peace, order and goodwill. Common to all is the conscious striving after definitive social justice, which for that very reason will become injustice. Here lies the most consistent expression of the irony of history. By the same token, here lies the tragi-comedy of puritan man.

Nothing is so elevating but at the same time so potentially destructive as the socio-political ideal. It is both dread and glory.

Part One: A Story Outline

1 Lost in Africa

It is a singular fact that for approximately the first century-and-a-half of European occupation of the bottom end of Africa there was a relatively small amount of change. The next century-and-a-half saw it all: the growth of peoples, institutions, possessions, tensions and, finally, conflict.

What Southern Africa had not known up to the closing decade of the eighteenth century – the clash of cultures, the struggle for ascendancy, the emergence of figures of true magnitude, Boer, British, Bantu, all within the context of, on the one hand, the Calvinist ethic, on the other hand, the barbarism of indigenous peoples – now became the tenor of succeeding ages.

Who were these reluctant early settlers, these primal ancestors of the people who in time would be known as the Afrikaners?

By the mid-seventeenth century, the voyages of men like Diaz, Columbus, Da Gama, Magellan and Drake had already for a century-and-three-quarters held Europe in a state of wonder. This astonishing opening-up of the new world, accompanied by conquest and colonization, had taken place in spite of almost incessant struggle between the peoples of Europe and their leaders. It had been the times of the Reformation, the Huguenot Civil Wars in France, the English Revolution, the painful and protracted rise of the Dutch Republic. It had finally been the formless torment of the Thirty Years War.

In 1648 in the *Friedensaal* of Münster in Westphalia peace was at last declared. It was also the formal end of the eighty years of resistance of the Dutch people to the imperial might of Hapsburg Spain.

The seventeenth century became the golden age of Holland. At the University of Leyden, where scholars like Hugo de Groot and Arminius taught, there were some 2000 students. Other fine universities were at Groningen, Utrecht, Franeker and Harder-wyk. Frans Hals, Jan Steen, Rembrandt van Ryn and many others, were interpreting their landscapes and contemporaries in luminous canvases. The theatre was lively and poetry flourished. Bredero, Huygens, Van den Vondel and others were being eagerly read and produced.

Ever since Diaz had charted the unknown on his way to India, the Portuguese had been the high adventurers on the oceans. In 1503, Antonio de Saldanha had been the first on record to anchor in Table Bay. He was also the first white man to see the wondrous view from the top of Table Mountain. The legendary Kingdom of Monomotapa lay somewhere in those blue distances; and the legendary golden city of Vigiti Magna lay there as well. It was a remarkable self-fulfilling legend, as time would prove.

The Dutch were the first to compete fully with the Portuguese. It was nevertheless only after the Jesuits had extended their missionary activities to the Zambezi (1560) and English ships had already put in at Table Bay (1591) that the Dutch found their way round the Cape to the Far East (1595). Seven years later the Dutch East India Company – the V.O.C.* – was founded. Soon the Dutch as militant traders were offering the Portuguese serious competition.

Health, the early voyagers had discovered, could be maintained by a sufficient diet of fresh meat, vegetables and fruit. The Cape was two-thirds of the way to Batavia, and the directors of the V.O.C. duly decided that a victualling station here would be of great assistance. They had been especially moved to this decision by the enthusiastic accounts of two returned castaways.

The Cape was founded neither as a colony of the United Provinces nor by conquest with the idea of opening up and developing the sub-continent. It was simply to enable a most unusual organization like the V.O.C. to pursue its imperial commercial interest, in the East generally but more particularly in the East Indies.

---

*V.O.C. being the abbreviated initials of *Generale Vereenigde Nederlantsche Geoctroyeerde Oostindische Compagnie*.

Capital was raised by national subscription. Local boards were established in the various states of the United Netherlands. There was a general directorate of sixty members, of which Amsterdam and Zeeland, with twenty and twelve directors respectively, were in the majority. A collegium of seventeen formed the board of control. The capitalism of the V.O.C. belonged to an older, simpler order than the vast consumer structures of present times. They were, in fact, in the tradition of the great commercial cities of the Netherlands, whose civic splendour and fine handicrafts had already established their fame in the Middle Ages. In the thirteenth century, cities like Ghent, Bruges, Leyden and Rotterdam had become the centres of large industrial populations. At the battle of Courtrai (1302) the people of the Netherlands resisted the nobility of France and won a victory for the common man.

The Flemish freedom-hero, Jacob van Aertevelde, however, saw his son killed and his people defeated at Roosebeke. The political and commercial greatness of the cities then declined. What the Netherlands subsequently experienced was first Burgundian, then Spanish Hapsburg, dominion. The worst period was the hard military rule of the Duke of Alva, veteran Spanish general, from 1568 to 1573. North and South in the Netherlands – the South being Catholic, the North being effectively Calvinist – were divided in 1579. The northern provinces were finally established as a confederation by the Union of Utrecht.

The Dutch spirit, having met the massive challenge of Spain, was now free to express itself in its full creativity. Law, art and literature would flourish, but so would commerce. The V.O.C. was the epitome of this.

The Company had the right to conduct its own military operations, to declare war and make peace. In October 1740, for example, it would indulge in the general massacre of Chinese in Batavia. It could enter into treaties, pass its own laws and administer its own territories as it thought fit. By 1619, it had established its imperial capital at Batavia, formerly Jakarta. From the thirties to the fifties, the Portuguese were driven out of Ceylon. Malacca was taken in the forties. Sumatra was gained by treaty in the sixties. In time, the V.O.C. had not only a great fleet of trading ships, but also a considerable army and navy of its own. Some thousands of functionaries served it. Each return fleet from the East Indies, sailing in convoy, carried merchandise from the East worth a fortune. Towards the end of the seventeenth century it was paying a dividend of some forty per cent.

For all practical purposes, the V.O.C. was an imperium within a state. It maintained its own Christian standards. Its Calvinism was that of the Synod of Dort (1618), which had been as much a scene of political conflict as theological argument. It was a workaday, down-to-earth Protestantism and it served its purpose. This was to administer to the personal spiritual needs of the Protestant Dutch. It included nothing like the fundamental social reconstruction of the Puritans of Old and New England.

This explains the vast difference in the earlier development of two groups of peoples in the new worlds, from largely the same Germanic backgrounds. Both found themselves in the seventeenth and eighteenth centuries in a wild and unbroken landscape; both crossed a still largely unchartred ocean to arrive there. The English Calvinist community went to New England; the Dutch Calvinist community to the Cape.

Already in the seventeenth century, towns in Massachusetts were expected to provide all facilities for lower education. Harvard College had been founded in 1636. The Congregational Church was jealously independent and exclusive. Much of the private wealth, which was to play such an important part in the history of America, had by the mid-eighteenth century already been assured.

Connecticut and Rhode Island were the first to point the way to civil and religious liberties. Here, too, education was soon a priority. Grammar schools taught the classics in Boston, New Haven and Hartford.

The New England landscape was cold and forbidding. Yet it had obvious advantages for vigorous economic growth. There was primeval forest providing an abundance of timber. There was good soil, once the trees had been cleared. There were rivers and harbours. Above all, and in spite of colonial status, there were royal charters, within which the communities could act more or less as independent polities. The culmination of these activities was the part played in the Declaration of Independence in 1776. As such, New England became a decisive force in the history of America and of the world.

Nothing similar was to take place at the Cape. By the end of the eighteenth century, the community here had politically and educationally made almost no progress. The freemen were living partly in relative isolation in their lovely Cape valleys, and partly at the eastern frontier, in even greater isolation.

In 1788 Spenlin, field chaplain of the Würtenburg regiment at the Cape, drafted in desperation a memorandum in which he proposed an Education Institute, with himself as its head, to meet the need for proper instruction. After all the years of V.O.C. administration, the only institutions of 'higher learning' at the Cape itself were a 'Latin School', revived after sixty-five years; an abortive Military School; and a private 'French School', run by one Ziegler. Neither had there been any broadening of school syllabuses since the founding of the colony.

In the inland Cape the position was even more unsatisfactory. Colonists living on distant farms had the choice either of educating their own children to the best of their ability, relying on the Scriptures and also, if they were lucky, on an elementary textbook; or of making use of inadequately-trained V.O.C. functionaries.

Why this tardy development?

Geography provides a partial answer. At the Cape there were no great forests. The rivers descended steeply from the mountains and were of almost no economic benefit. The soil seemed to be patchy, because it had never been properly examined. The only really good harbour was at Saldanha Bay, situated far from Table Valley in a waterless area. There were no prospects for local industries, such as the shipbuilding or whaling of New England. There were almost no opportunities for trade. The Cape was twice as far from Europe as Boston. Produce could only be sold to ships stopping over in Table Bay. The only export markets were in Batavia and Ceylon, and these were chancy.

Except for the handful of French refugees which came to

settle at the Cape during the last quarter of the seventeenth
century, there was never anything like organized immigration.
The prospects, judging from appearances, of the hinterland
being the seat of a viable Western community were poor. Such
independent immigrants as did arrive during the seventeenth
and eighteenth centuries were mostly wanderers.

All this retarded development. But it might well have been
overcome – as a later age would prove – were it not for the looming edifice of the V.O.C. In its great shadow, nothing could grow.
The remarkable thing is not that the Afrikaners as a people took
so long to emerge, but that they emerged at all.

The best that can be said of the early V.O.C. outpost in
Table Valley under Jan van Riebeeck was that it bravely struggled to make the Cape a worthwhile place to stop at on the long
voyage to India. Van Riebeeck's journal is the evidence of this.
It contains circumstantial accounts of erecting fortifications and
other buildings; of provision for visiting ships and for the
entertainment of their commands; of dealing with the wayward
Khoi-khoi (Hottentots); of establishing gardens and plantations;
of struggling in all this with inadequate labour; of punishing
those who failed to behave in a manner befitting servants of the
V.O.C.; of fighting the elements . . . and so on.

After more than ten years as commander of the settlement,
Van Riebeeck left at last in 1663 for Batavia. There he became
secretary for the Council for India. He nevertheless expressed
the hope that those remaining would help to make the Cape a
progressive settlement. He almost certainly did not have an
extensive community of Europeans in mind.

The Cape, from the start, was inordinately expensive. It was
no easy task feeding everyone in the service of the Company.
Ships, too, were at times few and far between. Rice and other
food had often to be imported.

In 1657 it had therefore been considered expedient to grant
a number of those employed by the Company rights as freemen.
Land for farming would be given them. They would also receive
other assistance. Nine, in this way, soon established themselves
on the banks of the Liesbeeck.

The position was clear. The Company needed a few independent producers, farming within defined limits, to supply the Company and help curtail expenses. The first freemen – the first burghers – can rightly be said to have formed the nucleus of what would in time be the Afrikaners.

After some brush with the authorities in 1707, a young man of Stellenbosch, one Hendrik Bibault, claimed special consideration on the grounds of his being a man of Africa. 'Ik ben een Afrikaander!'* he shouted exultantly to those who had come to arrest him. What he was saying in effect was that he belonged to the land as much as any Bushman or Hottentot.

The freemen were mainly Dutch and Low Germans, roughly in proportion of two to one. A sprinkling of Scandinavians, French and even a few English were included. During the first decade of the settlement, up until the departure of Van Riebeeck, some 235 had already found a fragile independence. The petty citizenry, mainly from the Netherlands and the neighbouring parts of Germany, who accepted service with the V.O.C., included a fair number of people who had been displaced by the Thirty Years War west of the Rhine, and the Eighty Years War in the Netherlands. These were adventurers, libertines and the like who took service, dreaming of riches awaiting them in the East Indies. There were many others, however, who had simply been impressed into service with the V.O.C. by the so-called *zielverkoopers*, the sellers of souls. The name was derived from the purchase of a *ceel* – seal – by the 'volunteer', being a promissory note against future wages. They were moved to this action by lavish hospitality and much talk of future riches.

Those who found themselves on their way, not to India but to the Cape, were, in the main, whatever their origins, part of a background where the struggle against oppression in its most uncompromising form had already continued for almost three centuries.

The coming of the French Huguenots in 1688 served to strengthen this tradition. They, too, were displaced people who had preferred to leave their ancestral environments and had undertaken the hazardous voyage to a remote and unknown country.

*'I am an Afrikander!'

In 1705, the Dutch/German freemen and the French Huguenots found common cause in opposing a progressive but corrupt governor in the person of W. A. van der Stel. He was the son of Simon van der Stel, most imaginative of the V.O.C. governors.

Old Simon loved the Cape. In 1699, when he was succeeded in the governorship by his son, he retired to the lovely Constantia Valley. There he developed orchards and vineyards and built a great manor house. Time was when the wines of Constantia were lauded by literary artists like Jane Austen, Klopstock and Baudelaire.

Simon had sensed the possibilities at Stellenbosch – so named by him – on the far side of the Cape flatland, separating the peninsula from the great mountain ranges to the east. He had a passion for planting trees, especially oaks. Some of them still grace the Cape landscape.

Trees are planted where men dream of the future, where they foresee permanence and development. The van der Stels were more enterprising, more bound to the Cape soil, than the normal run of V.O.C. officials. No doubt they recognized a potential in the land which few, if any, before them had considered. Simon's development of Groot Constantia was the testimony to this. So was his son's development of another great estate – Vergelegen in Hottentots-Holland – where the eastern mountains sweep down to the sea.

Dutch and Huguenot freemen were by this time living scattered about in the valleys of Stellenbosch and Drakenstein. As far as W. A. van der Stel was concerned they were of little import; in fact expendable. The very limited Cape market, which was dependent also upon the shipping in Table Bay, the governor needed for himself. After all, who were these burghers? They or their parents had arrived as nothing. They were still nothing. The same applied to the Huguenots, who had been brought out by the Company and were at the Cape on sufferance. Moreover, there was sufficient evidence that the freemen, under the pretence of barter, had been robbing the Hottentots. This had to be stopped.

But the freemen on their farms had long since outgrown whatever allegiance they had once felt towards the Company. The governor had sought to exclude them from the only livelihoods open to them, that of supplying the Company or the ships. He, of course, needed the markets for himself. His expenditure at Vergelegen, where he was employing the most efficient methods, was considerable.

For the freemen this was corruption and tyranny and called for action. The governor struck back. The leaders of the protest were arrested, locked up and banished mainly to Batavia and Mauritius. Four, however, were shipped to Patria, the United Netherlands. This proved to be disastrous – for the governor.

When he realized what he had done, he set off in a galliot in hot pursuit. The attempt to fetch the four back did not succeed, however, and the governor spent an uncomfortable night on an off-shore island.

In spite of feverish attempts to manufacture a counter-petition, the feast for van der Stel was over. The Council of Seventeen, having heard and accepted the evidence, acted accordingly.

On a dark night early in 1707, a young man named Van Emmenes went galloping through the streets of Stellenbosch on horseback, shouting: 'Victory!' Others came tumbling out of bed and soon the news was confirmed: the governor had been ordered back to the Netherlands. Freedom had triumphed.

As a political expression, however, it was an isolated incident. Revolt of firmer substance would have to wait until these expendables – the emergent Afrikaners – in their choice of isolation on the frontier had discovered in themselves a common identity.

It would take the English, more precisely the British, finally to effect this. But nearly a century-and-a-half would have passed before it could all come about.

Freedom is central to the human dilemma. So it is to the story of the Afrikaners. This does not mean that its human articulation would be a guarantee of its wholeness. For the human passion for freedom so easily becomes the invitation to irony, to a reversal of the rôles. In time the Afrikaners, too, following their deepest urges, would be led into stupendously difficult situations.

Trek or war, which would also become part of their history, would then be seen as relative simplicities. A time would come when, surrounded by vastly involved ethnic, sociological, economic and political factors, they would endeavour to meet it all by radical means. But in the early eighteenth century, when they were only just beginning to discover their own identity, the issues were elementary.

Here they were, a group of West European people, a mere fragment, which had found itself sharing not only a common landscape but also a common cause. What bound them together, in the deepest sense, was the Calvinist ethic. True enough, they had long since ceased to find a free intellectual discussion going on around them concerning this matter. Yet, rather strangely, the Calvinist tradition had remained alive.

The land, too, spoke to them in a language they collectively understood. It was a deeply appealing land. Its perspectives were vast. Its mountains in the distance were infinitely blue; its shores and seas awesomely beautiful; its far inland plains like another ocean. Everywhere there were wild animals: herds of antelopes, carnivores, elephants . . .

There had been a basic, unbearable contradiction to their remaining where they had been at the start, within the shadow of Table Mountain and of the Company. Only some remained in Table Valley and other parts of the Peninsula. These were individual families, developing patrician styles to suit those of the V.O.C. functionaries at the apex of the predominantly floating officialdom in and around the Castle of Good Hope.

Those who had settled in the Cape valleys of Stellenbosch, Hottentots-Holland, Drakenstein and the Land of Waveren (Tulbagh), not so distant from the Castle, had nevertheless to contend with isolation. Cut off from the brilliant academic life of the Netherlands, with no intellectuals, inadequate schools, no professional or merchant classes, hardly any public institutions, not a single publication of their own, the colonists were culturally severed from their own background. Only the church afforded them some relief. For the rest, as the eighteenth century developed, they gradually compensated by making furniture, and building houses that have captivated succeeding generations. In this, they were assisted by slaves from the East who became their close associates.

Materials for the houses and furniture were found locally: clay for the bricks; yellow-wood and stinkwood from the mountain ravines – in a noble combination – for joinery and cabinet-making; lime for the whitewash. The architecture was marvellously blended to the Cape landscape. It was John Ruskin who would later write that '. . . the only contribution to domestic architecture for several centuries was made by the Dutch at the Cape'.

Old Cape houses impress a modern viewer not merely because of their classicist or baroque charm, but also often for their sheer physical dimensions. Their spaciousness is strangely in contrast to the meagre proportions of the economy out of which they grew. Such was the isolation of these builders, who lived so distantly and self-sufficiently, that they knew next to nothing of Europe's tremendous Age of Enlightenment; nor could they have cared. The sixty-six books of the Bible were sufficient for all their educational purposes.

There they farmed in their deep valleys, between enchanting ranges of blue, sandstone mountains, superimposed on granite and cut by deep ravines, from which crystal streams emerged. They built their houses, tilled their fields and tended their vineyards. There was no reason to extend their lands, to increase production. What would they have done with the surplus? Sales of produce – of wheat and wine – were to the Company alone. They were wholly dependent upon the whims and manipulations of the V.O.C.

Often there had been talk of more white immigration, perhaps on the lines of the Huguenots. A high-ranking V.O.C. official, D. P. de Chavonnes, had once favoured it. White labourers could then be substituted for the slaves imported from the East. The plan was hardly workable. By the middle of the century, it was clear that more white settlers, not officially in the employ of the V.O.C. and left to their own designs, would only deepen the economic slough.

Apart from the Huguenots, the only sizable group to reach the Cape before the end of the eighteenth century were young German soldiers who had come out to help man the Cape garrison. The human stream remained slight. Even then it had divided. The surplus freemen, the grazier/hunters, finding the Cape Valleys already occupied – as they judged – looked eastwards and northwards and saw the mountains, range upon range, stretching away mysteriously. The clarity of the air added to their vision. From the slopes of the hills, from the tops of the mountains, they could see into measureless distances:

> *Spread to most distant ends as light*
> *where last strange stars fade out of sight*
> *each one in God is so diffused,*
> *no sign of pain could here be used,*
> *where all in all are lost in light.**

A modern Afrikaans poet, describing the journey of the soul in the twentieth century, would naturally use the language and metaphors of his ancestral landscape.

People whose parents or grandparents had been mainly petty citizenry of the ravaged lowlands of Western Europe – or who themselves had been – became hunters and graziers in a land of extensive mountains, valleys, plateaux and plains. Skills which they could not have been conscious of were called forth by the land itself. This was the more authentic Africa. It demanded the hardier pioneer and constant adaptation to the unknown quantities of a new, even stranger environment than the Cape.

It was no mass movement, as it had never been organized. It was rather a case of individual families, or small groups, moving off as subsistence required; following routes as necessity defined, usually to where the waters were. Fountains, *vleis*,† streams, pans ... this is where they settled.

At the Cape, and in the Cape valleys, the names of farms were inclined to be formally elegant, reminiscent of life in the V.O.C. or in the wake of it. There was Groot Constantia, Vergelegen, Meerlust, Schoongezicht, Libertas ... In the case of those whose background was French, it was reminiscent of Europe: Champagne, Languedoc, La Dauphine, Rhône, La Provence ... But the grazier/hunters named their places: Elandsvlei, Klaarstroom,

---

* N. P. van Wyk Louw (from *Dialogue of the Dead*, translated by William and Jean Branford).

† Small, shallow lakes.

Riviersonderend, Bitterputs Put-Sonder-Water, Soebatsfontein
...*

The movement penetrated into lands inhabited by Khoi-khoi and Bushmen. Game was hunted and so were the Bushmen. The Hottentots, herders themselves, whose numbers at various times during the eighteenth century had been severely cut by smallpox, moved ahead to other, more distant fields.

The Bushmen lived off the game; and when the game, after the new intruders had arrived, had soon been severely diminished, the Bushmen stole their sheep and cattle. Until well into the eighteenth century it was, at times, a deadly struggle. The Bushmen, as instinctive and immensely mobile as animals, used bows and poisoned arrows. The settlers found them thoroughly dangerous.

From time to time all sorts of administrative and legislative gestures were made from the Castle of Good Hope, signalling over great distances to those who were moving further and further away, that there was still an authority to which they owed allegiance. But as the century advanced, the torpor of the V.O.C. could only increase.

The two elements of the emergent Afrikaners, each moving away from the other, already shared a common speech. They were now using the language of Van den Vondel, Bredero, Grotius and others, the elevated High Dutch of the Golden Age of the Netherlands, in a new way. Their daily conversation with slaves, many of whom had come from the Malay Archipelago, compelled them to re-structure syntax, accept certain words from the languages of their servants, find apophthegms to express their observations and sentiments and build a new vocabulary. It was the growth of a vernacular. The British in the nineteenth century would refer to it as Cape Dutch or the *Taal*. It would become Afrikaans and play a decisive part in the steady growth of Afrikaner nationalism. It would also become the hallmark of resistance to anglicization and the British imperium and a literary language of great refinement, expressing itself in lyrical poetry of unusual beauty.

* Literally: Eland Lakelet, Clear Stream, River–without–End–Bitter Well, Well-Without-Water, Beg-For-Fountain...

Afrikaans, as it developed at the Cape, did not differ materially from Afrikaans as it evolved on the frontier. This is the more remarkable when one remembers that there were no means of mass, and very little of individual, communication between groups living at a distance from one another. For instance, a couple from the extended frontier around Bruyntjeshoogte, wishing to be married, would have had to undertake a three months' journey to the Castle of Good Hope and back.

Within the first century of Van Riebeeck's founding of the Cape station, the stamp of Africa was already on those who had been granted its 'freedom'. The Cape tradition of the Afrikaners had started and so had the frontier tradition.

Nothing in South African history was more of an exercise in futility than the attempts of the V.O.C. to assert its old authority over the frontier farmers melting away into the blue distances of Southern Africa. With only the rudiments of a public service being administered from the Cape, 'control' over the migrating families consisted largely of the 'recognition' of the occupation of *leningsplaatsen* – loan-places – selected by the occupier himself, measured mostly by riding a horse at a walk for half-an-hour in various directions.

The obvious advantage of the system was that it provided an otherwise landless class with the potential for obtaining land. There were disadvantages as well. It was excessively wasteful and encouraged people to believe that land, pasture and game were inexhaustible. Along with this went the growth of extreme individualism, so that communal centres were slow to come into being.

Survival meant pre-eminently becoming landed, building a dwelling, maintaining one's herds and flocks, in the face of many new problems. Above all there was the constant menace of the Bushmen who were raiding stock and killing slave-herdsmen and the whites themselves with their poisoned arrows. In 1775 the governor, Joachim, Baron of Plettenberg, was officially informed of the massive effort all through frontier areas against the Bushmen: in the Camdebo, the Swartberg, the Coupsveld, the Nuweveld, the Sneeuberg, lying around what was becoming the main settlement of Graaff-Reinet ... The Bushmen were far tougher than the Hottentots had been before smallpox had cut their numbers. They refused all attempts to come to terms. Hundreds continued to be shot. They kept coming back.

In the new district of Graaff-Reinet, *landdrost* Woeke reported in 1787 that frontier farmers within his area had in the course of five months lost more than 1200 head of cattle and 1500 sheep. Everywhere herders were being murdered. Woeke pleaded with the Company to send soldiers. But the frontiersmen, led by one Adriaan van Jaarsveld, took their own uncompromising measures.

There were other problems. Land seemed to be limitless and so therefore did pasture – as long as the summer rains kept coming. But drought, those early pioneers would learn, was always somewhere in Southern Africa. When the rains came and the sweet grasses grew, when even the high arid plateau of the Karroo bloomed and sheep grew shiny, it was Eden restored. When the rains stayed away and the heavens became a limitless succession of blue-white brilliance, *vleis*, springs, streams and rivers dried up – and the land faded. When the rains returned, the high plateaux sometimes became a chain of inland lakes. The rivers were torrents and the land drowned.

There were the years of the locusts and horse-sickness. These were also the years of the mass-migrating springbok, rushing far westwards to the Atlantic, to drown themselves.

In the early days in the gracious, tranquil Cape, these things did not exist. But life here on the frontier was far more demanding. Yet the grazier/hunters, in the pioneer roughnesses of their living, their excesses of contention and their fierce insistence on self-sufficiency, became deeply bound to it all. Even their great mobility did not prevent them striking root in this intractable soil.

All this was at a time when the Calvinist New Englanders had already passed through their own fundamentalist Great Awakening, and were now well on their way both to Benjamin Franklin's Art of Virtue, and the formulation of their high-principled belief in the Rights of Man. Across the Atlantic, another essentially protestant soul, Jean-Jacques Rousseau, was constructing in torment a similar secular faith, defining passionately and at length his own belief in man.

The frontier Afrikaners at that early stage in their development were also, inarticulately and instinctively, concerned with freedom. But the issues were still simple, instinctive and concrete, and were never theorized about. The Company had been outflanked by the sheer remoteness of the frontier. So the sole contention, except for neighbourly bickerings when the smoke of each other's chimneys became visible over many miles, was with nature and the Bushmen. It was an elemental struggle, without nuances, but with a variety of consequences.

As the frontier extended, the confession of Dort had been reduced to its own basic essentials. The word of God was the fountain of all knowledge, learning, morals and authority. The conclusion of the whole matter, as the book of Ecclesiastes had said, was to fear God and keep his commandments. Subtleties of human interpretation played no part in it. Each patriarchal head was his own theologian, consistory and educationist.

The expanding frontier, the vagaries of nature, the isolation of little clans under a lonely sky, horizon following upon horizon, made for an enormous turnover in land. In few countries in the world, Barrow observed at the beginning of the nineteenth century, did the inhabitants show such a propensity to buy, sell and exchange land, as at the Cape of Good Hope.

Graaff-Reinet became the seat of a *landdrost* in 1786. Private homes and public buildings, whitewashed, classicist or baroque, soon resembled those which had already been built in the Cape valleys. They were pleasant towns in which character had endured and mellowed. The most southerly of these, Swellendam, in 1747 became the first centre of positive political resistance by the emergent Afrikaners.

It came about exactly when the V.O.C., after almost a century-and-a-half at the Cape, seemed to realize that it had been unwisely neglecting its African charges.

In December 1779, after the frontiersmen had struggled to drive the Bushmen from the Bamboesberg, a commando under Adriaan van Jaarsveld clashed with Xhosa tribesmen who had been driving their cattle into pastures used by the colonists. The critical area was Bruyntjeshoogte on the upper reaches of the Little Fish.

As far back as 1702, hunters from Stellenbosch had already clashed with the Xhosa. They had killed a few, and had then robbed Hottentots of their cattle. Now, in October 1780, van Jaarsveld was preparing for a new and more substantive battle. The Council of Policy at the Castle was duly informed of Xhosa threats on the eastern frontier. In March of the following year the news was also received at the Cape that England had declared war on the Dutch Republic. The Council of Policy was suddenly faced with a double emergency; from beyond the ocean and from beyond the Fish River.

By the middle of 1781, a French fleet arrived in False Bay, to help defend the Cape against an attack by the British. A month later the British arrived – but in Saldanha Bay; and went off with five valuable V.O.C. ships as prizes. Meanwhile a group of 'Cape Patriots' had been patiently waiting in Amsterdam since October 1779, for the Council of Seventeen to hear their massive indictment against Company misrule at the Cape. Much of it was reminiscent of the charges at the beginning of the century against the younger van der Stel.

But more was stirring. In fact, the colonists in the far South were, like their kin on the eastern frontier, becoming politically restless. The dead weight of the V.O.C. could not be endured for much longer. It was only a small voice of protest, but indicative of deep stirrings everywhere. Ironically, the Cape was about to enter into a time of little glory.

Suddenly there was money for the asking. Not only had the French arrived to help protect the Cape, but also the Dutch put into port. The Commander of the Dutch fleet, Jacob Pieter van Braam, was heard to say in 1783 that he had never witnessed such prosperity anywhere such as that which obtained at the Cape. In fashion, the ladies were outdoing their Parisian counterparts.

Louis Michel Thibault, engineer and architect, was designing fine buildings which Herman Schutte, master builder, was erecting, and which Anton Anreith, sculptor and wood-carver, was decorating. In the homes of the burghers, van Braam recorded, there was locally-made furniture, hardly to be surpassed in Europe. Corn, wine and vegetables were in abundance. The drinking water was perfect and the climate a delight.

On the distant frontier, however, crisis was looming. The new sensitivity of the Company, like that of a dying man making a final attempt to expiate his sins, led to the proclamation of Graaff-Reinet as a new district on the eastern frontier, with Maurits Woeke as the first *landdrost*. But the following year was the dreadful one of 1787, with the militant Xhosa seeking pasture, pouring into the Zuurveld. The Bushmen, too, were raiding everywhere. As the decade closed, war threatened along the whole extended frontier.

With drought also in the land, C. D. Maynier, who had been appointed secretary to the *landdrost*, favoured a policy of conciliation with the Xhosa. Soon the burghers began to see in Maynier the personification of the Company and their mortal enemy. In Europe, Revolutionary France had reached the stage where the Terror of the Jacobins had taken over. So shrill were their voices, so penetrating, that the sound reached even beyond the blue heights west of Bruyntjeshoogte. For generations this had been utterly remote. Now suddenly, it was within reach of the modern world. 'Freedom!' those who had become isolated in Africa also suddenly cried.

On a morning in February 1795, an armed and mounted commando of forty burghers led by an outraged Adriaan van Jaarsveld appeared before the Drostdy at Graaff-Reinet. They demanded to see Maynier, who had meanwhile become *landdrost*. The farmers, van Jaarsveld declared, were most dissatisfied with the measures taken against the marauding Xhosa. Of the 120 farms in the Zuurveld two years earlier only four had not been overrun, plundered or destroyed.

Maynier arrived back at the Castle of Good Hope a month later, exhausted. The rebellious burghers of Graaff-Reinet, he said, were sporting the tricolour and employing democratic revolutionary terms. Although they still professed loyalty to the States-General, they would have nothing more to do with the Company. In June of the same year, burghers in the district of Swellendam, too, finally rejected the V.O.C. and declared themselves autonomous.

It was only a brief interregnum for the two abortive states. On 16 September, Admiral Elphinstone and General Clarke officially accepted the surrender of the Cape in the old government house at Rustenburg. The outpost, which had been a V.O.C. possession for 143 years, had become British with hardly a shot being fired. The first nine ships of the British fleet had already sailed into False Bay on 11 June 1795.

The emergent Afrikaners, for so long out of the age, were being brought back to it, haltingly. They were now facing black Africa in the form of the Xhosa; the world in the form of the British. It was the start of their 'century of wrong', but also of their heroic age.

2 The Heroic Age: Trek

Ahead of the Afrikaners lay now the nineteenth century. This was to bring them the new twofold summons: that of black Africans who were grazing their cattle in the same areas as the white frontiersmen, and that of the British, now established at the Cape, but still making up their minds whether Southern Africa would be of more than just strategic value to them. The technique of outflanking authority was, for the frontiersmen, no longer adequate. White and black were confronting each other on the eastern frontier. Both were laying claim to the same pasturage – the Zuurveld. Now white and white would also increasingly face each other with conflicting ideas: the one newly conscious of itself as a distinct community, the other seeing itself as an expanding imperial power.

On 2 February 1837, a few months before Queen Victoria as a girl of eighteen was suddenly called to succeed her uncle William IV on the throne of England, there appeared in the *Grahamstown Journal*, in the frontier district of Albany, a statement in English by one of the four outstanding leaders of the mass migration to the interior of Southern Africa of colonial farmers known as the Great Trek. Its author was Piet Retief who, later as 'governor' of the migrant community, and later still as its principal martyr, would play such a vital part in the history of the Afrikaners.

'A document has been handed to us,' an editorial note read in the *Grahamstown Journal* of the above date, 'purporting to be the cause of the emigration...'
Retief declared:

Numerous reports having been circulated throughout the colony, evidently with the intention of exciting in the minds of our country-men a feeling of prejudice against those who have resolved to emigrate from a colony where they have experienced, for so many years past, a series of the most vexatious and severe losses; and, as we desire to stand high in the estimation of our brethren and are anxious that they and the world at large should believe us incapable of severing that sacred tie which binds a Christian to his native soil, without the most sufficient reasons, we are induced to record the following summary of our motives for taking so important a step; and also our intentions respecting our proceedings towards the Native Tribes which we may meet with beyond the boundary:

1. We despair of saving the colony from those evils which threaten it by the turbulent and dishonest conduct of vagrants, who are allowed to infest the country in every part; nor do we see any prospect of peace and happiness for our children in a country thus distracted by internal commotions.

2. We complain of the severe losses which we have been forced to sustain by the emancipation of our slaves, and the vexations which have been enacted respecting them.

3. We complain of the continual system of plunder which we have ever endured from the Caffres and other coloured classes, and particularly by the last invasion of the colony, which has desolated the frontier districts and ruined most of the inhabitants.

4. We complain of the unjustifiable odium which has been cast upon us by interested and dishonest persons, under the cloak of religion, whose testimony is believed in England to the exclusion of all other evidence in our favour; and we can foresee, as the result of this prejudice, nothing but the total ruin of the country.

5. We are resolved, wherever we go, that we will uphold the just principles of liberty; but, whilst we will take care that no-one shall be held in a state of slavery, it is our determination to maintain such regulations as may suppress crime, and preserve proper relations between master and servant.

6. We solemnly declare that we quit this colony with a desire to lead a more quiet life than we have heretofore done. We will not molest any people, nor deprive them of the smallest property; but if attacked, we shall consider ourselves fully justified in defending our persons and effects, to the utmost of our ability, against every enemy.

7. We make known that when we shall have framed a code of laws for our future guidance, copies shall be forwarded to the colony for general information; but we take this opportunity of stating, that it is our firm resolve to make provision for the summary punishment of any traitors who may be found amongst us.

8. We purpose, in the course of our journey, and on arriving at the

country in which we shall permanently reside, to make known to the native tribes our intentions, and our desire to live in peace and friendly intercourse with them.

9. We quit this colony, under the full assurance that the English government has nothing more to require of us, and will allow us to govern ourselves without its interference in future.

10. We are now quitting the fruitful land of our birth, in which we have suffered enormous losses and continual vexation, and are entering a wild and dangerous territory; but we go with a firm reliance on an all-seeing, just, and merciful Being, Whom it will be our endeavour to fear and humbly to obey.

Retief signed, 'by authority of the farmers who have quitted the colony'.[1]

It would be relevant here to recall the terms of the American Declaration of Independence, insofar as they serve to put the Retief Manifesto, which may well be seen as the manifesto of the Afrikaner Trekker Community as a whole, into perspective.[2]

The Declaration reads:

When in the course of human events, it becomes necessary for one people to dissolve the political bands which have connected them with another, and to assume among the powers of the earth, the separate and equal station to which the Laws of Nature and of Nature's God entitle them, a decent respect to the opinions of mankind requires that they should declare the causes which impel them to the separation. – We hold these truths to be self-evident, that all men are created equal, that they are endowed by their Creator with certain inalienable rights, that among these are Life, Liberty and the Pursuit of Happiness. – That to secure these rights, Governments are instituted among Men, deriving their just powers from the consent of the governed. – That whenever any form of Government becomes destructive of these ends, it is the Right of the people to alter or to abolish it, and to institute new Government, laying its foundation on such principles and organizing its powers in such form, as to them shall seem most likely to effect their Safety and Happiness . . .

The Declaration goes on to say that governments long established should not be lightly changed. The long line of abuses and usurpations the American people suffered, however, constrained them to make a change. The abuses referred to are then dealt with individually. Of particular interest are the words:

He has excited domestic insurrections amongst us, and has endeavoured to bring on the inhabitants of our frontiers the merciless Indian Savages, whose known rule of warfare is an undistinguished destruction of all ages, sexes, and conditions.

The Declaration closes with an appeal to the 'Supreme Judge of the world' for the rectitude of our intentions 'in the name of the good people of these Colonies', and pledging the Lives, Fortunes and Sacred Honour of the signatories 'for the support of this Declaration, with a firm reliance on the protection of divine Providence'.

There are, indeed, important similarities between the Declaration and the Manifesto. These consist of the complaints of a colonial people regarding the abuse of authority on the part of a colonial overlord, in which *inter alia*, as they saw it, the barbarous and destructive behaviour of a still primitive people are favoured, to the general disadvantage of the Europeans living near them. There is then the further view that the yoke of such an oppressive authority should be removed: in the case of the Declaration by the establishment of independence *in situ*, in the case of the Manifesto by preferring a 'wild and dangerous territory', meaning the unknown in both human and physical terms.

More important than the similarities between the Declaration and the Manifesto, however, are the differences. They indicate clearly how two societies with largely similar spiritual backgrounds, contending with much the same kind of forces threatening their separate existences, were at a comparable point in history, and, within the same protestant ethic, at widely differing stages of development.

The Declaration is essentially a statement of socio-political fundamentals. It was, in fact, the first of its kind. These, according to the Declaration, are self-evident truths and bear certain inalienable rights. All men have been created equal and they have, as such, been endowed with the rights to life, liberty and the pursuit of happiness. The object of government, moreover, is to secure such rights by means of the consent of the governed. In effect, this means that the people, as the true political entity, should guard against any attempt to assail such rights. New government should only be instituted where this has happened. Moreover, the Supreme Judge supports the rectitude of these intentions. The people, conclusively, may rely firmly on the protection of divine Providence in the pursuit of their legitimate objectives.

To what extent the statement of such fundamental human rights, protected and sanctioned by divine Authority, constituted the first formulation of a secular faith (and radical politics) will be examined at a later stage. What is relevant here is the substantive difference between the American Declaration and the Retief Manifesto.

The Manifesto makes no attempt to formulate 'inalienable', therefore fundamental and absolute, human rights. The resolution to 'uphold the just principles of liberty' is still an *obiter dictum*. In the context of the times, it simply meant that there would be no re-institution of slavery. This is apparent from the further assurance, immediately following, that while taking care that no-one shall be held in a state of slavery, crime would be suppressed and proper relations between master and servant maintained. Other practical measures for assuring law and order, of keeping the 'colony' informed of these measures, of living 'in peace and friendly intercourse' with 'the native tribes' in the new country, are then set out. As organizational matters they were in substance the necessary measures to be taken by the migrant community to ensure orderly and civilized government.

The only absolute in the Manifesto is referred to obliquely: '... but we go with a firm reliance on an all-seeing, just, and merciful Being, Whom it will be our endeavour to fear and humbly to obey.'

The Manifesto makes no claim to certain 'inalienable' rights. There is no statement linking such rights with divine sanction. There is only the assurance that the journey to be undertaken will be in the fear of, in humility before, and in obedience to, the Lord.

The Declaration of Independence, on the other hand, is more than a statement of insurrection, it is an incitement to revolution. It is the articulation, as will be shown, of the New England spirit which had, in the words of Alexis de Tocqueville, 'interpenetrated the whole confederation'[3], extending its limits over the whole American world. In time, its impact would prove to be infinitely greater, extending over the whole world.

The Manifesto is a statement of revolt, not of revolution. The difference is a cardinal one, and will employ our fuller attention. Revolt, as Albert Camus has pointed out, is armed or other protest directed to an immediate situation, while revolution is a radical and therefore a *total* re-structuring of society by violent or other means.[4]

The Great Trek was the first massive revolt of Afrikanerdom, which by this time had become conscious of its own identity. It was primarily directed against the British authority whose measures, or lack of measures, threatened ruin to the society which it had come to govern. The minor insurrections at Graaff-Reinet and elsewhere which preceded it were, in a sense, mere preparations for the collective protest of Afrikaner frontier farmers in the middle thirties of the nineteenth century.

From 1803 there had been a brief restoration of Dutch power at the Cape. Following the Peace of Amiens, the colony was handed back to the Dutch, who had meanwhile constituted themselves as the Batavian Republic. In 1806, however, the British – the 'English' as far as the colonists were concerned – were suddenly back again.

The return of the British meant a re-imposition of autocratic rule, as was normal in colonies where Britain had established herself as a fast-growing imperial power. Government was by proclamation and the Governor himself held the supreme authority. The V.O.C. had held the Cape for 143 years, giving only grudging attention to its true development.

In 1806 the European colonists only numbered some 26,000. There was a slightly larger number of slaves, though fewer Hottentots. Problems abounded. Large areas were exposed to almost perennial drought; the soil on the whole seemed to be poor; and on the eastern frontier the Xhosa were constantly poised to overrun European-occupied land. Even the Bushmen had not yet been subdued. No wonder that the British were often almost contemptuous in their reference to the colony, in spite of Lady Anne Barnard's infectious enjoyment of the

Cape landscape at the time of the first occupation. The V.O.C. had held the Cape merely for the sake of an Eastern empire. Britain had decided to do more or less the same, because her occupation of India had been so rewarding. But the remarkable thing was that the British could never again be rid of either the Cape or Southern Africa as a whole. The 'English' and Afrikaners would continue to move around each other in a variety of attitudes. They would wish each other dead; but they would also desperately need each other.

Du Pré Alexander, Earl of Caledon, became at 29 the first British civil governor of the Cape. Like those who followed him, he was true to his people, class and time. Tory England was still in a state of delayed reaction to what 'undue political privileges' had led to in the late North American colonies. The Jacobin Terror, justified in the name of freedom, had served to strengthen this. Perhaps the English had also taken to heart what the traveller Barrow had once written: 'Such men [i.e. the frontiersmen of the late eighteenth century] will never become civilized until they are ruled with a rod of iron.'[5]

Caledon's youth in no way affected the generally imperious tone he set for British rule in South Africa for the rest of the century. One of his first measures was to regularize the life of the Hottentots. Henceforth, proper contracts of employment would be needed. Special provisions dealt with possible ill-treatment of servants. Caledon was not only determined to enforce positive respect of law, but considered it unquestionably necessary that 'British ideas', especially those which had become fashionable due to the activities in England of Wilberforce and other members of the Clapham Sect, should be inculcated into the Afrikaners. His successor, Sir John Cradock, took the cue and declared: 'I therefore anxiously hope that, in whatever Directions we may receive from Home ... there will appear the Desire to assimilate the Institutions of this country to those of England.'

One of the first attempts to discipline the colonists living on their farms in the frontier districts was the so-called Black Circuit, in the time of the governorship of Cradock (1811–14). For it would be the first serious exercise in the urge 'to dispense justice fearlessly'. To this purpose the Roman–Dutch law, so long in a state of animated suspense under the V.O.C., was revived. English procedure, however, would now be employed to administer it.

De Kiewiet made the following comment about the Black Circuit:

The Circuit Court, freshly created in 1811, announced a new era by making itself accessible to the Hottentot as well as the European population. Of the cases brought against European masters many were malicious, collusive, and false. Certain missionaries undoubtedly overreached themselves in trying to strike a blow for their protégés. But other accusations were proven. The sentences which the court pronounced against white masters shook the Colony with indignation...[6]

This observation provides an important clue to the build-up of resentment among the frontier Afrikaners, which eventually culminated in the revolt of the Great Trek. It also moved Piet Retief to justify the mass emigration in the way he did.

Judgements and perceptions in human things are, in the last resort, more than rational. This does not make them irrational. Sound sensitivities are both instinctive and intuitive. The frontier Afrikaners, contending with the Xhosa for the good pastures of the Zuurveld, then discovering to their dismay that 'certain missionaries [had] undoubtedly overreached themselves in trying to strike a blow for their protégés', were reacting to what they also divined to be basically questionable. Pre-eminent among the missionaries were Dr J. T. van der Kemp and Dr John Philip, both of whom had come to the Cape deeply imbued with the Evangelical spirit and determined to fulfil their calling in a far away country. Charity, they believed, was more to the point abroad than at home.

The sponsoring body was the London Missionary Society. This was the fruit of the English Evangelical Movement and it was fired by the 'religion of the heart', appearing as a latter-day revival of grass-roots Puritanism. The London Missionary Society was, in short, a reaction to the massive well-being and deep complacency of the Established Church.

In 1828, Dr John Philip saw the triumph of his endeavours when, as a result of a visit to England in which he aroused the

Evangelicals to new fervour, he convinced the British authorities
to repeal the proclamations of Caledon and Cradock, thus placing
the Hottentots on an equal footing with the white colonists.
This was the famous '*Ordinance Fifty*', the heart of which was the
abolition of the legal colour bar. Philip attacked not only the
Afrikaner frontiersmen, but also the authoritarian Tory governor
at the Cape, Lord Charles Somerset. The matter was compounded when he published, also in 1828, his *Researches in
South Africa*. In this the Xhosa and the Hottentots were praised,
the colonists and officials generally and heartily damned. All this
took place at a time when Mr Gradgrind was still a dominant
feature of the British industrial landscape. Before long Karl
Marx, in the British Museum, would ponder it all deeply. It
may well have been that the distant colonists on the frontier
sensed, even if they did not understand, the ambiguity.

The Afrikaners were, in the years leading up to the revolt of
the Great Trek, getting the worst of both British worlds. On
the one hand they had to cope with dedicated missionaries;
on the other, they were being governed in a most imperious
way by men for whom British ideals were the ultimate goal,
regardless of their applicability to Afrikaners.

The philanthropists – in the eyes of the frontier Afrikaners –
sought their downfall by discrediting them before God and man.
The Tory governors, more especially Lord Charles Somerset,
sought their downfall by repression and anglicization.

There had been the affair at Slachter's Nek. A small insurrection of frontier farmers had taken place in 1815: the same
year as the battle of Waterloo and the surrender of Bonaparte.
After a lengthy trial, in which it appeared that the accused had
actually considered an alliance with the Xhosa to resist the
'English', five were sentenced to death. At the public execution
on an exposed hill overlooking the Great Fish, the ropes of four
of the accused broke at the first attempts at hanging them.
Amid scenes of great emotion and pleas for mercy, the condemned men were again taken to the gallows. This time they
died.

Martyrdom in any form is a self-sowing plant. It is beyond
calculation, therefore beyond rationality. What comes up after a

season is dismaying. But the wind takes the new and prolific seed along and scatters it wide.

For the next twenty years, the frontier Afrikaners were never long without trouble. In 1818–19 the Xhosa, now under Ndlambe, once more devastated the Zuurveld. They also, massively but unsuccessfully, attacked the new frontier town of Grahamstown. The Xhosa were eventually driven back, but at a high cost. All of which pointed the moral: opposing lines of settlement, whether Afrikaner or British, were struggling against the Xhosa for the control of the same natural resources of water, grass and soil. The 5000 British settlers who came to live on the eastern frontier would soon come to learn this.

The Afrikaners on the whole, however, had more to deal with. 'Ordinance Fifty', being the work of Dr Philip was, primarily, aimed at them. So was his *Researches in South Africa*. It gave rise to increasing bitterness among the settlers. Meanwhile, the policy as originally formulated by Cradock 'to assimilate the Institutions of this country to those of England' had received a powerful impetus in the governorship of Somerset. He knew what was right for the country and he needed no advice. It was a fact that, in the thirty years since the second and final coming of the British in 1806 to the year of the Great Trek, in spite of the Cape being primarily expedient for the further exploitation of India, more real progress had been made than during the 143 years of V.O.C. rule. Huge districts like Stellenbosch, Swellendam and Graaff-Reinet were subdivided and new ones proclaimed. Land-tenure was reformed, quit-rent and finally ownership being substituted for the old system of loan-farms. Neither did details like pipe-borne water and a public library fall outside of Somerset's Olympian scope.

By 1828, a new Charter of Justice had established an independent judiciary. Ironically, the Roman–Dutch civil law, which under the V.O.C. had been static, had suddenly, whether by design or not, been given a potential which would have the effect of restoring it as a cardinal institution. Somerset imported both Scots schoolmasters and Scots ministers of the Church of John Knox. There was no secret about his motives. The colonists had to be anglicized thoroughly, once and for all. The language of the courts would henceforth be exclusively English. By 1837, the Dutch Reformed Synod had a majority of Scots ministers. Somerset had ruled by proclamation in 1822 that after five years English would be the sole official language. The judiciary, church and schools all had to serve the purpose of turning the Afrikaners into British colonials.

Somerset's understanding did not match his drive and energy. Only two of his schoolmasters – William Robertson and James Rose-Innes – survived the experiment. In the Church, the Andrew Murrays, Colin Frasers, Morgans, Sutherlands and Robertsons in time founded their own Reformed tradition. Increasingly it, too, became an Afrikaner heritage. Towards the end of 1834, abrasive Xhosa unrest once more erupted into violence. It was the Sixth Frontier War. From distant Capetown, Colonel Harry Smith rode swingingly to Grahamstown in under six days, averaging more than a hundred miles a day. The war lasted until September 1835 and included the death of Hintsa, Paramount Chief of the Xhosa. Once more the Zuurveld was in ruins, the newer British settlers suffering as much as the Afrikaners. What complicated things for the latter was the emancipation of 36,000 slaves in the colony, valued at over £3,000,000. Less than twenty per cent of these were from the frontier districts. Compensation at less than half the estimated value could be claimed by the owner. Those claims recognized were payable in London.

So it became the Great Trek. With the coming of the British all contours, human and physical, had hardened. The frontier Afrikaner community, partly settled, partly semi-nomadic, had already, since the twenties, migrated seasonally to beyond the Orange. They felt themselves far more confined in their freedom of movement and expression than in the capricious days of the dying V.O.C. The expansive frontier Afrikaner nature, rarely discerning neighbouring smoke nor needing it, felt itself cramped in its new style. It was threatened, both by the militant Xhosa and especially the unreasonably authoritarian British. Land was no longer freely available to those who had the urge for possession, the stamina to make the trek, and the capacity for marking off their lands' limits on horseback. Insufferable officials, speaking a strange language, were there to regulate and require obedience.

Easily the worst of the new colonial policy was the way it interfered with the already generations-old relationships between master and servant. The British talked of equality and put strict limits on employers' authority. The Afrikaners felt that this was abominable. Did they, the British, in their own country equate servants with masters and masters with servants? In any event, here it was worse, for the servants were neither white nor always Christian. A niece of Piet Retief, Anna Steenkamp, accepted as such among leaders of the Trek, expressed an important part of the general motivation most succinctly. 'The shameful and unjust proceedings with reference to the freedom of our slaves,' she stated, was the precipitating cause of the Trek.

And yet it is not so much their freedom which drove us to such lengths as their being placed on an equal footing with Christians, contrary to the laws of God, and the natural distinction of race and colour, so that it was intolerable for any decent Christian to bow down beneath such a yoke, wherefore we rather withdrew in order thus to preserve our doctrines in purity.[7]

British manners imposed by British authority therefore meant, above all, intensification of a black threat, a confinement of land, the loss of various kinds of freedom and a free hand to dangerous, often indictable, elements. They were objecting not so much to laws, many Trekkers maintained, as to lawlessness.

Secret preparations were already being made in the early thirties. In 1834 a commission under Pieter Lavras Uys travelled up the east coast to Natal to spy out the land. He found only a few British traders at Port Natal and fine, depopulated land between the Tugela and the Mzimvubu. So he brought back a favourable report. The secret preparations for the Trek went on, many blind eyes being turned to it by conniving officials.

The revolt slowly took form through the Trekkers outflanking the opposition, as De Kiewiet put it.[8] With much coming and going north and south of the Orange, with the Colonial Governor,

The Puritans in Africa

Lord Glenelg, in 1836 entering into an unfavourable frontier settlement, at least for the Afrikaners, the swell became a wave. Some thousands of Afrikaner colonists somehow seemed to find each other and formed a discernible body of migrating people. In time some nine per cent of all colonial whites, approximately 6000 people, had joined the Trek, with about 4000, mostly coloured, servants. It was a true *Volkswanderung*, resembling the Goths of the fifth century B.C., transporting their women and children in wagons while the warriors went on ahead. It was colonization in a time when the concept was accepted in all European countries without significant question; although John Calvin, among others, had summarily rejected it.[9] It was colonization with a difference, by virtue of mass migration and the seeking of land for a new polity in a 'wild and dangerous territory'. It did not involve military conquest by seaborne troops going to a far country. For in the mid-thirties Southern Africa generally was still suffering acutely from the effects of what in Nguni terms has become known as the Difaqane. This, as Leonard Thompson has described it, was the massive Southern African catastrophe which struck many of the inhabitants of the highveld between the Drakensberg, the Kalahari desert and the Limpopo, between 1822 and 1836.

'These disturbances', Thompson says,

were a result of the rise of the Zulu Kingdom, for the primary agents of destruction on the highveld were three bands of refugees from Shaka: Hlubi led by Mpangazita and Ngwane led by Matiwane, who operated in the southern sector between the Vaal river and the Maluti mountains; and Ndebele under Mzilikazi, most of whose operations were to the north of the Vaal river. Several of the Sotho communities who were displaced by the Nguni invaders became secondary agents of destruction – such as Tlokwa in the southern sector and Phuthing, Hlakwana, Fokeng, and Taung in the northern sector ... This time of troubles on the highveld is known as the Difaqane, a word meaning 'forced migration'.[10]

By the end of the twenties, almost every Sotho community in the Transorangia had been completely disrupted. The whole social and moral order had collapsed. 'Thousands of the inhabitants,' says Thompson,

34

had fled – some to the north, where they caused destruction beyond the Vaal, others to the south-west where they obtained a footing, among the Griqua, or took service with white farmers in the Cape Colony, or joined southern Nguni chiefdoms. In most of the Vaal-Orange area itself the old settlements were abandoned, the stock was destroyed, the fields ceased to be cultivated, and in several places the landscape was littered with human bones. Demoralized survivors wandered around singly or in small groups, contriving to live on game or veld plants. Even cannibalism was widespread.[11]

The culminating movement in the Difaqane, however, was the rise of the 'Ndebele conquest state': when a rebellious Zulu in the army of Shaka* had fled before his wrath to the highveld, soon overpowering the Pedi, the Kwena and the other Sotho. By the early thirties Mzilikazi's outposts extended to the Limpopo, the Crocodile, the Vaal and the Malopo, over an area of about 30,000 square miles. Here he governed as an absolute ruler in a well-ordered Nguni (Ndebele) state, having as his subject element mainly the Sotho.[12]

The rise of Mzilikazi was essentially the expansion of Nguni power and influence at the expense of all who dared to oppose it. The missionary, Robert Moffat, who seemed to have been Mzilikazi's single friend, enjoying peculiar trust and admiration from the despot, said of him: 'The evils now coming upon the Matabele (*Ndebele*) are only what I expected. Mzilikazi has ruled with an iron sceptre, and his warriors have, full often unprovoked, shed the blood of thousands . . .'[13] It would be superficial, however, to see Mzilikazi merely as a tyrant. He was rather an extremely militant, highly effective, black absolutist ruler, no

* The tyranny of Shaka is best illustrated by the way in which he had mourned the death of his mother, Nandi, whose illegitimate son he was. On hearing the news of his mother's death Shaka 'stood for about twenty minutes in a silent mournful attitude with his head bowed upon his shield on which a few large tears fell – the only occasion on record on which Shaka had been shown to possess any human affection. Then "after two or three deep sighs, his feelings became ungovernable, he broke into frantic yells, which fearfully contrasted with the silence that had hitherto prevailed." This signal was enough. A wailing was set up which continued throughout that night and the next day, increasing all the time as fresh regiments arrived on the scene. Forty oxen were slaughtered as an offering to the spirits of the tribe; and when Shaka ordered the execution of several men on the spot, the multitude commenced a general massacre of those whom they thought were not displaying sufficient grief . . .'
(See Eileen Jensen Krige, *The Social System of the Zulu*, London, 1936, Chapter 1.)

better nor worse than most such rulers have been in the course of history.

A most interesting situation had been created. From the early twenties to mid-thirties, Nguni expansion had ranged over a wide area of Southern Africa. It had produced one completely dominant figure in the person of Mzilikazi, established at his royal *kraal* at Mosega, around the headwaters of the Marico river on the Western highveld. The Difaqane had left enormous areas virtually a human wasteland. Into this 'Pax Nguni' another kind of expansion came to intrude: that of the emigrating Frontier Afrikaners, out to seek some place of their own in the 'wild and dangerous territory' where they could establish a pure Afrikaner state.

Of course, they were well-informed of the situation in the north. Hunting parties had often returned with news, and some early Trekker families had been murdered near the Vaal. Leaders like Gert Maritz, Pieter Lavras Uys, Hendrik Potgieter and Piet Retief – who joined the Trek early in 1837, to become its elected 'Governor' – might well have foreseen that a clash with Mzilikazi was inevitable. As such it was a calculated risk. A Griqua commando had already, notably during the attack of Phuthing and Hlakwana hordes during the Difaqane on Dithakong near Kuruman in June 1823, demonstrated how guns and horses used by determined men could deal effectively with a far greater number of assegai-wielding warriors.

The clash came on 16 October 1837, at Vegkop ('Hill of the Fight') when a force of 6000 Ndebele bore down on a small party of emigrants, defending themselves for the first time in a *laager* – an enclosure of covered wagons, forming a fort. With the women loading alternate guns, and some forty men riding out to meet the attackers, cleverly remaining out of range of the assegais, shooting from the saddle with their flint-lock muzzle-loaders, the attack was at last beaten off. The defenders had been outnumbered by a hundred to one; but the superiority of guns and horses to vast numbers had conclusively been proved. The Ndebele were defeated but made off with many thousands of sheep, goats and head of cattle, all of which had been grazing beyond the *laager*. A few months later, a multi-racial commando

under Hendrik Potgieter, comprising 107 whites and forty
Griquas and Korannas, also sixty Rolong cattle drivers, rode
some 200 miles to Mosega, to exact fitting punishment from
Mzilikazi. Daniel Lindley, the American missionary at Mosega,
who would later join the Voortrekkers as their preacher, described the remorseless way in which the attack was carried out.
Mzilikazi himself escaped as he was elsewhere at the time; but in
all, upwards of 200 Ndebele lost their lives. Few of the men on
the *kraal* escaped the fury of the commando; and many women,
according to Lindley, were also shot. Returning to the *laager* in
the Transorangia, the avengers took away some 6000 head of
cattle. Lindley and his party accompanied the commando back
to the Transorangian *laagers*.

But Ndebele power was still largely intact, in spite of some destructive harassing by fellow Nguni from the distant east,
inspired by Dingane, overthrower of Shaka and now the un-
disputed lord of the Zulu Kingdom. A little more than a year
after Vegkop, Potgieter, at the head of a powerful commando of
330, once more attacked Mzilikazi, this time from beyond the
Vaal. In nine days of relentless fighting, the Ndebele Conquest
State itself was conquered. Mzilikazi, sizing up the position
quickly, decided that his empire could still be safe if he took it
elsewhere. He was, strange to relate, emulating the Voortrekkers
themselves: outflanking a troublesome opposition and moving
away, to establish himself beyond their reach. Beyond the
Limpopo, Mzilikazi then founded a new royal *kraal*, naming it
Kwa-Bulawayo – 'The Place of the Persecuted One' – after
Shaka's Old Great Place in the Valley of the White Umfolozi.

What might have been predictable from the start of the Great
Trek was the conflict within the Voortrekker *maatschappij*.*
This was between leaders whose strong-willed individualism
had been compounded by the fact that there had not been a
single organized trek-party, but rather a sequence. Each party
was led by a regional leader, taking along with him kinsmen,
neighbours, dependants and coloured retainers. When the
various parties eventually met at waters to *laager* together, the
leaders often disputed bitterly. They argued passionately about

* Society, community.

37

the objectives of the movement, their physical destinations and the general running of affairs. Most controversial of all was Potgieter, who was at one and the same time the most robustly anti-British and the most headstrong. He preferred a trek-route to the Transvaal Highveld, rather than one down to Port Natal, where some British had already settled. Gert Maritz, most worldly-wise of the Trekkers – he had been a successful business-man at Graaff-Reinet – and the elected president of the 'Council of Policy', was the special butt of the Potgieter temperament.

Division took on a more substantial shape in October 1837. Potgieter and his commando – among them the later hero of Blood River, Andries Pretorius – were disporting themselves on the highveld among the scattered Ndebele – when Retief decided to cross the Drakensberg with a party and go down to Port Natal. It was a reconnaissance meant to investigate the prospects for a Voortrekker state among the green hills of Natal. Behind them they soon left the Drakensberg – *Qhuathlamba*, as the Zulu referred to it: 'Jagged-and-Heaped-Up-like-a-Cluster-of-Spears' – still flecked in places with late-winter snow. Over this great barrier, Retief envisaged, the combined treks would in time descend. Should an agreement be reached with the Zulu King-dom, the Trek could assemble in the land below the Tugela. Here the basis would be laid for a new and civilized polity.

On 19 October Retief and his small party were at Port Natal. Here they were welcomed by an Englishman, Alexander Biggar, who was to die in the cause of the Voortrekkers in Natal. Here Retief also learned, to his surprise but not to his dismay, that Dingane had already granted the land they sought to the mis-sionary, Allen Gardiner. 'The great Book of God teaches us,' Retief nevertheless with fine provocation informed Dingane a week or two later,

that kings who conduct themselves as Umsilikazi [Mzilikazi] does, are severely punished, and it is not granted to them to live or reign long; and if you desire to learn at greater length how God deals with bad kings, you may enquire concerning it from the missionaries who are in your country.[14]

Dingane, being only too well-informed of what had happened at Mosega, had at the same time taken note of the fact that

Mzilikazi had been chased beyond the Limpopo and now had every reason to fear. His cattle had been raided by mounted people dressed and equipped like white men, he said. Retief would have to see to the return of such cattle before there could be any further discussions.

By a clever ruse, Retief, some time later, enticed Seconyela, chief of the Tlokwa, to meet him in the garden of the missionary, Allison, in the eastern Transorangia: whereupon he arrested Seconyela, informing him that a condition of his freedom was the return of Dingane's cattle and the handing over of all horses and guns with which the raid had been effected. It was a successful operation. But on the way back to Mgungundlovu, with the accompanying Zulu listening, there was, perhaps, too much optimism expressed on the coming establishment of a Voortrekker Republic of Natalia.

The assembled Trek had, indeed, by this time come over the Drakensberg and were settled at various points along the upper Tugela. Confidently Retief and his mixed party – seventy-one Boers, thirty Coloureds – set out once again for Mgungundlovu. This time Retief carried in his shoulder pouch a document ceding certain land, ready to receive the mark of Dingane. The cattle recovered from the Tlokwa also went along. On 3 February the riders were at the Great Place of the Zulu: an amazing collection of beehive huts arranged in huge concentric circles.

Dingane received the commission in a friendly enough manner, showing nothing of the deep fear which, in fact, had taken hold of him. The guns Retief had seized from Seconyela had not been sent to him. His representatives who had accompanied Retief had much to tell of the efficacy of a Boer commando. A few days more of bargaining followed, with the missionary, Francis Owen, who was stationed at Mgungundlovu, secretly warning Retief that the situation was perilous.

Retief deemed his confidence well-founded, however, when Dingane in fact put his mark to the deed of cession. The Voortrekkers were thereby granted all the land between the Tugela and the Mzimvubu, including 'the place called Port Natal'. On Tuesday, 6 February, Retief and his party were invited to Mgungundlovu to drink beer and watch a display of dancing.

The Puritans in Africa

In the prevailing spirit of goodwill, the invitation was accepted. It was, however, an agreement to destruction.

The performance seemed to be a pageant of a Zulu army attacking the enemy in the form of an *umkhumbi*, or semi-circle. Suddenly it was pageant no longer. Dingane himself rose and shouted: '*Bulalani abatagati!*' – 'Kill the wizards!' The horns of the *umkhumbi*, fortified by other warriors who came streaming out of the huts, closed in upon Retief and his men. White and Brown were soon overpowered and then dragged out of the *kraal* to the hill called Hlomo Amabutha. Here they were massacred.

Still innocent of what had taken place, the immigrant encampments below the Drakensberg now lay at the mercy of the Zulu. Various Trekker groups had formed separate *laagers* (but hardly defensive ones) around the upper waters of the Tugela and two of its main tributaries: the Blaauwkrantz and the Bushmans. Of the leaders, only Gert Maritz had established a reasonably strong position in a sinus of the Bushmans. Uys had gone off to the Transorangia to fetch his people. Potgieter, who had for some time been on the highveld at the Suikerbosrand, had sullenly and haltingly trekked down to Natal to re-establish contact with the majority in the *maatschappij*.

In the early morning of Saturday, 17 February, the Zulu *impis* fell upon the *laagers*, grouped along the tributaries of the Tugela.

Maritz had on 15 February suddenly realized that all was not well: Retief should have been back from Mgungundlovu. From *laager* to *laager* he rode, warning the people to be on their guard. He made little impression. Even when the first shots were heard in the distance that early morning of 17 February, they were taken to be shots of welcome for the returning Retief. Soon the dogs everywhere were barking 'as if fighting with leopards'. Then, out of the night, the Zulu appeared. The first rage of onslaught struck the *laagers* between the Blaauwkrantz and Moordspruit.

Here the momentum also spent itself, so that the Retief *laager* some few miles away to the north-west was left untouched. To the south the Zulu were checked by Maritz, whose *laager* had been the most prepared. The result was something like the battle of Vegkop. Outnumbered men rode out to engage the enemy, then drew them nearer to the *laager* for concentrated fire.

40

In all about 300 white Trekkers – men, women and children – and about 250 coloured servants were killed. Sheep, cattle and horses, in their thousands, were driven away. Among the dead was George Biggar, elder son of Alexander, who had settled at Port Natal.

The news soon reached Potgieter and Uys, the former partly, the latter completely, still on the inland highveld. They hurried down to Natal to help form a punitive commando. It was the worst possible combination. With a leadership which contained built-in dissension, the outcome could have been foreseen. At Italeni the commando was ambushed and humbled by the Zulu. Afrikaners still refer to this expedition as the *Vlugkommando* – the Commando of Flight. Particularly dismaying was the death of Pieter Lavras Uys, in spite of the heroic action by his twelve-year-old son, Dirkie, who ran to his father's aid when surrounded by the enemy. Father and son fell side by side.

More or less while this was taking place, an expedition from Port Natal, nominally under the command of Robert Biggar (brother of the dead George), led sixteen fellow Englishmen, some Hottentots and 1500 rebel Zulu across the Tugela and engaged a Zulu army of several thousand. In a furious clash Dingane's army triumphed again, leaving 1000 of their fellow but rebellious Zulu dead, and thirteen Englishmen, including Robert Biggar. Of this battle McCall Theal has said: 'But no lion at bay ever created such havoc among hounds that worried him as this little band among the warriors of Dingane before it perished.'

For the immigrant community of the Boers, things had come to a pass. Trying to carve out for itself some place in Southern Africa where it could find a future, it had been massacred, defeated and riven by deep dissensions. Not even the death of Pieter Lavras Uys could put a stop to long-standing bickering and acrimony among the leaders. Potgieter, who in the eyes of many had badly mismanaged the punitive expedition against Dingane to the point of fresh disaster, packed up once again and re-crossed the Drakensberg with a large party. As far as he was concerned, the Trek in Natal either had to do likewise or stay and suffer the consequences.

Food was short and, to make matters worse, torrential

summer rains started falling. This was a blessing in disguise. Had the weather been fine, the Zulu might well have attacked again. With Voortrekker morale at a low point, the Zulu could easily have disposed of the remaining Trekkers. Instead, these somehow reconstituted themselves. Quite remarkably, they soon set about ploughing, sowing and doing all the things which indicated an intention to remain. They even drafted a constitution for the new Republic of Natalia, and founded its capital, naming it Pietermaritzburg: after the leaders Pieter Retief and Gert Maritz. Most remarkably, even while Dingane, with two great victories to his credit, had every reason to be not merely defiant but dominant, the site for the capital of the Republic of Natalia was chosen. Plots were offered to the Trekkers. Theal compared this action to the successful sale by auction in Ancient Rome of land on which a Carthaginian army was encamped.

It displayed optimism where there was every reason to despair. Retief had died at Mgungundlovu; Uys had died at Italeni; Potgieter had gone off to the highveld in disgust. In September 1838, Maritz died of illness on the Little Tugela, after a visit to Port Natal. He was only 41.

Deputies had been to the Cape Colony to seek assistance. In September they returned with a great many letters from relations, friends and loved ones. They also brought newspapers. Best of all they brought the news that Andries Pretorius, at the head of several influential men from Graaff-Reinet and other Cape frontier centres, had decided to come to the assistance of their fellow Frontier Afrikaners.

No time was to be lost. During August of that year some 10,000 Zulu had, for the second time, attacked the *laager* on the Bushmans. In spite of illnesses and insufficient food and the fact that the *laager* contained mostly widows and orphans, the onslaught was beaten off after two days and nights of terrible fighting.

During the last week in November Andries Pretorius arrived with sixty mounted men and a cannon. Within three days the Council of Representatives of the People had appointed Pretorius as Commandant-General.

He was different to the other leaders of the Trek. He was

clean-shaven and wore clothes with a certain style. At Graaff-Reinet he had been regarded as a wealthy man. Generally, he conveyed the impression of being a sophisticated man with far more than just frontier experience. Before the end of the month he was at the head of a commando of 470 men and fifty-seven wagons on their way to Mgungundlovu. Among them was Alexander Biggar, father of George and Robert, who had already fallen before the Zulu assegais, and 'whose grief for the loss of his sons was inconsolable'.

'The commando resembled an itinerant prayer-meeting rather than a modern army on the march,' Theal says, 'for the men were imbued with the same spirit as the Ironsides of Cromwell, and spoke and acted in pretty much the same manner.'[15]

In the evenings, a *laager* would be formed and the commando would gather for prayers. On Sunday 9 December, there was a day of rest. Sarel Celliers – the old Prophet of the Trek – was the author of a solemn vow, expressed in public on behalf of all, that should the Almighty grant them the victory in the coming struggle, a church would be built and the day ever after be commemorated and observed as a Sunday.

A week later, Sunday 16 December, was no day of rest. Some 10,000 Zulu had again appeared. The *laager* was strategically placed in a bend of the Ncome. With incredible bravery the Zulu unleashed attack after attack. Fire from the single cannon and more than 400 muskets carved them down. Eventually, with a sortie from the *laager* of mounted men, firing and loading from the saddle, the Zulu were driven off. The Ncome became a river of blood. For ever afterwards it was known as Blood River. Some 3000 Zulu had fallen, and only three of the commando – including Pretorius – had been wounded. But ten days later, at the White Umfolozi, Dingane's *impis* almost succeeded in a masterly ambush. Pretorius and his commando were visiting a deserted Mgungundlovu and had discovered the bones of Retief and his company at Hlomo Amabutha. They had also found the deed of cession still in Retief's shoulder pouch.

... but the Voortrekkers fought their way out, losing only five men and killing about a thousand Zulu, and thereby giving an even more

43

impressive demonstration of fire-power [*than at Blood River*], for the battle was on terrain selected by the Zulu and the Voortrekkers were without wagons.[16]

On the commando's side there also fell Alexander Biggar. All the male members of an English family, a father and his two sons, had now fallen in the Voortrekker cause in Natal.

An alliance was now formed between the Afrikaners and the rebel part of the Zulu nation under Mpande, half-brother of Dingane. By decision of the *Volksraad*, now meeting in Pietermaritzburg, an expedition to crush finally the power of Dingane had become necessary: to ensure the survival of the embryonic Voortrekker state.

In January 1840, Mpande's army of about 10,000 moved into Zululand, commanded by Nongalaza. Mpande himself – as a safeguard – was part of the mixed commando under Pretorius, consisting of 300 whites and 460 attached Africans and Coloureds. Dingane was well-informed of the approaching threat to his dominance. He thereupon dispatched a special envoy, Dambuza, who was accompanied by his servant, Kombazana, to sue Pretorius for peace.

It became another excruciating incident in the still persistent theme of the persecuted becoming the persecutors, and then becoming the persecuted again . . .; of blood being requited with blood alone.

Dambuza and Kombazana, having arrived at Pretorius' *laager*, were immediately arrested and hauled before a hastily assembled court-martial. Chief prosecutor, witness and judge in the trial now became Mpande, who for obvious reasons wished the elimination of the ring-heads immediately surrounding his adversary for the Zulu throne, his half-brother, Dingane. Dambuza, said Mpande and those of his immediate circle, had been Dingane's chief advisor at the time of the visit of Retief and his commando to Mgungundlovu. He had also, according to them, been prominent in the matter of the subsequent ferocious attack upon the *laagers* among the headwaters of the Tugela. Pretorius found Mpande plausible enough and allowed matters to take their tragic course. Dambuza, now finding himself the victim of action 'contrary to all law and justice',[17] nevertheless acted with the greatest calmness and dignity. He did not refute what Mpande had said, neither did he wish to defend himself. He did point out, however, that he had come as an envoy to talk about peace. He would not ask for mercy but pleaded that Kombazana be regarded as his servant, obeying his orders. Kombazana, however, thereupon refused to suffer any other fate than that of his ring-head master.

Sentence of death was announced and Pretorius solemnly preached to the condemned, recommending them to pray to Almighty God for forgiveness of their sins. To this Dambuza answered that his only obedience was to Dingane, and that the great Lord of which Pretorius had spoken would surely approve of his conduct. One last request he wished to make, however: that he not be killed by boys or small men, but by warriors of large physique.

That same day the two prisoners, who had come as envoys, were manacled together, naked, and shot. Two white members of Pretorius' commando fired at them from a distance of sixty paces. Kombazana was killed instantly; but Dambuza, with a shot through the body, rose at once, still manacled to the limp body of Kombazana, and proudly once more faced his executioners. Further shots were fired; and then Dambuza, too, was dead.

This act of Pretorius was subsequently deplored in the *Volksraad*, as he had clearly exceeded his authority. Those who disapproved of what he had done, however, were in the minority and the matter was allowed to drop. Pretorius, the hero of Blood River, the commando leader of great courage and charisma, had here done something which McCall Theal, an unstinting admirer of the pioneer Boers, described as a great mistake as well as a great crime.[18]

The rebel Zulu army, led by Nongalaza, moved into Zululand and finally overcame the forces of Dingane near the Mkuzi river. Shortly afterwards Dingane himself fled northwards, where he was killed by the Swazi. Pretorius then proclaimed Mpande King of the Zulu, to become a vassal to the Republic of Natalia. The commando returned with 36,000 head of cattle and also many children, captured by the Zulu to be apprenticed as servants.

Had the Zulu threat to Natal, to Southern Africa generally, been finally broken by this Aeschylean sequence of events? It would be true to say that it was effectively subdued for at least the next generation. That Blood River and what followed put an end to Zulu power once and for all, however, is a myth. The force which finally broke the Zulu as a nation of exceptional militancy was the imperial English.

The decisive 'ruin of Zululand', as Miss Colenso was to describe it,[19] turned out to be one of the most important chapters in the far-reaching, high-souled history of Victorian imperialism. In its entirety the Anglo-Zulu War of 1879 far exceeded in its cost in human lives and in money the First Anglo-Boer War, which was almost immediately to follow.

It was the rise of Cetshwayo, nephew of Shaka, out of the stagnation of the Mpande vassalage and what followed, that brought on the struggle. The British had at first been extremely reluctant to expand imperially into Natal; but in 1844, after the collapse of the Republic of Natalia, the province had been incorporated into the Cape Colony. Immigrants kept coming in a steady stream; but by the end of the seventies the white community of about 8000 was becoming uncomfortably aware that a highly-trained Zulu army of some 40–50,000, now armed with good rifles, were poised to move on the borders of Natal. What added to the general nervousness was the view in high circles that an independent Zulu Kingdom of such militant power was a serious obstacle to the ideal of a British Federation of Southern Africa, as dreamt of by Lord Carnarvon and others. War with Cetshwayo, it was believed by the colonial authorities in Natal, had become inevitable.

On 11 December 1878, the British sought to determine the boundaries of Zululand once and for all, demanding at the same time the extradition of certain murderers and fines for other crimes committed. Most important, however, was the injunction that the Zulu military system be done away with and that a British resident be stationed in Zululand. For all practical purposes this amounted to a declaration of war. Cavalry, infantry and artillery, under Lord Chelmsford, 'to exact from Cetshwayo reparations for violations of British territory' then invaded Zululand in four separate columns. The British had, however, hopelessly underestimated the strength of Cetshwayo's army, having ignored the sound advice of Paul Kruger, who had been Vice-President of the South African Republic immediately before annexation by Great Britain in April 1877. At Isandhlwana, the invading forces suffered a major disaster. Nearly 900 British, officers and men, and 800 supporting Zulu were destroyed. Panic-stricken colonists took ship for the Cape. Greater disaster might have followed had not a fortunate telegraphic appeal to London brought immediate results. The shock of Isandhlwana had alerted the whole British world. From many corners of the Empire – Ceylon, Mauritius, the United Kingdom itself – troops arrived. Naval brigades employing artillery and rocket-tubes were also sent to assist. The Zulu threat was generally regarded as a supreme danger to the whole of Southern Africa.

Many moving incidents took place. There was the death of the Prince Imperial of France who had volunteered for service. Pieter Lavras Uys, son of the Uys who had fallen at Italeni, and leader of a Boer commando in the war, was also killed.

The final engagement took place at Cetshwayo's royal *kraal* Ulundi on 4 July 1879, when Chelmsford set out to settle matters before being superseded in his post by Sir Garnet Wolseley. The full power of the imperial troops, with nearly 800 artillerymen using thirty-six guns, was now directed against a Zulu army of some 20,000. It was only with a supreme effort that victory was at last obtained.[20]

It was an English rock which finally caused the Zulu ship of state to founder. The power which the Voortrekkers had checked in the late thirties and the early forties was only finally broken in 1879. In doing so, Afrikaners and Anglo-Saxons were increasingly sharing a common experience. The Zuurveld of the eastern frontier of the colony, the green hills and forests of Zululand, provided the common ground. Africa itself was the catalyst: its vastness, mystery and dismaying complexity of human motives.

Back in the forties, the Voortrekker Republic of Natalia had not survived its premature birth. For a year or two it had seemed as if the Land of Promise would be realized in Natal. By 1840 the Republic had extended to beyond the Drakensberg, so as to include Winburg in the Transorangia and Potchefstroom in the Transvaal. The *Volksraad* was operating on a rudimentary but reasonably effective scale. There had been encouraging support from influential quarters. Daniel Lindley, who had returned from Mosega with Potgieter's punitive commando, was now the official pastor of the Trekkers. He became their devoted *predikant*, an American with Puritan antecedents among the Boers.

With autonomy having a semblance of reality, Pretorius, in effect leading the Republic, was determined to consolidate what had been gained. In 1841 he led a commando southwards to the Mzimvubu to recover cattle allegedly stolen by the Bhaca, causing the loss of some thirty lives among the blacks. The neighbouring Mpondo chief, Faku, thereupon appealed to the British for protection. What may also have contributed to action was the policy of segregation which the *Volksraad* had accepted for the Republic. It was nevertheless the same policy which later in the century would be applied with much greater thoroughness by Theophilus Shepstone, according to some, South Africa's greatest administrator of Africans. 'Surplus' blacks would be moved south, the *Volksraad* had decided. By June 1842, the British under Captain T. C. Smith were back in Port Natal and were being beleaguered by the Boers. Richard King undertook an epic ride from Port Natal to Grahamstown to fetch aid. The news which the British authority on the eastern frontier of the Colony received was not only that of immigrant Boers threatening Port Natal, but also that the *Volksraad* had had dealings with a view to Dutch intervention. At the end of June 1842, the *Conch* and *Southampton* arrived at Port Natal with reinforcements. Under cover of the ships' cannons the troops, led by a Cape Afrikaner (but one of the by-now-anglicized community) Lieut.-Col. Abraham Josias Cloete, were soon ashore. Andries Pretorius, who had since the days of Blood River known so much military success, had now no alternative but to retire.

The anger and bitterness with which the Afrikaner community in Natal received the news was expressed on 8 August, when 400 Voortrekker women led by Johanna Smit, sister of the dead Gert Maritz, presented a petition to Henry Cloete, brother of the lieutenant-colonel, and Her Majesty Queen Victoria's commissioner in the district of Port Natal. The Afrikaner women, Mrs Smit defiantly declared, would much rather walk barefoot back over the Drakensberg than submit to the English. Freedom or trek was their demand.

But the formal surrender by the *Volksraad* had already taken place on 15 July. After six years of intense and complicated revolt against British colonial authority, the Trekkers had discovered themselves to be almost exactly where they had started. Boer and Briton had already found themselves to be inextricably linked to each other under the sapphire skies of Southern Africa. Their attitudes toward each other would range from hatred to love and back again. But, whatever happened, they were stuck with each other.

Much the same sort of relationship had already developed between Boer and Bantu. On the battlefields of Natal, around the *laagers*, among the green hills, in the deeply undulating valleys and thickly wooded *kloofs*, their blood had wetted the same African earth. A time would come when also the fallen Zulu would be remembered with humility by an Afrikaner poet:

> When warriors again go out to war,
> the hilltops pulsing with their savage dance,
> the shields thunder and the spear points flash
> high in the sun:
> then you sleep on
> and you sleep sound,
> your feathers scattered far by sun and rain,
> your body with its tender coppery gleam
> perished, and you?
> The grasses still will bend,
> the cattle low, and life will call,
> but you?
> Here where you lay, sheep graze in morning dew.[21]

3 The Heroic Age: The Wars of Independence

Had it all been a case of things absurdly coming to naught? Had all the mutual violence, the loss of life and property, the fine sentiments, the martyrdom, the solemn vow before the Battle of Blood River, the requitements in blood, been a mere exercise in futility? Had these immigrant pioneers, who would become the most vital element in the history of the Afrikaners, in their triumph over the Zulu Kingdom, in the summary justice they meted out to those who had caused them injury, in the questionable practice of child 'apprenticeship' (especially when punitive expeditions returned to the *laagers*), in their enforcement of segregation in church and state, merely been acting more or less in the way the British imperium had been acting towards them?

'The Great Trek,' Leo Marquard has said,

had divided South Africa politically into British colonies, Boer republics, and African tribal lands ... the Great Trek brought African tribesmen into armed conflict with Boer commandos; but after each local conflict the social life of the African was not greatly different from what it had been. He might lose some of his land or he might be subjected to Boer rule; but he continued to live his simple tribal life. When he went to work on Boer farms he found the ways of the white man strange, but he continued to do the kind of things he had been accustomed to: he tended cattle and sheep, grew maize and vegetables, and lived the unhurried seasonal life of a farm; he kept his social customs of initiation and marriage dowry; he ate his customary food and drank kaffir-corn beer brewed by his womenfolk. His Boer master knew his language and was good-naturedly tolerant of his ways. In spite of the vast and obvious difference between Christian white and heathen black, there was much in common between the Boer farmer and the African farm labourer, and each had the leisure to adapt himself to the other's habits. The relationship between the two was patriarchal and personal.[1]

In this traditional social structure of the frontier – even when it was still in a state of mobility, when the inland dominion of Afrikanerdom in the form of the South African Republic (the Transvaal) and the Orange Free State, was still rudimentary – there was as yet nothing of the cultural destruction of a subject people which would cause so many of the colonial peoples of the twentieth century to react in violence and bitterness.

The very nature of early Afrikaner society was un-colonial in the sense in which Fanon and a great many other kindred spirits of our time have looked at the phenomenon. The Afrikaners themselves had revolted against colonialism. For anything like this to come about in the evolving Afrikaner societies, a fundamental change would have to come about in their own economic structure. This was to happen, but at a date far removed from the frontier days of the Afrikaners.

Even in the days of slavery, before the Trek had started, there had been a great deal of intimate going-about with each other (*verkeer*) in the communal life of the white Afrikaners and their non-white slaves or servants. In history the phenomenon is as old as Rome or Athens, as a distinguished student of the classics, a modern Afrikaner, has pointed out:

Let us apply this to the historical situation in our own country, particularly as regards the social history of the Afrikaner people. Have we ever paused to ask ourselves what the full significance is of the circumstance that generation after generation of our Afrikaans ancestors were nurtured at the breasts of Indian, Hottentot and negro women, and received a good part of their early education from slave and Hottentot men who, ignorant of classical traditions, acted unwittingly as their trusted and beloved 'pedagogues'? What strange love was imbibed, to be passed on to future generations? What stories were learnt? And the language they heard from the lips of those slaves – was it not the *lingua vernacula*, the Cape Dutch, of the slaves, the Cape vernacular? Truly, our forbears may be said to have imbibed the vernacular language together with the vernacular milk . . .[2]

It was in this spirit that non-Whites, not only at the Cape or in the greater Cape but also in the distant inland, towards the eastern border districts on the Great Karroo, formed, as Hugo says, 'an integral and indispensable part of civilized society'.

Children of all races played together; prayers were shared by all; and in the older settled district of the Cape, there was until the second half of the nineteenth century no separate 'Mission Church' for the Cape Coloured people of the Reformed faith.

The movement of the immigrant Afrikaners to the interior of Southern Africa back to the inland highveld between the Vaal and the Orange, and beyond the Vaal, was something unique in the history of the West. This was not like the Conquistadores – Cortez in Mexico or Pizarro in Peru – unremittingly subjecting a culture with an already high degree of development to the Spanish imperium and mind. Nor was it the 'destruction and frenzy' of the Spaniards who hunted Indians with bloodhounds, of which Alexis de Tocqueville speaks. It was not even the equivalent of what this same observer testifies to in his classic assessment of pioneer America in its dealing with its own indigenous peoples: '. . . It is impossible to destroy men with more respect for the laws of humanity.'[3]

In the old order of Afrikanerdom, also as a *maatschappij* on trek, the patriarchal or semi-feudal structure naturally meant a hierarchy in which ex-slaves and recent primitives occupied the bottom rungs. By the beginning of the second half of the nineteenth century, most of the immigrant Afrikaners were back on the central highveld. By 1855 there were roughly four groups north of the Orange: those in the Transorangia, still looked upon as British subjects by the Imperial authority and those in the Transvaal. These included the Andries Pretorius people in and around Potchefstroom; the Hendrik Potgieter group, now under Stephanus Schoeman, in the shadow of the sub-tropical Zoutpansberg; and more Potgieter people in the east, towards the verdant, feverish lowveld.

During the preceding decade, the British had been busy developing Natal as an extension of the Cape Colony. They were at the same time deeply embroiled in another particularly destructive war, on the eastern frontier: the seventh. Sir Harry Smith, the driving spirit in the very determined suppression of the Xhosa by British soldiery, nevertheless had time and men enough to intervene when the Afrikaners beyond the Orange, led by an irrepressible but now ageing Andries Pretorius, compelled the British Resident at Bloemfontein, Major Warden, to capitulate. At Boomplaats Sir Harry at last put an end to the long line of military successes of the much-seasoned Commandant-General. The clash was short and sharp, and Pretorius soon realized that the odds were against him. Having heard that Sir Harry had offered a prize of £2000 for his capture, he retaliated by offering 1000 cattle for anyone bringing him Sir Harry. But the hero of Blood River's remarkable career as a commando leader had come to an end. Like the rest of his company, he retired to his farm. Five years later, seeing few signs of a stable society around him in the Transvaal, he died. He was 54.

Not long after Boomplaats, Warden was back in Bloemfontein. The British soon discovered, however, that the Boers were the lesser of their worries. The Sotho in the east, led by the wise and formidable Moshweshwe, were proving to be difficult. The Xhosa, too, supported now by Hottentots, were here in the early fifties, steadily defying a still essentially reluctant authority, which was, however, deeply committed to suppressing them.

The moment for the Afrikaners was propitious. In 1852 a convention, meeting on the farm Sand River, acknowledged the independence of the farmers north of the Vaal. Perhaps some 40,000 had already settled there. A meeting of Whites, gathering that same year in Bloemfontein, decided in favour of British sovereignty. The British, however, were set on getting rid of their burden. The next year a special commissioner arrived in Bloemfontein, calling upon the inhabitants to take over the government. It was all rather un-British, at a time when the spirit of the imperium elsewhere was on the ascendant. Between the Orange and the Vaal there were not more than 15,000 Whites.

The Free State, being nearer to the relatively-settled Cape and on the whole to the demanding, imperious British, soon became a stable political entity. Professionals and businessmen, many of British stock, arrived. A constitution was drawn up with 'sixty-two crisp articles'. Most fortunate was the election of Sir John Henry Brand of the Cape as President in 1864. He was a Cape Afrikaner, one of the older tradition. For the next twenty-four years he would govern wisely and well: so well, in fact, that

James Bryce, first Viscount, who visited the Boer republics in the nineties, in the account of his journey declared the Orange Free State to be a model state. [4]

In the Transvaal things were never good. In the middle forties a constitution of sorts *au pis aller* had been drawn up, mainly to provide for the annual election of a *Volksraad*, trying to exercise both legislative and executive powers. Before and after Sand River it was abundantly clear that the Transvaal administration, with no centre from where it could establish a permanent public service, was more or less chaotic. The old Trek leaders, Pretorius and Potgieter, took the lead desultorily and ineffectually. When both died, early in the fifties, their mantles, now rather tattered, fell on their sons, M. W. Pretorius and Piet Potgieter. The latter died two years after his father; and then only the younger Pretorius remained.

To the west of the Transvaal lay the unknown Kalahari Thirstland; to the north the equally unknown Trans-Limpopo. Within the Transvaal all was still peaceful. The highveld tribes had not yet recovered from the reign of Mzilikazi. In the south-east the Zulu under Mpande were still docile. In the west were the elusive, secretive Portuguese.

What the Transvaal lacked were the 'English'. For a quarter of a century they would be more of a memory than a reality. The Free State would have the 'English' and it would be to the Free State's advantage. The British would be, if not within the boundaries of the republic, then more or less continually on its borders. They were in and around Basutoland, the country of Moshweshwe, who would ask for and be granted British protection. In time they would become an integral part of Griqualand West, and the diamond fields.

The rise of the Transvaal and of the northern Afrikaners within the greater body of Afrikanerdom was to coincide almost exactly with the extension of British imperial interest into the far inland highveld beyond the Vaal. That was only to come about in the late seventies. Lack of mephistophelean interest in the Afrikaners beyond the Vaal would provide no opportunity for:

> *Ein Teil von jener Kraft*
> *Die stets das Böse will, und stets das Gute schafft.* [5]

The 'good' would have to wait until Great Britain had sufficient reason to extend her imperial influence over those corners of Southern Africa.

Meanwhile, what was happening in the world? In 1848 the *Communist Manifesto* had stated:

The bourgeoisie, wherever it has got the upper hand, has put an end to all feudal, patriarchal, idyllic relations. It has pitilessly torn asunder the motley feudal ties that bound man to his natural superiors, and has left remaining no other nexus between man and man than naked self-interest, than callous cash payment.

Strangely, the primitive Calvinists on the inland highveld of Southern Africa might well have provided Marx with a most interesting field of study. It was British activities on foreign soil, like the Crimean War (1854–6) and the Indian Mutiny, which perhaps gave the republican Afrikaners an opportunity to go their way. The French were heard to compare the Mutiny to the Charge of the Light Brigade: '*c'est magnifique, mais ce n'est pas la guerre.*' But the British were nevertheless capable of waging war. This was demonstrated by the Mutiny when the Bengal Army, resisting further erosion of the Indian soil, rose to restore the empire of the Great Mogul.

The spirit of the age was enigmatic. During the first half of the century there had been signs enough in the West of quests for a more humane society. Robert Owen, for instance, had made New Lanark a model of enlightened industrialism. The British, whatever their other shortcomings, had already adopted legislation improving the condition of factory workers. Marx and Engels had, in their *Manifesto*, spoken ringingly to, and on behalf of, the alienated working-class. In Paris, Louis le Blanc had bloodily sought to employ many thousands of jobless workers in his *Ateliers Nationaux*, under a red flag.

Now here in the second half of the century it soon became apparent that the Age of the Common Man had not yet arrived. On the contrary, the already established forces of nationhood and capital were everywhere re-aligning their strengths, regrouping and re-asserting themselves. In America the socio-political ideal of life, liberty and the pursuit of happiness had come into destructive conflict with the feudal, patriarchal society of the south.

Before the end of the decade Victoria would be proclaimed in Delhi *Kaiser-i-Hind*, Empress of India. As far back as 1857, Lord Canning had already become the first of the Viceroys. But the British were by no means alone among Europeans in these foreign adventures. In 1860 a combined British and French force had attacked the city of Peking, plundered the old Summer Palace and destroyed its treasures. This was during the Second Opium War.

Britain, France, Germany, Belgium ... In turn they would all, in increasing measure, seek platforms in Africa, spheres of influence, areas of exploitation. It was, in the language of the diamond diggers themselves, soon to appear a rush, not a scramble. Britain had come originally to the Cape because of her interests in India, but was now becoming sensitive to her own Southern African destiny. The eastern frontier of the Cape Colony had required increasing money and military attention, as it extended up to Natal. In 1857 Natal was granted representative government, a year or two after the Cape. Early in the seventies, on Zandfontein Farm on the banks of the Vaal, some way above the river's confluence with the Orange, a diamond of 83.5 carats was found. Rumours of gold discoveries in the Transvaal were also by now frequent enough. A German geologist, Carl Mauch, had made a well-substantiated claim of having made a gold strike on the banks of the Tati. An objective observer viewing the progress of things on the sub-continent at, say, the first half of the seventies, and relating it to the developing spirit of the age, could have foreseen the political future, at least in its general outline. Boer and Briton would not each continue to go their own way. With the Bantu they shared a common situation. Only at times did it seem as if they were each acting out their own soliloquies. They were essentially on the same stage, performing in the same play.

The relatively well-ordered Orange Free State would, surprisingly, last as a sovereign state up to the turn of the century.

Not that things for the Free State were ever uneventful. There had been constant trouble with the Sotho. The First Basuto War had not gone too well for the Republican forces. Moshweshwe, from the Mountain of the Night, Thaba Bosiu, an almost impregnable fortress, frustrated the burghers in their attempts to subdue him.

By 1866 the Free State commandos were once more facing Sotho forces more numerous than themselves. Again Thaba Bosiu proved to be impregnable; and the commando leader, Louw Wepener, heroically lost his life. It was only after Paul Kruger arrived opportunely from the Transvaal with a commando, that the Basotho were subdued. Kruger was later to become Transvaal State President. The following year, however, war broke out afresh. It ended suddenly when Britain decided to take Moshweshwe and his people under Imperial protection. President Brand protested. The Free State had borne the brunt of Sotho depredations and Britain was now claiming the benefits.

The Colonial Office had all along been prompted by missionaries (like David Livingstone) and others, to re-establish British authority beyond the Orange. Why were they ignored? Why was Britain only prepared to take peripheral action? They were concerned merely with protecting the Sotho, and the Griquas under Nicolaas Waterboer, when the ownership of the new diamond fields in 1871 had become a sharp issue.

For the new diamond-rich lands between the Orange and Vaal, which, according to the Free Staters, were indisputably part of the Republic (having been so described at the Convention of Bloemfontein), were now included in Griqualand West, which had been annexed to the Cape Colony. This was as a result of arbitration on the issue of ownership. In April 1871, the lieutenant-governor of Natal, Robert William Keate, had decided between the Free State, Waterboer and also the Transvaal. The award went to Waterboer. The consequence was annexation. There had been a time earlier in 1871 when a Free State commando and Cape Mounted Police had faced each other at the diggings. The most that could be done after annexation, President Brand ruefully decided, was to go to

London and protest. This proved to be only partly successful. Britain paid the Free State £90,000 to relinquish her claim. This was accepted by the Free State.

Once more, this raises an awkward question. Why had Britain, with ever-widening and deepening imperial power, moved so apologetically, as the case of the diamond compensation had shown, on the borders of a puny little republic? Britain had protected Moshweshwe and Waterboer and had 'stolen' the diamond fields. They had made their imperial presence felt. The Free State, nevertheless, retained its independence.

The question is even more relevant with regard to the Transvaal. The Free State, at least, was well-ordered. In the Transvaal, however, a happy anarchy existed by comparison.

M. W. Pretorius had accepted the mantle of his father. In 1857, rather high-handedly, he claimed authority over all the land between the Orange and Vaal as part of his political legacy. When the Free State rejected this claim, they sought the aid of Pretorius' rival in the North, Schoeman of Zoutpansberg. Soon a Free State commando faced one under Pretorius near the Renoster River, not far from Vegkop, where Mzilikazi had once attacked the Voortrekkers. Paul Kruger, however, took the lead in a last-minute attempt to restore brotherly amity, and succeeded in doing so. An armed clash was avoided and peace restored.

But there was no subduing Pretorius. In 1860, in spite of his former assertiveness, he was elected as the successor of President Boshoff in the Free State. A federation of the two republics was his expressed intention. The *Volksraad* at Pretoria, however, was an immediate obstacle. Choose between the two presidencies, they said. This is what Pretorius did. He resigned as head of state in the Transvaal, while in no way abandoning his activities there. An unlikely ally was found in Stephanus Schoeman, his old opponent. Soon afterwards a rebel meeting at Potchefstroom rejected the *Volksraad*, declaring Pretorius to be still President of the Transvaal, Schoeman being his understudy.

By the beginning of the sixties, two factions had defined themselves. On the one hand there was a constitutional government with W. J. C. van Rensburg as President and Paul Kruger as Commandant-General, especially strong at Potchefstroom, with its strictly Reformed Calvinists, and at Lydenburg. Ranged against it was Pretorius *in absentia*, represented by Stephanus Schoeman and Jan Viljoen. Four years of political conflict followed. On a balmy highveld morning, in January 1864, commando stood against commando, Calvinist psalm sounded against Calvinist psalm and brother rode against brother. The constitutional army (*Staatsleër*) of Paul Kruger fought the people's army (*Volksleër*) of Jan Viljoen. After the fighting the *Volksleër* counted five dead and thirty wounded. In Kruger's forces two had been killed, eight wounded.

Pretorius, who had meanwhile resigned from his Free State office, suddenly emerged as a peacemaker. This was strange, for the whole civil struggle in the Transvaal had mainly revolved around his rather mediocre personality. Even more startling, in the perspective of history, was his subsequent re-election as President of the Transvaal.

In the far North the Venda erupted, retaliating for raids on their property (by Boers, they said). Kruger could hardly raise a commando of 400 men. Schoemansdal at the Zoutpansberg was abandoned and black rebellion spread from the Limpopo to the Olifants. A highveld version of Moshweshwe might well have seized the opportunity for imposing a black polity.

Living in such fine isolation, in the manner of the grazier/hunters of the eighteenth century, these most northern of the Afrikaners seemed to have got lost in Africa for the second time. They had come back over the Drakensberg from Natal and discovered the highveld to be bountiful. They chose their farms, spreading over a vast area. The soil was arable and game was plentiful. They went off on great hunting expeditions – westwards to the Crocodile, northwards to the Limpopo, eastwards to the lowveld . . .

In the bushveld and lowveld the trees bore an excellent crop of veld-fruit. The rains were much more reliable. The highveld in a good summer was a sea of grass. The Blacks, generally, were distantly located. The 'English' had gone off . . .

There was too much peace. Splendid self-sufficiency makes for triviality.

There had been the unseemly *broedertwis* – argument between brothers – culminating in the futile little civil war. It had lasted but a day. It was typical of the uninspiring leadership of M. W. Pretorius. For some years the *Volksraad* was like an amateur road show, meeting here and there, with not much to do, because there was no money.

The state of the *volk* became apparent when M. W. Pretorius at last (in 1872) bowed his way out, to no-one's great regret. The Transvaal now needed a president, a 'learned' man. Sir John Henry Brand of the Free State had declined an invitation. So the offer went to another Cape Afrikaner – a minister who had been charged with heresy by the Cape Church and found guilty. His eventual appeal to the Privy Council had succeeded, however, and he had been reinstated. He was a liberal in the full nineteenth-century sense of the word.

How Thomas François Burgers came to be President of the South African Republic is one of the singular chapters in the story of the Afrikaners. Burgers supported the positivism of Auguste Comte and the empiricism of J. S. Mill. The tenor of his preaching was to break with the theology of the Reformed Church.

Only a minority of bed-rock conservatives in the Transvaal had reservations. They included Paul Kruger. But the need of the Transvaal was so great, that Burgers was persuaded to stand for election. He won by 2964 votes to 388, against William Robinson.

It was a bizarre situation. Here was this Calvinist farmers' republic, patriarchal, semi-feudal, economically bankrupt, politically primitive, being led by a man who had conducted long public debates pleading for a secular faith. He taught and wrote like a rationalist, looked like a mystic. To have such a man lead such a society was to guarantee failure.

To the credit of Burgers it must be said that, when he entered the ' conditions of confusion and anarchy',[6] he really had the most courageous intentions. He sought to develop the new Lydenburg goldfields, founded a newspaper (*De Volkstem*), a library, a botanical garden and a college for secondary schooling. He travelled to Europe. The British distrusted him; but the Dutch and Belgians fêted him. He was given a honorary doctorate by the University of Utrecht. He was even knighted. His main object, however, was to raise money for the building of a railway from Delagoa Bay to the Transvaal border. He spent £60,000 – two-thirds of the money he had been able to raise in the Netherlands by debentures – on railway material, most of which was then left to rust in Flushing awaiting shipment, only some of it eventually reaching Delagoa Bay. The President had once entertained ideas of changing the coat of arms and the flag of the Republic. What he did manage, however, was to get a Dutch composer to write a successful national hymn.

Shortly after taking office he had purchased a nugget of Lydenburg gold – there had been something of a gold rush in the Eastern Transvaal – had it coined, the pieces bearing on them the Transvaal arms and his own likeness, then presented each member of the *Volksraad* with one. So, too, he did to every head of state who recognized the independence of the South African Republic.

Having extolled the virtues of the Transvaal as an area for European settlement, Burgers returned at last, bringing with him some lecturers for the intended State Gymnasium in Pretoria, also a Superintendent-General of education. Alas, as McCall Theal was to remark in another context, there was unfortunately nothing for the new dignitary to superintend.

Back on the highveld, Burgers personally but quite disastrously led a reluctant commando against the recalcitrant Bapedi chief, Sekhukhuni, in the mountain country near Lydenburg. The Bapedi had been building up a considerable supply of firearms since 1866. Initially the commando had been able to dislodge the enemy from certain strongholds. When Sekhukhuni himself was attacked, however, resistance stiffened and the whole commando began to disintegrate, the deserters justifying their behaviour on the grounds that the Lord could not possibly support an expedition led by such a God-questioning man as Thomas François Burgers.

'The military force of the republic had completely broken down,'[7] Theal records; and shortly afterwards the *Volksraad* met in the most depressing circumstances. The country was hopelessly bankrupt. Trade had almost completely ceased. Gold-diggers at Lydenburg, and English and German residents of the villages, were often behaving as if there were no republican authority. The Bapedi were ultimately brought to some order, not by republican forces but by volunteers led by a free-wheeling Irishman called Aylward. He was assisted by the Berlin missionary, Merensky, who had influenced Sekhukhuni to sue for peace.

In these confused conditions, some ultra-fundamentalist Afrikaners of the far west had decided that for them the Transvaal held no future. A 'moving spirit of trek' had by the mid-seventies set them off in various groups on one of the most hazardous and strange journeys in the history of Western man. Straight into the Kalahari Thirstland they went, following the sun, believing that somewhere beyond the last horizon they would eventually discover Beulah, Land of Rest. There they would establish themselves in final self-sufficiency, free from the God-taunting ideas of the President; out of reach, too, of the English. For there had indeed been talk for some time of the English returning to the highveld. Disraeli's Colonial Secretary, Earl Carnarvon, having succeeded in the unification of Canada, had for some time been thinking of repeating his success, this time in Southern Africa.

At a terrific cost in human lives and material loss, these people went on trekking for the next five years, crossing in the process some 2000 miles of the most difficult terrain in all Africa.

The Thirstland of the Kalahari held its terrors, but the great fever marshes of the Okavango swamps even more so. By 1879 the remnants of the original 500–600 had gathered at Namutoni on the Great Etosha Pan of South-West Africa. The country was in a state of almost unabated war, with Nama – Hottentot – and Herero concluding a half-century of mutual near-destruction. The Thirstlanders had not yet reached their Land of Rest. They moved off into the wild and almost inaccessible country of the Kaokoveld, still following the sun. There they were visited by a remarkable man, Will Worthington Jordan, who became their guide, counsellor and friend, as well as their physician. He was a hunter-trader, linguist, amateur medico and dreamer of a new and civilized order in a war-torn country. In the new immigrant Boers from the Transvaal he thought he had found just the right material. Only with them as a nucleus, he concluded, could peace and development come to his beloved South-West Africa.

The saga of Jordan's journey with the Thirstlanders to a remote highland in Portuguese West Africa, Catholic Angola rather than Calvinist Beulah, is not in the mainstream of Afrikaner history. Essentially, however, this mid-eighties story of tough, principled Afrikaners jealously preserving their own version of the Reformed tradition, has a significance for all history: that of man, at any price, pursuing 'the impossible dream'. The finest turn of irony in the chapter of the Thirstlanders was the remarkable fact that Will Jordan, born and raised at the Cape, who later became in his manner of dying a martyr in the cause of the irreducibly hard core of white Afrikanerdom, was coloured.

The British came to the Transvaal in 1877 peacefully, almost casually. Lord Carnarvon's London conference with a view to a South African federation had finally collapsed. The British press had for some time been publishing details of Transvaal's inability to manage its own affairs. This was demonstrated especially by the clumsy campaign against the Bapedi and the chaotic conditions of the national finances. The following January, Sir Theophilus Shepstone, acting as a special imperial commissioner to the Transvaal, arrived with a party of twenty-five mounted police and eight officials: among them being the romantic novelist H. Rider Haggard. For sleepy Pretoria this was the social event of the decade. There were balls, banquets, a whole series of festivities, to make Shepstone and his party feel at home. The President, it seemed, had by this time privately made up his own mind that the only thing that could really save the Transvaal was British annexation.

Shepstone took things in leisurely style, enjoying both the autumnal weather and the hospitality and ignoring the mutterings of some suspicious souls like the new Vice-President, Paul Kruger. He was by no means alarmed by the presence on occasion of a commando of 300 in the streets of Pretoria. Nevertheless, he promised the President that he would take no further steps, if certain reforms could immediately be undertaken. The President obliged.

Still in two minds about the whole affair, however, Burgers soon ran into trouble with both Sekhukhuni and his own *Volksraad*. The former now refused to sign a peace treaty; and the latter, supported by the commando outside the President's house, was belatedly insisting on independence. Meanwhile Cetshwayo and his formidable and well-armed Zulu regiments were massing on the south-eastern border. Before the end of the decade the British in Natal would feel the full force of Zulu military power.

With the Utrecht farmers protesting, and Cetshwayo withdrawing, Shepstone, after a sojourn of two-and-a-half months in Pretoria, took the final step. As a last resort, desperately, the executive council offered a treaty with the other states of South Africa. It was too late, however. On the morning of 12 April 1877, Rider Haggard, who might well during the previous weeks have been thinking out his story of *King Solomon's Mines*, hoisted the Queen's flag over the little capital. There was an immediate protest from Burgers and the *Volksraad*, of course: but it was a formality, at least as far as the President was concerned. After more than three decades of shaky, often improbable, existence, the South African Republic had collapsed. The comedy had ended.

The shock, a delayed one, spread steadily through the languid body of the polity. A year after the annexation, one Gerrit Kok, in the style of the highveld fiefdom, was welcoming hundreds of guests from many parts of the Transvaal to enjoy his hospitality under the pleasant oaks on his farm Doornfontein, situated on the highroad between Potchefstroom and Pretoria. They had arrived to protest against the annexation. Commissions had been sent out to various parts of the Transvaal to test the people's feelings. The former Vice-President, Paul Kruger, and Dr E. P. J. Jorissen, whom ex-President Burgers had brought from Holland to help staff the new State Gymnasium, had travelled to London to make known the feelings of the

Transvaal to Lord Carnarvon. It was all to no avail. What Her Britannic Majesty had decided, the deputation was informed, could never be undone.

After the meeting at Doornfontein, Kruger went again to London, this time accompanied by Commandant-General Piet Joubert and the State Secretary, Eduard Bok. The highveld slumber of the most northern Afrikaners was now fast coming to an end. What civil war, the obstreperous Venda and the intractable Bapedi, even the eloquent, progressive, Calvin-rejecting Thomas François Burgers could not do, the English would do. In various places in the Transvaal British garrisons arriving from Natal were soon set up. At the same time there had been a continuation of the *volksvergaderings* – meetings of the people – with burghers coming from afar to attend. This led to a massive get-together of 6000 people at Wonderfontein at the end of 1879. With the *Vierkleur* flying in the breeze, the meeting solemnly pledged itself to the cause of freedom; at the same time, anew, to the honouring of the law and the development and progress of the country. Ex-President Burgers had meanwhile retired to the Cape Colony, there to receive a British pension until his death in 1881.

While the ex-President went farming in the Karroo, the Transvalers were preparing for battle. At Paardekraal, between Potchefstroom and Pretoria, some 10,000 burghers assembled on 8 December 1879. Ironically the British had not only drawn this reaction from them, they had also enabled many of them to leave their farms in comparative safety. The previous year, Sir Garnet Wolseley, governor of Natal and the Transvaal, had eventually subdued Sekhukhuni. The *volksvergadering* decided to restore the *Volksraad*, appointing a triumvirate to administer the country. It consisted of Vice-President Paul Kruger, Commandant-General Joubert, and ex-President M. W. Pretorius. A great heap of stones was raised at the spot after days of high oratory. As at Blood River, this would mark a new determination and a new trusting in God. On 16 December, the day of Blood River which the Voortrekkers had vowed to commemorate (but had largely forgotten during the 'dark age' of the Transvaal), the *Vierkleur* was raised at Heidelberg. The triumvirate now demanded that the government of the country be handed over to them. That same day the first shots in the War were exchanged. Part of the British garrison at Potchefstroom capitulated within two days. Another part, outside Potchefstroom, under Colonel Winsloe, valiantly withstood the Boer siege until 21 March of the following year.

Four days after the *volksvergadering* at Paardekraal, a major battle was fought at Bronkhorstspruit, not far from the capital. The battle, lasting only ten to twenty minutes, was nevertheless violent and bloody. The British force of 300 lost almost half its men.

The British regiments in the south now retired in the direction of Natal. Commandant-General Joubert then led the main Boer force to Laing's Nek on the Natal border, to prevent General Sir G. Pommeroy Colley, Governor of Natal, from entering the Transvaal. Colley was twice defeated within eleven days. Joubert drove him back from Laing's Nek on 28 January. On 8 February, General Niklaas Smit had the better of things at Ingogo. Colley was then prepared to accept the proposal of Paul Kruger that a Royal Commission decide on the future of the Republic.

Unreasonably, he demanded an answer within forty-eight hours, which was impossible. Burning inside because of his two defeats, Colley then secretly climbed Majuba Mountain with a force of 550 men, thinking he had a commanding position. Having sighted the British on the roughly conical peak at daybreak, Joubert then called for volunteers to remove them. Smit and 200 men – among them the later-to-be-famous Christiaan de Wet – set off without delay and took five hours getting up the mountain. From the top the British had difficulty in seeing the attackers. On the other hand, the defenders could barely raise their heads above the summit rocks without drawing lethal fire. When the attackers eventually stormed the final ridge, many tried to get off the mountain where it was steepest, and fell. In all, ninety British soldiers lay dead that morning on the summit and slopes of Majuba. Many others were wounded or taken prisoner. One burgher lost his life and five were wounded.

It was the end of the First Boer War, the First War of Independence. The generation of sterile isolation in the Transvaal had been left behind. Life now moved on to a more creative plane. In the heat and blood of battle all hesitancy, much mediocrity and a plethora of pettiness had finally been transcended.

It was the definitive form of Afrikaner revolt, its shape that of a burgher commando. Along with it, once again, figures of stature would rise. But it would never have come about had not Theophilus Shepstone run up the Queen's flag so presumptuously that fresh highveld morning in Pretoria. Though they did not know it at the time, the British were shaping a nation.

Everywhere in South Africa things were now stirring. Not only had there been unrest in the Transvaal, which had led to war. In Natal the Anglo-Zulu War had far exceeded in size and cost the first Anglo-Boer War, and had caused the final collapse of Zulu power.

In contemporary Great Britain, the ideals of the collective political system and of individualist economics had been engendered by the same protestant ethic. They had already been well established before the end of the seventeenth century. But it would need the imperial vehicle for the political ideal truly to set it on a course which would conquer the world. The temper of Victorianism was infallibly Puritan. 'Training its pupils to the mastery of others through the mastery of self', R. H. Tawney says of the age, 'it prized as a crown of glory the qualities which arm the spiritual athlete for his solitary contest with a hostile world, and dismissed concern with the social order as the prop of weaklings and the Capua of the soul.'[8]

It was a remarkable quirk of history that a fragment of a West European people should suddenly provide the field for the 'glorious picnic' of the imperial idea. For more than two centuries, they had lost themselves in Southern Africa. Concerned with nothing but their own veld-confined challenges, they had faced up to problems of a purely local nature. The 'spiritual athlete' driven onwards by the unsurpassable ideal of Anglo-Saxonism, Empire and capital, to serve the individual and the collective, was Cecil John Rhodes. The negation of all this was the strictly Reformed Church *Dopper*, soil-rooted farmer and statesman of the *volk*, Paul Kruger. Rhodes and Kruger were both originals. In the most classical way they represented the Faustian situation.

Everything the Afrikaners had faced in the 230-odd years of their presence in Southern Africa – the near century-and-a-half of V.O.C. indifference, the arrogant policy of anglicization by Somerset and his successors, the twofold pressures of British and Bantu on the eastern frontier (with the British predominating), the campaign against Mzilikazi, the conflict with Dingane and the Zulu, the various minor clashes with the colonizing British, dissension within the *volk*, expressing itself in many ways, at many times, the First War of Independence – all this would be overshadowed by the events of the last two decades of the century; by the culminating struggle of the Anglo-Boer War, the Second War of Independence. This would form the climax of the heroic age and the Afrikaners in revolt.

In the discovery of fabulous diamond riches in Kimberley's 'blue ground', and the later discovery (1886) of the even more fabulous, deeply-hidden gold of the Transvaal's Ridge of White Waters, the legend of *Vigiti Magna*, somewhere in the heart of Southern Africa, had fulfilled itself. The country had been spurned by the V.O.C. for a long time because of its apparently meagre natural resources. It was regarded by Great Britain, too, as being very much of a burden, devoid of almost everything which had made North America, Australia and New Zealand worthwhile fields for colonial development. But it had suddenly proved itself. The stone which the builders had rejected now showed all signs of becoming a key-stone in the soaring edifice of Empire.

Of Rhodes it could be said that, in a way beyond rational comprehension, his presence in the South African situation, his sudden, unforeseen development as a personality, his 'immense and brooding spirit' co-ordinated strangely and most remarkably with the discovery of South Africa's great mineral resources. He was the right man at the right time.

Rhodes, the son of a vicar in Bishop's Stortford, Hertford-shire, had been seized by the idea of Empire as the most satisfy-ing expression of the messianic role of the Anglo-Saxons. His drive and finesse in matters of business even got the measure of Barney Barnato in the end. Barnato's capitalism was what the Afrikaners would call *opslag*: annual plant-growth after copious rains, bursting prolifically through the soil in even the oddest places. Rhodes's capitalism was the logical conclusion of a messianic dream.

He was, in fact, of all the figures which appeared in the English Puritan lineage, the most complete embodiment of capitalism rising in close conjunction with Puritan man's secular religion. Money for Barnato, too, meant power; but in a primitive way. Money for Rhodes, as for all who retain roots in the 'protestant ethic', was part of a socio-political ideal allied to the ideal of money. It provided the definitive certitude, the fixed pole-star of his life.

He had arrived in South Africa as a sickly youth, whose schooling had been cut short. Prepared to go farming as a last resort, he found himself at the age of 18 on the Kimberley diggings in the company of the toughest breed of fortune-seekers ever to gather in Southern Africa. At the age of 27 he returned to England to take a degree at Oxford, commuting for ten years between there and Kimberley. He soon controlled not only the South African diamond industry, but also ninety per cent of all world production. Gradually, he came to control effectively the gold-mining industry in Johannesburg. At the age of 37 he had reached the peak of local political office and became Prime Minister of the Cape Colony. The economy of a sovereign independent country now consisted in considerable measure of the personal financial interests of a foreign head of state.

Rhodes was a man of many parts. He was a dreamer who directed his gaze from the eastern slopes of Table Mountain to the far north – beyond the Limpopo and Zambezi – con-templating his own words: 'thy hinterland lies there'. He was also the Man of Empire who brooded on the prospect of painting the map of Africa red from Cape to Cairo. At times, he was

Rhodes, the apostle of Anglo-Saxonism, who saw in his race God's ideal type, serving God's purpose.[9]

Then there was the ruthless, idealistically calculating business-man who, when the B.S.A. Company was badly in the red in 1893, knew that it was either Lobengula's head or the Company's.

Rhodes, the skilful statesman, presided over a cabinet in the early nineties as talented as any in the history of Southern Africa (Hofmeyr, Sauer, Merriman, Rose-Innes). He incorporated British Bechuanaland into the Cape Colony, and concluded the Swazi Convention, all to secure the colonial base and the idea in which he believed. He did this at the expense of the Transvaal and its ageing President.

Rhodes in the mid-nineties was Prime Minister of the Colony, the head of the British South Africa Company, also of De Beers and of Consolidated Goldfields – utterly confident that it was now only a matter of time before the Transvaal, too, would be privileged to share in the great design of a British South Africa.

There was Rhodes treading the road of necessity – for he had both surveyed and constructed it – to the border of the South African Republic at Pitsani where 'Dr Jim' – Jameson – stood ready with his mounted column, as he had once stood ready against Lobengula and the Matabele. Desperately he tried to stop the ill-starred expedition when it had already become too late.

All along too there had been the Rhodes of the Victorian-Puritan conscience conjuring up new dimensions to philanthropy, to the point where his still largely unmade fortune (1877) had been willed as an endowment, ensuring the extension of the Empire through all the world, including America, so that the true *Pax Britannica* could at last come about.

He was also a man of the Cape. He loved it so much, in fact, that he could never tire of buying up decaying, but still splendid, Cape Dutch manor houses, restoring them to pristine beauty and laying also the foundations of a great deciduous fruit industry.

His special friendship with Bondsmen Afrikaners was part

of this same love. The Afrikaner Bond had come out of the Afrikaans Language Movement but, as it grew older, it moved strangely nearer to Rhodes. So, a time came when J. H. (*Onze Jan*) Hofmeyr, and especially the Rev. S. J. du Toit, were well within the Rhodes sphere, to the annoyance of many of their republican kinsmen in the north.

The friendship between Rhodes, Hofmeyr and du Toit was more than expediency. There was, in fact, the common heritage of the particular protestant ethic which they shared, although they could hardly have recognized it. In the case of Rhodes, it had already evolved to the point where the 'rise of the economic virtues'[10] had combined with a new socio-political ideal: that of the British universal state. In the case of the Cape Afrikaners it had reached the relatively primitive point of a gathering resistance to the dominion of others. The English had been at a corresponding point in their own development at the time of Mary Tudor and the Puritan exiles in Europe.

At a time when the Transvalers were trying to solve for themselves the puzzle of Thomas François Burgers, the Thirst-landers were following the sun and the Free Staters were minding their little model state, the Cape Afrikaners had for the first time begun to give expression to their own revolt. Once again it was on a cultural level.

In Paarl, one of the oldest settled parts of the Drakenstein Valley, some local farmers, descendants of the Huguenots, led by the Rev. S. J. du Toit, himself of Huguenot descent, formed themselves into a *Genootskap van Regte Afrikaners* – an Association of True Afrikaners. Their object had pre-eminently been the recognition and use of the vernacular as opposed to the elevated High Dutch, still regarded as the language of press, pulpit and school.

The situation was akin to that in which John Calvin had found himself in the sixteenth century. The facts of a profound change in man's economic life had to be accepted. The pretence of the Church that nothing had really happened to require an overhaul of basic attitudes had to be challenged.

The Cape Afrikaners had long been merely on the periphery of their people's resistance to 'the Imperial factor'. But now suddenly they had become more directly involved. The Afrikaans Language Movement was, in a sense, their own war of independence.

Finally, there was the defeated Rhodes, dying on the shores of False Bay, in the simple cottage which he preferred to the splendour of Groote Schuur. In his last days he could see distantly over the expanse of the Atlantic in the embrace of the Cape mountains: towards Hottentots-Holland; towards Drakenstein, the valleys which he had still found time to love.

What has been said here of Rhodes in a story outline of our subject has only been given because of the light it throws on S. P. J. Kruger. Kruger was the definitive republican Afrikaner of his time, as Rhodes simultaneously was the archetypal imperial Englishman. They had much in common, the two men, like the peoples from which they sprang.

A strange socio-political situation obtained in the Transvaal, after the confirmation in 1886 that the gold-reef underlying the Ridge of White Waters was not only fabulously, but also uniquely, rich. As De Kiewiet has pointed out,[11] it was both the richest and poorest gold-ore in all the world; no 'geological cream' lying near the surface to be scooped off, but fine gold-particles dispersed through the deep-lying conglomerate of quartzite. The ready availability of a cheap source of labour and power – coal – made the exploitation of this vast deposit of gold-bearing rock possible in a way the world had never previously seen.

It was a case of a simple rural society, only five years after its third-of-a-century of highveld slumber, suddenly being shaken to perennial wakefulness by the arrogant industrialism and aggressive capitalism of the nineteenth century; overlain with the messianic content of the Anglo-Saxon dynamic. That the farmers' republic of the Transvaal, aligned to the 'splendid stepping of the ox'[12], was in any way able to stand up to the immense onslaught on its traditional way of life, was in itself a reason for wonder.

Before the official proclamation of the goldfields in 1886, Kruger as a natural leader had only to deal with the far simpler matters of relations within Afrikaner society and with the immediate and uncomplicated matters pertaining to the colonizing British.

With no formal education at all – as a boy he had been part of the Great Trek – he nevertheless had a great natural sagacity. Like Abraham Lincoln, what he knew he learnt from a close and intelligent bond with his natural environment.

In the earlier republic he had played a solid enough role. He had distinguished himself in the campaigns against recalcitrant African chiefs like Makapan. When the Venda had erupted at Schoemansdal and a crowd had set free J. H. du Plessis after he had been convicted by *landdrosts* of seizing Venda cattle, he had led the white inhabitants out of their far-northern enclave. He had ridden at the head of a commando to assist hard-pressed Free Staters in one of their many struggles against Moshweshwe and the Basuto. He had tempered M. W. Pretorius in the latter's ill-considered attempt to force the Free State into union with the Transvaal. Several times he had undertaken the 7000-mile journey to the Colonial Office in London to plead the cause of his people.

Kruger had spoken at Wonderfontein in 1879, pacifying his deeply anxious people who had gathered there, consequent upon the annexation of Transvaal. He had spoken to them in the year before the First War of Independence, inspiring them in mea- sured tones to resistance. He had also spoken at Bronkhorst- spruit, Laing's Nek, Ingogo and Majuba and in April and December at Paardekraal. He was one of the triumvirate established to lead the Transvaal. In 1881, with the victory shouts of Majuba still ringing all through Southern Africa, but with British 'suzerainty' weighing heavily on the farmers' republic, he had spoken again. And new stones were now added to the cairn at Paardekraal.

All these things had happened, and Kruger had not yet spoken to, or on behalf of, an emergent Afrikaner nation. This had not yet come into being. Those descended almost completely from the Free Burghers and Huguenots of the seventeenth century, also from the small number of immigrants, mainly from Ger- many, who had arrived in the eighteenth century, had by the last quarter of the nineteenth century fallen into cultural disarray.

The Puritans in Africa

They were using three different languages. Many of the Cape Afrikaners, especially those living in or near Capetown, had become so anglicized that they regarded English as their home-language and English culture generally as their own. In church, schools and public matters generally, High Dutch was used. But the real language was the vernacular, called Afrikaans. Kruger could only begin to speak for greater Afrikanerdom when he – the farmer/hunter, commando leader and people's orator – was suddenly confronted in the mid-eighties with the massive change in the life of his country. Now, for the first time, because the world outside had come to the highveld with aggressive intelligence, the conditions were forming for Kruger to speak to and on behalf of a wider society.

Gold, and its impact upon the highveld rural society and its Old Testament patriarchy, lifted him into the dimensions of international statesmanship.

Modern criticism looks more favourably upon Kruger's mining policy, De Kiewiet says.

... Much more successfully than the Lieutenant-Governors of Griqualand West did Kruger succeed in compelling the acceptance of the idea that the gold in the earth was a public benefit and not the booty of capitalist enterprise. Thus an old man who in his youth had walked with the oxen of the Great Trek won for himself a meaningful place in the history of the relations between the state and industry. But in 1895 mining capital looked with little love upon Kruger's strict rule.[13]

In encounter it was Rhodes who usually had the better of things. There was the time when the two far-western mini-republics, Stellaland and Goshen, had been jostled between annexation by the Transvaal or the Cape Colony. In Goshen S. J. du Toit had tried to force the President's hand by hoisting the *Vierkleur*. Goshen was in fact annexed provisionally; but du Toit was soon told by the President to lower the flag. In order to remove all mention of 'suzerainty' Kruger had, at the Convention of London, been compelled to forfeit all but a part of his claims to the territories. Rhodes needed an open road along the Western borders of the Transvaal to Matabeleland

74

and Mashonaland. Kruger also surrendered his claims to the far north, beyond the Limpopo, preferring to consider an outlet to the sea at Kosi Bay, in the fever country of north-eastern Natal.

The real occasion for contest was the Raid. Rhodes, drawn to take the step by his Anglo-Saxon dream, retained sufficient judgement to realize at the eleventh hour what was happening. The lines had been cut south of Mafeking. The mounted column was already on its way to Johannesburg. Kruger had waited for the 'tortoise to poke out its head' and it was neatly cut off – at Doornfontein. The subsequent arrest and trial of the Reform Committee in Johannesburg on charges of high treason prepared the stage for the climactic act in the heroic age of Afrikanerdom.

The characters had now finally been drawn into mutual, tragic involvement. Some – Rhodes, Kruger, Chamberlain, Jameson – had been clearly defined. Others – Milner and Steyn – were taking shape in the wings and would soon be in the centre of the stage. Rhodes was to fade into the background, concern himself with matters in Matabeleland/Mashonaland, talk with Wilhelm II, dream of a great fruit industry at the Cape and lovingly collect cultural treasures . . .

The coldly brilliant, unrelenting Milner was to take his place at the heart of the Empire. Steyn was to support Kruger, but in no way add to or subtract from the epitome of the Afrikaner of the age.

The skirmish at Doornkop was over before the Uitlanders could properly piece the news together. There were dead on both sides: but Jameson and his police had been all but routed. Sixty of the Reformers were arrested. The ringleaders were charged with high treason and, pleading guilty, were sentenced to death. Kruger had to deal with his more impassioned countrymen who wanted the lot court-martialled and shot. Instead, he had the sentences commuted. Jameson and his lieutenants were handed over to the Imperial authorities to be punished. The Reformers – including Rhodes – however received only token censure in London and were generally regarded as heroes.

Conflict in South Africa, almost everybody believed, was now inevitable.

In spite of everything there had been a good deal of sound law-making in the Transvaal between the Raid and the War. The Press Law, the Aliens Expulsion Act, the Immigration Act, as E. A. Walker says, gave the authorities very few powers which were not exercised by a British Home Secretary.[14] There was also hard, practical administration. Rejecting the testing right of the courts as in the Brown judgment had been, indeed, the only way to prevent legal chaos and immense expense. Kruger, *de oude scherpe vossengeest* – the keen old fox of a spirit – as his friend and great admirer, G. A. A. Middelberg, Director of the N.Z.A.S.M. (the Netherlands Railway Company) lovingly referred to him, had since the advent of the 'English' learnt well the game of political chess. He as a *Dopper* could smell money-making humbug as soon as it appeared over the distant highveld horizon. And his native shrewdness got the measure of most of his opponents.

Kruger had many moods. Finger-wagging anger when Joseph Chamberlain roundly declared that, in spite of the London Convention of 1884, British suzerainty over the Transvaal had never lapsed. Grunting forgiveness, when 800 Uitlanders who had taken up arms against the Raiders were enfranchised. Or he could be generous. At the time of the Queen's jubilee, he closed the public offices, released the two remaining Reform prisoners and sent his congratulations to the regal old lady whose portrait still adorned many a Boer home.

He could also be a strong-willed authoritarian. Kruger finally sacked Chief Justice Kotze, because he insisted on the Court's right to test Republican legislation. The president and *Volksraad* would govern, Kruger said, not the judges, nor the law.

There was even the straight-faced Kruger who once solemnly opened a synagogue in Johannesburg – he was partial to the Jews – 'in the name of the Father, the Son, and the Holy Ghost'.[15] Among his special friends he counted Sammy Marks to whom he granted the right to distil whisky, and from whom he received by way of genuine appreciation two ornamental lions, to be mounted outside the President's house in Pretoria.

And then there was also Kruger at a state banquet, when everybody was most correctly busy with the turkey, unconcernedly enjoying his glass of *zoete melk* – fresh milk – and a huge slice of blood-red watermelon.

'He sat there happily,' Middelberg records, (p. 69),

with a new green sash on, embroidered with the coat of arms of the Republic, receiving many a toast, until he, at last, had the opportunity of replying. He spoke like a patriarch, at length. He spoke of God's guidance and of the problems his *volk* would have to face, so as not to be pounced upon by the enemy. He spoke of not angering the God of their fathers by dishonouring his commandments. How many a tear did I not see at all this in the eyes of sturdy farmers and ordinary worldlings. And I myself would not have been able to say a word for having been so deeply moved ...

'Casting all your care upon him; for he careth for you. Be sober, be vigilant; because your adversary, the devil, as a roaring lion, walketh about, seeking whom he may devour.' So he once cabled to Wilhelmina of the Netherlands, quoting the Bible.[16]

'... The President is ill,' Middelberg wrote to relations in Holland in 1897.

He sat at home in his chair, clad in a nightshirt and a red sleeping cap. He had folded his hands and his eyes were fixed in their gaze. Then the members of the executive council entered and proceedings got under way. Twice this week I have been present on such occasions. It was like a painting. Suddenly he (the President) would be awoken out of his drowsiness. Then he would sharply pass judgement on what had just been said. On such occasions he would be extremely lucid, so that I had difficulty in countering with an argument. Even more comic was his way of eventually conceding. Usually he would sigh, and appear deeply tragic, feeling himself too spent to even grumble.[17]

Around this Falstaff of the highveld, as Middelberg saw him, burghers like the people Frans Hals once painted would gather where his train stopped to question him at length, the President standing on a *kist*.

... They were against the railway, against the dynamite factory, against Leyds, against all that was the government. Kruger always remained in good temper; always had a quick reply; always had those with a sense of humour on his side; always knew how to answer a question by pretending to understand it in a completely different sense.[18]

Even more revealing of the essential Kruger than Rhodes was Her Majesty's High Commissioner in South Africa, Alfred, Lord Milner. Milner, born and partly trained in Tübingen, a graduate from Balliol, became the consummate imperialist, believing utterly in the redemptive task of Great Britain and the Anglo-Saxon race. 'If I am also an imperialist,' he declared on occasion, 'it is because the destiny of the English race, owing to its insular position and long supremacy at sea, has been to strike fresh roots in distant parts of the world.'[19] The land itself tempered Rhodes so that even after the Raid he never lost his love for it. Milner, by contrast, was above the land.

His most revealing moment came in replying to an address by loyal Bondsmen at Graaff-Reinet in 1898 while touring the Cape Colony. Worthy Graaff-Reinetters had welcomed the presence of His Excellency, the Governor and High Commissioner; and had expressed regret at the circumstances which compelled them to seize this opportunity to give His Excellency the assurance of their loyalty and deep attachment to the British Empire.

'I am glad to be assured that any section of Her Majesty's subjects are loyal,' Milner responded, calmly and coldly. 'I would be much more glad to be allowed to take that for granted. Why should I not? ... Well, gentlemen, of course you are loyal. It would be monstrous if you were not. And now, if I have one wish, it is that I may never again have to deal at any length with this topic.'[20] The Bondsmen were put to shame.

In that same year – 1898 – Kruger was returned with an overwhelming majority for his fourth term of office. Kruger and Milner eventually confronted each other at the famous Bloemfontein Conference in May 1899, shortly before the outbreak of the Anglo-Boer War. Milner had already summarized his determination to put an end to Boer hegemony in the Transvaal in his famous dispatch to London on 4 May. The spectacle of thousands of British subjects in the condition of 'helots' in

South Africa, he declared, was undermining the prestige of Great Britain.

President Steyn of the Free State, doing his best to create an atmosphere of goodwill, arranged for a first meeting at the Presidency, on the morning of 31 May, at eleven.

'President Kruger did not keep us waiting,' Steyn later recorded.

... but it was well a quarter of an hour or twenty minutes after eleven before Lord Milner and his entourage showed up ... He made no apology; and President Kruger probably did not even notice it. President Kruger arose and offered him his hand, so as to greet him in the manner of the Afrikaners. Milner simply walked past him and shook hands with my wife and me, after that with President Kruger. This happened in sight of many people. Milner was, of course, correct in first greeting the hostess, but who would have taken it amiss had he in the circumstance have offered his hand to the aged, simple man ...[21]

'I mention these things,' Steyn concluded, 'merely to indicate how different were the characters of the two men in whose hands Providence had laid the fortunes of South Africa.'

Steyn urged Kruger to continue making concessions wherever possible. With Fischer and Smuts he made a plea for a simple five-year franchise. Regarding the difficult matter of the dynamite concession, the existing situation had to be drastically reviewed. To this Kruger agreed. It was perfectly clear, however, that neither of the two Presidents had any real illusions that Milner would unbend. Steyn, in fact, had suggested that he concentrate on the dynamite question. Milner had thoughtfully answered, 'Yes, I may try that.' Almost immediately after, however, he indicated the true issue when he said: 'What is the dynamite question after all? It is the franchise that must do it.'[22]

Steyn had sensed the real issue from the start. It was the continuing march of imperialism through history.

Kruger had been right when, at a tense moment during the Conference, he had declared that what Milner wanted was not the franchise, but his country. 'No historian of feeling,' De Kiewiet says, can read the records of these years without halting reflectively at many points where the elements of compromise approached one another, where the old President showed that the desire for understanding was alive in his heart, where even mining magnates admitted the benefits of the republican régime and sought to co-operate with it.[23]

From within the South African Republic itself, however, there had been sharply critical opposition from the Afrikaner side. The most outspoken comment on Kruger's intransigence came from bold young journalists writing for *Land en Volk* in opposition to the Kruger press, which took the form of the established *Volkstem*. Most aggressive of the rebels was Eugène Nielen Marais, destined to become one of the most eminent of Afrikaner poets. In 1891 he had at the age of 19 become editor of *Land en Volk* and was so sharply and intelligently critical of the Kruger order, that the old President had him thrown out of the press gallery by a majority decision of the *Volksraad*. It even happened that Marais was on occasion arrested in the public gallery for *lèse majesté*. This led to a public indictment, but Marais was found not guilty. He continued his journalistic activities to the outbreak of the war, resuming them in 1902.

Meanwhile the leaders of the Afrikaner Bond at the Cape, J. H. Hofmeyr and A. J. Herholdt, who was also a member of the cabinet, did their utmost to have the new Franchise Law in the Transvaal revised once more. The State Secretary, Reitz, who had also been President of the Free State, announced on 19 August that Milner's demand of a five-year franchise with retrospective power would be met. The conditions were that Great Britain would no longer concern herself with the internal affairs of the Republic; and that its sovereignty be respected, while all points at issue be subjected to arbitration. Chamberlain agreed soon enough to accept the proposals, but rejected the provisos on the ground that the parties were bound by the Convention of London and the substance of suzerainty. From everywhere news was being received of troop movements on the borders of the two republics. From everywhere voices of protest were now sounding, also in Great Britain. Of these, Olive Schreiner, the sister of the Prime Minister of the Cape Colony, was among the most articulate. '. . . the true born South African man, whether Dutch or English,' she had once written, 're-minded us of nothing so much as those huge shaggy watchdogs, which lie before their master's houses placid and kindly, whom you may stumble over and kick, almost with impunity; but when once you have gone too far and he rises and shakes himself, you had best flee . . .'[24]

War finally came on 11 October 1899. At the same time it was the dénouement of the personal tragedies of Rhodes and Kruger. The tragedy of Rhodes was that of a man who dreamt deeply, constructed vastly, but had insufficient understanding of the traditional world of Kruger. He was a man who tried to force the time to fit his vision. The tragedy of Kruger on the other hand, was that of a man of heroic virtues, who had in-sufficient understanding of the world of Rhodes and the modern forces of which he was a part. He resolutely turned the clock back in order to maintain his tradition intact.

What they shared was the common ground, the soil of the land itself. Sympathy in the viewer is the mark of tragedy. In the final loneliness of exile both Kruger and Rhodes would give rise to it in a way beyond their knowing.

Against the eastern slopes of Table Mountain Rhodes in sculpture looks out into the blue distance, to beyond Van Rie-beeck's Great Mountain Range of Africa; to the far north, to the land which, in spite of everything, he loved but lost. Deep in an armchair, with a rug over his legs, a huge open *Statenbijbel* on his lap, his hand resting on a page, eyes also fixed in the distance, face drawn but serene, Kruger in sculpture seems to reflect on the greatness of God and the littleness of man. He, too, remem-bers the land he loved but also lost.[25]

With no place for man to hide, all triviality, self-sufficiency and mediocrity had finally been abandoned. Never more would the Afrikaners be allowed to revert to it. The active principle of their century of revolt – the 'English' – would in increasing measure be among them, be part of their lives, in ways far more difficult to define than the single-minded imperialism of the late nineteenth century. The 'English' would form a lasting, challenging presence in the tight pattern of urges, dreams and ideals. For the British this, too, would mean being captured by something far greater than the urban comfort from which most of them had emerged. The Southern African landscape, human and physical, would imprint itself upon them also.

The Boer War, Field-Marshal J. C. Smuts later correctly pointed out, was unique. Its human interest far surpassed its military value. For the British, the war started disastrously when, in the second week of December 1899, mobile Boer commandos rapidly invaded Natal and the Cape Colony. In the North-Eastern Cape, General Gatacre was defeated in the Stormberg. Further to the west, Kimberley and Mafeking were encircled by Boer forces. Most catastrophically, at Magersfontein, also in the west, Lord Paul Methuen sent in an army of 12,000 men in a frontal attack on the Boer positions. In a bloody battle 8000 Boers, led by the leonine figure of General Koos de la Rey and General Piet Cronjé, the hero of Doornkop at the time of the Raid, severely defeated the attackers.

But it was nevertheless General Buller's defeat at the Tugela – the scene of so much struggle in the history of the Afrikaners – which was the severest blow suffered by the British in that second week of December. Like Methuen, Buller, too, thought a frontal attack would sweep the Boers before him. But the young General Louis Botha, based at Colenso, and facing a far superior British force of 23,000 men, supported by forty-two guns, drove back Buller, who suffered more than 1000 casualties. About a month later, in January 1900, this remarkable success was repeated at Spion Kop, against an even more powerful British army. This time there were 1653 British casualties with more than 300 dead.

What kind of people were these Boers? Winston Churchill, at the time special correspondent of the *Morning Post*, was to ask himself.[26] The lasting image he carried with him, he was to write, was that of seeing them riding through the rain of an early morning, independent marksmen, each one accustomed to making his own decisions, carrying fine weapons, and led with judgement and ability. As they rode, so they lived. They had neither commissariat nor ammunition columns. They were as mobile as the wind, relying on an iron constitution and the stern God of the Old Testament which would surely scatter the Amalekites ...

Churchill caught a timeless moment, recording how above the beat of rain on the corrugated iron roof of the shelter in which he was being held prisoner, he suddenly heard the sound of voices raised in song. The Boers were singing their evening psalm. The notes, sonorous and strong, almost threatening in their volume, were more suggestive of anger and disdain than love and grace. It was chilling and disturbing in its effect. It made Churchill think that the war, after all, was unjust: that the Boers were better men than they who sought to conquer them; that Heaven was not on the side of the British; that Ladysmith, Mafeking and Kimberley would fall; that the garrison at Estcourt would be destroyed; that foreign powers would intervene; and that it would all be the beginning of the end. At that moment, listening to the deep and measured cadences of the psalm, sung in the manner of the Huguenots riding to battle or the English Calvinists preparing for the Civil War, the future greatest Englishman of his time despaired of the Empire. It was only when, as Churchill later soberly recounted, the early morning sun at last and once again shone in at the windows of the buildings, that all things were restored to their true colours and dimensions and he could once more view the world about him with equanimity.

The early Boer successes in the pitched battles could not last. The odds against them were too great. Ladysmith, Kimberley and Mafeking were relieved. The Boers had wasted much time, men and many of their meagre resources on pointless sieges. Some severe reverses followed. Cronjé's surrender with 4000 burghers at Paardeberg was a catastrophe. Lord Roberts of Kandahar marched through to Bloemfontein; and, in September, he formally annexed the Transvaal.

But as Johanna Brandt, one of the 'Petticoat Commando' of Boer spies, said to a war-weary Tommy thanking God that the war was over, the struggle had only begun.

What, in memory, particularly endures? There was Marthinus Theunis Steyn, President of the Free State, who had tried so hard to appease the opposing parties in May/June 1899, and who himself became a combatant. He was like General de Gaulle, who, some forty years later, was to inspire his occupied country to resist, whatever the odds.

For almost two years Steyn lived with General Christiaan de Wet's commando, mostly in the open veld and off the land, often sleeping under the stars. In the bitter cold of winter and the sweeping rain of summer, they undertook enormous journeys, following de Wet, who always led them to safety through the widely-strung lines of the enemy. In February 1900, with Kruger, he directed an appeal to Britain to stop the war; but Salisbury rejected it. From then on he appealed no more. With de Wet, he rode across the Vaal to the Magaliesburg to attend a meeting with the other Boer leaders in October 1900. There he argued in favour of a Boer invasion of the Cape Colony. In January 1901, he was back in the Free State with de Wet. Once, at Reitz, on an early morning in July 1901, he was surprised by the British. He was saved by his black squire, Ruiter, who had warned him in time.

There was de Wet, who had gained a world-wide reputation as the most tantalizing of the Boer guerrillas. At regular intervals he struck the enemy unexpectedly, then disappeared. His easy, down-to-earth personality, his unusual intelligence, the very relish he seemed to convey in his incalculable appearances and disappearances, captivated all, including many of the enemy. Poplar Grove, Sannaspos, Roodewal ... These were names neither de Wet nor the British could ever forget. The brilliant guerrilla led his commando to the Transvaal, back to the Free State, down to the Orange and the Cape Colony, and over to the North-West Colony, where he met Hertzog, returning with him to the Free State. He swept through the land capriciously, destructively and inspiringly. To the very end he evaded capture.

There was Gideon Scheepers, who had been born in the Transvaal, but at the age of 23 had been sent by de Wet as the leader of a small commando of twenty men to support the invasion of the Cape Colony. Some Cape rebels joined him and the group fought courageously and well for almost a year. Then the young commandant fell ill, so that his men had to leave him at a farmhouse and send a message to the British to come and fetch him. The British obliged, captured Scheepers, then treated him in hospital. After he had recovered, he was tried by court-martial on various charges pertaining to rebel activities and finally executed.

There was *Oom* Koos de la Rey who, in his own *milieu*, the Western Transvaal, remained unbeaten up to the end of the war. Long after the British had established their authority in the two capitals and the central districts, he still effectively controlled things in the west. In March 1902, he and Kemp defeated an army division of Lord Methuen, understudy to Kitchener. Soon after, Methuen's camp at Tweebosch was surrounded and attacked. Among the 860 prisoners was the commanding officer himself. More than 400 dead were left lying in the veld. Methuen himself was wounded. De la Rey decided to set him free and had him taken to a British hospital. When some of the burghers objected, reminding their leader of what had happened to Gideon Scheepers, de la Rey said that it was his Christian duty. Thereupon Methuen was sent to Klerksdorp in an ambulance wagon.

Louis Botha succeeded Joubert as Commandant-General of the Boer forces when Joubert died on 28 March 1900. He faced Roberts in the last pitched battle of the war at Dalmanutha. In March 1901 he met Kitchener at Middleburg in an attempt to negotiate a peace settlement; but the arrival of Milner in Johannesburg spelt failure for the meeting. The latter's conditions, Botha decided, could not be met. Instead he protested against the condition of women and children in the camps and also against the use of Bantu as spies and scouts. In the last quarter of 1901 he led his commandos through the eastern highveld, evading capture.

There were the Boers. There were also the British ...

Horatio Herbert, Baron Kitchener of Khartoum, had taken over from Roberts and was faced with one of the most difficult military and administrative tasks in the history of the Empire. The camps, the farm burnings, the immense cross-country drives, trying to force the commandos up against lines of hastily-constructed forts (blockhouses), the building up of the British Army in South Africa to nearly a quarter of a million, were all the stern measures of a dedicated soldier, determined to put an end to an unpleasant but necessary task. But there was also Emily Hobhouse, representing in her own inimitable way the essence of her race, protesting in ringing terms, and ministering personally like another Florence Nightingale, to those who had borne the brunt of the war, the women and children.

John X. Merriman, later Prime Minister of the Cape Colony, was a model of English Colonial excellence, a connoisseur of the Old Cape, a wine-farmer and politician. He never stopped being Milner's conscience. At the beginning of 1901, together with W. P. Schreiner he had sought to address the British House of Commons on the subject of the war. He remained the consummate Anglo-Saxon to the end, but – perhaps for that very reason – was a steadfast friend of the Afrikaners.

The Tommy Atkinses marched in their drab khaki over limitless land, weary unto death, sometimes receiving food and shelter from Boer women who took pity on them.

Some 26,000 of these women were to die in the camps, together with some of their children, six times more than those who had fallen on commando. There were the burghers themselves, and their incredible 'long rides' over the length and breadth of Southern Africa. The epic ride of J. C. Smuts's commando after invading the Cape Colony to the far west is a classic case. Week after week the commando crossed great mountain ranges, plains and rivers, suffering from illness, exposure and the destruction of war. It was often harassed and split into fragments by the enemy, only for the parts to find each other again. They crossed great mountain ranges, plains, rivers. They suffered from illness, exposure, the general wear and tear, the destruction of war. They eventually found their way to the far south of the sub-continent, where in the closing months of the struggle the Boers, contrary to all calculations, seemed to have re-established themselves.

With Smuts and others individually leaving the Western Transvaal at the beginning of August 1901, the full commando eventually gathered at the Vet River in the Eastern Free State. In the face of the enemy they crossed the Orange into the Cape Colony near the Basuto border, entering the Stormbergen in nasty weather. Numbed by the cold, wet to the skin, ever on the move, the commando neither slept nor ate for more than forty hours. Finding themselves at last in the wild and inaccessible Zuurbergen, the commando almost succumbed to a man after eating poisonous veld-fruit. While still suffering acutely, they were attacked by the enemy.

At the beginning of October they nevertheless considered pressing on to Port Elizabeth. At Doornbos, near Somerset East, the enemy was heavily defeated, more than 200 'lovely horses' being captured. From there they crossed the great central plateau of the Karroo, eventually reaching the far-western districts of Calvinia and Sutherland.

'So our commando reached this district,' Smuts reported, after enormous hurt, trouble, and danger had been endured. Within two months we had travelled through nearly all the districts of the Colony. We had crossed dangerous mountain ranges in the face of the enemy, and I had been enabled to ascertain completely the present political and military situation in the Colony.[27]

The distance covered was upwards of 2000 miles.

'In the course of one of these skirmishes,' Deneys Reitz recalled, 'Duncker, riding beside me, was shot through the chest. We plugged the bullet-holes with pieces of his shirt, and he rode on with us for the fifteen odd miles that we had to go before we overtook the commando. He was then sent to a farm among the foothills, and completely recovered within a few weeks . . .'[28]

Reitz tells the story of the execution of Colaine (Colyn), who as a Boer had made an attempt to join the commando, but who was, in fact, in the pay of the enemy.

On the way he spoke to us. He said he knew he deserved to die, but he was a poor man, and had taken blood-money to keep his wife and children from starving . . . We blindfolded him and placed him at the head of the grave. Realizing that this was the end Colaine held up his hands, and in a low tone recited the Lord's Prayer, while the firing party silently ranged themselves. As he came to the final 'Amen', they fired. With a convulsive jerk he pitched backward into the grave, and the frightened Hottentots quickly covered him with earth.[19]

But there were happier moments, too, with the commando gathering on the banks of the lower Olifants. Reitz remembered:

The sea lay only twenty-five miles from here, and the day after my return, he [Smuts] sent word to the units quartered within reach that all who had never seen it were to be sent to him. Some sixty or seventy men arrived within the next forty-eight hours, and with these we set off for a small inlet on the coast called Fishwater. Towards afternoon they caught a glint of the ocean through a gap in the dunes. Few of the men had ever seen a bigger stretch of water than the dam on their parent's farm. Mounted on their horses they looked in wonder on the Atlantic, then, like the Greek soldiers, rushed forward in a body, crying 'The sea! The sea!' each wanting to be first on the beach.[30]

Soon they were frolicking in the waves, some on horseback, shouting and laughing, with the long bitter war suddenly only a distant memory. A coloured fisherman inquired from Reitz where they were going. 'To England,' Reitz replied. 'We are crossing tonight to capture London.'

'My God, baas, don't do it,' the reply came. 'The water is over your head and you will all be drowned.'

They sat around great fires of driftwood, talking and joking about what they had heard and seen until far into the night. The news had reached them that men from the commando of General Maritz had, at Lambert's Bay, a few days previously, taken potshots from the shore at a British cruiser lying offshore. They had conducted the only naval battle of the entire war.

Smuts's commando spent a few more days holidaying, helping the local fishermen drag their nets, swimming in the surf. At last they returned along the river to their starting-point. The war was still on.

Some time later in Namaqualand, and with much of the North-Western Cape again under Boer control, the news reached Smuts that he should proceed at once to the North for peace talks at Vereeniging, on the north bank of the Vaal.

They were all there to deal with Milner and Kitchener: Steyn, Botha, Smuts, Hertzog, de Wet, de la Rey . . .

'I still see the drawn and sombre faces of the hitherto unyielding officers,' J. D. Kestell,* beloved *veldprediker* – field preacher – wrote,

> deputed to uphold our independence. I still see them gazing as if into emptiness. I still see the imponderable question engraved on their faces: Was this the bitter end of all our suffering, our struggle, of all our faith and strong appeal to God?
>
> General de la Rey had on the previous day exclaimed in the meeting: 'You speak of faith – what is faith? ... Lord, Thy will, not my will be done!' ...
>
> I saw lips tremble of men who had never flinched before the enemy. I saw tears welling up in eyes which had been dry when they had seen loved ones laid away into the cold earth.[31]

It was between eleven p.m. and twelve midnight on 31 May 1902.

Kitchener shook hands with each of the Boer delegates as they left the conference chamber. 'We are good friends now,' he said. Outside, the story goes, de Wet shattered his rifle over a rock.

The news was conveyed to ex-President Kruger in Holland. It was the start of his true exile. It was also the end of an old order, and the slow, hesitant beginning of a new one.

A quarter of a century later an Afrikaans poet would write about the statue of Kruger:

> The moon shines mistily on stone and clay:
> Strange light upon the past for him who led
> An Afrikanerdom that passed away.[32]

---

* John Daniel Kestell, clergyman, educationist, author, academic, cultural leader, was the son of the 1820 settler John Kestell, a cartwright from Devon, who set up business in Pietermaritzburg. He married a Trekker woman (Dorothea Weyers) in 1842, and joined the Dutch Reformed Church.

4 The Coming of the *Burgerstand*

For the Afrikaners, the nineteenth century had been the age of revolt, being on the whole a creative reaction to blows, pressures and penalizations. This had initially been African; but as the century advanced it became predominantly Anglo-Saxon.

Each of the three principal periods had produced figures of lesser or greater magnitude. In the time of the Great Trek there had been Piet Retief, Gert Maritz and Andries Pretorius ... Appearing out of the fire of Majuba, out of the massive development of deep-level mining on the Rand, there had been the definitive figure of Paul Kruger. There had also been the array of figures, given form and stature by the culminating struggle of the Anglo-Boer War: Steyn, de Wet, Botha, de la Rey, Smuts, Hertzog ...

Growth in the life of nations, like that of individuals, it has often been said, becomes increasingly subtle and hazardous with progress upwards. In many cases, as with the Afrikaners, it means that once a traditional society has been disturbed beyond repair; as *embourgeoisement* – becoming an urban and suburban middle class within an industrializing society – takes place, the problems to be met are increasingly and primarily of an inner nature. The difficult landscapes and militant enemies, which characterized a time of pioneers, patriarchs, feudal lords and heroes, make way for a struggle with the self. Essentially it is a question of whether the ethic of the one-time oppressor is accepted or not.[1]

This means that among those who belong to a defeated, subjected people there can most obviously and most easily be the reaction of enduring and growing resistance. It becomes 'nation-consciousness'. In its most uncompromising form, it becomes militant nationalism, finding its sustenance in a burning resentment. It has no theories, only the belief that the group has suffered injury, that there must be redress: power must be wrested from the oppressive opponent. Only in this way can things be righted.

But resistance can transcend militancy and confine itself to a will to throw off the shackles of national bondage by constitutional means. There is no less resentment; but on the whole the attitude represents a genuine love for the national idiom: of what belongs peculiarly to a people. As such it can be seen as an authentic desire for identity.

Between the militant nationalists, prepared for almost any means, including violence, in their struggle for power, and the patriots reasonably rejecting political bondage because it is unworthy of the free intelligence which is the human being, a spectrum of related attitudes may emerge.

The urge to power of the militant nationalists finds its opposite extreme in the attitude among those of the defeated, who for reasons of expediency believe that, in not being able to beat the opponents, it would be better to join them. Here again there may be related authenticity in the form of a genuine urge to reconciliation. Between these poles there is also a spectrum of attitudes.

To sum up: a subjected, defeated people may react hazardously by resorting to power-seeking militancy, or by 'collaborating'. It may also react creatively by 'being itself', and yet seeking reconciliation.

In broad outline this forms the dominant theme in the process of the *embourgeoisement* – the *verburgerliking* – of the Afrikaners: from the Peace of Vereeniging to the present day.*

In different terms it meant the transition from a heroic age of revolt and resistance, to a revolutionary age in which an attempt was made to re-structure not only Afrikaner, but South African society generally: radically, fundamentally, rationally and for all time.

'For a century and more Afrikanerdom had managed to preserve its life through heroic action', a post-Second World War

* It also becomes the dominant theme in the growth of Black Consciousness, in the post-Second World War world.

observer has stated. 'It now thought to prolong its existence by heroic thought against the whole world. The Age of the Generals was past and done with forever. Afrikanerdom would endeavour to maintain its existence through the age of the politicians.'[2]

In the new federation towards which Milner was striving, the British way would predominate, by virtue of its inherent excellence. The only way to deal with the threatening flood of Blacks was a healthy white population, maintaining a high level of competence and production. The Rand was the key to it all. And the key itself could only properly be entrusted to an Anglo-Saxon hand. Bright young men from Oxford were imported to assist. Ignoring the demands of Sir Henry Campbell-Bannerman and others for his recall, refusing the offer, too, of the Colonial Secretaryship, Milner preferred to return to the task of reconstruction, but on British lines. The shattered Afrikaner communities had to be financially assisted. The repatriation of prisoners of war from distant Ceylon and St Helena brought them back to deserted farms and the ruins of what had once been their homes.

A united South Africa within the Empire was also their best guarantee. British colonists were imported to promote progressive farming; the mines were restored to their former dynamic; the railways extended; representative government promised... In loyalty, intelligence and sheer hard work, Milner gave all he had for the sake of a British South Africa. He was fighting a losing battle.

Everywhere there were signs that the Afrikaners were neither adjusting to their subjection nor co-operating whole-heartedly in the achievement of the new vision. Milner had done his best to be helpful. He had even incurred the displeasure of organized commerce, when he had protected the returning burghers in their time of need from exploitation by merchants and storekeepers.[3] Every possible means was being employed to rehabilitate a broken people. It had not been unreasonable to expect positive results. Like so many Cape Afrikaners, some had, indeed, begun to play their part in the British community of peoples. But there were also many signs of enduring resistance. On 14 July Kruger died at Clarens, Switzerland. Through Botha he sent a last message to his people.

'Look to the past,' he had said, 'for all it contains which is fine and noble. Let that then be the measure of your ideal; and let your future be the endeavour to realize it.' Kruger's body had been brought back to the Transvaal. Generals de Wet, Botha, de la Rey, and ex-Vice-President Schalk Burger, who had succeeded Kruger after his departure to Europe, had led the cortège. A great crowd in Church Square, Pretoria, had listened in deep silence to moving funeral oratory.

In 1904 the *Het Volk* party had been founded in Pretoria by Botha and others. A new *hereniging* – reunion – of Afrikanerdom was its prime objective. In the Cape, J. H. Hofmeyr had already turned the Afrikaner Bond into the South African Party. Hofmeyr, on returning from Europe, had been in favour of a High Dutch revival. But a second and even more powerful enthusiasm for the vernacular had taken hold of the country. Eugène Marais, who in the nineties had written so sharply and critically of Kruger and his administration, also returned from Europe. In a single poem he put it beyond all doubt that Afrikaans had become a language in its own right.

> *O koud is die windjie en skraal.*
> *En blink in die dof-lig en kaal,*
> *so wyd as die Heer se genade,*
> *lê die velde in sterlig en skade.**[4]

In education the enormously improved facilities were not proving to be wholly acceptable to the ex-Republicans. Private schools had been opened in the Transvaal to provide 'Christian-National' education on Calvinist lines.

The massive effort to establish the two colonies as worth-while entities in a British order suddenly seemed to have got the better of Milner. There had been the attempt of the mines to ease a critical shortage of unskilled labour by the importation of

*O cold is the slight wind and sere.
And gleaming in dim light and bare,
As vast as the mercy of God,
Lie the plains in starlight and shade.
(Translation by Guy Butler)

Chinese. Milner had opposed it, but had finally agreed. In Britain, the Liberals were about to form the Government. The South African ideal had suddenly lost its shine. On 2 April 1905, a tired and disillusioned Milner at length departed from Pretoria. Crossing the highveld by train, with the late sun sinking into an ocean of grass, he might well have considered how war here had indeed changed all, but not as he had envisaged it.

Afrikaner nationalism, still largely inchoate, was nevertheless a force to be reckoned with. Conclusive evidence came in 1907 when *Het Volk*, led by Botha, beat the 'Vote British' Progressive Party at the polls. The issues were almost as simple again as they had been in the field between Boer and British. Botha's cabinet included the war heroes J. C. Smuts and Koos de la Rey. The opposition was led by George Farrar, who had been a Reformer.

But a National Convention with a view to Union, then Union itself in 1910, and the developments within the next few years more clearly defined the various attitudes which overshadowed the *verburgerliking* of the Afrikaners. The National Convention included as delegates the war heroes de Wet, Botha, Hertzog, de la Rey, Smuts and Burger. But there were also four ex-political prisoners of the Raid: Hull, Farrar, Fitzpatrick and Jameson. There was also John X. Merriman, formerly Prime Minister of the Cape Colony, who yielded the premiership to Botha, so as to 'bring in the Transvaal'.* The predominant mood was that of conciliation; and Botha was the leading protagonist. His cabinet included ex-Republican Boers, British and Cape Afrikaners. Botha, Smuts, Hertzog and Fischer took office alongside Leuchars, Gubbins, Burton, Graaff, Sauer and Malan. Together they led the South African National Party. But even Jameson, as leader of the Unionist opposition, was no disruptive element. Together with Steyn, Botha, Smuts and Hertzog, he attended a luncheon at Buckingham Palace to mark the occasion of Union. Queen Alexandra wore the Cullinan diamond, the most splendid in the world, presented to her by the Transvaal government: by Louis Botha, his fellow Afrikaners but political opponents, would say.

---

* Hofmeyr had died, and Steyn's ill-health ruled him out as a candidate for the premiership.

How lovely was the South African garden: lawns trimmed, flowers in bloom, young and sturdy trees in leaf. The head gardener himself and his closest associates were all Afrikaners.

Had the Boers won the peace after all? Had the confidence once expressed in *Een Eeuw van Onrecht* (*A Century of Wrong*), issued by Reitz and purportedly written by Smuts, been vindicated? It had stated that the Republican flag would fly again, but this time from the Cape to the Zambezi.

Viewing the garden from a distance, noting especially that the real force in the development was the second-in-command, Smuts, an onlooker might well have concluded that those rooted to this soil through centuries had, indeed, triumphed.

From a closer vantage-point, however, the view was different. It showed that the garden, in fact, was an exotic one. Trees, shrubs and flowers were predominantly non-indigenous. The style was English; and the native gardeners were happy to have it that way.

Nevertheless the vigorous, indigenous plant of nationalism which had already been discovered in *Het Volk* had struck root here as well. In the garden of conciliation it would soon make its presence felt.

The prime mover was Hertzog. In the days of the Orange River Colony, he had already insisted on a greater role in education for the Dutch language. In the Transvaal, Smuts' Education Act had only required mother-tongue instruction up to standard III for Dutch-speaking children. Thereafter English was to be the medium in all but two subjects. Students had to be fluent in it before they could be promoted. But Hertzog, as Minister of Education, had managed things in favour of the Afrikaners generally. Mother-tongue instruction had to be given up to standard IV. After that, half of the principal subjects were to be taught through the medium of Dutch, the others through the medium of English. A requirement that teachers should be bilingual drew protests from the 'English'. But Hertzog, deeply conscious of the disadvantages of his people, campaigning for the *eie*,* was not to be deflected from his course.

* The word means the particular cultural idiom of a people: what belongs to them distinctively.

It was not only in education that the Afrikaners were reminded that they were subservient. The public service was essentially British. The work of Milner in this regard had by no means been undone. Bilingualism was merely a statutory gesture and there were many high officials who regarded a mere 'working knowledge' of Dutch as being sufficient. The newly born language, Afrikaans – the vernacular – had as yet no official standing.

National symbols – flag and anthem – were British. In no way was the Republican tradition reflected. The representative of the Crown in South Africa was a Governor-General, as British if not as powerful as any colonial governor since Caledon. Even the Supreme Court, with its own Appellate Division, was not the final arbiter in the administration of justice. The Privy Council in London still had the last word.

The heart of the matter was that, in Hertzog, Afrikanerdom had found an articulate voice insisting on the priority of the *eie*. If the policy of conciliation meant that the *eie* was to suffer, then the policy of conciliation had to be rejected. There was no doubt in the mind of Hertzog that, in spite of their apparent political dominance, the Afrikaners still had a long way to go before they could make up their cultural and economic leeway. Except for a small percentage, they were almost exclusively still a rural people. The cities, populated since the second quarter of the nineteenth century with more and more British immigrants, predominantly from the urban middle classes, were seats of Anglo-Saxon culture. Many Cape Afrikaners had become anglicized since Somerset had pursued anglicization as an official policy. Old families had accepted all the English graces. The Afrikaans *eie* had become foreign to them. They refused High Dutch and used the vernacular only when addressing servants. Thus anglicized, they had become a *haut bourgeosie*.

Neither was the general process confined to the Cape, nor to the cities. Many inland towns in the Cape Colony had already developed English-speaking communities. Sturdy *plattelanders* regularly corresponded with each other in meticulous English.

They read *The Illustrated London News*, sang *God Save the King*, sometimes even spoke nostalgically of going 'home', when they meant England, like so many of the English.

Trade, commerce and industry had established its most powerful generating centre during the development of deep-level mining on the Rand. In style, and very largely in content, it was wholly Anglo-Saxon where it was not Jewish. The 'English' moreover had an almost complete monopoly of the industrial skills. Technical training was almost exclusively 'English'. The British generally, like the Jews, had a long tradition of successful commercial enterprise. The big financial institutions, such as banks and insurance companies, for example, came from Britain. Living in towns and on farms in the country, the Afrikaners as a group were economically still nowhere. Except for a relatively small professional class – mostly teachers, lawyers and ministers of religion – they were confined to their traditional occupation and way of life. Not for nothing had they acquired the name Boers – the Farmers.

But Afrikanerdom's rural wholeness could not possibly last. Rural surplus population, on the whole a distinct, rootless class living on the land of others and known as *bywoners*,* would be the first to start drifting to the cities. The destruction of the war had increased their numbers and the cities offered prospects. They would, however, only form the forlorn vanguard of a far more inclusive migration. As such, within a generation, it would become the break-up of a traditional society and the drift of a people towards centres which to them were culturally still foreign.

While all this was taking place, and while a man like Hertzog was increasingly concerned with the economic handicap of his people, also with their cultural estrangement in the Anglo-Saxon cities, there was as yet almost no awareness of a similar situation affecting a potentially much bigger group. These were the various African peoples whose own ancestral societies had suffered the impact of industrialization. The Afrikaners, with

---

* *Bywoners* – share-croppers of a kind – were there from the start when the grazier/hunters moved off to the eastern frontier of the Colony. They were the unlanded.

their own war-heroes leading the government, were still much
too busy orientating themselves towards their erstwhile con-
querors.

The rediscovery of the *eie* is in the modern world a well-known
political *motif*. It lies at the heart of movements like Black
Power, of Black Consciousness generally, emphasizing that
'Black is beautiful'. It is, in effect, nothing more than an aspect
of the human urge to be oneself and to live in accordance
with one's essential nature, as a free intelligence with a particular
idiom.

The Afrikaners were split. Hertzog opposed his former
comrades in arms. They believed in conciliation, while he
emphasized the priority of the *eie*. The Afrikaners were still far
from the days when they would cast their political thinking into
the heady sphere of a socio-political doctrine.

Hertzog's revolt was still legitimate resistance; and Botha's
striving for conciliation was legitimate outwardness. Without
being conscious of it, Afrikaner politics was still well within
the tradition of the original Calvin. Civil government, said the
Reformer, was a provisional order in which no absolute claims
could be suffered: to be conducted, within the necessary
authority of government, in the mood of charity, equity and
natural law. As such, political struggle is no conflict of ultimate
power, leaving in its wake domination and subservience. Rather
it is creative contest, in which changes of government could
happen without catastrophe.

In the process of internalization of the problems facing
Afrikanerdom, the dividing lines of their situation were becoming
increasingly apparent.

During October 1912, Hertzog presented his point of view
in a series of addresses. 'South Africa is to be ruled by Afrikaners,' he kept stating, but added that this included those
English-speakers who were rooted in the country.

'South Africa first' he demanded at De Wildt; and Col.
Leuchars, a Briton from Natal, resigned in protest from the
cabinet. Thereupon, Botha disbanded the government and, on
reconstituting the cabinet, rejected Hertzog.

In November 1913 the split became final. At the South

African Party Congress in Cape Town a straight vote was taken. The Commandant-General won and the ex-Free State General left the hall with his followers.

Among them was General de Wet, who stopped at the door. 'Adieu!' the ex-commando leader called out with sonorous defiance to those who remained behind. The doors closed behind him. The two categories of Afrikaner political thinking had finally established themselves. 'Sap' and 'Nat' were now defined.

The following month, on 16 December, the anniversary of the Battle of Blood River, the Women's Monument at Bloemfontein was unveiled. It had largely been the inspiration of ex-President Steyn who had sought to honour the memory of those who had died in the camps. Emily Hobhouse came out specially from England to perform the ceremony, but ill-health kept her at Beaufort West. Steyn himself, who was to have delivered the main oration, was too ill, and his speech had to be read. But the 'Glorious Trio' – de la Rey, de Wet, Botha – who after the Boer War had travelled to Europe to raise funds for their people, were together again.[5]

For a moment it seemed as if the tensions of the previous two years had been left behind and that Afrikanerdom was once more united. De Wet addressed the crowd of 20,000 in a short piece of characteristic oratory. When the applause and cheering eventually died down, Botha's turn arrived. But by now many of the audience had wandered off to a hill near the monument. There they sat down, turning their backs on the speaker. It was a bitter moment for the man who, in the company of de Wet and de la Rey, had once reminded crowds of admirers that they – the 'Trio' – had not come to Europe to rejoice, but as the 'delegates of a most unhappy people'.[6]

Worse things were to come. On 4 August 1914, the First World War broke out. Within a month the Union Parliament, hardly four years old, was called upon to decide between support for Britain and risk an Afrikaner rising, or remain neutral, and risk resistance from the British. But the British, for all practical purposes, were a unity; and the Afrikaners were deeply divided. Boer and British had made an honourable peace, Botha and Smuts decided; now they should stand by one another.

Early in September Parliament in Cape Town also formally decided to invade South-West Africa. Less than a week later Christian Beyers, Commandant-General of the S.A. Defence Force, resigned in protest. Within a few days he and his old comrade in arms, de la Rey, were on their way to Potchefstroom to attend a protest meeting. Between Pretoria and Johannesburg a road block forced them to stop: the police were on the look-out for a gang of motor-car bandits who had been terrorizing the Rand. Beyers drove on and the police fired. A ricochetting bullet struck de la Rey and killed him.

It was a sad end for a man who belonged so magnificently to a heroic age, but who did not fit into the new pattern of issues being driven ever deeper inwards. The same could be said of de Wet, who soon became the central figure in the ensuing 'armed protest' of determined, irreconcilable Afrikaners.

October 1914 was a crucial month. Maritz, who had fought with Smuts in the North-Western Cape to the bitter end, broke away with a Defence Force commando, announcing that he was crossing over to the Germans in South-West Africa. Beyers declared at Steenboksfontein that the Afrikaners would protest by a show of arms, even at the cost of his life. At Vrede, de Wet said that he would join Maritz and also raise the *Vierkleur* in Pretoria. Some time previously Beyers had addressed a meeting on Kruger's birthday (10 October) and had had his words drowned in the audience's singing of *Rule Britannia*. The old warrior de Wet, joining forces with Christian Beyers, was soon in the field again. Kemp, emulating Smuts's 'long ride' of the Anglo-Boer War, managed to cross the Kalahari Thirstland and reached German South-West Africa. Maritz had meanwhile been operating with considerable confidence in the North-Western Cape. He and Kemp raised hopes for some while that once again the commandos would ride through all South Africa.

It was not to be. Maritz and his men escaped to German South-West Africa, thence to Angola and finally to Portugal. Here they lived in exile. With rash courage the leaders of the 'armed protest' in the Free State and the Transvaal gathered their followers – some 12,000 – and rode to battle. Among the first to be killed was de Wet's own son, Danie. Viewing the body the old leader remarked that he preferred it this way to his beloved son's falling in the cause of the English in South-West Africa.

It was not Boer against Briton, it was Boer against Boer. But the legend goes that Botha, when awaiting the attack by de Wet's force, seeing through his field-glasses mounted men approaching, announced to his fellow officers that *die Engelse kom* – the English were coming. At Mushroom Valley near Bloemfontein the government forces fell upon de Wet's commando, and the fight was soon over. Beyers, escaping to the north, was drowned while attempting to swim the flooded Vaal. De Wet surrendered: a defeated man who had lost his beloved boy, and had been but the shadow of the once famous commando leader. He and many others were tried and sentenced. One man was condemned to death – Commandant Jopie Fourie, a Defence Force officer, who had thrown in his lot with the rebels. In spite of desperate pleas for clemency, Fourie was shot. 'Do not shoot me in the face,' Fourie was said to have finally requested. 'I have a large Afrikaner heart.'

Once more Afrikanerdom was in turmoil. Within the space of a few months de la Rey had been shot, de Wet's son had fallen, Beyers had been drowned, Fourie executed while de Wet, Kemp and others were in prison. The 'armed protest' had been totally crushed. By the middle of 1915, when Botha had successfully concluded the South-West Africa campaign as part of South Africa's contribution to the war effort, 3000 Afrikaner women gathered in a solemn procession in Pretoria to petition the Governor-General, Lord Buxton, for the immediate release of de Wet and his fellow prisoners from the Johannesburg Fort.

But the British commitment to South Africa was every bit as wide and deep. In addition to the campaigns in German West and German East Africa – where Smuts conducted an epic contest with Lettow-Vorbeck – between seventy and eighty thousand men served in Europe in the Allied forces. The troubles of the Afrikaners were suddenly as nothing compared to the massive slaughter on the Western and Eastern fronts in the northern hemisphere. The rebels, who had faced charges of high treason and heavy claims for damages, had been helped financially by a movement of co-operative assistance (*Helpmekaar*) in which J. D. Kestell, the old *Veldprediker* of the Commandos, had played a prominent part.

The Afrikaners' struggle had been eclipsed by world events. There was much bitterness in the country. But the services of the Afrikaners, too, were required on a much vaster front. Smuts, taking leave of his East African campaign, was invited to join the War Cabinet. Soon Winston Churchill was referring to him in appreciative terms. The Boer War General, the Cape Afrikaner, who had carried on the struggle against the Empire up to the closing months of the war, had within half a generation reached a position where David Lloyd George was to describe him as the father of the British Air Force. Botha himself, after his triumphant South-West African campaign, was to join his deputy.

It was unique in history: two leaders of a vanquished enemy were within half a generation advising in the inner councils of the victor. Botha, so the taunt from the highveld rang, had donned the silk stockings of British aristocratic regalia.

At Versailles, the two ex-Boer War generals were distinctly unhappy about the harsh terms proposed. On 28 June 1919, Botha jotted down on a piece of paper: '... Today I remember the 31st day of May, 1902.' It was a shout from the heart of one who knew the hurt of defeat; and the even greater hurt of taking up arms against former comrades.

On 30 May 1919 Smuts wrote to Woodrow Wilson: 'There will be a terrible disillusion if the peoples come to think that we are not concluding a Wilson Peace ...' Three days earlier he had written to his wife: 'Dearest Mamma, ... the Peace Treaty fills me with such despair and repugnance that I am sometimes really furious with the leaders ...'[7]

Like Milner, Botha suddenly seemed to weary of his burden. A few months later, after a short illness, he died at Pretoria. Smuts, who had been offered the position of British Ambassador in Washington, declined and hurried back to his own country after a three-year absence. He was there to help bury his friend to whom he came 'as close together as it is ever given to men to come . . . the largest, most beautiful, sweetest soul of all my land and days'.[8]

Smuts, succeeding Botha, now discovered what had, in fact, been happening while he had been away. Afrikaner nationalism had been growing at the expense of conciliation. In *Die Burger* the movement had found an intelligent new medium, pleading the Afrikaner cause. In the 1915 election the Nationalists polled only 16,000 votes less than Botha's South African Party. A little more than six months after Botha's death, the Nationalists won more seats in the new parliament than any other group. The Labourites, too, under Col. Cresswell, had gained impressively. Compromise was necessary and for a time there was talk and hopes for a new *hereniging* – reunion.

Maybe Smuts himself realized by this time how clouded his view of the domestic scene had become. He was a lover of the land, attached to its mountains, flora and fauna. Inevitably, however, he had lost contact with the deep stirrings of his own people. He saw the veld, but not the *volk*.

In his career Smuts had consistently displayed the many sides of a complex personality. In the commando days, he had demonstrated his application to a single task, his pitiless pursuance of both means and ends, but also his great intelligence. These qualities were particularly apparent in his style of leadership of the burghers during the 'long ride' and in the condemnation and execution of Colyn. (See p. 87.)

The same qualities he would repeatedly demonstrate as statesman and politician. In 1908 he had finally clashed with Mohandas Karamchand Gandhi, who would find in the disabilities of the South African Indians – indentured labourers and their descendants – both the stimulus and the training-field for what was to shake British India and stir the world.

It was the beginning of *Satyagraha*. Jopie Fourie had been executed in 1914. That year, too, there had been a general strike in the Transvaal and Natal. A state of martial law had been declared, and nine ringleaders had been summarily deported.

Smuts had been attacked on all sides, but had always skilfully countered.

In 1920 he had dealt with the Israelites, a religious sect of Xhosa who had illegally occupied land at Bulhoek near Queens-town. After peaceful methods had failed, the offenders had been forcibly removed, with much loss of life.

In 1922 Smuts was suddenly faced with a strike by the Mine Workers' Union, 'full of disinherited Afrikanders from the land',[9] resisting an attempt by the Chamber of Mines to meet a falling gold premium by eliminating the high cost of skilled or semi-skilled white labour through removal of the colour bar.

Smuts appealed to the Chamber to reopen the mines. 'Scabs' began drifting back to work. In February Hertzog proposed in Parliament that legislation be introduced to prevent diminution of the sphere of white employment. It was decided, however, to institute an impartial inquiry. What had been smouldering in the minds of the Afrikaner miners now took flame. It was simply the old situation they had known for a century-and-a-quarter: capitalist 'English' using Blacks to get the better of the Afrikaners . . .

So commandos were formed and there was wild talk of pro-claiming a republic.[10] For some days during the first week in March most of the Rand was in the hands of the rebels. The 'Council of Action' even sought contact with the Third International. Afrikaner sentiment had suddenly, strangely, found common ground with international Communism. It was, in fact, an early expression of what would, in the latter half of the century, become commonplace in the Third World: nationalist thought and sentiment aligning itself to Marxist theory.

Smuts called up the Defence Force. Soon Afrikaners were again shooting Afrikaners. Within ten days some 200 lives had been lost. But the revolt was at an end.

The strikers, a Commission later decided, had hoped for support from the *platteland*. In this they had been encouraged by the idea of a restored republic. What the Commission was, in fact, affirming was that the Afrikaner miners, as uprooted *plattelanders*, had already formed an Afrikaner proletariat. They were *in* the city, not *of* it. They were alienated both culturally and economically in a strange new community in which they occupied, as far as the Whites were concerned, the bottom rungs.[11]

Mining provided those rungs most readily. Overwhelmingly, it was the only alternative to subsistence farming or *bywoner*ship. In mining, mainly as unskilled or semi-skilled workers, they had soon begun to form a body of wage-earners. By the twenties, there were already many others who did not even have the measure of permanency the miners had acquired.

The relatively sudden appearance of an Afrikaner proletariat gave a new index to what had always merely been the ties of blood, language and soil. Here was now the common experience of being indigenous have-nots in cities of 'foreign' haves. The reaction to this was a discernment, dim and as yet unexpressed, of a wider, communal sharing. They were not merely nationalists, they were *socialist nationalists*. This would generally become true of all the Hertzog Afrikaners.

But the strike had suddenly also heralded a new complexity in colour relations. White Afrikaners and black Africans were no longer in the simple relationships of advancing frontiersmen and counteracting tribesmen; or white patriarchy and 'non-white' appurtenance. In the long struggle against the English, awareness of a similarly emergent and competing black proletariat had remained subconscious. But now it had surfaced, and could never disappear again. The transition from proletariat to a *bourgeoisie* would in the case of the Africans be considerably slower. This would be because of their non-literate background, but also because of positive measures consciously employed by a white establishment to retard the process. The Africans would be kept on the periphery of things: their labour would be regarded as being adjacent to the new industrial community, not part of it.

The full import would only gradually force itself upon the consciousness of the Afrikaners. Meanwhile they were far too busy with their primary objective, facing up to their own estrangement from the dominant group, the moneyed English.

At the beginning of the twenties very little divided the followers of Hertzog and those of Smuts. People still trusted men, not 'principles'. Once again there was talk of *hereniging*: a distinct hope that divided Afrikanerdom could once more be united.

Not long after the strike, in September 1922, a last attempt at reconciliation, at Bloemfontein, also came to nothing. The estranged, have-not Afrikaners of the cities instinctively opted for Hertzog, not Smuts. Smuts was now irrevocably associated not only with the Empire, but also with the capitalist structure of non-Afrikaner South Africa.

For many years a favourite figure of caricature in the Afrikaner press was a vulgar, opulent character called Hoggenheimen.[12] It was also indicative of the socialist tendencies which formed a powerful element in Afrikaner nationalism and which brought about a remarkable new partnership: a coalition between British socialists – the Labour Party – devoted to the cause of the white workers, and the Nationalists. It was a triumph for Hertzog.

Here he showed himself to be a truly creative politician, capable of synthesis. The right to secede from the Empire had been an important theme in the Nationalist manifesto. For a while, this was left to itself. The form of government was not important, but independence was. In a hearty exchange of letters between Col. Cresswell – the Labour leader – and Hertzog, they agreed that the 'greatest danger' for South Africa was 'big finance'. For a while, the Afrikaners' cultural aspirations and republican sentiments were left unstressed. The economic betterment of the people was the primary concern. The 'English press' soon came up with charges of an unholy alliance between Christian Afrikaners and (British) Bolshevists. But the government itself was in trouble. There was a sluggish economy, a plague of locusts, muddle in provincial finance. A by-election at Wakkerstroom was unexpectedly lost. Smuts went to the country, and the outcome was momentous. The National/Labour Pact was returned. And Hertzog was the leader.

Travel-weary by now, Smuts decided, philosophically, that anyway it was about time for a rest. He, too, was a creative politician. He himself had been defeated in his old constituency, Pretoria West. Soon, however, he was back in the Assembly as leader of the Opposition. Hertzog had generously allowed a by-election at Standerton, for which Smuts had been nominated and for which he was returned, to remain unopposed.

Revolt, resistance, triumph, renewal, counter-revolt, counter-renewal ... Politics was still a reasonable contest; and nobody saw disaster in a change of government.

Smuts, in good spirits, went botanizing with his friends John Hutchinson of Kew and Rudolph Marloth of Cape Town. At Marloth's home in the Gardens, they sat talking science and philosophy until deep into the night. One result, eventually, was *Holism and Evolution.*

Afrikaner socialist nationalism – a merely descriptive term for these present purposes – was granted almost a decade of practical, reasonable government. The Hertzog Afrikaners had gained the government with the aid of British socialists. This was because they themselves, representing the 'disinherited Afrikanders from the land', had a natural sympathy for the white proletarian workers, who were almost completely Afrikaners. The flow of the 'disinherited' to the cities was going apace. The signs were everywhere. The 'Poor-White Problem' was becoming uncomfortably urgent. It was by no means only the growing proletariat of displaced Afrikaners coming to the new industrial areas. Behind them still on the *platteland* was a considerable reservoir of rural poor: people who had lost not only the means but also the will to make a decent living, many of whom who were, too, on their way to the cities. There was a growing feeling among intellectual Afrikaners that the problem was getting out of hand; that soon a considerable part of Afrikanerdom would, economically and spiritually, be beyond redemption. It needed deep study leading to action. Also vitally necessary were the Church and other public bodies. Above all a government was necessary, concerned with the lot of those who had largely been the product of a difficult history, in a hard land.

In the early thirties a special commission sponsored by the Carnegie Corporation of New York investigated the problem. Essentially it had been a question of part of the early grazier/hunters slowly moving eastwards and northwards in the old Cape Colony, the least adaptable elements floating along in the stream of immigration. Either they served the stronger elements as *bywoners*, or else they had been pushed ahead to marginal lands of the new frontier areas. War, natural disaster, even the normal increase in population in a community with predominantly a subsistence economy, soon turned them into a human surplus.

For them there were three possibilities. They could remain where they were. But the ownership of the land to which they were attached was becoming subdivided to a point insufficient even for subsistence. They could try their luck on the various diamond diggings, especially those in the far Western Transvaal. Finally, they could find their way to the towns and cities, hoping for some employment in the strange 'English' world of mines, factories and shops.

No largely Afrikaner government coming to power at this time could be anything but socialist and nationalist. It had a special responsibility for indigent kith and kin. It was also conscious of the fact that the oldest, most tried, section of the white population did not own the richest of the land.

Socialist nationalist legislation of the early Hertzog era included an act to provide South Africa with its own national flag, while still retaining the Union Jack to fly alongside of it: a compromise in pursuance of the *eie*, which at times caused turbulent feeling in British areas like Natal. It included, too, the official recognition of Afrikaans, which by now had indisputably become a literary language.

There was legislation to provide for the special interests of farmers and mineworkers and to deal with the promotion of South African industry. There was also legislation to deal with drought-relief, irrigation, diamond-cutting and other new industries. The most 'socialist' of the new measures, however, was the establishment of a nationalized iron and steel industry, based on the country's huge reserves of coal and iron ore. This pleased the Labour Party for obvious reasons, while irking the believers in free enterprise, who were also the champions of existing economic links with Britain and the Commonwealth.

There were also various 'socialist-nationalist' measures designed to protect the new white Afrikaner proletariat from competing Africans. A black proletariat had also been formed by the disrupting forces of a changing economy, population growth, war and natural disaster. White Afrikaners and black Africans opposed each other in a far more subtle way than was ever possible on the frontier. This the strike had shown. In the pioneer days defence for the Whites had meant *laagers*, guns and sorties. Now it became the political expedient of 'civilized labour'.

It meant legislation such as the *Wages Act* (1925) and the revived *Mines and Works Act* (1926), also known as the *Colour Bar Act*. It was discrimination, of course, and, quite apart from the moral issues involved, it was debatable on the practical grounds of whether it was wise to let Poor-White and African workers fight it out for themselves, as fight they would.

Basically, there were no mere racial motives in Hertzog's measures. This was demonstrated by his attitude towards the Coloureds, largely from the Cape. In a speech at Smithfield, on 13 November 1925 on 'Native policy', he had said of the Coloureds: '... They came about and exist in our midst. They know no other civilization ... They use the languages of the whites ... There can be no question of segregation.'

No nationalist editorial commentator could as yet fundamentalize the difference between the approaches of the 'Sap' opposition and the 'Nat' government as follows:

> The latter has always made itself known as a party with an ideal. Its opponents who do not know the difference between the two, have already accused us of ideological obsession, but in so doing they were not able to detract from the power with which loyalty to its fundamental principles has invested the National Party.[13]

The Hertzog Afrikaners had no conceptualized, rationalized programme to follow religiously. They had no central idea or policy, unfolding logically, step by step, to final and full realization. They were primarily concerned with things in terms of practical realities.

There were certain facts in the general situation of the Afrikaners which Hertzog had to face, for which he had to legislate and to administrate. They had been a defeated people. Their traditional society, in the process of defeat and post-war reconstruction, had been shaken to its foundations. New means of production and ways of living had developed. In the process many had lost all stability. Already some 17.5% of all Afrikaners were living in penury. They had been leaving the *platteland* in increasing numbers, and had gathered in fringe-areas of the cities. They had already formed a wage-earning class; and, alongside but also below them, another had been forming. It was black.

The dominant white classes of the cities were no comfort, because they, too, were strange. The cities were still citadels of Anglo-Saxon culture and British economic power. The new immigrant Afrikaners were, in fact, strangers in their own country: hesitant, fearful of using their own language in shops and businesses, and confined very largely to the humbler areas and jobs. They were without the fine schools supported by the English churches, the institutions and amenities generally, which the English took for granted. For this reason, moreover, they were exposed to the rivalry of non-white South Africa. The increasing competition from black Africans, which took place primarily in the cities, affected them in the first instance. The great mass of the established English middle class lived and worked in areas where the problems of colour were items in the daily newspapers. In spite of all the leaders of Union so far having been ex-Boer War generals, South Africa was still a British country.

'To the Afrikaners,' David Welsh points out,

towns were pre-eminently the places of the oppressor. Many attributed their rural poverty to the financial power of the English and Jewish groups ... The Afrikaner in the towns regarded himself as a foreigner among aliens ... The language of industry, commerce, and officialdom of the towns was overwhelmingly English. Even the former Trekker capitals of Pietermaritzburg, Pretoria and Bloemfontein, had been 'captured by the language and way of life of the foreigners'.[14]

All this was difficult to define and impossible to legislate for. It lay outside the normal field of politics. It was one thing to accept the equal status of Afrikaans by act of parliament, it was another to establish its use. Attitudes were private matters; and so were the languages people used in their businesses, or whom they employed. For Hertzog the promotion of the *eie* and the development of the country towards full independence were mainly concerned with the elimination by act of parliament of what still remained of British colonialism.

In 1926, Hertzog had inspired the declaration by Lord Balfour, a leading minister in the Conservative Government, that the status of the dominions was one of complete equality with Britain.

De jure, many inequalities still remained. There was the subordination of the South African Appeal Court to the Privy Council. There was, too, the *Colonial Laws Validity Act* of 1865, ruling that no colonial law was to conflict with a British one; the right, in theory at least, of the British government to reject dominion legislation through the advice of the Governor-General.

In the Statute of Westminster of 1931, aided by a fellow Afrikaner (Smuts), a Canadian (Laurier) and an Irishman (de Valera) Hertzog was again the enlivening spirit. The Crown was now the only link between the equal partners of what, for them, had ceased to be the Empire and had become the Commonwealth. It was another triumph for the man who was devoted to the cause of restoring the full independence and dignity of his people, but in a way which would not disrupt the accord it had found with British South Africa.

Employment opportunities had been created for the displaced Afrikaners streaming to the cities. Like the police and the public services generally, the nationalized railways would absorb many. New manufacturing and processing industries served the same purpose.

Nevertheless, times were difficult. There was a world depression. South Africa, too, could not escape it. The end of the twenties and early thirties also saw an almost catastrophic drought. In the Free State, cosmic dust-storms swept the land like doom itself.

The natural development in the political thinking of a man whose struggle for the *eie*, for 'South Africa first', full national autonomy and the rejection of colonialism, had by the turn of the decade largely been vindicated, might well have been a synthesis with those who with equal honesty had been working for the cause of conciliation. After all, the working arrangement with British socialists had already indicated as much. In 1926, Barlow of the Labour Party had even successfully proposed the abolition of British titles.

Conditions generally favoured political compromise. In the deep of depression, the price of yellow maize had fallen by half. Wool was fourpence a pound. Drought lay over the land like darkness at blazing midday. The disinherited from the *platteland* were streaming to the cities. The noble efforts of the Church to keep indigent Afrikaners on the land at new irrigation projects on the banks of the Orange River, could only affect a small part of the 300,000 the Carnegie Commission would estimate the Poor-Whites to be. The predominant literary work of the time was the novel *Ampie* by Jochem van Bruggen. His comic vision of the Poor-White was redemptive only to the discerning.

What precipitated synthesis was the crisis following the abandonment by the United Kingdom of the gold standard. Hertzog, strongly supported by his old comrade-at-arms, Havenga, held the view that it was in South Africa's interest as the world's greatest gold-producer to remain where she was. But capital was, alarmingly, fleeing the country; and Smuts likened it to a wounded man shedding his life-blood. At the height of the crisis, Tielman Roos, an Appeal Court judge, dramatically left the sheltered precincts of the law and returned to the political arena. He demanded an all-party government and a departure from the gold standard, soon winning public support. In the ensuing turbulence, the government gave way. The gold standard was discarded and coalition became a fact.

It was the start of what Hertzog's biographer, Van den Heever, would refer to as the 'Great Experiment of Fusion', the start of a prosperous and creative period in the life of the country.[15] It was the start also of one of the most bitter chapters in the history of Afrikanerdom. A man who had given everything for the cause of the Afrikaners, groping their way into the twentieth century, was now to experience the trauma of uncompromising opposition by fellow nationalists: on the grounds that he had, in the matter of the *eie*, capitulated for the sake of doubtful conciliation with traditional enemies.

But fortune favoured the Great Experiment. With Fusion in 1934, the depression lifted, capital – off gold – came bounding back; and so did the rains. The two Anglo-Boer War generals, Hertzog and Smuts, now led the new United Party. Smuts was prepared to serve as Hertzog's deputy. For the latter, however, there was now a new opponent, a Cape Afrikaner, a man whose whole background was different from every Afrikaner who had yet led the Union.

In and around the Anglo-Boer War, D. F. Malan had been a young man in his mid-twenties studying theology at Stellenbosch and Utrecht. Unlike Smuts and Hertzog, who had also had a Cape background before moving to the North, Malan's interest in the struggle of the two Republics had been academic. After graduating as a doctor of divinity he had entered the Dutch Reformed Church. In 1915, he became editor of *Die Burger*. Two years later he entered politics. When the Pact government took over in 1924, he became Minister of the Interior, Health and Education.

It can be said of Malan that he represented the beginning of a fundamental change in the course and nature of Afrikaner nationalism. Malan was born and spent his childhood in the same kind of *platteland* – Riebeeck West – as Smuts. But he became essentially the articulation of the rising *burgerstand*. He was one of an emergent political élite drifting to the top of a tenuous urban middle class, closely following the Afrikaner proletariat: already, partly, arising out of it.

The quality of Malan's intellect was different from that of both Hertzog and Smuts. Hertzog had been a jurist and judge, while Smuts had been one of Cambridge's most distinguished scholars. But both were still really rooted to the veld, the soil. Smuts always returned to his farm Doornkloof at Irene, as did Hertzog to his farm Waterval, also on the highveld. Smuts was later, posthumously, to say of Hertzog: 'Even in the midst of the most bitter political struggle, our personal relations were excellent ...'[16] The story goes that there were times when

Hertzog and Smuts, while their respective parties were locked in debate on some deeply contentious question, would meet in the precincts of Parliament and have a lively discussion on veld-grasses and their nutritional value. They shared not only love of the land, but also a great many friends. In Hertzog's study at Waterval there were pictures on the wall of Kruger, de la Rey, de Wet and Steyn. They had also been Smuts's comrades.

It was natural for Hertzog to regard the new kind of Afrikaner politician with some suspicion. He had complained bitterly of ministers of the Dutch Reformed Church, who had entered politics. He was obviously thinking particularly of Malan in this regard; but there were also others. What Hertzog vaguely felt about Malan, was the first indication of a reaction to the theologizing of Afrikaner politics.

It was, perhaps, epitomized in the claim by the new Nationalists that they followed 'principles and not people'. It indicated the remarkable way in which the process of internalization had proceeded, more or less keeping pace with *verburgerliking*. The close disciples of Malan were all similar intellectuals: N. J. van der Merwe, T. E. Dönges, Eric Louw, C. R. Swart, J. G. Strijdom, H. F. Verwoerd...All except Verwoerd were urbanized Afrikaners, but a generation removed from their own *platteland* nurseries. Verwoerd had been born in Holland.

None of the inner circle of the new Nationalism had anything remotely resembling the war experience of Smuts, Hertzog, Reitz, Kemp and others in the United Party. They had been born in the *platteland* and had studied at South African and European universities. They had returned and had become members of a new political intelligentsia, proceeding forth from the *burgerstand*. The re-modelled Nationalist Party held them together, but also an older, in a sense more inclusive, organization – the Afrikaner *Broederbond*.

The *Broederbond* had originally been designed as a service organization on the lines of the Rotary Club. It was there to help Afrikaners through their experience of alienation when coming to the Anglo-Saxon cities. Like the Freemasons, the organization was religiously-based and observed certain rituals. Like the Rotary Club it offered its services to its own special community. Where the *Broederbond* differed from the other two organizations was in its distinctive Afrikaner idiom. Its religious and cultural content lay wholly within the protestant ethic.

At Smithfield in 1935, Hertzog, after breaking with Malan, had denounced the movement. 'The *Broederbond*,' he said, 'is a serious threat to the peace and order of the Union ...' Malan, he took note, was a member of this 'ethically questionable' secret society, which operated only for a 'chosen group', those who claimed to be better Afrikaners than anybody else.[17]

For more than thirty years, Hertzog had accepted the growing burden of serving his people and country. He had given all he had. In the Anglo-Boer War he had been among the successful commando leaders who had invaded the Colony, and had ultimately managed to establish Boer control over a large part of the north-western territory. Havenga, who had been his young military secretary, had later testified that, in fact, the whole guerrilla strategy had been inspired by Hertzog. He had even been de Wet's instructor.[18] He had led a ragged band of burghers over the endless Karroo, often being forced to proceed on foot, because of horse-sickness. In many encounters with the British, his commando had miraculously survived. His most notable victory had been the capture of Calvinia on 10 January 1901. This town was later to be represented in parliament by D. F. Malan. Meanwhile, his wife had suffered deeply in a British concentration camp.

After the war, in the days of the Orange River Colony, he had fought and won the battle for equality of the languages in the schools. At De Wildt, in 1912, he had stood under a korri tree and had announced his championship of the *eie*. All who gave their unconditional loyalty to South Africa, he said, were Afrikaners. In 1924, he had formed a most successful coalition with English-speaking Labourites. He had fought for and established iron and steel and other industries. He had expanded the railways. He had cared for the dispossessed of his people. He had fought, against the most impassioned opposition, for a national flag. He had been the decisive factor behind dominion sovereign independence and diminishing colonialism. South Africa had been hit by drought and depression and his people had suffered. He himself had gone through difficult times, but he had always survived. He was still deeply, reverently attached to the *eie* and to the ideal of national unity. He visualized both great cultural traditions flowing in two parallel streams. With Smuts, he had found a *modus vivendi*. They were fully agreed on the deep necessity of encouraging a true South African spirit, a feeling of national self-respect. After the many years of un-relenting political conflict, the country overwhelmingly supported Fusion.

The only serious opposition came from the Cape Nationalists, under the leadership of Malan. In a speech at Stellenbosch on 29 June 1934, Malan had openly accused Hertzog of dealing on his own initiative with Smuts, who had been rejected by the *volk*, at the cost of principle.

'Principles?' Hertzog angrily expostulated. What did these political *parvenus* know about principles when they libelled a man of the stature of Smuts in the way they did? They, the Malanites, were, according to themselves, the only true believers. Hertzog himself had become 'the poor old general'.

'So it continued,' Van den Heever recounts, 'in leading article after leading article ... in an endless stream of letters to the press ... This is what party politics had become in South Africa.'[19] Hertzog himself gave no quarter. His intolerance and angry invective towards his former political comrades remained unsurpassed. His abhorrence was unmitigated and complete.

What, Hertzog was to inquire with mounting bitterness, had these 'super-nationalists' ever done for their country to warrant their fantastic claims? All they ever seemed to do, he might have thought, was to gather in the *Koffiehuis* in Cape Town. There they sat, morning after morning, listening to the pronouncements of a man who had watched the Anglo-Boer War from the comfort of the Netherlands ...

Hertzog was right in judging the behaviour of the new political intellectuals as being – to use a modern term – one-dimensional. They were concerned only with Afrikaner ascendancy in an Afrikaner nation. But he was wrong in trying to explain every-thing in terms of an unadorned power struggle. What he failed to recognize was the intimation of revolutionary thought among the political intellectuals of the expanding *burgerstand*. Increasingly it became for him a personal struggle.

In the *Koffiehuis* discussions tended to be directed to the idea of a completely new South African order. It would not only be a republic, it would be an Afrikaner republic of a particular kind. Its shape could not yet clearly be seen, but it would be fundamentally different to what had always obtained.

What was being discussed in the *Koffiehuis* was only a reflection of ideas being deeply considered in the *Broederbond*. The themes of Afrikaner estrangement in the cities and the still-backward position of Afrikaans culture had been debated many times. So had the relevance of the link with the British Crown and the remaining British symbols of flag and anthem. But a new theme was soon to be of overriding importance: that of colour. What had for so long remained scarcely recognized – the awareness of colour in an urban context, as a huge shapeless black/brown proletariat – was now returning to the surface. At the time of the strike it had come and gone, generated by the sudden but transitory heat of revolt. In the gathering evolution of a revolutionary idea, however, it could only increase.

Hertzog's 1936 legislation had by no means disposed of the 'Native question'. There was also the matter of the Coloureds, who were mainly confined to the Cape. Hertzog had repeatedly said that they should be regarded as an integral part of the white community. Whites and Coloureds were being allowed to mix and even to marry, the new Nationalists objected. It was all wrong. It was a serious threat to the survival of the Afrikaners. Colour relations now required *radical* thought.

The whole nature of an evolving revolutionary idea was still strange to the Afrikaners, even when they were already drawing its outlines. To Hertzog it was a blank. What really limited his vision was his personal involvement in the struggle and his deep, bitter feelings about the distrust of those who had done so little for what he saw as the true interests of South Africa. His answer to what often showed itself as spiteful opposition was to take even more of the burden of things on himself. The weight Atlas was carrying, however, was already inordinate. Inevitably it became a kind of autocracy.

Only a strong United Party government, Hertzog believed, could have been able to deal with the 'Native question'. The 1936 legislation had considerably enlarged the reserves, partly as compensation for the removal of Cape 'natives' from the electoral roll. In the Senate, the Africans would have white representation. Coloureds would remain part of the white electorate.

Great new roads running through the country had been built. The airways had been vastly improved. Agricultural marketing had been completely overhauled...

The measure of Hertzog's government was still sound, practical reason. The country had fully recovered from the depression of the early thirties and the drought. Proof of public satisfaction was afforded at the general election in 1938. The United Party, losing a few seats, nevertheless obtained a clear majority.

The Nationalists had hoped to do better. An ill-considered poster depicting the evils of mixed marriages had badly boomeranged. South Africa did not like it. There was still tolerance in the land.

Malan had tried to convince South Africa that he, Hertzog, had abandoned the true principles and interests of the Afrikaners. He had been supported by a most effective press, but had made little headway.

What, abandon the struggle for the *eie*? For the full autonomy of the country? Had he, Hertzog, not established by the Status Acts the sovereign independence of the country once and for all? Had he not incurred the wrath of Stallard's Dominion Party, when *Die Stem van Suid-Afrika* had become the only national anthem, *God Save the King* being reserved for special occasions? Had he not likewise seen to the pre-eminence of the national flag? Had these measures not caused dissatisfaction even within the United Party? The answer came in the form of the centenary celebrations of the Great Trek.

A symbolic trek of ox-wagons had been organized to move from various points in the country, converging gradually on Pretoria, at the site of the intended new Voortrekker Monument. An extensive sequence of functions, graced by people in Voortrekker dress and beards, took place as the ox-wagons proceeded on their way to Pretoria. Pageantry and oratory reflected a fresh and powerful wave of Afrikaner feeling. It became a massive demonstration of the new nationalism.

The Rand Strike of 1922 had been the first announcement of the presence of an Afrikaner wage-earning class. But the masses gathering round the ox-wagons in the new Afrikaner suburbs were the sign that a great many picks, shovels, carrying-hands, loading- and unloading-hands had already been exchanged for blue-collars. And a great many blue-collars had already been exchanged for white. The *burgerstand* had come. The symbolic Ox-Wagon Trek was also its triumphant announcement that it had come to stay.

The Poor-White problem was being solved, not by a return to the land, but by a speeded-up process of integration of the dispossessed into industry. In the suburbs, however, Afrikaners were still being confronted with the dismaying affluence of the English. In spite of their own flag and anthem, the formal acceptance of Afrikaans as an official language, the Statute of Westminster and the Status Laws and more than a decade of Hertzog rule, practically all public notices were still in English alone. In order to use their language in businesses and shops, even in many departments of the local, provincial and national public service, city Afrikaners had to resort to special organizations for *taalhandhawing*. They used their own language in public places, deliberately and often provocatively. In return, they were frequently insulted. In the Supreme Court of South Africa the almost exclusive language in civil matters was still English. The delivery of a judgment in Afrikaans was invariably news. In every cinema and public concert-hall performances were still being terminated grandly by the playing of *God Save the King*, while a sun-bleached Union Jack fluttered tremulously on the screen.

All this and very much more needed humour, but instead it served to fill the new Afrikaner immigrants with a consuming sense of inferiority. Even the fact that the country since Union had never been governed by any other than Afrikaners could not dispel it. In the immediacy of everyday life, the evolving *burgerstand* still felt themselves to be strangers in the land of their fathers. Inferiority bred resentment which in turn generated a new kind of nationalism. This was something which Hertzog, in spite of his incomparable services to Afrikanerdom, could not really understand.

In the world of the *platteland* Afrikaners, attitudes had not yet reached the stage of being defensive, grimly resentful or visionary. Between the bucolically expressive but seldom intolerant nationalism of the *platteland* and the tight nationalism of the *burgerstand*, there was a world of difference. The very fact that Hertzog chose to make his important policy speeches at Smithfield in the Free State was indicative of the distance which had grown between him and the new Afrikaners.

The outbreak of World War II in September 1939 provided the climax, too, of the Hertzog drama. Subjected for so long to an unceasing and often heartless attack by the Nationalists and their outrageously efficient press, Hertzog was suddenly faced with an issue like a chasm. It was a matter of *hereniging* with his militant fellow Afrikaners, or support for Great Britain to the point of entering the war.

'Bring together what belong together, because of inner conviction,' Malan had incessantly preached. His words now seemed to have acquired a prophetic character. In a moment of apparent truth, in a time loaded with old and renewed antagonisms, Hertzog decided in favour of neutrality.

The 'great experiment of Fusion' was at an end. Smuts was suddenly the old Smuts: the man who was to play successfully the same Olympian part in this great war as in the last.

The vote in Parliament went against Hertzog. South Africa was, with the Allies, at war with Germany. There was a great upsurge of Afrikaner emotion: it was 'England's war'. There was an undefined feeling that the new political order which had developed in Germany and had led to such spectacular results held out promises, too, for Afrikanerdom. The tradition of socialist nationalism, in which Hertzog had played such a great part, now prepared them for long-distance appreciation of national socialism.

'According to his [Hertzog's] insight,' Van den Heever says,

'... its [National Socialism's] fundamentals were to be found in the constitution of the old Republic of the Orange Free State.'[20]

It was a strange, general *malaise*. Everything Hertzog had so strenuously opposed in the new Nationalism of Malan cried out against it. But in the turmoil of emotions, utterances, writings, charges and counter-charges perspective was no longer possible. In a way, Hertzog had been affected by exactly what he had been fighting.

There was a memorable meeting three days after Smuts had taken over. At Monumentkoppie, the site where the new Voortrekker Monument was to be erected, Hertzog and Malan, before a cheering multitude, demonstrated their new solidarity. The character of a people, Hertzog said on this occasion, was more than its armies.

It was all too unreal to last. Afrikanerdom was floundering around, trying to find firm ground for its treading feet in the rising world-flood.

Malan generously offered Hertzog the leadership of the party of *hereniging*. Soon, however, some of the most powerful of the new political intellectuals were working to undermine Hertzog's intended leadership. 'Principles,' they again demanded, 'not people!' It was a remarkable adumbration of a long period in the political history of the Afrikaner, when 'principles' would be preferred to people.

In Europe, the Germans were poised to start their all-conquering *Blitzkrieg*. A para-military organization, having much in common with National Socialism, had also spread through Afrikanerdom. It was the *Ossewabrandwag*; 'The Ox Wagon Guard'. It was the prelude to the coming fundamental change in political belief, part of the founding and growth of a secular religion which was intended to save Afrikanerdom and perhaps the world. Meanwhile, Europe was locked in conflict; and the fall of France was imminent.

Hertzog, rejected by the Free State congress of the new *Herenigde* National Party, left the hall in Bloemfontein, followed by a small number of his faithful supporters, among them Havenga. Thirty years previously he had done more or less the same thing in Cape Town. Then Christiaan de Wet had accompanied him.

He resigned from parliament and retired to his farm. The burden for Atlas had, at last, become too great. To remain erect he had to discard the burden. He could only face the ensuing loneliness with as much fortitude as possible.

In his woodcutter's jacket he was to be seen at times on horseback riding through the warm veld of his large estate. Then again he would be seen giving instructions to one of his black farm workers. Then one would discover him, a thin and lonely figure, standing among the thorn trees . . .[21]

He arrived on his own one night at a Pretoria hospital and asked to be admitted. The receptionist, taking down the details for registration, failed to recognize the frail, bespectacled man with the grey, bushy moustache. He had given his occupation as that of a farmer. J. B. M. Hertzog died at Waterval on 21 November 1942.

Darkness had settled on an occupied Europe. In Germany itself, the Jews were being sent in their millions to the gas chambers. It was all being done in the name of radical politics: a messianic, millennial idea, a socio-political ideal, the ultimate theology of politics.

No Afrikaner political leader in the tradition of nationalism was as yet able to understand this. The tragedy of Hertzog – and the potential tragedy of Afrikanerdom – had still to be put into a meaningful perspective.

Part Two: Roots and Relations

Part Two: Ideas and Relations

5 The Original Calvin

To say that the key to the Afrikaners is Calvinism is not enough. As is the case with all apostles there are as many Calvins as there have been restatements or 'revisions' of the original philosophy. Relevant to the Afrikaners of Southern Africa are: the Synod of Dort early in the seventeenth century; the rise of Puritanism; and the neo-Calvinism of Kuyper, Dooyeweerd and others, in the Netherlands of roughly our own time.

We shall examine each of these in turn, but a fuller perspective can only develop if we look, primarily but briefly, at the original or primitive Calvin in the *milieu* in which he wrote, spoke and directed.

Calvin was outstanding in a number of ways. There were several elements of overriding importance in his enormous influence, which reverberated from Geneva in the latter half of the sixteenth century through all subsequent history. Among them were his separation of the functions of church and state and his acceptance of the profound contemporary changes in society's social and economic conditions. The nature of his religious belief was also highly significant. He took particular delight in the words of St Augustine that the first, second and third precepts of the Christian religion were humility.[1] He also believed that man left to his own designs was a devil, and that God alone was sovereign and good. Man's utter dependence on Grace, Divine election *and* Christian liberty were at the heart of human existence, according to him. This was a mystery, calling to mind what Samuel Johnson was once reported to have remarked on the matter of predestination: that all logic accepted it, and all experience rejected it.

The social humanism of Calvin arose out of such fundamentals. This is the more remarkable when viewed from the vantage point of an age, with so much burning concern for the 'wretched of the earth', in a great variety of revolutionary forms. On this subject André Biéler has written a monumental study.[2]

The view of R. H. Tawney that Calvin's Geneva was a theocracy which made of 'Geneva a city of glass, in which every household lived its life under the supervision of spiritual police'[3] is reduced to only a partial truth in the light of Biéler's work. For although Calvin's voice in the affairs of the city-state was a clear, persistent and authoritative one, it was never that of a visionary who had worked out a total blueprint for the reconstruction of society, primarily seeking man's redemption by the 'human engineering' of a socio-political system. It was rather that of a spiritually most gifted leader who constantly sought to examine the temporal society of civil government in the light of humility as a Christian precept. In this way, he dealt 'piecemeal' with the renewal of his particular community, as K. R. Popper has discussed in another context.[4] Church and state were nevertheless autonomous institutions, each operating in its own circumscribed field. This remained fundamental to the Reformed faith. Calvin himself, Biéler says, sometimes departed from his own basic tenets as far as this was concerned, as in the case of Miguel Servetus. In these cases, he sought the aid of the state to deal with the enemies of the true faith because he, too, was still partly exposed to the spirit of the age.[5] The list of martyrs who had ended their lives at the stake or on the scaffold of the Inquisition had already by that time become a formidable one.

Calvin indeed sought the regeneration of Genevan society, but never in the utopian sense. Civil government, as the final chapter of his *Institutes* most definitively shows, was concerned with an order which moved within strict limits, which could never lay claim to its own absolute values and which, in fact, was guilty of trespass when it pretended to prescribe its own manmade ultimate ideals for its citizens. 'We are subject to men who rule over us,' Calvin said, 'but subject only in the Lord. If they command anything against Him let us not pay the least regard to it nor be moved by the dignity which they possess as magistrates . . .'[6] Unto Caesar should be rendered whatever was his as long as he did not exceed his authority and present himself as God. This would be so precisely where Caesar sought to usurp the work of Providence, and when the 'royal office' behaved as if it were the 'apostolic ministry'.[7] Magistrates are the ordained guardians of the civil order of whom 'it should be their only study to provide for the common peace and safety'. The function of the Church, on the other hand, was not that of the everyday business of running the polity, but 'great Kings should not think it a disgrace to them to prostrate themselves suppliantly before Christ ... nor ought they to be displeased at being judged by the Church.'[8] The enormous impact of Calvin on the Genevan society, one which has lasted until the present day, should primarily be seen in this light.

The social and economic life of Western man had, at the time of Calvin, long been in a state of metamorphosis. Great leadership has always been distinguished by the ability to recognize – rationally and intuitively – the changing tenor of the times and to act creatively in accordance with it. In essence, this means the ability to move a society towards the acceptance of a new synthesis of seemingly opposite forces. Calvin was an outstanding example of this.

The Middle Ages had been a time of feudal lords, pious and learned clergy, largely confined to their monastic seclusion, and also of toiling peasants in serfdom. Consummate craftsmen erected soaring monuments in stone, while an emergent society of burghers uneasily explored the new fields of commerce, criss-crossed with trade-routes from the Far and Middle East, the lands around the Mediterranean and deeper Africa. By the twelfth century a new class of professional traders, frowned upon by the Church and despised by the nobles as bourgeois rich, were coming together in guilds, preparing the ground for new political and economic institutions. This would in time come to be known as representative government and bourgeois capitalism. What Johan Huizinga has described as the Autumn of the Middle Ages had a relatively sudden onset. The beginning of the fourteenth century saw the Papacy in exile at Avignon. Plague, famine, war and peasant revolt raged incessantly over most of Western Europe. The autumn with its fading light soon became a winter of inexpressible gloom. The last quarter of the century brought the Great Schism in the Church, when for nearly three generations a double succession of Popes ruled in Rome and Avignon. In all, the age was a tired one. Even its violence was torpid.

All creation was crying out for renewal: socially, politically, economically, spiritually. In the century-and-a-half that followed, it came about in a variety of ways.

In Italy the rebirth of humanism appropriately expressed itself in a new passion for classical learning, literature and art. Out of the rubble of antiquity the Renaissance had flowered.

Martin Luther, on a pilgrimage to Rome at the time, had no eyes, however, for the glories of neo-classical art, arising everywhere. His offence at the shallow ostentation of Pope Alexander VI and those around him was too great. Alexander was not only Pontiff, he was also War Lord and Emperor.

The Holy City itself was a blasphemy. The Church was obviously very sick indeed. Ironically, while the Church still ranted on about the sin of usury, the Papacy, as Tawney says, had become the greatest financial institution of the Middle Ages.

New worlds were meanwhile being discovered. In 1492 Christopher Columbus had crossed the Atlantic. Six years later Vasco da Gama rounded the Cape on his way to India. Within less than a generation, Magellan was preparing an expedition to sail around the world. In the same year (1518) Hernando Cortez landed with the first of the Conquistadores on the coast of Mexico. At Wittenberg, in Germany, on 31 October 1517, Martin Luther had hammered his ninety-five theses as subjects for debate on the door of the church attached to the castle of Frederick of Saxony. The beating of his hammer was at the same time the announcement that Western man had arrived at a divide in history.

As indicated, it was John Calvin, not Martin Luther, who in time gave the Reformation its most penetrating shape. This was because of his deep awareness of the currents of the age. It was not merely a question of the sick body of the Church, its abuse of powers and betrayal of its calling. It was also a question of its obdurate refusal to recognize that the socio-political and economic institutions of the Middle Ages were no longer valid. For some centuries they had been showing signs of dissolution. In the fifteenth century they had been moribund. Here in the sixteenth they had finally collapsed. All that now remained was the magnificent pretence.

Calvin's *Institutes*, the first edition of which appeared in 1536, was as much a restatement of St Augustine as an acceptance of a profound change in what Marx, at a later stage in history, would call the 'means of production'. In the last resort, this means a development in the cultural practices of the wider community. It requires a contemporary spirit to recognize and accept this. A traditional way of life must be adapted to meet the fresh requirements of an age. New wine needs new bottles. It is the inner discipline of faith.

Geneva as a city, however, saw the new development in mainly secular terms. Like Venice, Genoa, Antwerp and the cities of the Hanseatic League, it had become by now a wealthy centre of trade and manufacture. Its burghers had successfully rejected the overlordship of the Duke of Savoy. Geneva was now an independent state. Its people had taken eagerly to the new liberty. Optimism went like wine to the head. And in the process many were exploited.

Into the shining, prosperous landscape around Lac Léman a scandalized William Farel at last brought the lean ascetic figure of Calvin. He had heard the call and he never hesitated.

The *Génévoises* did not take kindly to Calvin during his first sojourn in the city. Incurring the anger of the patrician Council and others for his forthright criticism of conditions, he was soon forced to leave for Strasbourg. There he lived in exile for three years, working assiduously on the *Institutes of the Christian Religion*. In 1541, however, he was invited to return to Geneva. The city could not do without him. His wise counsel, his ascetic but quite irresistible dynamic, were needed not only for the Reformed church, but also for the community as a whole.

Calvin's return changed things for the city for all time. Except for the period in Strasbourg, he spent the rest of his life in Geneva. Nothing was either beyond his notice or his censure. It is important to emphasize again there was no question of a socio-political 'unfolding', step by logical step, towards an utopian end. It remained a constant but *ad hoc* examination of behaviour in the life of the city, both public and private. In the *Sermons*, in the *Commentaries* on the Old and New Testaments, in his vast correspondence and other writings, in the *Institutes* itself, the behaviour of the human creature was examined in its entirety.

But it was not so much the thorough and conscientious detail of Calvin's vision which marks it as one of the decisive influences in Western history. Rather it was his unerring sense of the needs of the age, the changed fibre of society. It was also his ability to formulate it for all concerned in terms of basic Christian precepts. Tawney misjudges the position when he says that Calvin, except for the matter of interest, 'made few innovations to the details of social policy'.[9]

What distinguished his approach from that of the Middle Ages was not merely the question of usury, or the amount of new religious zeal he was able to inspire. The shape and spirit of the age itself had changed, and he recognized it like none of his contemporaries did; immensely more than Luther, for instance, who thought mainly of a return to a former state of innocence or holiness: and far more than Melanchthon, who had already pointed out some of the real aspects of the new economy.

The economy of the civilized world had become a money-economy for reasons which had nothing intrinsically to do with the greed of man. It was rather a matter of sound practicality induced by the growth in populations and the discovery of the new world. As such, it had to be accepted in humility and honesty as a new field in which God could be served. The same could be said of the change in the relationship between state and church. The old medieval unity between the two entities was no longer true. It had become a great unworkable pretence and was now a nexus of abuse. To bring about the restoration of both the religious and civil order, the falsities which had developed had to be finally exposed, then rejected.

For Calvin, the restoration of society had to take place on the firm foundations of the Christian faith. This meant a renewed clarity about man's true calling in the world. It also meant an unambiguous recognition of the many practical measures by which this could be demonstrated.

Calvin's insistence that church and state both have their clearly defined fields of activity, constituting autonomous behaviour, does not mean that they are to be sealed off from each other. What it does mean is that each entity has its own particular function in the wider concept of the Christian religion.

The state is the secular power which is merely a provisional order. As such it is like the law, which is the state in a particular mode. The special mission of the state is that of ensuring a minimum of good conduct of governing with charity, equity and reason, but without trying to include the Kingdom of Christ within the elements of this world. (Cf. p. 127 and note 8).

'There is a twofold government in man,' Calvin says in the closing chapter of the *Institutes*. This *double régime*, as Biéler refers to it, is precisely there because man will abuse his freedom.[10] A minimum code of behaviour (*morale minimum*), like the rules of the road, will need to be enforced. Civil Government is not the apostolic ministry. (Cf. p. 127, note 7).

The civil order is preferably democratic without being essentially so. Above all, the state has strictly defined limits. Although even an unjust régime should be obeyed because all authority is from God, in exceptional cases even revolt is justified. Insurgents may well be the messianic saviours when God himself has raised up inside or outside the nation. This may happen when the disorder or injustice of the government in power is greater than that of the rebels. God condemns revolt, but serves himself at times by using insurgents as a judge over those who have exploited them.[11]

While the state has no spiritual authority over the Church, the Church has a particular political mission. It prays for those in power, even when they persecute the Church. But it censures authority when it exceeds its bounds, remembering always that the Church should defend the poor and helpless against the rich and powerful. Should the Church find it necessary to range itself against the injustice of the state, it must be prepared to become politically suspect, even to the point of persecution. By such resistance the Church then contributes towards the restoration of an authentic social order. Spiritual liberty requires social and political liberty.[12] The Church is therefore intimately concerned with the renewal of society. This is a regeneration in Jesus Christ, and it is particularly expressed in the social relations of labour.[13] All Christians are necessary reformers of a disordered society.[14] This operates in the fields of worship, doctrine and morals. The Church alone is the arbiter of morals.

Material goods are a sign of God's grace, and in Christendom material things also have a spiritual value. Temporary benefits may well be pledges of the coming kingdom. They should therefore not impoverish our spiritual life, but should help to restore it.[15] Even though material goods are a sign of God's grace, we should never be tied to them. God's grace may be bestowed on us in this way, but we can do without it. Prosperity in itself is no proof of merit, neither is poverty proof of demerit. To be materially deprived, on the contrary, may well be the occasion for spiritual enrichment.[16]

There is no need for the kind of asceticism practised in the Middle Ages. The attitude of the Gospels is rather one of simple contentment with what God puts at our disposal and offers for our use from day to day. Trust in Providence, however, should never justify indolence or want of foresight, or on the other hand febrile, inordinate activity. The worship of goods, investing them with a sanctity of their own which may serve our selfish ends, is the idolatry of Mammon.[17] To this the only antidote is faith in Christ.

There is a certain mystery about poverty which should be taken into account. The poor are the victims of sin, and they are in a sense the agents of God, testing man's obedience. A society is ultimately judged by its attitude towards its poor. Christ himself was *le pauvre par excellence*. The poor can be seen as visitors of God. Poverty as such, however, is not sanctity. More important is the spirit of poverty.[18]

Of equal importance is the acceptance of the new economic order. Monopolists who lay claim to material things for their own selfish ends are in a sense murderers of their fellow men.[19] To deny your neighbour what is his due in the form of goods and services, is to rob him.[20] Speculation, too, is an untenable practice. In fact, money readily becomes the means of oppression and as such it is evil.[21] There is, however, another extreme: the spiritualized life which ignores acting in any material way.[22] But the material world is an integral part of the Christian life. What must be remembered, however, is that there is only one proprietor: God himself. In his relation to material things, man should be neither a communist nor an individualist.[23] By the same token there is no justification for a monastic existence.

The material things of life are not, as such, the bearers of evil. On the contrary, money, too, is the fruit of man's labour. It is the pursuit of profit for the sake of profit that detracts from the order of God. There is no point in referring to specific usages among the Jews. The requirements of the ancient Jews and those of modern man are two different things. Aristotle is of no real assistance here. The true directory in assessing the worth of action is that of love.[24]

Man's free labour completes the work of God. For this reason, too, slavery is objectionable.[25] Exploration should be for the sake of evangelization, not for the sake of colonialism, which is exploitation.[26] In Christ all barriers of race have been abolished.[27]

Labour is a vocation of God, and in free labour man fulfils himself.[28] The alienation of labour comes about when it is directed towards the wrong ends.[29] This does not mean that work is always pleasant. On the contrary, it may be either pleasant or unpleasant; but Christ is always the liberator of the pain which work might cause.[30]

Labour is no merchandise to be traded at will.[31] Those who labour should be paid a proper wage, and neither the market price nor the legal minimum is an indication that it is just. Towards the proper remuneration of those who labour, contracts and arbitration may serve usefully.

The abiding theme in all Calvin's writing is that God has given man will and intelligence by which the powers of analysis, knowledge and creativity have also been conferred on him. Whether these gifts are employed in manual or intellectual labour makes no difference. They are always to be used in the service of God and of society.

In the fields of both science and art, man's activities can be directed towards the wrong ends. There is the ever-present danger of idolatry. The same applies to the commercial life of man. In all man does, there is this critical ambiguity. He may serve God (and so society), or serve himself (and the devil) and so become alienated from his proper calling. This is the price of our freedom.

It was not merely Calvin's thought, but also his personality which impressed itself lastingly on the Genevan community. Intellectually scintillating, severe in his demands not only towards others but also himself, just, truthful, steadfast, loyal, often brusque, yet at times also cheerful and even light-hearted, those around him seemed to be similarly affected. It was a personal style which, like the thought which it carried, would often be repeated in times to come in all those circumstances where a faithful vision was employed to meet intolerable circumstances. These would vary from the arrogant, self-sufficient dominion of the high and mighty, the powerful and moneyed, to the grey conformity, the spiritless mediocrity, the self-comforting smugness of bourgeois man.

Geneva had been in a state of disorder while Calvin was in banishment, working steadfastly on his *Institutes* in Strasbourg. He had been called back to Geneva and had returned in triumph. He himself had lived through a time of deep personal stress. He had married the widow Idelette de Bure, and their only child, a son, had died within the first year of their marriage.

The *Institutes*, Tawney says, had become a Protestant *Summa*, and the reformed programme of renewal had become 'thoroughly medieval'.[32] Indeed, the *Institutes*, like the *Summa*, is a systematic theology, characterized by a sense for the practicalities of life and a fundamental respect for the incarnate world. But Calvin went much further than Thomas when it came to daily matters of statecraft and government. The sermons and commentaries dealt especially with this aspect. Tawney himself says that Calvin 'drafted the heads of a comprehensive scheme of municipal government, covering the whole range of civic administration, from the regulations to be made for markets and crafts, buildings and fairs, to the control of prices, interests and rents.'[33] This is hardly medieval.

Calvin was by no means a mere throwback to the Middle

Ages. There was admittedly a return to medieval fundamentals, but coloured by innovations. His presence not only marks the beginning of a new money-economy, which before him had never been fully accepted by Christians, but also the beginning of the state in its modern sense. And, of decisive importance, he marked the beginnings of social humanism.

Calvin insisted that man's frailty was an essential theological truth. He came to this conclusion after looking around him and noting that humanity's normal condition was not peace and goodwill, but indiscriminate violence to the persons and properties of others. The doctrine of the elect, based on the firm foundation of God's sovereign will, could also be seen as the corollary of this.

What about Calvin's enormous effort to reform his own society? The Puritans of a later generation were to rationalize their own positive, radical efforts to rebuild society, not as a justification for election, but as the consequence of it. Calvin's piecemeal reform of his own society over the best part of a generation had the ring of St Augustine about it. Human freedom only became relevant when man's complete dependence had already been acknowledged.

Following St Augustine, Calvin, too, insisted on the free intelligence of the human creature. The *Institutes* abound with admonishments, not to abuse God's gifts, to be obedient, to requite God's goodness, to accept the authority of the moral law, to divest ourselves of ourselves, and so on. The consciences of believers may rise above the law, and may forget its righteousness. The conscience, free from the law's yoke, may cheerfully obey the will of God.[34]

Calvin's tireless debate with his theological adversaries in the *Institutes* was a reaction to the depravity of the age, where the enormous edifice of the Church seemed to have become a monument to man himself. His uncompromising emphasis on Divine election was, in fact, a counter to the total, sinful experience of the Church where redemption could be obtained for a sufficient consideration. Humility as the first, second and third precept of the Christian religion, however, required the rejection of *all* the human certitudes. So strong is the emphasis on Grace-alone in the *Institutes*, that the chapters devoted either directly or obliquely to human liberty would either be ignored or not sufficiently noticed by Calvin's immediate Puritan heirs. What in Calvin is still essentially a mystery, the dichotomy between grace and freedom, would be disregarded by the Puritans in favour of the certainty of the elect. While, as Max Weber points out, for Calvin there could be no final human knowledge, in this life, of one's election,[35] for the Puritan heirs, revising their Calvinism, it would become a case of believing as if everything depended on God alone, and acting as if it all depended on man alone. Not only did de Bèze, Calvin's immediate successor in Geneva, regard the recognizability of election as of absolute importance, but the Westminster Confession of 1647 also assured its Puritan subscribers of the *certitudo salutis*, the certainty of Divine favour.

Such assurances which had always been the prerogative of kings and monarchs, and in time to come would still be claimed by them, now also became the belief of the new middle-class man. It would increasingly appear in a variety of forms; and interchangeable terms for 'Divine' would be 'Supreme Being', 'History' and 'Destiny'.

Seizing on the element of Grace-alone in Calvin, ignoring its greater context and also its ultimate mystery, this claim to certainty by his heirs was to become the kernel both of a new bourgeois capitalism and an unending sequence of radical political systems promising redemption.

The former theme was exhaustively examined *inter alia* by Max Weber and R. H. Tawney, and there is little that can be added to it. What is not fully realized, however, is that the radical politics of which Michael Walzer writes in his study of the 'revolutions of the saints'[36] either precedes or runs concurrently with the 'spirit of capitalism', individual or collective. Bourgeois capitalism and revolutionary or radical politics both have their roots in the same protestant ethic.

Man pursues his vision of happiness and seeks final security in the total framework, the all-providing political system. This is politics bursting its bounds and presenting itself as a secular 'apostolic ministry'. Calvin would have regarded this manifestation as wrong-headed and spurious.

Alongside of this, however, and serving as its true alternative, is the fixed certainty of money, no longer in the form of merchant-prince, patrician or royal monopoly of riches, but in the far more comprehensive form of a new bourgeois capitalism.

All this would become in time part of the story of the Puritans in Africa, as we shall see: part of the story of the modern Afrikaners seeking to establish their own design for living, identity, survival and happiness.

To this end, we need to recall not only the salient facts about those times and societies which are generally regarded as having been the antecedents of the Afrikaners. Far more significantly, we need to know the salient facts about the model of all political radicalism: the Anglo-Saxon revolution.

6 Rebels not Revolutionaries

Anglo-Saxon Calvinism of the sixteenth and seventeenth centuries was, by virtue of its rapid development into Puritanism, essentially different to the Calvinism which obtained in the Netherlands, France and Scotland: those countries which, in a descending order, are usually associated with the reformed heritage of the Afrikaners. To be sure, the heroic age of the Afrikaners had a most definite link with the Protestant spirit of the sixteenth- and seventeenth-century Dutch, who had so decisively resisted the imperial power of Catholic Spain. It was also connected with the equally heroic Huguenots, who were engaged in protracted civil war with Catholic France. Much of what took place during the treks, battles and wars of the Afrikaners during the nineteenth century found its spiritual inspiration in the Netherlands and France, from which they had so largely emerged. The Scottish Reformed tradition, introduced by Somerset after the British had finally occupied the Cape, was, like that of the Netherlands and France, associated with resistance to tyranny.

The resistances in the Netherlands, France and Scotland were heroic, but in themselves confined. The Anglo-Saxon revolution, however, beginning in the time of Mary Stuart and the exiled English Calvinists in cities like Frankfurt, Strasbourg and Geneva, reached its climax in 1776 in America with the Declaration of Independence. All subsequent history was affected by it.

For a fuller appreciation of the heroic age of the Afrikaners, the histories of the Reformed Netherlands, France and Scotland are instructive. The Anglo-Saxon Revolution is of primary importance to an understanding of the modern Afrikaners, striving to secure their society 'for time and eternity'.

The Netherlands – especially its Nordic north – was particularly receptive to the message from Geneva in the mid-sixteenth century. There were essentially two reasons for this. A long history of foreign dominion – Burgundian in the fourteenth and fifteenth centuries, Habsburg towards the end of the fifteenth – was one. But there was also the fact that cities like Bruges, Ypres, Ghent in Flanders; Dordrecht, Leyden, Haarlem, Delft, Rotterdam in Holland; and Middelburg in Zeeland had, since the Middle Ages, known their own proud tradition of vigorous commercial independence. They knew a splendour of their own.

By the end of the fifteenth century, the Netherlands had been drawn into the amorphous collection of states and dominions which constituted the Habsburg empire. Charles V was an absentee monarch, popular enough in his way; but he demanded more and more money from his lowland provinces, to keep his clumsily constructed empire going. Ghent was the first to resist, at precisely the time when Calvin's voice from Geneva was unmistakably being heard. Ghent was, however, humbled by force of arms and then heavily fined. By this time, Charles was ruling over all seventeen provinces constituting the Netherlands of the time.

The resistance in the Netherlands, and especially in the seven provinces north of the Scheldt, was still mainly a broad national movement against the intolerable burden of a foreign intruder. To this end, religion – the Reformed creed as formulated in Geneva – proved to be a source of particular strength. The constitution and operation of Calvin's Christian Socialist Republic excluded the idea of absolute hereditary privilege. This was even more the case where the royal authority was not inherently part of the social structure, but a destructive force from outside.

In every sense the pronouncements and writings of Calvin would be employed to support resistance. Christians, he had stated, were the necessary reformers of a disordered society. He had condemned religious nationalism as one of the destructive forces in the Church,[1] but true patriotism required *de vivre et de mourir pour maintenir l'Evangile et la liberté de la ville.*

His constant warnings against the 'insolence of luxury' were particularly relevant where the ostentations of Charles were only too apparent. So, too, was his clear pronouncement that obedience to the authorities was always limited by obedience to God. In cases where the disorder or injustice of the government was clearly greater than that caused by revolt, the latter was justified.

In the Netherlands nobles, lesser nobles and rich burghers, both Protestant and Catholic, were united in their opposition to the Habsburg hegemony, spiritually supported by its Spanish Inquisition.

A time came when William the Silent, Prince of the House of Orange-Nassau, together with the counts of Egmont and Horn, petitioned Margaret of Parma, Charles' illegitimate half-sister, governing in his absence abroad, for more rights for the States-General. They came as 'beggars'. And 'beggars' (*Gueux*) was soon the name employed with pride in all the impassioned field-preaching which followed. With Calvinist burghers and gentry forming armies and William of Orange trying in vain to mediate, with 'images' in cathedrals being stormed and broken, Margaret of Parma, employing German mercenaries, retaliated viciously. At Antwerp the Calvinists, still much of a rabble, were badly defeated. This was only the prelude. In 1568, the Duke of Alva was on his way. The Eighty Years War of the Netherlands against Imperial Spain had now properly begun.

Alva was a soldier in the most uncompromising tradition. The very mention of his name has, for centuries now, aroused strong feelings. For Alva, Spain and the Holy Catholic Church were inseparable absolutes. Those who questioned or opposed them had to be eliminated.

Egmont, Horn and twenty other leading figures of the reform movement were arrested and beheaded. A Council of Blood tried insurgents generally. Many fled the provinces as Alva pursued his relentless course. By the early seventies he had saved the Netherlands for God and Charles.

But the Beggars had now become Sea Beggars and were effectively raiding Spanish strongpoints and lines of communication from England and East Friesland. In 1572, fortunes changed dramatically. The Sea Beggars seized Brielle at the mouth of the Maas. Three months later the Spaniards had been driven out of the whole of Holland except for Amsterdam.

Alva nevertheless left a path of blood as he marched through the Lowlands. Of significance now, however, was the increasing part being taken by the ordinary burghers. The resistance was fast becoming a popular national movement. Above all, it constituted a great urge to be politically free. There was no stopping the Dutch now, and at the end of 1573 Alva's fleet was defeated on the Zuider Zee.

Decades of struggle, however, still lay ahead. A sharper division between the Catholic South and the Protestant North – although, strangely, by the end of the sixteenth century only twenty per cent of the population were definitely Calvinist – had now become apparent.

The loose federation of the seven northern provinces of the Netherlands, with Holland and Zeeland forming its most stable elements, became the Dutch Republic.

Philip II of Spain, who had succeeded Charles V on his abdication, rightly saw William as the most powerful element in the Dutch resistance. In 1584, William of Orange was assassinated by an impassioned young Catholic.

William's eldest son had been taken captive by the Spaniards and was being held in Spain. His second son, Maurice of Nassau, who was to succeed him, had not yet come of age. The *stadholder*ship now passed to two 'regents': Paul Buys, advocate of Holland, and the patrician, Johan van Oldenbarneveldt.

An attempt by William of Orange to obtain French intervention in the struggle against Spain had failed. But a year after his death the English appeared on the scene. Led by Elizabeth's Leicester, they proved to be no more helpful than the French had been, in the person of the Duke of Anjou.

Three years later, in 1588, however, the English struck a blow for the Seven Provinces when unexpectedly and stirringly the Spanish Armada was defeated. Maurice of Nassau and William Louis, *stadholder* of Friesland, took great heart and the Dutch army was moulded into an excellent fighting force. Soon there were practically no Spanish garrisons left in the northern provinces.

By the close of the century the Seven United Provinces were an emergent world power, worthily taking their place in an alliance with England and France. Prince Maurice, at the head of the House of Orange-Nassau, still co-operated quite happily with the elder statesman, Oldenbarneveldt, and led the Dutch army to even further triumphs. Philip II, by this time, had begun to accept the situation and was (secretly) allowing the Dutch to develop their trade with the Far East. Before long, the V.O.C. had been founded.

The war had by no means come to an end. As the century ended, Prince Maurice, at the instigation of Oldenbarneveldt, attacked Dunkirk with some success. With James I of England trying to marry his son to a Spanish *infanta*, and compromising his Calvinist education for the sake of peace with Spain, the Protestant Dutch were suddenly without their English allies. Nevertheless, their position was still strong enough to arrange, in 1609, a twelve-year truce.

After the long struggle against imperial Catholic Spain, in which the Dutch Calvinists had played such a decisive part, it was inevitable that some kind of spiritual reappraisal would take place. It took the form of the Synod of Dort (Dordrecht) in 1618–19. Ministers of religion, theologians from the universities, elders, political commissioners from the States-General and visitors from England, Switzerland and some German states arrived for the deliberations.

Dort provided the occasion for many tensions and antagonisms, profound differences of opinion in theology, but also, most persistently, in politics. As in the case of Servetus in 1553, for reasons which were both theological and socio-political, a death-sentence reminiscent of the Inquisition was pronounced. The victim this time was one of the most eminent sons of the republic. It was Oldenbarneveldt.

From the start the Synod proved to be deeply schismatic. The issue outwardly was mainly the old one of the doctrine of the elect, encompassing the scope and availability of God's grace, and the freedom of the human creature.

On the side of the Arminians and free-will were Olden-barneveldt and Hugo Grotius, a philologist, theologian and poet, but above all a great jurist. On the side of Gomarus and Grace-alone was Bogermann, chairman of the moderature of the Church, and Prince Maurice, head of the army. The conflict was deeply compounded by political issues.

The climax of the lengthy proceedings was reached at last when the two parties, angrily facing each other in the *Kloven-iersdoelen*, heard Bogermann demand the ejection from the premises of Arminius and his fellow Remonstrants. '*Ite! Ite!*' Bogermann thundered. '*Dimittimini!*' So the Arminian Remon-strants were cast into outer darkness.

Bogermann and Arminius had once been students together in Geneva. Calvin himself might have remarked on all this that the struggle was irrelevant. Both Grace-alone and freedom were right; for the seeming dichotomy was beyond human compre-hension.

Such would also be the effect of Dort on the Reformed con-fession of the Afrikaners. Dort had fixed the canons of Dutch Reformed theology for all time to come.

The Synod was still in session when Prince Maurice ordered the arrest of Oldenbarneveldt and Hugo Grotius. A special tribunal was constituted, not so much to try as to condemn.

Oldenbarneveldt was summoned to appear before his accusers on no less than sixty occasions. No legal aid was allowed him. On 13 May 1619, the day after he had finally been pronounced guilty, the 71-year-old statesman was executed in public at The Hague. His death moved the Dutch people deeply. Oldenbarneveldt had served his country well in the days of the Spanish terror. He had been a man of great dignity and charac-ter.

The lot of Grotius was happier. He had been sentenced to life imprisonment and was confined to the Castle of Loevestein. His clever wife, however, managed to effect his escape in a chest. Thereupon he fled to Paris, where he later became the Swedish Ambassador.

In 1621, the twelve years of truce with Spain were at an end and hostilities started anew. Four years later, Prince Maurice was dead and his more open-minded younger brother, Frederick Henry, became *stadholder*, Prince of Orange. The quarter-century of his reign now became the Golden Age of the Netherlands. It was the flowering of creativity following upon a successful resistance to the challenge of Spain. Learning, literature and commerce flourished as never before, as few other countries of the West had experienced them. This was while a great part of Europe was locked in one of the most destructive and formless struggles of all history: the Thirty Years War. It was in the closing decade of this expansive, highly creative time that the Dutch, now supremely confident, made the decision to establish an outpost at the extremity of Africa, serving the fleets of the V.O.C. on the long voyage to the East Indies.

The struggle of Protestant France, too, comprised resistance, revolt, civil war and martyrdom. It never grew into more than that. The revolutionary movement was contained by the power of a fearsome authoritarianism which only, eventually, experienced nemesis in the form of the Jacobin Terror.

It was no coincidence that Jean-Jacques Rousseau had a Genevan background and considerable regard for its Reformer. If the Huguenots could not finally reform France, the *philosophes*, the social idealists and the revolutionaries of the late eighteenth century did. That was when the revolution happened.

French Calvinism started at the top, appealing especially to the political élite and nobility. It was concerned not so much with the establishment before God and man of a commercial middle class, as with the affirmation of the old feudal order in a new form. The feudal lord was now to become a Calvinist magistrate.

The Huguenots were, indeed, an army before they were a church. They were saintly soldiers passionately committed to *vindiciae contra tyrannos*. It was a rebellion of the Huguenot nobles leading Protestant soldiery, advocating the existence of an élite state within a state. It was never a rising of an alienated people reacting to their own rejection, aligning themselves to a socio-political ideal worked out for them by an intellectual élite.

Indeed, some of the phenomena attached to the Huguenot cause would, in the history of the Afrikaners, become manifest again. These would include soldiers riding out as a motley band to do battle with the enemy, singing their psalms, praying movingly in public, honouring their own articles of civilized warfare, and looking to history (Franco Gallia) to provide 'the earnest, active Huguenot with a multiple legitimacy' in his own cause. These things would also, in the late nineteenth century, become part of the Boer life on commando in the heroic age.

The first French Reformed synod took place in Paris in 1559, a few years before Calvin's death. It was modelled on the democratic polity of Geneva. Within three years, Protestant confidence was sufficient to challenge the royal establishment, not only in matters of faith, but also politically. At Amboise even a plot to kidnap the king was seriously considered. In any event, Catholic France was sufficiently impressed to consent to talks with the rebels at Poisay. In 1562, an official guarantee of religious liberty was obtained.

That very year, however, a bloody slaughter of unsuspecting Protestants by the followers of the Duke of Guise took place in a barn at Vassy. At this stage, the Queen Regent, Catherine de Medici, for her own reasons was still a moderate, and prepared even to endure the defiance of the Duke of Guise. The Protestants were loyal to the crown, their spokesman, the Prince of Condé, assured the Queen, but they would resist with arms for the sake of conscience. Soon it was civil war, with the Protestants eventually marching on Paris and procuring the peace of St Germaine in 1570 by virtue of their strength. A Reformed France, like a Reformed Netherlands or Scotland, now seemed a distinct possibility.

What decided matters in favour of a Catholic France was the Massacre of St Bartholomew on 24 August 1572. Catherine de Medici, who for reasons of expediency had been not unsympathetic towards the Huguenot cause, now decided, for similar reasons, that she had had enough of Admiral Gaspard de Coligny and other leading Huguenots. She herself had arranged the marriage of her daughter Margaret to Henry of Navarre, who was the titular head of the Huguenot movement. The marriage – so nearly all France believed – would at last bring real peace between the Catholics and Protestants.

With the Protestant élite gathered from all parts of Paris, it was a rare opportunity to eliminate their threatening power. Catherine, with the efficient aid of hired assassins, had all the assembled Huguenots slain, with the exception of Henry of Navarre and the Prince of Condé. The prince, incidentally, was an heir to the throne.

The blood-wedding was the start of a general massacre. Everywhere in France, Huguenots became fair game. Soon it was national frenzy. Driven back on their heels, the Huguenots in desperation formed a new united opposition. They closed their ranks and became an autonomous unit within the state, prescribing and obeying their own laws of civil administration. In spite of all the violence done to them, their resistance was still formidable.

There was an agreed truce in 1573 and general amnesty was granted. Three years later, however, the civil war re-started. With brief intervals of comparative peace, it lasted to the mid-nineties, when Henry of Navarre succeeded Henry III, to become King of France. In 1598 there was, at last, positive triumph when the new Henry IV sanctioned the Edict of Nantes, granting the Protestants in France the right to worship according to their own consciences.

In 1610 Henry IV, like Henry II before him, was assassinated. Power returned to the Catholic party, and the Protestants were once more forced to take up arms in their own defence. By the end of the first quarter of the century the most formidable opponent in the history of Protestant France appeared upon the scene: Cardinal Richelieu. The Huguenots were the saboteurs of truth, he said. They had to be suppressed in the name both of God and France.

What surprises the reader of history is that on receiving the assurance that the Huguenots were loyal subjects, the civil authority again granted them liberty of conscience. In 1643, the Edict of Nantes, which had long been their guarantee of freedom, was once more affirmed.

But the Catholic clergy refused to abide by it. A new means to continue the attack on heresy was devised. While the Edict stood, there was one way to effect this and that was to insist on the strict terms of the Edict itself. In the legal war which ensued, all liberties which had not explicitly been granted the Huguenots were systematically denied them. There was no end to the proclamations strictly circumscribing the privileges of the dissidents. Torture was re-instituted as the right means to serve the true faith.

Pressures all through France increased and Louis XIV saw no more reason why his peace should any longer be disturbed. The Edict had become a bother. In 1685 he revoked it.

Nearly half-a-million French Protestants fled their country. Like expatriates, exiles, refugees from despotism through the ages, they took with them a wealth of character. They, too, had long been tempered in the fires of persecution. The spirit of Huguenot resistance impregnated much of the Western world. The Cape, too, and the Afrikaners of Southern Africa would benefit from this.

Like the Dutch and French, Scottish influence in the Reformed tradition of the Afrikaners had behind it a history of resistance to a foreign intruder. Up to the middle of the sixteenth century the Scots were still largely attached to Anglo-French royalty. But John Knox, who had been a kind of Marian expatriate on the Continent, finally returned to his native soil at the close of the fifties and became the heart of protest. For the same reasons as the Dutch and French Calvinists had questioned royal hereditary rights, Knox rejected the established order. Mary of Lorraine was still on the throne as regent. Her daughter Mary was preparing for succession, while Elizabeth was a confident newcomer to the English throne. This inspired the holy wrath of the Reformer's preaching. Images were broken, monasteries destroyed, and a French army taken on in combat. When it had finally departed from Leith and Edinburgh, papal authority was at last abolished. Elizabeth put her chagrin at John Knox's excesses behind her and indicated her support for this measure.

The kirk grew. Knox based his first *Book of Discipline* on

the 'Ordinances of the Genevan Church': 'that perfect school of Christ' he so admired. The church was to be reorganized on Presbyterian lines. The young would be instructed; schools and universities would be brought into the Reformed sphere; the poor would be fed. Within seven years of the return of John Knox from Continental exile, the kirk was the only church in Scotland.

Mary died in 1568. Apart from the upheaval in the church, there was little change if any in the socio-political organization of Scotland. In 1570, Knox was still declaiming in St Giles against the presence of the French. Two years later he died, 'weary of the world, and the world of him'. In the same year the *Second Book of Discipline* had been published. Again it was a document concerned almost exclusively with church polity.

Of importance here is that Mary's departure did not mean a republican Scotland. On the contrary, a Queen's party was defiant until the capture of Edinburgh Castle in 1573. The young James VI of Scotland had the throne retained for him by a series of regents. When he eventually also succeeded Elizabeth on the English throne, adding immense power to the government of Scotland, which he had already assumed in 1581, the Scottish Reformation was socio-politically at an end.

7 Revolution and the Puritan Spirit

Calvinism found its true historical dynamic not in France, nor in the Netherlands or Scotland, but in the Anglo-Saxon world. By this we mean that the development of Puritanism out of the English Calvinist ethic became one of the prime forces in all Western history. While the spirit of the heroic age of Afrikanerdom has obvious links with Dutch, French and, obliquely, with Scottish antecedents, for an understanding of the Afrikaners of our own time, we need to take note of the essentially different way in which Calvinism developed in its Anglo-Saxon context. It becomes a case of the birth of revolution from the soul of Puritanism. As such it goes to the heart, too, of the profound change in the life of Afrikanerdom, when in the twentieth century the *burgerstand* had finally developed in the once almost exclusively Anglo-Saxon cities.

There was the storm of English Puritanism in the sixteenth and seventeenth centuries, culminating in the English Revolution. With the death of Cromwell and the Restoration, the movement was not at an end: its centre was transferred across the Atlantic to New England, where for generations afterwards it gathered strength. Its definitive embodiment was the American War of Independence and the Declaration which followed. The greater movement, properly starting with the return of the Marian expatriates in the second half of the sixteenth century and ending with the formulation of the American Rights of Man, could be described as the Anglo-Saxon Revolution.

The internal dissensions which in a short space of time split the English Puritans into Presbyterians, Independents (Congregationalists), Separatists and Baptists, were of lesser significance as far as the Puritan impact on history was concerned.

What transcended their theological differences was their common urge to save the world and build a New Jerusalem. 'Whole classes of people,' William Haller says,

would yet be affected: not only in the first two centuries of the movement itself, but for ever after that. It was a new way of life, overrunning all the divisions which from time to time seamed its surface ... Eventually it was to subdue English civilization to an attitude of mind, a code of conduct, a psychology, a manner of expression, the vitality of which far outran the particular forms of religious life which sprang up from time to time in the course of its irresistible advance.[1]

The Anglo-Saxons would become, incomparably, the most vital of Calvin's heirs.

The English Reformation had roots extending further back than that of any other society. Its original voice was the clear and fearless one of John Wyclif (1320–84). Midway through the fourteenth century, he anticipated Luther – who was to follow nearly two centuries later – by attacking the Church for its worldliness and corruption. The Lollards, as his followers came to be known, took the Franciscans as their model. They found support, too, in the writings of William of Ockham and other scholars and set for themselves the ideal of evangelical poverty. In this dominion of the poor and humble, the true spirit of Christ would be realized. Wyclif continued his preaching throughout England, more or less as John Wesley was to do more than four centuries later, and largely for the same reasons: to resist the power, wealth, pomp and pride of the Church and its stultifying complacency. Inspired by Wyclif's translation of the Bible, and with the nobility and House of Commons lending their support, the Church sought an answer in official condemnation.

In 1395, eleven years after the death of Wyclif, the Lollards proclaimed their beliefs. Believers had to be without material possessions; worship without trappings; the clergy without their spurious views on chastity and their sterile auditions of confessing sinners. Only three things really mattered: loving God; dreading Him; and trusting Him. Persecution was inevitable. The University of Oxford, in time a stronghold of these original non-conformist views, was eventually purged by decree of the Church.

The century was one of social unrest, particularly in England. These were revolts against the whole system of social inequality, which was an injustice compounded by the Church. John Ball (1360–81) of Kent kept telling English yeomen and English peasants of their rights as men. As long as goods were not in common, he declaimed, and as long as there were villeins and gentlemen, things would never right themselves in England.

For the Lollards, the Church and its failings were of primary concern. What eventually happened at Wittenberg on 31 October 1517 did not cause the English reformers too much surprise. After all, they had already been protesting at the iniquities of the Church for some generations. Lollardry was never eradicated in England. It was gradually outshone by the brighter lights of Luther and, conclusively, by that of Calvin.

'The reformers or Puritans were Calvinists,' Haller says. 'What Calvinism did for them was to supply a current formulation of historic doctrine in lucid, trenchant terms, strikingly supported by the success of the state which Calvin's genius had called into being at Geneva.'[2]

The eclipse of the Lollards, as suggested, was caused by Calvinism. It formulated what had for two centuries been deeply felt and experienced, but never articulated in terms for all to understand.

Because of the powerful Reformed tradition in England, starting some three centuries before the Pilgrim Fathers set sail for Plymouth, no other society was so well prepared to change the world, either directly or indirectly, than the broad community of Anglo-Saxons. Without them, Calvin's influence would have been immensely more localized.

Henry VIII, in creating his own diversion by dressing up his personal and political rejection of Rome to look like reformation, stole the emergent Puritans' thunder. However, it was Mary Tudor who finally, by virtue of her total opposition, set them on their course. Her royal authority would once more be unconditional. Her cause was also that of Catholic restoration. The sweet smell of burning heretics hung over the fair English landscape. Some 300, in the course of three years, were put to death; humble folk, gentry and nobility. Those with the means and friends to assist them fled to the Continent. They lived in exile in cities like Leyden, Frankfurt and Geneva.

Elizabeth succeeded her rigid half-sister and steered a sensible middle course between Papal excommunication and her own approval of the expulsion from Cambridge of Thomas Cartwright; between rooting out the Catholics as traitors to the state and dispatching Leicester with an army to the insurgent Netherlands; between scattering the Spanish Armada and containing those most difficult of people, the Puritans.

The century changed, as did the supreme, secular authority. But James I of England, also James VI of Scotland, was a disappointment for those who had pinned their hopes on his Calvinist training. At the Hampton Court gathering in 1604, he dismissed Presbyterianism.

The Puritans had judged the position wrongly. In spite of the religious motives interwoven in it, the true struggle in the land was still that between king and parliament. James was most certainly not going to accept any derogation from his royal powers. The Puritans were wiser and angrier, especially when James announced to everyone that kings were justly called gods, for they exercised 'a manner of resemblance of Divine power on earth'.

The profound change which Western Europe had undergone socially and politically, the disruption of old feudal patterns and rural living, the rise of urban communities finding their livelihood in commerce and independent agriculture, had discovered in Calvinism a creed of immense relevance.

The demands of Calvinism, from the start, had been rigorous, uncompromising and urgent. It naturally attracted the temperamentally active: being like a great fine-meshed seine, netting its most valuable haul in Anglo-Saxon waters. In England a sturdy development had taken place, as part of her long tradition of reform, of those classes which

combined economic independence, education, and a certain decent pride in their status, revealed at once in a determination to live their own lives, without truckling to earthly superiors, and in a somewhat arrogant contempt for those who, either through weakness of character or through economic helplessness, were less resolute, less vigorous and masterful, than themselves.[3]

Such were the strong-spirited yeomen, firmly rooted in their land. Typical also were the traders of the newly industrialized areas: London and Middlesex, Norfolk, Sussex, Essex, Northamptonshire and Lancashire. It was in these urbanized areas of an expanding textile industry that 'Puritan islands', as Tawney says, arose like little Genevas from the surrounding sea of Roman Catholicism.

As a Calvinist himself, James I was essentially in agreement with his opponents. Yet he would not suffer them to speak their minds too loudly. Ecclesiastical tribunals were kept busy depriving the outspoken of their livings, commanding them to be silent, with James watching from the side-lines. The intellectuals at Cambridge, however, were still in possession of their fellowships. A great deal of pamphleteering and sermonizing continued.

... the number steadily grew of those who viewed with disapproval what they regarded as the extravagance and corruption of the court, the insolence of upstart favourites, the pride of prelates, the venality of judges, the extortionate practices of monopolists, each and all subservient to the crown ... Englishmen were becoming ever more aggressively English. That meant that they hated Spain, despised France, dreaded the Pope and embraced Protestantism ...

The people wished to know what to do to be saved. The preachers told them to trust in Jesus Christ and to put on the whole armour of God. Yet behind the thinning veil of doctrine and image the Puritan Revolution was gathering momentum. [4]

From 1629 to 1640 England was subject to Charles I's interpretation of the 'Divine Right of Kings'. This doctrine effectively stifled Parliament and prevented its meeting. A group of intellectuals leading the new urban middle class felt alienated by the high-handed action of the privileged. At the same time, it resented the growth of corruption and social decay. These feelings, set alight by a passion for reform and godly justice, burst out into open rebellion. For some it meant martyrdom – William Prynne, John Bastwick and Henry Burton ...

Until Milton employed his literary gifts against prelacy, it

was Prynne's pen which cut most savagely into the body of the
Established Church. It was Laud, Archbishop of Canterbury,
Charles' spiritual advisor, against whom he directed his fury.
For his fanatical espousal of the Puritan cause he, smiling defi-
antly, had his ears cropped.

But, in time, justice would be done. For Laud himself, when
Parliament, as the Long Parliament, had at last re-established
itself, was beheaded on Tower Hill, having been spared the
brutalities usually meted out to those guilty of high treason.
Strafford, with Laud the most powerful of Charles' supporters,
suffered the same fate, as Charles himself was to do.

In all there were three periods of drastic communal upheaval
and sudden changes of fortune in the extended Anglo-Saxon
Revolution. There was the Cromwell uprising leading to the
short-lived English Republic. This was followed by the conclusive disruption of the Stuart dynasty, leading to the enthrone-
ment of William and Mary, succeeded by the Hanoverians.
Finally, there was the American War of Independence.

The first of the Puritan Commonwealths lasted for a remarkably short time. In the proper sense, it ended with the death
of Cromwell in 1658. What preceded it was the immensely intricate history of the rise of the English *bourgeoisie*, held together
and led by intellectuals trained in the Calvinist ethic. Their
struggle was with a decadent monarchy, as shown in the conflict
between King and Parliament. In the early forties Cromwell's
New Model Army proved their moral and military superiority
at Marston Moor and Naseby. A truncated Parliament exacted
terrible justice from the 'first of the Cavaliers'. Charles serenely
met his death on a scaffold near Whitehall. Never before in
history had the common man expressed himself so unequivocally
and assertively. Thereafter came the Ironsides, subduing, in
quick succession, both Ireland and Scotland and establishing
naval supremacy over the Dutch. They came to the aid of the
Huguenots of southern France and scattered the Spanish fleet
with great daring, this time at Tenerife.

But suddenly, before his time, Cromwell died. Though the

Commonwealth quickly followed him, its implications were to reverberate through many centuries and in many lands.

Gathered together in this first Puritan movement were two distinct categories. One was primarily concerned with recovering freedom by socio-political means. The second sensed that the loss of freedom was basically a matter for the individual, and saw the issue in moral and religious terms.

In the first category one kind of power would necessarily have to be substituted for another, while at the same time moral justification, dwelling on the concept of freedom, would accompany it. In the second, power would be transcended and essential freedom sought in the individual and his relationship to God. Denis de Rougemont, writing in the Reformed tradition, has described this accurately when discussing the pursuit of freedom in our own time as a man-made abstraction:

... to build a régime on the fine word freedom is tantamount to the politics of collective romanticism; which is the politics of power, as Machiavelli formulated it ...

... The freedom we [should] die for is not the freedom guaranteed by the political order. Freedom loses its golden rays the moment it is defined by a lawmaker: in the same way as a film star is no longer a star to the man whom she has married. Behold the great illusion which the goddess at the port of New York symbolizes, shedding her light without favour on all the children of men. Watch her more closely: this goddess in the abstract, so much the more sentimental. She appeals to religious feelings, referring, not without pathos, to emptiness. How many immigrants have not wept in passing her ...

In truth we should say about our time as a whole: freedom-in-general is no Cause, even in the political field, whatever the sacrifices or the rhetoric attached to it. Freedom is rather the original sign of our humanity.[5]

Since the model of the original Puritans there have always been two kinds of seekers after freedom. The inspired revolutionary is motivated by the heroic task of reforming the world and is totally absorbed by his sense of mission and vision of the future. But there are also those who divine the true meaning of human freedom, whether this is ever formulated in precise terms or not.

In the history of Anglo-Saxon Puritanism this is represented, on the one hand, by the parliamentary Puritans and, on the other, by figures like Milton, Newton, Baxter, Bunyan and Locke.

The Puritan politicians were a political entity. Though thoroughly imbued with Puritan principles, they were also strongly influenced by the humanism of the Renaissance. Part of their legacy was also the strongly nationalist idealism which had grown to maturity in the time of Elizabeth. In those days there had been not only the Puritan resistance within the Church, but also what might be described as a Puritan party at the Elizabethan court.

'This was made up of the great peers and their adherents, conspicuously anti-Catholic, potentially when not openly anti-clerical, intellectually liberal, and strongly individualistic and nationalistic in temper and policy.'[6]

Essentially it was England and the English soul for which they cared. The rottenness of things which ultimately became apparent with the coming of the Stuarts could not be endured: not so much because it was un-Christian as because it was un-English.

But, of course, the Anglo-Saxon Puritan movement was essentially a resistance of the newly emergent middle classes. The intellectual leadership had come from this same social environment: as in the cases of Prynne, Bastwick and Burton, to the point of martyrdom. As the movement approached the phase of armed conflict, however, the political leaders moved into the foreground. There were close ties of neighbourhood, interest and family. Robert Greville, Lord Brooke, the Earl of Warwick, the Earl of Lincoln, Sir Henry Vane, John Pym, Hampden, and finally Cromwell himself were joined together in a complex variety of ways.

From the point of view of the modern Afrikaners, too, the transition from a God-fearing but also deeply patriotic group to a militant, often nationalist, radicalism, leading eventually to a new despotic rule, found its original model in the history of the English political saints of the seventeenth century.

The Presbyterians, being much too refined, were soon banished. The King was executed. There was a final, deeply-felt transition from ecclesiastical matters and theology to saintly politics. The finest sentiments and most noble intentions of the

English radicals were contained in arguments and concepts like the popular will and the basic rights to life, liberty, property and conscience. In Lilburne a theorist appeared who could formulate and intellectualize all these strands. It was, as Max Weber would say, worldly asceticism. In Winstanley the ultimate conclusion was expressed: nothing would suffice except a complete social and economic reform.

The Puritan soul, still active in the hearts of men who were essentially concerned with substituting power for power, had emanating from it particular expressions of idealism. These were: a Bill of Rights; no interference in essential liberties; the *Agreement of the People* (1647) ... The Lord Protector and Parliament would have strictly limited powers, the *Instrument of Government* (1654) said. But ideals *à outrance* are the royal road to autocracy and tyranny: they are so fine and unquestionable, nobody else except those in power can be entrusted with them. Conscience still moves and there are assurances of the hard measures taken being merely temporary: all is there for the ultimate good. But the ultimate good never comes.

What comes in its place is tragi-comedy. The English Commonwealth was the first act in the stupendous cycle of revolutionary movements the world would see over and over again.

John Milton forms a remarkable bridge between the world of the Puritan radical and the world of those discovering the true meaning of freedom. When the Civil War finally set in, Milton already had a considerable record of spirited opposition to the hypocrisies of royalty and church. At Cambridge he had been a student rebel, expressing himself with unusual virtuosity in public speeches and seized with a fervour for reform. What is especially notable about Milton is his loyalty to the cause of Puritanism, the Commonwealth, of radical renewal in the society of his time, while being different to those who were his brothers in the struggle. He was different to the point of being a one-man resistance.

The state, he maintained, could keep the peace, but it could never make men good or wise. Above all, the Church should be free. For freedom was at the heart of everything. And the uncompromising claim to be counted among the elect – for here the Puritans saw a certainty which surpassed all others – was rejected by Milton. An arbitrary Deity, he said, could never command his respect, even though he be sent to Hell for it.

The true stature of the man and the artist appears after the collapse of the Commonwealth, and the hanging in public of Cromwell's body. With the capital city blighted by the Great Plague, he hid from persecution in relative poverty, suffering in the flesh, but even more deeply in the soul. In fact, he was 'eyeless in London among a nation of slaves'.

The results of this purgatory were *Paradise Lost*, *Paradise Regained* and *Samson Agonistes*. Like Samson, who was eyeless in Gaza, Milton was able to re-discover the true meaning of faith, and to conquer despair.

Sharing with Milton the remarkable release of creative powers which were the fruit of the true English Reformation in the seventeenth century were Newton, Bunyan, Baxter and Locke. Isaac Newton's Royal Society must be seen as one of the lasting monuments of human culture, representing the shining intervals in history when man transcended his anxieties and lived in love with the created world and its people. Other such periods were the rise of Athens; the emergence of the guilds out of feudalism; the great voyages of discovery; and the development of truly representative government. Bunyan's allegory on the journey of the soul, *The Pilgrim's Progress*, has retained its validity both as literature and theology through the centuries. Richard Baxter's *Christian Directory*, another Protestant *Summa* and a companion to Calvin's *Institutes*, intrigues the modern reader for its relevance in an age when 'abundance' and 'growth' have become more and more questionable. And John Locke's cool look at the true nature and extent of politics is immensely to the point in a world where the revolutionary ideal is once more presenting itself in a variety of forms. Like Newton, Locke arrived at a time which was patently both right for him and for his society.

More than a century earlier, Hooker had said many similar things. But perspectives were still in a state of flux and not conducive towards the rational arrangement of thought. With Locke, meaningful elements had converged. As Hooker, too, had argued, civil and ecclesiastical laws had to bear the test of reason; and civil law was best expressed by public approbation.

Political organization could be constructively explained by the hypothesis of a social contract, said Locke. This had been entered into by the members of the human community for the sake of law and order. On the same grounds, Hobbes had concluded that absolute government was absolutely necessary. At the very most, Locke said, the social contract could establish but a limited authority. The Hobbesian contention of *homo lupus homini*, as the original state of man, was similarly to be rejected. Peace and reason did, in fact, once prevail. Man lived under natural law, following a body of rules determined by reason, honouring the rights to life, liberty and property.

The remarkable thing about Locke is that this prophet of the English Enlightenment and founder of the liberal tradition of parliamentary democracy, who inspired many struggles for liberty all over the world, represents, too, the most positive, creative and permanent elements in Calvinism.

For example, he questioned radically the Divine Right of Kings and the absolutism of Hobbes. This revolt exactly echoed the central thought in primitive Calvinism. God alone was sovereign, and any pretence to absolute human authority in civil government was untenable. The closing paragraph in the *Institutes* put this beyond doubt.

'We ought to obey God rather than men' (Acts v. 29). Let us console ourselves with the thought, that we are rendering the obedience which the Lord requires, when we endure anything rather than turn aside from piety. And that our courage may not fail, Paul stimulates us by the additional consideration I (Cor. vii. 23), that we were redeemed by Christ at the great price which our redemption cost him, in order that we might not yield a slavish obedience to the depraved wishes of men, far less do homage to their impiety.

Power, said Locke, was justified only in terms of the public good which it served. Directed therefore to a good beyond its own interests, government was a trust. As such it was liable to be forfeited where it exceeded its bounds and became tyranny.

Locke's preference for an elected legislature and government by the people likewise finds its counterpart in the Reformed faith with its new home in Calvin's Geneva. While expressing a personal appreciation for aristocracy, either pure or modified by popular government, Calvin admitted that in such a system there was great risk of a lack of 'acuteness and prudence' on the part of the ruler.

The Christian analogy to this is man being called by God to subdue the earth by his labour. Created in the image of God, man was at the head of all creation. The point of departure of the whole anthropology of Calvin was the fundamental biblical axiom that man could not know himself outside the self-knowledge that God affords him. Man, in other words, is a creative intelligence.[7]

All men, Locke insisted, are, under the law of nature, endowed with the basic rights of owning property, of thinking and expressing themselves in freedom and of worshipping as they please. All these rights are contained in the basic right to adequate protection by the ruling authority.

This is an expression in secular terms of a central thought in the Reformed Christian anthropology:

That the consciences of believers may rise above the Law, and may forget the whole righteousness of the Law. That the conscience, free from the yoke of the Law, may cheerfully obey the will of God. That they may not be bound by any religious scruples before God about things indifferent ...[8]

God's providence does not abolish but sustains the clear exercise of the responsibility of human freedom.

In Locke especially the Anglo-Saxon Puritan Revolution achieved a positive synthesis.

What is regarded in some quarters as Locke's most original contribution to social and economic thought, his theory on labour, is a secular paraphrase of the Christian position, also to be found in Calvin. Labour, as a creative human function, is applied to property, said Locke, and the result is something of greater value. The enrichment by labour of the world around him affords the labourer the full value of his production.

*   *   *

The Puritan Commonwealth in England had come to fruition, had had its day and disintegrated, all within the space of something like a decade. It had never become the fulfilment of the English radical dream. The epicentre of the Anglo-Saxon Revolution now moved across the Atlantic. If Old England had discovered itself to be unequal to the task of building the Godly Commonwealth, New England enthusiastically accepted it.

No change in the composition of those participating had taken place. Essentially they were still the same kind of people who had dreamt of, worked and struggled for the reform of England. Their basic motives remained unaltered. If of the earlier Milton it could be said as William Blake said:

> I shall not cease from Mental Fight,
> Nor shall my Sword sleep in my hand,
> Till we have built Jerusalem
> In England's green & pleasant Land.

the more so it could be said of New England as a whole.

Perry Miller remarked about this '. . . they did not set out to become provincial communities on the edge of civilization but to execute a flanking manoeuvre in the all-engrossing struggle of the civilized world. The Lord was granting them the greatest opportunity afforded to any people since the birth of Christ . . .'[9]

The 'howling wilderness' of New England, demanding immense stocks of courage, perseverance, resourcefulness and faith in their calling, had taken on in renewed and immensely increased measure the life of the spirit, which had played so important a part in Old England since the start of the fourteenth century.

At a time when Richard Baxter had already outgrown his own conception of an earthly state of Christian civil polity, the New Englanders experienced an overpowering sense of vocation towards it. This was the very purpose towards which they strove, collectively and individually. In so doing, they felt themselves ennobled in a world pervaded by unrighteousness. The Westminster Confession assured them anew, in terms clearer than those of the Reformer of Geneva, of their particular participation in the 'indubitable certainty of grace'. Here was certainty in an unassailable form for their earthly sojourn.

As in the case of the Afrikaners of later times, the New England Puritan community was structured around the concept of a visible and demonstrable election. This meant the unequivocal rejection of free-will, as once formulated by the Dutch Remonstrants, who were Arminians, and the joyous affirmation by godly behaviour of divine election: the acceptance of grace as being the whole of all that is positive and creative in human affairs. 'Acceptance' itself, of course, could hardly be accommodated in a system of complete determinism. But, as history has shown, it was exactly such communities which set about things in a most active and positive way: re-shaping society in its most 'Christian' form; setting things right for both God and man; believing utterly, in the words of Peter:

> But you are a chosen race, a royal priesthood, a consecrated
> nation, a people set apart to sing the praises of God who
> called you out of the darkness into his wonderful light ...¹⁰

It was the ultimate *noblesse oblige*; and therefore God's election had to be honoured in this world, too, by the governmental evidence of godliness.

The Anglo-Saxons in New England, discovering themselves to be indubitably the true people of God, set about organizing their society with tireless devotion to prove it.

Calvinism in its primitive form appealed to different kinds of people at odds with the sickness of the age. Included were those imbued with a godly fervour and impatience, to restore wholeness and happiness to this world, justifying morally thereby their deep need of power; and also those who wished for nothing more than a restoration of the essential truths of the Gospels, exactly the kind of humility which Calvin himself had described as being the first, second and third precepts of the Christian life. Out of this ambiguity grew the Puritan mind.

For those primarily concerned with the setting right of the polity, the many unaccommodating statements in the *Institutes* where Calvin with his own peculiar positiveness joined issue with the proclaimers of free-will had a particular appeal. For example:

Those therefore, whom he has created for dishonour during life and destruction at death that they may be vessels of wrath and examples of severity, in bringing to their doom, he at one time deprives of the means of hearing his word, at another by the preaching of it, blinds and stupefies them the more ... For while we maintain that none perish without deserving it, and that it is owing to the free goodness of God that some are delivered, enough has been said for the display of his glory; there is not the least occasion for our cavilling.[11]

The militant reformers, who had also inevitably found their piety expressing itself in terms of fundamental social reform, would naturally align themselves spiritually with the concept of election. Vocation, which was also election, was after all the best guarantee for worldly success as well. Herein lay the ultimate certainty.

Calvin himself, however, balanced the positive affirmations of the dependence of the human creature on Grace-alone by the considerable attention he gives to the matter of self-denial as the sum of the Christian life[12] and to Christian liberty where conscience '... being free of the yoke of the law itself, voluntarily obeys the will of God ...'[13] As for attaining certitude in this life of election: 'Because we know not who belongs to the number of the predestinated, or does not belong,' he says when concluding his refutations of the 'calumnies by which the doctrine [of predestination] is always unjustly assailed', 'our desire ought to be that all may be saved; and hence every person we meet, will desire to be with us as a partaker of peace ...'[14] This accords with what Max Weber says when discussing Calvin, and to which reference has already been made: 'The elect differ externally in this life in no way from the damned ... The elect thus are and remain God's invisible church.'[15]

While the Anglo-Saxon Puritan movement had moved violently through the first acts of its revolutionary cycle in Old England, across the Atlantic there were those who had been even further refined by the great net of Calvinism. They entered into their Holy Commonwealth, in the firm belief that here at last, bound unto the Covenant of Grace, they could walk in blameless obedience.

However, Quakers, Anglicans and Anabaptists also arrived,

and for them the idea of a Puritan theocracy was meaningless. The Puritans at first ignored them, but were soon declaring that God's word did not allow Christian States to tolerate such adversaries of the truth.

Clerical élite like Cotton Mather looked upon Quakers as the moral and social scum of the earth. Eventually, three of these new nonconformist souls were forfeited. They included proud Mary Dyer who returned to Massachusetts to suffer execution. What was happening in the new Commonwealth with surprising rapidity was the disintegration of the holiness of the saints. Surreptitiously, the elect had become an élite. This also meant that they relatively soon became an ecclesiastical oligarchy.[16]

Grace with Calvin, as with St Augustine, was the central component in the life of regenerate man. Whatever doubt there might still have been concerning the visibility of this favour here below, the Puritans in New England, precisely as they became an ascertainable élite, put recognition beyond all doubt.

'With this conclusion,' Perry Miller says, 'they went beyond Augustine (*and therefore beyond Calvin*), for he would never have said point-blank that the presence of grace could be verified by external symptoms ... Yet Augustinian theology, in other hands than Augustine's tends towards this deduction...'[17]

Western Christian man, seeking power and finding his guarantee of identity, survival and fulfilment in his control over the lives of others (which would threaten the life of the dominant group), has always tended to claim divine sanction for his behaviour.

It was the Puritan Mind which finally gave political messianism the kind of collective sound which struck terror into the hearts of those on the periphery and inspired the faithful to an intensity of devotion. The divine right of kings was also that of the elect. It would, before the close of the eighteenth century, become the divine right of the people.

It was the start of the socio-political ideal.

By the first quarter of the eighteenth century the austere dignity of church-going Bostonians, 'the favoured few of the Lord',[18] provided a spectacle which was both comforting and disturbing. It was comforting to those who felt themselves secure and justified, losing themselves whole-heartedly to God on Sundays, and devoting themselves equally to their new burgeoning businesses from Mondays to Saturdays. It was disturbing to a small minority, still remembering something of an earlier time when things were simpler.

Putting the matter of divine approval beyond all doubt was the development within New England Calvinism of the idea of a threefold covenant, the Church, the Civil Government, and Grace itself. No man was debarred from accepting the fullness of this grace, if he would but condescend to God's conditions. The covenant theory, Perry Miller says, was a subtle device, within the framework of election, for arousing human activity.

... it permitted man to conceive of divine grace as an opportunity to strike a bargain, to do himself a good turn, to make a sure profit, as an occasion that comes at specific moments in time through the agency of natural means, through the ministry, and the plain, demonstrative sermon. Ergo, whoever does not close the deal when he has a chance, cannot blame God for his own stupidity.[19]

The Covenant theology of New England did not intend to undermine the basic tenets of Calvinism. Spiritual leaders of the Commonwealth like John Cotton, however, had already expressed themselves strongly on the fundamental issue of free-will. Cotton had entered into debate with Dr Twisse, the conscientious Moderator of the Westminster Assembly. The latter solemnly argued in favour of the orthodox Calvinist position. According to this, God elects or rejects according to his own good pleasure, by virtue of his own absoluteness. To Twisse's dismay Cotton had declared that it was to the greater honour of God to be gracious and just than to be wise and powerful. He wished to clear the Orthodox doctrine of predestination from such harsh consequences as would be derived from absolute reprobation.

The generation of Cotton, Hooker and Bulkley were under greater compulsions to clear God of the charge of arbitrary government ... The upshot of all the New England preaching of the threefold Covenant was the pragmatic injunction permitting ministers to inform their congregations that, if any of them could fulfil the Covenant, they were elected. The ultimate spirit of these theologians, the practical point of their intricate system, was summarized by John Preston in one amazing sentence: 'The way to grow in any grace is the exercise of that grace.'[20]

The primary attitude of this exercise, common to all its postures and styles in every time and place, is that of vocation. In the New England Commonwealth, Puritan thrift allied to the system's peculiar psychological stimulant to activism (confirming one's own acceptance of the Covenant, therefore one's own election) had meanwhile brought about the growth of Yankee prosperity. The wilderness was receding and in the towns a genteel affluence was spreading. In the Church itself the rigorous demands for public acceptance of the Covenants were being eroded, so that an 'unregenerate' second generation was already thrusting upwards. By the turn of the century, the Covenant had become what has been described as a Half-Way Covenant.[21] The course had been set. It was a course which would lead not only New England, but the Colonies generally, to the new humanist ideals of the American Revolution. As such it would prove to be a true culmination of the greater Anglo-Saxon Revolution.

Spiritual leaders like Increase and Cotton Mather did their best to stop the rot. The theocracy had ended in 1692 with the termination of the Massachusetts charter. The Mathers continued writing pamphlets in support of a moribund cause. Early in the new century, their publications were so many obituaries for what had already passed away.

John Wise, of Ipswich, Mass., unwittingly gave expression to the profound change which came over the Community of Saints. He was far more than just the standard Congregationalist clergyman. His sensibilities reached much further than his parochial responsibilities. He had been a soldier in Canada; and, while still a student at Harvard, had become absorbed in the reading of legal and political works. While writing his tract *Vindication of the Government of the New England Churches*

(1717), as part of his opposition to the Mathers, he was in fact articulating far weightier issues. Here was a visible directive in the developing final phase of the radical Anglo-Saxon movement.

'A man in making himself a subject,' Wise wrote, 'he alters himself from a freeman into a slave. Also the natural equality of men amongst men must be duly favoured; in that government was never established by God or nature, to give one man a prerogative to insult over another . . .'[22]

Wise had led the citizens of Ipswich to resist the levy of royal taxes. For this he was tried and convicted, fined and put in bonds to keep the peace.

'Honour all men,' he insisted. 'The end of all good governments is to cultivate humanity, and promote the happiness of all, and the good of every man in all his rights, his life, liberty, estate, honour, etc., without injury or abuse done to any . . .'[23]

The ringing tones of the Declaration of Independence, and all that in turn it inspired, can readily be discerned here.

The *Vindication* was widely read and, together with other essays, consistently re-printed. Had John Wise been born when he died (1725) he might well have become as famous as Thomas Paine or Thomas Jefferson. In any event, the re-publication of the *Vindication* in 1772, 'transformed it into one of the bibles of the American Revolution'.[24]

The central, captivating fact is that in John Wise a 'complete reversal of Puritan philosophy' found its first expression. The civil order was not justified in the greater context of the Kingdom of God. The primary task of the state was to 'cultivate humanity and promote the happiness of all and the good of every man in all his rights.' Neither were the churches justified in isolating themselves from all this.[25]

The thrusting, testing social conscience, which had been part of the social humanism of Calvinism from the outset and had expressed itself militantly but amorphously in Cromwellian England, was now perceptibly assuming a final shape.

In essence it was the urge to power: the unexpressed belief that only by man's conscious, determined, courageous efforts could the desired state of the 'happiness of all' be brought about. But power in its naked form is incompatible with the Puritan mind. Only a high-souled intent of ensuring the 'good of every man in all his rights' could make it acceptable. For this was the justification. As the basic Calvinist concepts were human frailty, depravity and the utter goodness and sovereignty of Providence, the obvious answer was to claim divine approval. To this the great emphasis which had been laid on divine election lent itself. The other values in the Gospels, such as utter humility and self-denial, were pushed to the background by a kind of spiritual Gresham's Law. Nothing, all experience has since demonstrated, is so destructive to the Christian message than great ideals. They are the very soul of revolution.

There was to be one short-lived return to the old passion, from the new Horizontal to the ancient Vertical. This was the Great Awakening of which Jonathan Edwards was the central figure. The essential doctrine of Calvinism had by no means wholly disappeared. There still remained those who were, by temperament and natural proclivities, not radicals, but fundamentalists of the calibre of the Lollards, their primitive originals. They feared God, loved Him and trusted Him, claiming nothing while offering all.

Jonathan Edwards himself tried to stem what by the middle of the century came to be almost communal hysteria. It was a great wave of emotion and piety which swept through the land like a tidal wave. As such, it proved to be very temporary.

'When the inevitable reaction came, it left the Puritan philosophy in a much more precarious position than ever ...,' Schneider says. 'New England, instead of making religion the business of life, returned to the life of business.'[26]

Jonathan Edwards himself was defeated in his attempt to restore the Covenant of Grace. Retiring to the wilderness to write philosophical works, trying to re-build the metaphysics of Puritanism, Edwards could nevertheless view from afar the way things were going in his beloved country. He had preached the all-sufficient Sovereignty of God. He had spoken deeply, movingly, of man's need for utter humility. This was the authentic voice of Calvin. But he had also, in the true Puritan tradition, emphasized that this did not mean passive resignation. The 'setting in' of the Spirit of God was to be eagerly awaited. It was a progressive sort of waiting, and it tended to promote not humility but hubris. Edwards had never spared himself to awaken anew the true Calvinist sense of sin; but all around him his fellow countrymen were becoming increasingly self-reliant. 'He defended the glory of God to those who were beginning to revel in their own glory.'[27]

De Tocqueville, as acute an observer as has ever visited North America, epitomized it all as follows:

Men sacrifice for a religious opinion their friends, their family, and their country; one can consider them devoted to the pursuit of intellectual goals which they care to purchase at so high a price. One sees them, however, seeking with almost equal eagerness, material wealth and moral satisfaction; heaven in the world beyond, and well-being and liberty in this.[28]

The 'well-being' was very much the steady growth of the 'economic virtues', as Tawney has referred to them. In the end, Benjamin Franklin was its most influential and articulate apostle and drafted its catechism.

Franklin's Art of Virtue promoted: temperance, silence, order, resolution, frugality, industry, sincerity, justice, moderation, cleanliness, tranquillity, chastity, humility . . .

This was the Complete Puritan in his secular dress. It pointed the way to health, wealth and wisdom. Here were the beatitudes for those who would, in time, found the Great American Fortunes.[29] The founding dynamic of the modern pragmatic spirit would also be found here. It would evolve with revolution.

But there was also liberty . . .

This took the form of a fast-spreading passion for political freedom, incubated in the 'hotbed of disloyalty', as an assertive, un-English George III had come to regard Massachusetts. There was increasing outrage, after the failure of the Stamp Act, at the behaviour of a remotely controlled British authority, making its military presence felt up and down the New England coast in the most provocative way. George III, who had come to the throne in 1760, wished to prove himself a king of English substance, if necessary at the expense of the Colonies. It was perfectly calculable that the primary reaction would find its centre in that part of the new American society, where the stream of resistance to royal arrogance ran deepest. It was, in fact, power answering power.

In the place of the glory of God as the object of all human striving, there should now be, as de Tocqueville described it, 'heaven in the world beyond, and well-being and liberty in this one'. Temporal happiness became primary; and inevitably there was a corresponding loss of the acknowledgement of sinfulness and a growth in the comfort of innocence.

The tremendous success of the American Revolution – the ultimate phase in the greater Anglo-Saxon Revolution – would, in time, confirm all this. Gone, finally, was the 'sense of sin'. In its place there was now the thrilling, inspiring ideal of freedom.

The cradle of the new revolutionary idea was very much Harvard University, more especially a library which served magnificently the needs of the astoundingly intellectual colonials.

The Puritan faith had long been disintegrating. In the two decades preceding the Declaration of Independence, it rapidly made way for the new religion: the ineducible, inalienable Rights of Man, of which freedom was the heart.

'The principles of New England,' de Tocqueville says,

spread at first to the neighbouring states; they then passed successively to the more distant ones; and at last, if I may so speak, they *interpenetrated* [de Tocqueville's italics] the whole confederation. They now extend ... [he was writing some sixty years after the Declaration of Independence] ... their limits, over the whole American world. New England has been like a beacon lit upon a hill, which after it has diffused its warmth immediately around it, also tinges the distant horizon with its glow.[30]

It could well have been prophesied from the start. 'These men,' de Tocqueville remarks, 'possessed, in proportion to their numbers, a greater mass of intelligence than is to be found in any European nation of our time ... The other colonies had been founded by adventurers without families ... Their object was the triumph of an idea.'[31]

> By the rude bridge that arched the flood
> Their flag to April's breeze unfurled,
> Here once the embattled farmers stood
> And fired the shot heard round the world.

But Emerson, in so describing the fateful happenings at Concord on the night of 18 April 1775, could never have imagined the distant corners, the future ages and the strange ways in which the North Bridge shot would yet reverberate in the history of Western man.

Neither the 'common sense' of Tom Paine, nor the Virginian deism of Jefferson, would provide the true spiritual force of the Revolution. Like the Lollards who had become eclipsed by the advent of Calvinism in England, so Paine and Jefferson, believing, respectively, in the deity of reason and the reason of deity, were absorbed in the Puritan Ideal.

The Puritan sense of sin diminished, as the secular religion of Ideals and Virtues finally established itself. So the very rationality of both Paine and Jefferson found their common genius, not rebuked, but transcended.

'Under their hand,' de Tocqueville said of the new Puritan radicals, 'political principles, laws and human institutions seem malleable, capable of being shaped and combined at will ... Thus in the moral world everything is classified, systematized, foreseen and decided beforehand ...'[32]

On the two levels of the political ideal, and the more steadily advancing one of prosperity, the same basic motives were diligently at work. The Kingdom of Man was being built. The architects were New Englanders, the contractors and artisans, Virginians.

'Whether our nation interprets its spiritual heritage through Massachusetts or Virginia,' Reinhold Niebuhr has written, 'we came into existence with the sense of being a "separated" nation, which God was using to make a new beginning for mankind ... they believed in either case that we had been called by God to create a new humanity. We were God's American Israel.'[33]

For both Jefferson and his fellow Virginians, as well as the new radical Puritans, the creation of a 'new humanity' was basically the pursuit of the political ideal. It was, however, decisively the evidence of rising prosperity everywhere which affirmed the promise of the future.

For the Virginians, prosperity increasingly became the basis of virtue. And for the Puritans, virtue was the visible evidence

171

of God's grace. The outer forms of a traditional faith still prevail long after man has finally re-shaped it all to his own ideals. Virtue in the Puritans' terms became the basis of prosperity. It was the restless, anxious mind of man, expressing itself in various styles and places, which here found an essential *rapport*.

When Jefferson, Washington, Henry, Madison and Lafayette had finally reduced the Puritan idea to the noble terms of the Declaration of Independence, then to the more business-like terms of the Federal Constitution, the construction was complete.

Two things had been stated: the enduring need for revolution, which was also the first abstraction of freedom, and the American bourgeois ethic. The latter would take longer to be recognized. It was responsible for the rise of capitalism; not so much its protestant ethic, as the secular manifestations which grew from it.

When the American Revolution definitely established the great principle of the sovereignty of the people as the basic article of the Belief in Man, it represented the crowning performance of the reforming Anglo-Saxon Mind. It had all started effectively in England in the time of Elizabeth, with the return of the Marian exiles from Geneva, Frankfurt, Dieppe and other cities. Here in America, at the end of the eighteenth century, it would reach its logical conclusion.

'The people reign in the American political world as the Deity does in The Universe,' de Tocqueville declared. 'They are the cause and aim of all things; everything comes from them, and everything is absorbed in them.'[34]

Vox Dei had become *vox populi*. *Vox populi* as *vox Dei* would then inevitably become capitalism's basic rationale.

The Declaration of Independence indeed echoed the words of Locke, as in a sense it also echoed those of Calvin. What had happened, however, was that Jefferson and others had restated Locke's ideas in dogmatic terms. Locke was concerned with how to order man's political and social life in rational terms. But Jefferson re-defined this preoccupation in terms of eternal principles. To what extent this still constitutes the all-encompassing idea in the great American society, may be judged from the words of an acute modern observer:

It is more than success, more even than a miracle: it is, to paraphrase Lincoln, the achievement of a superior Destiny placed by the Almighty into the hand of his 'almost chosen people', to spread a great promise to all the people of the world in all time to come.[35]

The promise itself had said:

We hold these truths to be self-evident, that all men are created equal; that they are endowed by their creator with certain inalienable rights; that among these are Life, Liberty, and the pursuit of Happiness – that to secure these rights, Governments are instituted among Men, deriving their just powers from the consent of the governed.

This was already a far cry from primitive Calvinism in which there was no question of man's 'inalienable rights'. Man's legitimate attitude was composed of humility and gratitude. He had no claim whatsoever to his own fundamentals or to lay any other foundation than the one that had already been laid by Jesus Christ (1 Cor. 3:11).

'This feeling of predestination, and of selfwonder, served by unchanging rites and rhetoric,' Clément remarked, 'has astonished even the most sympathetic observers of the American republic, from Alexis de Tocqueville to Sir Denis Brogan. The certainty that American institutions are the best in the world – even when some of their defects are acknowledged – expresses itself in an "American creed" and prolongs itself in an "American Dream".'[36]

But a people's dream of survival, identity and fulfilment is not so much destroyed by its enemies, as by the incalculable upsetting of the roles: the subtle undermining of its best-laid plans, loftiest ideals and most inspiring dreams by the tragicomic sequence of events. It remains true for all men, in all places, at all times; but the more so for those who have been endowed with the imagination and intelligence to plan, to dream, to construct. Lucifer was a fallen angel.

From Calvin to the Puritan theocrats of New England – whose American heirs are still to be found in the modern Protestant Establishment; to the Jacobins, sealing their contract with humanity with the blood of the guillotine; to the Communist International declaring boldly the Age of the Worker; to the modern Afrikaners, also attempting to usher in the true and lasting Kingdom of Man – at least in Southern Africa – what ultimately defeats us is irony. America, sowing the seeds of abundance, and reaping the despoliation of the American environment; and Soviet Russia, sowing the seeds of ultimate brotherhood, and reaping yet another mighty imperium, are outstanding cases in point.

What Reinhold Niebuhr has said becomes even more relevant in the light of these developments.

Escape from our ironic situation obviously demands that we moderate our conceptions of the ability of men and nations to discern the future; and of the power of even great nations to bring a tortuous historical process to, what seems to them, a logical and proper conclusion.[37]

... The perplexity arises from the fact that men have been preoccupied with man's capacity to master historical forces and have forgotten that the same man, including the collective man embodied in powerful nations, is also a creature of these historical forces. Since man is a creator, endowed with a unique freedom, he 'looks before and after and pines for what is not'. He envisages goals and ends in life which are not dictated by the immediate necessities of life. He builds and surveys the great cultural and social structures of his day, recognizes the plight in which they become involved and devises various means and ends to extricate his generation from such a plight. He would not be fully human if he did not lift himself above his immediate hour ...

But if we imagine that we can easily transmute this logic into historical reality we will prove ourselves blind to the limitations of man as creature of history ... The most important of these is the fact that human communities are never purely artifacts of the human mind and will ...[38]

... The inhumanities of our day, which modern tyrannies exhibit in the nth degree, are due to an idealism in which reason is turned into unreason, because it is not conscious of the contingent character of the presuppositions with which the reasoning process begins, and in which idealism is transmuted into inhumanity because the idealist seeks to comprehend the whole realm of ends from his standpoint.[39]

The relevance of this in an essay on the Afrikaners of Southern Africa will become clear when we deal specifically with the growth of their own 'idealism in which reason is turned to unreason': in the secular manifestation of Separate Development. To be scandalized because of the inhumanities of apartheid may too often indicate innocence. It would be far better to understand it all, not as an isolated phenomenon in a 'very strange society', but as essentially part of the general picture of Puritan man, willing power but at the same time seeking divine approval. The way to this is the ideal of social and political organization.

For the purposes of the main theme of this book we need to look pertinently if quickly at the most important of the secular manifestations which in history grew out of the original Puritan spirit.

8 The Socio-Political Ideal

Und sie laufen ! Nasz und nässer,
Wird's im Saal und auf den Stufen.
Welch entsetzliches Gewässe !
Herr und Meister ! hör mich rufen ! –
Ach, da kommt der Meister !
Herr, die Not ist grosz !
Die ich rief, die Geister,
Werd' ich nun nicht los.

Goethe's sorcerer's apprentice (*Der Zauberlehrling*), calling up the spirits to obey his, not the absent master's, will becomes the appropriate allegory. The activated spirit proves to be most uncomfortable about the premises. Having spoken the magic words, setting the ghostly forces to work carrying water, the apprentice then discovers that he has forgotten the incantation necessary to reverse it all. The water-carrying soon becomes an embarrassment, at last a flood. Only the return of *der Meister* can put an end to it.

After the rights of man, centring around an abstract idea of freedom, had been reduced to the clarity of well-defined ideals, there was no limit to them. Their very conceptualization gave them a mobility capable of penetrating the most distant spheres.

It was, like the scientific spirit – also a product of the Christian West, as A. N. Whitehead has shown[1] – no longer the prerogative of the originators. Societies, far removed from the Calvinist–Puritan tradition, would be equally affected. In time even the Maoist Far East would look here for its final absolutes of belief.

It could perhaps have been foreseen that the first country to be inspired would be France. After all, Calvin had been the 'classic Frenchman', as Lewis Mumford says,[2] and Geneva was essentially French. In France itself, the Calvinist heritage, even if the Huguenots had finally been dispersed, had not wholly disappeared. What remained was the collective memory of *vindiciae contra tyrannos*. Those living on the periphery of massive, insensitive privilege, with sufficient intelligence to understand the nature of their own estrangement, would share in this. They would also add to it their own accents.

The *philosophes* of the Enlightenment had, of course, themselves been dabbling in variations on the theme of freedom: from the debunking of power and its excesses by Voltaire to Montesquieu's noble sentiments on liberty. It was Jean-Jacques Rousseau, however, maybe because of his own Calvinist background, who proved to be the most disturbing influence. Every prospect pleased, including man, and only the system was vile. Strife and moral confusion were the necessary consequences of excessive inequalities, money and the growth of government.

The Age of Reason, generating its own ironies, at last presented Europe with the articulation of sentiment in the form of Rousseau. It also produced the most violent performance of unreason yet witnessed in the world of Western man.

The theme was the defeat of tyranny, the restoration of liberty, the reign of the people and the definitive abstraction of freedom. The lines had tentatively been written by the *philosophes*, but conclusively by Rousseau.

Rousseau's emulators were, at a critical stage, assisted by the presence of a man like Benjamin Franklin, who soon became the darling of France. This was not so much because of his wit and social graces, as for his thought. Finally it was the Marquis de Lafayette who, on 11 July 1789, presented a statement of human rights to the National Assembly modelled closely on Jefferson's Declaration of Independence.

If France, in a variety of ways, had helped the national consciousness of the United States of America to evolve, the latter responded most effectively. What had left Europe generations earlier now returned with a new refinement. It was also the very freshness of the pioneer spirit, the semblance of Eden restored, which gave it its moving power.

It was no accident that the Jacobins soon came to resemble the American radicals more than any other. Robespierre, the model of the lean and hungry intellectual dreaming of a new human order, had absorbed the essence of Rousseau, who in turn had been influenced by the American idealists.

Calvin, the Puritan preachers, and Rousseau, Walzer says, can be grouped together: their legislative effort had as its goal the replacement of a decaying order. But Calvin, as we have shown, had no earthly order to unfold programmatically. He had no secular fundamentals, for the polity was a provisional order and could lay no claim to its own absolutes.

From the Puritans of New England there is a steeply rising curve leading to Robespierre, who becomes the classic and absolute revolutionary, displaying all the characteristics of the political saint, obsessed with a holy vision, carried forward by a terrible urge to save mankind.

His fanaticism was unsurpassed. His unusually sympathetic voice compelled attention. His personal integrity was a model for all. He was named the Incorruptible. Louis should die, he said, so that the country might live. In saying this he went to the heart of political messianism.

The inhuman, death-dealing things which duty necessitates are only temporary. The end will justify all. The ultimate happiness, which is also served by extreme measures, will sanctify everything. Faith in the cause calls for unquestioning loyalty, whatever the present cost.

Danton and Desmoulins as relative moderates, with a penchant towards practicality in politics, and others like them were sent to the guillotine. Nobody would accuse him, Robespierre, of being what in modern terms would be described as a liberal. The Reign of Terror would proceed unabated: that was the only way in which the universal ideal of Rousseau could be realized.

Overriding this ideal there is always a greater concept guaranteeing the final validity of it all: the Supreme Being or Supreme Force. In the case of Robespierre it was necessary at last to honour the Supreme Being in a great festival on 8 June 1794. At the same time, those who had previously similarly honoured the Goddess of Reason (Hébert and his fellow atheists) were rooted out.

The motives are in every respect those which would be present in all movements aimed at re-building the world in a perfect shape, whether by violence or persuasion. The Jacobin Revolution and the Reign of Terror demonstrated for all time to what terrifying ends noble but extreme means will lead. From the Festival of the Supreme Being to 28 July, when Robespierre himself ended his life on the scaffold, the Terror became a great wave of slaughter. Heads rolled as if on a production line. The Revolution had very soon become the madness of Organized Man, symbolized by the machine of the guillotine. As such it soon devoured its own geniuses. Among them was Robespierre. The taunt which had been thrown at him only two days previously, when addressing the Convention for the last time: *'C'est le sang de Danton qui t'étouffe!'* had only really here become relevant.

Political idealism in the form of messianism inevitably begins with concern for the oppressed and the exploited, for their estrangement from something in which they ought to share as human beings but do not. These are relative terms and may vary from resentment at the treatment of one's own people at the hands of an alien intruder, to a burning sense of injury and disregard on behalf of various kinds of 'wretched of the earth'.[3] Initially, this resistance to the outrageous arrogance of power (for that is what it really is) is expressed in general terms. The intellectuals who take the lead, however, gradually find their ideas crystallizing (as Afrikaners like to say) to certain well-defined concepts and principles. The socio-political gospel, announcing the coming kingdom of man, has then been clearly stated. All that remains is to work actively, faithfully, with complete devotion, towards the unfolding of the idea, which will restore all to their proper places and, at last, establish righteousness.

No idea could possibly develop its dynamic were it not for the element of truth contained in it. Precisely because it has humanist qualities, it relates in one way or another to freedom. It may be the rights of man; *liberté, égalité, fraternité*; the Marxist concept of labour as an expression of man's emancipation from alienation, his return to himself, his self-realization; or the insistence on the individuality (or identity) of cultural groups (or nations) as expressed in Afrikaner Right-wing political idealism of the present day.

They all deserve the name radical, because they all attempt to restore totally the essence of the human creature – freedom. That what is pursued is but a caricature of the real thing, does not affect the passionate devotion to their purpose.

Marxist-Leninist Communism, like the formulation of the democratic ideal in Revolutionary America and Revolutionary France, became yet another people's and therefore democratic ideal to emerge from the Christian West. ' ... Marxism stands within the Biblical tradition,' Marthinus Versfeld says.

It is this tradition which, building on Hegel and Feuerbach, Marx has secularized. Marx endeavours after a unity of man and nature which corresponds with the unity of man and God in the Incarnation, and which aims at a humanism of the world which Christians regard as the fruit of the incarnation ... Nobody nowadays can endeavour to translate into real life the saying that you cannot serve God and Mammon without making use of Marx's analysis of the structure of Mammon. Finally his conception of the proletariat as the people chosen by history to overcome alienation and redeem the world is a secularized theology of the elect. [4]

Marx, thirsting after righteousness, was true to his own Hebraic tradition. Like Ezekiel quoting the Lord Yahweh, he could cry:

> Trouble for the bloodstained city.
> I too plan to build a great fire.
> Heap on the wood, light it,
> cook the meat, prepare the spices,
> let the bones burn.
> Set the pot empty to heat on the coals;
> let the bronze glow red-hot,
> the filth inside melt away,
> the rust inside be consumed. [5]

For this very reason Marx comes close to Calvin.

The material things of life are not, Calvin had written, as such the bearers of evil. On the contrary, money, too, is the fruit of man's labour.[6] It is pursuit of profit for profit's sake that detracts from the order of God.[7]

Man's free labour completes the work of God.[8] Labour is a vocation of God, and in free labour man fulfils himself. The alienation of labour comes about when it is directed towards the wrong ends. This does not mean that work is always pleasant. On the contrary, it may be either pleasant or unpleasant; but Christ is always the liberator of the pain which work may cause.

The rich and powerful, unfortunately, often abuse their power to oppress the weak and poor.[9] The abuse of the poor and the oppression of the weak, of all who occupy a lowly condition in society, is exactly the opposite to the divine order which we as Christians ought to respect.[10] Labour is no merchandise to be traded at will. Those who labour should be paid a proper wage and neither the market price nor the legal minimum is an indication that it is just.[11]

Because man tends to abuse what God has given him, Israel instituted the sabbatical year,[12] in which they allowed fields and vineyards to lie fallow. This was also to serve as a reminder that the earth belongs to the Lord, and that man has no unlimited use of it. Man has been given dominion over the earth, but outside Christ he becomes estranged from it. God has given man will and intelligence by which the powers of analysis, knowledge and creativity have also been conferred on him. Whether these gifts are employed in manual or intellectual labour makes no difference. They are always to be used in the service of God and society.[13]

The new life of man in Christ is, however, no mere individual but rather *a communal life* in which social relations have been fully restored: in which an end has been put to the divisions between rich and poor, male and female, different races and nationalities. The most lowly can glory in his high place; and he who is rich can glory in his smallness.[14]

Calvin's and Marx's anthropologies have, indeed, so much in

common, it could hardly have been coincidental. As in primitive Calvinism, so too in primitive Marxism, there is a reconciliation between freedom and determinism. Calvin, relying mainly on St Augustine, proclaimed at the same time God's absolute sovereignty and man's freedom. Both were equally certain. Marx did something similar. For God's sovereignty, however, he substituted history.

K. R. Popper's conclusion that the historicist (and therefore Marxist) optimism must rest on faith alone (since reason is denied the role of bringing about a more reasonable world), is probably the ultimate refinement in the emergence of the various socio-political ideals from the Puritan tradition.[15] It needed something far more like the original Calvin than either the Rights of Man, or *liberté*, *égalité*, *fraternité*, to abandon God altogether, and yet restore the primacy of faith. Marxism provided this.

The *Communist Manifesto* was the credo of one who had in himself all the necessary elements. Here was a scholar of enormous dedication, burning integrity and consuming anger. Around him as he sat there reading, thinking and writing in the British Museum, the new industrial society was forging ahead. It had been stimulated and compounded by a newly-burgeoning imperialism. The Puritan mind, in the ultimate form of the new aggressive 'economic virtues', produced Victorianism. Riches were pouring into Britain from its far-flung domains, where conquest, sustained by a sense of mission, had established Christian order. At the same time, people were labouring at home in the most appalling conditions. The contemporary of Marx was Dickens.

Anger, born from indignation at social injustice, is the flame which builds up the pressures of power which may explode in revolution. An older power is then upset by a younger. But it was precisely Marx's Hebraic-Christian conscience which required the coming cataclysmic change to be justified in terms of faith alone. What mankind needed, he sensed, was a new (secular) theology of the elect. The ordaining power would then no longer be God but history. History was on the side of the true creators, the workers. The general course of history had been plotted by Hegel, and it was a *via necessitas*. It led to the coming reign of the Absolute.

The progress of history came about by tensions building up between thesis and antithesis, between old and new cultural practices and means of production. Straight-line reforms were impossible. The dialectical struggle was necessarily a class struggle, because classes were marked by the creativity or non-creativity of their labour.

The coming clash was certain. The opposing forces would produce a new synthesis. The proletariat, as the elect, would inherit the earth. The new earth itself, when finally the state as an interim measure had withered away, would be man's real and lasting heaven. Marxism is the most complete secularization of the Puritan ethic. Its end, too, as contemporary history has amply demonstrated, is a massive new bureaucracy and a new tyranny.

But, of course, especially in a time when almost all radical movements are from the Left, we need to remind ourselves that the most cataclysmic of the socio-political ideals of modern times has been from the Right. It is National Socialism, the particular secular manifestation of the Third Reich.

To understand what took place in Germany between the two World Wars needs reference to the writings and preachings of three early minor prophets: Paul de Lagarde, Julius Langbehn and Moeller van den Bruck.[16] The nature of the power which all revolution seeks to replace is inevitably, because of its inherent corruptibility, dull, mediocre, indulgent, respectable, materialistic and hypocritical. The power of the revolution itself, on the other hand, is necessarily young, arrogant, dedicated and idealistic. In the heyday of Bismarck's Second Reich, with bourgeois industrialism as the culture of cities, the particular Germanic expression of it all was *Gemütlichkeit*. Nietzsche, of course, would prove the most devastating critic of all this, precisely because he was also a poet. Of more immediate effect in the growth of a Germanic ideology, as Fritz Stern has shown, however, were the three minor prophets mentioned above.

The intensity of thought and feeling which marked the writings and speakings of de Lagarde, Langbehn and van den

Bruck culminated in their pleas, expressed or implied, that the German nation accept its divinely ordained mission. Each in his own way laid the foundations of the Third Reich.

These three writers were passionately concerned with the search for a new secular creed which would provide the German *Volk* with a total plan for liberation from its spiritual sterility. All the familiar phrases of socio-political gospelling, in greater or lesser degree, were now at last to be expressed in a peculiarly German idiom.

Lagarde's was a rhetoric of resentment. He had lived in England and was filled with profound admiration for the English. He despised what he called the tawdry *Lumpentheologie* of German Protestantism, especially Lutheran pietism. Germany needed a new sense of destiny, returning to the mountain peaks of the spirit. God's will for Germany was a Christian heaven and a German earth. A new national temple would be built where there would be collective acceptance of a divinely ordained mission. The call was for faith and order, especially for Prussia, because history was on her side.

Langbehn, Lagarde's close disciple, likewise pleaded for a new, reformed Germany, where simplicity, subjectivity, individuality (familiar values in the Puritan West) would be re-established in the place of the dullness and mediocrity of a Philistine society. Langbehn's criticism was especially directed against what he saw as the prime evils of the new bourgeois life: *carrière machen* (pyramid climbing, status-seeking, as nowadays Vance Packard would say), 'Americanization' and Mammonism.

'But in his thundering against bourgeois life,' Stern says, 'one can hear the peculiar note which the National Socialists later tirelessly blared forth. The bourgeoisie had become "rootless", estranged from folk and nature, had lost its *Volkstümlichkeit* and childlike nature.'[17] An Age of Art should replace the currently prevailing Age of Science.

It is not only the line leading to the Third Reich which those with hindsight can detect. Langbehn's passionate search for a new Beauty for his *Rembrandtsdeutsche*, his fierce rejection of all pedantry which killed the 'vital spirit' of a people, his war against the 'poison of commerce and materialism', raises echoes not only of Rousseau and Marx, but also, more remarkably, of Jonathan Edwards and his Great Awakening. It was precisely on a theory of beauty, harmony, proportion and love – the 'Rembrandt virtues' – that Jonathan Edwards erected his own Calvinist/Puritan idealism.[18] 'Only the love of beauty and of those beings in whom beauty is reflected makes life worthwhile. To it the wise man surrenders . . .'[19]

Langbehn's ideal type at one time lived on the North-Western plain of Germany. They were the noblest and toughest of an idealized peasantry. Calvin himself had once written with equal feeling and piety of the peasantry, working in God's glorious theatre of nature. They were, Langbehn said, akin to great culture heroes like Rembrandt and Shakespeare. They were – it is intriguing to note here – also akin to the South African Boers, who were 'the only surviving old Germans'.[20] Langbehn's *Niederdeutsche* hero was also to be found among the Calvinist Afrikaners. Neither soil, nor speech, nor state, but the *Volk* in its oneness is the Fatherland, Langbehn declared.[21]

The *Volk* was the hidden repository, as the People were in Revolutionary America; the People generating a General Will in Rousseau's pre-Revolutionary France; and the Proletariat in the writings of Karl Marx. It was the mythical receptacle of character, strength and belief in the future. Langbehn, like Rousseau, and Hitler more than a generation later, was formally a Catholic, but temperamentally a pietistic Protestant, although like Lagarde he despised what he regarded as the bourgeois cant of the Lutheran church. He might well have paraphrased Marx's description of such institutions as being the opium of the *Volk*. It was, finally, that most dangerous of all combinations: the romantic spirit with the reforming mind. It led to the famous *Fahrten ins Blaue*, a kind of early 'Counter-Culture', which was also a reaction to a flatulent Mammon. The *Wandervögel* sang their songs while exploring Nature, discovering, as at Woodstock in the late sixties, a 'transcendent togetherness'. The vital point was the *Erlebnis*, the 'trip', as the moderns would say: a deep experience of 'belonging'. The difference, of course, was that with these German puritan-souled romantics, the critical unit was the nation.

Here was the true mediator of salvation. It was the people, the proletariat, in other terms.

In the various socio-political gospels, whether of the right or left, the collective has proved to be the hallmark of its true nature: spiritual *Kitsch* as substitute for the Word become Flesh. Holy scripture in the case of Langbehn was his book *Rembrandt als Erzieher*.

Moeller van den Bruck completed the trio. The book here bore the prophetic title *Das Dritte Reich* (1922). It was the logical culmination of both Lagarde and Langbehn. It was also the articulation of 'conservative revolution'. There was the same loathing for the dullness, flatness and liberalism of bourgeois life. The same passion existed for a new national holiness, the heroic Germanic ideal. There was the same rejection of reason and a deeply emotional reverence for the spirit. All would find its utmost expression in the God-called leader. This was the *Führergedanke*, and the effectiveness of the thought is a historical axiom. The Third Reich in the writings of Moeller van den Bruck became the coming 'Kingdom of Man'.

It was politica idealism of the Right at its most articulate, the great Germanic Dream. Its promise was eternal peace, a new deep consciousness of Christian unity within the nation. It had been predestined. *Schicksal ist stärker als Staatskunst.*[22]

'... long before Hitler, long before Versailles,' Stern says, 'there appeared in Germany deep national frustrations, galling cultural discontents, which inspired nationalist fantasies and utopias which found ready assent among this German élite ...'[23]

It was again the intellectual élite preparing the way for revolution. The conditions accompanying their appearance were similar to what Marx had described as a change in the means of production. This could also be expressed as a change in a people's cultural activities. Walzer has described it as the transition from some or other form of a traditional to a new kind of society. Urbanization, industrialization, the growth of a new middle class, has so far consistently provided the right *milieu* for revolution.

A change in the nature of man's creative work takes place and new insights, new attitudes and practices have to be sought.

It was the case in England and America (which must be seen as a single movement), in France and also in Germany.

The German 'heroic vitalists' were doing essentially the same thing. The industrial revolution had, too, penetrated deeply into German life. *Embourgeoisement* – according to Lagarde, Langbehn and van den Bruck – had overtaken Germany like a disease.

Nietzsche, who was much less of an immediate success as a writer than Lagarde, Langbehn or van den Bruck, was primarily concerned with personal, not national, rebirth. According to Nietzsche it was neither the group, nor the *Volk*, but the creative genius which determined the ascent of man. The supra-national was the real, creative, health-giving entity. Langbehn expressed the antithesis of this in his insistence that Germany take its rightful place as *magister mundi* for the sake of general human salvation. Nietzsche's penetrating criticism of the *deutsches Wesen* culminated in his towering condemnation of Richard Wagner. On the other hand, Langbehn, who nevertheless admired Nietzsche's character, declared that he could not read a page of his writing without becoming physically ill.[24] Artificial nationalism, Nietzsche said, was just as dangerous as artificial Catholicism. The English with their bad food, their Puritan Cromwells, their pietistic Wesleys, their industrial slums, their money power, were even worse than the Germans. They only thought of 'happiness' ...

No wonder that when the Third Reich finally came to the formulation of its *Weltanschauung*, it was not Nietzsche with his *Übermensch* who contributed so substantially to the rise of the Germanic ideology, but Lagarde, Langbehn and van den Bruck. They constituted a vulgarization of Nietzsche.[25]

The heart of world-reform was for them the nation. The German *Weltsendung* was the noblest of missions, and society would be reborn by the *Sachlichkeit* of the Prussian spirit. Soul-destroying Western Liberalism would be finally effaced.

There is abundant evidence, Stern says, of the direct influence of Lagarde and Langbehn on the most important of the National Socialist ideologists.[26] Moeller van den Bruck again was the dominant figure of the 'conservative revolution' in the Weimar Republic. Of course, the idealism of these early prophets was adulterated as the tyranny of the Third Reich grew, and they were eventually repudiated. But such is the fate of all political idealists. They eventually get buried in the bureaucratic super-structure all tyranny needs. Things were no different with the Jacobins and Marxists.

What is noteworthy in the case of the Third Reich is that here the organism at the heart of the socio-political gospel became the *Volk*, the nation. Previously it had been the people, the proletariat.

Scratch an ideology and you find a collective. Scratch a collective and you find a band of intellectuals with a vision of the Kingdom of Man, being *Ersatz* for the Kingdom of Heaven. With their eyes on Utopia, let these intellectuals then scratch each other. Soon they will uncover all the articles of faith constituting their idea, their particular gospel.

The socio-political ideal allied to power, like capitalism, as the prime belief of life, shot forth out of Puritan soil as a vigorous but hazardous mutation of Calvinism. Its fruits looked decep-tively fine, promising, in fact, eternal life. The effect of eating them, however, brought about a sudden deadly consciousness of nakedness.

Can we now, as Walzer has done,[27] draw an abstract idea from the revolutionary movement of radical politics, whether of the right or the left? The following may serve the purpose.

A power structure, having lived through its prime, to which old but still remunerative privileges attach, needs an increasing reliance on its own functionaries and abstractions to bolster its position. This means inevitably both bureaucracy and oppression. As long as the structure is a simple hierarchy of upper and lower classes, lords and liegemen, masters and servants, the haves and have-nots, the time for radical renewal has not yet arrived. It is only when the break-up of ancient traditional structures takes place that the true potential for revolution is released.

An intellectual élite, emerging from a new middle class, then articulates the repressiveness, slackness, mediocrity and in-justice of the old order. Painstakingly, they also explore the present, past and future, and rationalize the shape of the new kingdom, which would utterly reverse the old. Preparing to challenge it, they centre all their thinking on the re-establishment of total social justice. Justice, as expressed in the formulation of an abstraction of freedom, becomes their justification of power.

The ideal is that of the completely new society. The band of brothers also demand from themselves the most rigorous discipline and unswerving faith. Sacrifices are called for; and should it mean martyrdom, so be it. Persecution could only serve to strengthen the spirits of those who have accepted their destiny.

At last the hour arrives. It is the reward of faith, and the hour of fulfilment. Often it means bloodshed, sometimes to an inordinate degree. The old order, however, may be so advanced in its decay that if left to stew in its own juice, it collapses at a touch, destroyed by its own 'inner tensions'. Power has now been transferred, the old making place for the young: an ideal has been attained.

It is, however, not yet *the* ideal. The new society is still an infant. When the complete design has at last been realized, and the new order established, man will have arrived at his true home.

As a temporary measure, it is proposed, the new order will also need authority: uncompromising, even drastic, where the need arises. This, however, is not oppression, for its true intent is to serve the high ideals of the revolution. It is merely a passing discomfort which will disappear as the vision is translated into reality.

What now happens is that the total nature of the revolution in turn will also require an increasing number of functionaries to make it work. Surreptitiously, no, mysteriously, the new authority then gradually adopts the attitudes and methods of the old, in spite of its finest intentions to avoid the bureaucratic morass. This is unavoidable because all 'human engineering', as Popper calls it, like the mythical Tower, will require a myriad of operators who, precisely because they are labouring at an abstraction of fulfilment, will increasingly fail to communicate with each other. It becomes the confusion of tongues.

The whole should then be seen as yet another case of striving man's great socio-political ideal inexplicably getting lost in the ironic intricacies of history.

Part Three: The Afrikaner Revolution

9 A Band of Brothers

We have examined the development of the socio-political ideal, the evolution of political fundamentalism out of the Puritan mutation of Calvinism and drawn an abstract in broad terms. We should now look more closely at the development of a similar movement in Southern Africa.

From what has been said, we would primarily need to trace the growth of ideas among the *burgerstand*, as it evolved in the urban areas of South Africa after the Peace of Vereeniging. Indications have already been given of the appearance of an intellectual élite within nationalist Afrikanerdom, led by the most formidable opponent of Hertzog, D. F. Malan. The very tension which grew between these two champions of Afrikanerdom would indicate some profound change in outlook. As will be seen, it was mainly that of the scope and function of politics. It was the first stirrings of Afrikaner revolution.

At the turn of the century, only some ten per cent of the Afrikaners were living in towns and cities. In 1970, only some twelve per cent were still living on the *platteland*.

It was the Second World War which finally shattered this traditional society. In a way, it set the seal on the process of urbanization and industrialization, of *verburgerliking*. Afrikaners from the thinning ranks of manual workers and the growing band of office-workers 'trekked up' to join Smuts's new South African Army. Soon Afrikanerdom was as much at war in Abyssinia, Madagascar, the Western Desert of North Africa and Europe, as South Africans of British stock. This was in spite of energetic opposition to South African participation in the war by the new National Party under Malan, and a militant reaction on the part of the para-military organization, the *Ossewabrandwag*, with its Nazi sympathies. It was also in spite of the open defiance by the extreme right of this movement, to the point of sabotage; and the national trauma caused by the climax of the Hertzog tragedy.

'A great percentage, if not the majority,' F. A. van Jaarsveld says, 'of the white military forces consisted of Afrikaners. Men from both language groups fought shoulder to shoulder on the battlefields and elsewhere against the threat from outside.'[1]

Afrikaners soon played leading roles in the operations. A *plattelander*, Dr H. J. van der Bijl, who had become a brilliant industrialist and head of *Iscor*, was put in charge of war supplies by Smuts. The production of munitions and other military requirements was soon organized to a point of high efficiency. In East Africa, Brigadier (later General) Dan Pienaar led the South Africans in the conquest of Abyssinia. Addis Ababa, entered on 4 April 1941, became a part, too, of South African history. As did the Western Desert where South Africans, now serving in the British Eighth Army, distinguished themselves at Sidi Rezegh, Taub el Esem, Bardia and Sollum. Rommel's Afrika Korps, pursuing the retreating Eighth Army, changed course and attacked Tobruk where 25,000 men under General Klopper were forced to surrender. For a great many, it was shock and misery. But at El Alamein, in 1943, South Africans, fighting under General Bernard Montgomery, helped prepare for the final defeat and capture of the Afrika Korps. That same year, South Africans fought in Italy under General Evered Poole, and as part of the British Eighth and the American Fifth Armies. Elsewhere South Africans – Afrikaners, too – were distinguishing themselves. In the Battle of Britain 'Sailor' Malan, as one of the Few, contributed to its epic and heroic qualities.

Above all there was Smuts, who had been made a British field-marshal in 1941. The fifteen years of withdrawal – from 1924 to 1939 – were at an end. At the age of 70, his rôle was once more that of the commando leader of the Long Ride, the East African adventure versus Lettow-Vorbeck: '... imparting courage and energy to civilians and soldiers, and keeping a firm grasp in military and strategic matters.'[2] Winston Churchill sought Smutsian approval on all major questions. By Smuts's side was Ouma – Granny, the Boer woman of Doornkloof. Like her husband, she received the outside world at the sprawling corrugated iron-and-wood homestead, which had once been a Boer War officers' mess. She wore flat-heeled shoes, workaday dresses, but never a hat, and moved about the war scene, from South to North Africa, like Mother Courage in a new key. When the war ended, the combined South African forces numbered about a third of a million. Of these roughly a third were Afrikaners, a third from British stock and a third African or Coloured.

Smuts's United Party was firmly in power, supported by Stallard's Dominionites, who were loyal to the British Empire and spiritual heirs to Jameson's Unionists. It must have seemed to Smuts as if his concept of a South African nation as part of the greater British Commonwealth had truly taken shape in the fires of the war. He could afford to be generous. The most passionate of the extreme right were filled with 'perhaps a kind of romantic longing for heroic deeds in the interests of Afrikanerdom'.[3] Comic indeed was the spectacle of these newly citified descendants of the burghers of the Heroic Age playing at soldiers, while the rest of the country was locked in the world-wide conflict. Smuts, casting a glance now and again with his pale blue eyes at the *Stormjaers*, with an odd bomb or two set off in public places (occasionally with serious consequences) for good measure, must have shaken his finely-sculpted head rather sadly, remembering greater days and worthier causes.

It was not only the new imitation of the old commandos (the *Ossewabrandwag*) which gave the impression of being a complete exercise in futility. It was also the scandalized vocabularies of the new political militants, protesting so burningly at times against 'detention without trial'. They also cried against the internment of the most active of the would-be saboteurs, who had rejoiced noisily at the news of British reverses and German triumphs, and who listened intently to the nightly outpourings of Radio Zeesen.

In 1943, the draft constitution of the future Republic, couched in suitably solemn language, was published by a group of young political intellectuals in the North. Its terms were uncompromisingly radical. It enshrined the Afrikaner Dream: a complete restoration of the old Republican Order but with additions. The world of the city, with its manifold phenomena inimical to the true Afrikaner heritage, would be re-structured in terms of the 'traditionally Calvinistic' world-view of the Afrikaners. The non-Whites would firmly but justly be returned to their stations.

The draft was published in *Die Transvaler*, the new Nationalist daily in Johannesburg, for which H. F. Verwoerd was writing dissertative editorials on the new and heroic task of the Afrikaners. In the first of these he had written: '*Die Transvaler* has come with a calling. It has come to serve a nation by making the voice of loyal and sublime nationalism resound to the farthest reaches ...'[4] Verwoerd later denied that he had in any way been responsible for the draft constitution of the Republic, saying that he had merely allowed the young Republicans the freedom of his columns to state their views.[5] This freedom was allowed by the grace of Smuts. In 1938 Verwoerd, surprisingly, had already indicated a broader kind of nationalism, directed towards the 'white nation' rather than the *Boerenasie* – the Boer Nation – of the militant Republican intellectuals. 'It is the unity of all who can think, feel and work together for their own and only fatherland, South Africa,' said Verwoerd. 'It is the solidarity of people of one mind and feeling, who may truly be called members of the nation; it is only in this real unity that domestic peace and bonds of friendship will be able to be found.'[6] This was, however, but a fleeting indication of the Verwoerd to come.

Meanwhile, he was very much a part of the disarray into which conservative Afrikanerdom had fallen. '... hardly ever before,' van Jaarsveld says, 'had there been greater confusion, internal division, and political impotency. It was a condition which reminded one of the period of civil war in the Transvaal from 1860–1864.'[7] Among those who opposed the war were the Nationalists under Malan, the Afrikaner Party which had been formed by the close followers of Hertzog and led by N. C. Havenga, and the *Ossewabrandwag*, led by van Rensburg. Smuts, supremely confident, had the position well in hand, finely judging just how much latitude he could allow the more adventurous of his opponents. With the true sickness of the

Third Reich becoming increasingly apparent, even Malan, who came to refuse all associations with the *Ossewabrandwag*, was being grouped with the enemy. On the whole, the Nationalists were being accused of supporting the Third Reich. They failed to share the general enthusiasm for the war effort and were concerned only with the inner politics of Afrikanerdom. This caused their fellow Afrikaners, supporting Smuts, unkindly to call them *Malanazis*.

The future looked empty for them. So much was this the case that Michael Roberts and A. E. G. Trollip in 1947 published a political study of the Afrikaners under Malan, Havenga and van Rensburg, and called it *The South African Opposition*.[8] A year or so later, what they had judged to be a permanent political minority in parliament had, *mirabile dictu*, become the government.

The impotence, confusion and disarray of his opponents had also lulled Smuts into a sense of false security. What he saw was only what was taking place on the surface. In a sense, it was the price he was paying for having lived and moved for so long on a world platform. As a national leader and as a field-marshal in perhaps the greatest struggle of the age, there was even less possibility of his understanding the dangerous earnestness of the new élite the *burgerstand* had produced; or of the way in which their nationalism differed profoundly from anything which hitherto had been a part of the South African political landscape. Smuts had long since lost all real contact with the thinking of a large and important part of his own people.

Hertzog, too, was out of touch. Nothing in his background could enable him to grasp what was happening. But it was more so in the case of Smuts. He had only watched the Afrikaners' cultural struggle casually, from a distance. When, in 1943, the Smuts Government was returned to Parliament with a comfortable majority, the *Oubaas* – the Old Master – could well have looked forward to a successful conclusion of the war, then perhaps to a peaceful period of new expansion and growth in a united South Africa. After that he would be able to retire happily to his beloved mountains; to the veld, the grasses, to philosophy ... He might even spend time visiting old friends:

the Churchills, the Roosevelts; even Queen Frederika of Greece.

It was Atlas again, the giant carrying the burden, his own world, on his sinewy shoulders, not fully realizing how fatally self-reliant he had become and not having any idea of what great stumbling-blocks would appear under his own feet. With eyes fixed on the 'distant prospect', he could not watch his own step.

A lot was taking place beneath all the mad comings and goings, the endless and impossibly involved infighting among the nationalist Afrikaners. The *Herenigde* National Party,[9] the Afrikaner Party and *Ossewabrandwag* all joined in what must have seemed to many on the side-lines as a political free-for-all. Roberts and Trollip carefully describe the detailed intricacies of all these manoeuvres, from 1939 to 1945. An agreement between the *Herenigde* Party and the *Ossewabrandwag* at Cradock in October 1940 divided the spheres of activities in nationalist Afrikanerdom. The Party was to see to the political side of things, while the *Ossewabrandwag* was to look after the non-political and 'cultural' interests. More indicative of anything else was the eulogistic article on J. F. J. van Rensburg about a year later in the *Münchener Illustrierte Zeitung* as a true friend of the Third Reich.[10]

Malan soon saw which way the wind was blowing and, from the middle of 1941, began his sonorous, cadenced exposition of the new thought in Afrikanerdom. It was a time of frequent meetings, endless scurrying about, rhetoric and bitter accusations and counter-accusations. While the rest of the world was embroiled in the war, these Don Quixotes jousted with steel-bladed windmills above the sun-baked South African veld.

Smuts, soldier, statesman, philosopher and world-figure, seemed serenely oblivious to all this. Whether it was a complacency induced by supreme confidence, the shrewdness of the wily politician or a lack of sufficient contemporary sense, is debatable. It was, probably, a combination of all these things. Smuts had his gaze fixed on the fine new world which would arise from the ruin of the war and in which the British Commonwealth of Nations would play such a tremendous role. He could hardly take parochial politics too seriously. The more adventurous of his opponents had had to be curbed by internments and imprisonments. For the rest, as he was fond of saying: 'the dogs may bark, but the caravan moves on'.

But the barking of the dogs was mostly so much misleading fury. There was a quieter, more effective and earnest core of people meeting within the innermost *binnekring* of the *Broederbond*, thinking, talking, into the small hours of the morning. This marked the steady driving-inwards of Afrikaners' political thought and sentiment. Afrikaner politics was slowly but fatally being theologized. There was a growing urge to set the South African world aright, once and for all, to reconstruct it and redeem it in terms of a newly-defined Afrikaner *lewens-en wêreldbeskouing* – a world-view.

It is not wholly correct to say that the Dutch Reformed Church was (or became) the 'National Party at prayer'. It is more correct to say that the National Party was itself becoming, if not a church, then a party imbued with religion – a secular religion – at its very roots.

The tendency to associate Afrikaner thinking in the war and post-war years with National Socialism was only partly due to distinct words and behaviour on the part of certain Afrikaners expressing overt sympathy with the Third Reich. As we have seen, what happened in Germany was just another of the various systems of radical politics promising redemption, rooted in Puritanism.

Now it was happening here. The Afrikaners' whole history had been delayed for 143 years by the sterile parade of the V.O.C. They had lived through a heroic age in the nineteenth century. But only after the impact of the Anglo-Boer War had finally disrupted their traditional *platteland* society, had they begun to be an urban people. Gradually, through four decades, the full awareness of their new situation grew on them. The cities were Anglo-Saxon, for such was their culture. The great mass of Afrikaners, expatriates from a disintegrating *platteland*, had found refuge in the ragged edges of the cities.

For more than a decade – from roughly the mid-twenties to the mid-thirties – they had been almost exclusively concerned with *handhawing* – maintaining and extending their own cultural position *vis-à-vis* the English. At the time of the strike in 1922, they had reacted militantly to the threat of black workers being used by the mining houses for the sake of cheaper labour. It had only been a temporary flare-up; for the threat of competing Africans as a co-existent proletariat had never really got under way. The forceful, dynamic Clements Kadalie from Nyasaland had founded the Industrial and Commercial Workers' Union in 1919. Rousingly, he campaigned for better wages for Africans and for removal of the colour bar. Even when he seemed to be most effective, he caused no particular anxiety among the Hertzog Afrikaners. In fact, Hertzog, as Edward Roux has told us, wrote him a friendly letter, enclosing a personal contribution to his funds. Even D. F. Malan found the opportunity to send an encouraging telegram.[11] Kadalie visited England where he enlisted support from British trade unionists. A special advisor was seconded to the Union for this purpose; but on Kadalie's return to his adopted country he found his movement in a state of schism. The I.C.U. drooped, faded, then died.

Legislation and statements of policy dealing specifically with racial matters had been both practical and economical during the régime of the Pact. From 1924 to 1933 special measures adopted included an act providing for segregated areas of African residence, service contracts for Africans and influx from tribal areas to the cities. This still permitted, however, African freehold within all areas except the Free State and certain proclaimed areas under the Gold Law.[12] Acts were passed about 'native' administration, instituting special courts for customary African Law and making it an offence to promote feelings of hostility between black and white.[13] Another act instituted an African Development Fund;[14] yet another reserved many skilled occupations in mines and works for 'Europeans, Cape Coloured, and Mauritius Creoles, or St Helena persons'.[15] There was a policy requiring 'civilized' rates to be paid to as many Whites as possible even if they did unskilled work;[16] an 'immorality act' prohibiting intercourse between Whites and Africans, but not between any other races;[17] and an act controlling riotous assemblies, again prohibiting the engendering of feelings of hostility between black and white.[18] Seven, in all, in some nine years, contrasting with more than 200 special measures to regulate matters of race from 1948 to 1971, all of which will, in due course, be more fully dealt with. An interesting feature of the earlier period is that the positive acts of discrimination affected only Africans, not Coloureds or Asians. It is also interesting to note, from the vantage point of this present age of Afrikaner rule, that these acts, put on the statute book from 1924 to 1933, were conceived and executed in partnership. The partners were Afrikaners still in the style of the Age of the Generals and sound British socialists, dedicated to the cause of labour. The still relatively mild forms of positivist segregation were by this time a well-seasoned British South African tradition. Theophilus Shepstone, Administrator of Natal, devised it as far back as 1847, as David Welsh has so cogently reminded us.[19]

In the 'golden period' of Fusion (1934–9), Boer and British came together in an even wider context. But with a duo of Boer Generals, Hertzog and Smuts, still leading the country, legislation materially affecting race relations was even more restricted. There was Hertzog's act on the representation of 'Natives' in 1936. African voters in the Cape were put on a special roll to elect a limited number of white members to the House of Assembly and the Provincial Council; and Africans generally in South Africa were given the powers to elect four white senators.[20] To supplement all this, in the same year, another act provided for $7\frac{1}{2}$ million morgen* of land to be added to the Reserves, creating a special Native Trust to administer the areas.[21]

The nationalist Afrikaners were preoccupied with the 'all-white' political issues of Fusion. They were devoting time, energy and talents to the cultural struggle against British influence, and were deeply committed to the solution of the problem of their own rural poor, gathering in increasing numbers in slum areas of the cities. As far as they were concerned, the still-silent black/brown proletariat had moved off-stage. But where to?

This question nags and worries the observer. And the answer is whispered: only to the wings, shortly to return. The black

* 1 morgen = 2.117 acres.

and brown Africans were slowly and silently consolidating their positions in the cities, existing alongside the Afrikaners fighting their own cultural struggle and seeking to reinstate their own disinherited, the rejects of a disintegrating *platteland*. And we have already briefly seen how in 1937 the 'others' were suddenly remembered when election posters demanded an end to 'mixed marriages'. But they were not yet important from the vantage point of Afrikaners seeking political power from Fusionist, predominantly 'English' South Africa. The Second World War not only conclusively shattered the traditional society of Afrikanerdom, it suddenly forced it to face up to the black/brown presence. This, too, had formed massively on the tattered edges of the cities. It was coming together in conditions infinitely more formless, squalid and huge than the recently arrived 'Poor-Whites' from the *platteland*. It was this other immigration to the cities which was becoming a looming fact also of Afrikaner existence. Smuts, thoroughly enjoying his conduct of the war, showed almost no awareness of this. It was an aspect of his error of having lost contact with the thinking and feeling of the main body of his own people. From the middle thirties onwards, he might have discerned the shape of things to come, had he been able to understand the new underlying social trends.

The tragedy of Smuts proved itself in the end to be of the same order as those of Kruger, Botha and Hertzog. Atlas stumbled, not only because his burden became intolerable, but also because he came to regard himself as the only one fit to carry it.* No-one was there to take his place, because he overshadowed his own time to such an extraordinary degree. For this same reason, he could only be judged by his own standards.

Meanwhile, in the *Koffiehuis* in Cape Town, D. F. Malan and his group of eager, efficient young nationalist intellectuals – mainly lawyers, journalists from *Die Burger* and professional

---

* Atlas, in Greek mythology, brother of Prometheus, was one of the Titans who took part in the war against Zeus. He pays for this by being condemned to support the heavens: probably because this was his style, in any case. Prometheus, who likewise suffers a tragic fate because of his inordinate striving, has laid siege to the Fire of Heaven, which he wishes to present as a gift to mankind. In both cases the tragic error is that of trespass. Nietzsche in his *The Birth of Tragedy* indicates this difference in the style of the tragic hero.

politicians – sat around their coffee tables. They often listened to the measured tones of *Doktor*, but mostly to each other: discussing, not only the form and content of the new nationalism, but also, as a necessary corollary, the coming Republic. They regarded the increasingly urgent question of race relations as being of paramount importance, as it formed part of their deepening concept of the Afrikaner nation. They pondered how the other groups, white, brown and black, would fit into the new all-encompassing design. At the Afrikaans universities, similar groups of dedicated academics were labouring in their studies, adding deeper dimensions to the discussions of the men in the market-places of politics and journalism. Among the students, the new nationalism was being nurtured by a consecrated band of the nation-conscious *Afrikaanse Nasionale Studentebond*.

Three academic figures especially had constantly been addressing them, Dr N. Diederichs, Dr P. J. Meyer and Dr G. Cronjé. Of these Diederichs spoke in words of passionate oratory, Meyer in blunter, but equally effective, rhetoric. Cronjé, in a dry-as-dust style, expounded the most thoroughgoing analysis of the new political sociology with deep theological overtones. To all of them the present writer was once a witness.

Diederichs, at that time a professor of political philosophy at the Grey University College of the Free State, had published his study of nationalism as a world-view, in 1936.[22] It was, in many respects, to form the corner-stone of the great theorizing which was to arise from the fundamentals of the nation.

At the secret heart of all this activity was the deep inner circle of the *Broederbond*. Nothing so stirringly spoken by Diederichs, Meyer and Cronjé could find public utterance, before it had been the subject of intense pondering and discussion by this 'band of brothers', so completely devoted to the cause of alienated Afrikanerdom. Its members were the true spiritual progenitors of the new Idea which had already been born in 1935, somewhat prematurely, perhaps, but nevertheless lustily enough to provide the promise of vigorous future growth.

Diederichs' treatise on nationalism as a world-view, as the

basis of what would soon become the concept of 'Apartheid' or 'Separate Development', was the first sustained statement of theologized politics to come from an Afrikaner. Trained at various European universities, he was, however, in spite of obvious German influences, sufficiently rooted in his own Reformed tradition. His political philosophy, 'nationalism as a world-view and its relation to internationalism', was to become the first chapter in an evolving secular doctrine. It was the core of the Afrikaners' 'new politics', aligned not to Calvinism as to be found in the *Institutes*, but to its Puritan mutations, with later neo-Calvinist accretions.

'Nationalism rejects this concept of freedom ...', Diederichs had written, '... on the grounds of its doctrine that the individual in itself is nothing, but only becomes itself in the nation as the highest (human) community.'[23] He was remonstrating against liberalism.

Calvin, it should be remembered, had consistently stressed the value of the individual. The whole meaning of the Reformation, as restated in Geneva, was a revolt against the collective aspect of the Church and the insistence that, in the matter of salvation, there should be nothing between the individual soul and God.

Abraham Kuyper, once Prime Minister of the Netherlands, whose writings were to play such an important part in the development of neo-Calvinism among the Afrikaners, had correctly epitomized the spirit of the original Calvin when, in the first of his *Stone Foundation Lectures* at Princeton in 1898, he had said:

Hence we cannot recognize any distinction among men, save such as has been imposed by God himself, in that he gave one authority over the other, or enriched one with more talents than the other, in order that the man of more talents should serve the man with less, and in him serve his God. Hence Calvinism condemns not merely all open slavery of women and the poor; it is opposed to all hierarchy among men; it tolerates no aristocracy save such as is able, either in person or family by the grace of God, to exhibit superiority of character or talent, and to show that it does not claim this superiority of character or talent, for the sake of self-aggrandizement or ambitious pride, but for the sake of spending it in the service of God. So Calvinism was bound to find its utterance in the democratic interpretation of life; to proclaim the liberty of nations, and not to rest until both politically and socially every man, simply because he is a man, should be recognized, respected and dealt with as a creature created after the Divine likeness.[24]

Diederichs carefully spelt out the difference between the old nationalism (as under Hertzog) and the new. This was not the kind of nationalism, he said, which expressed itself on public platforms or at the polling booth. This was a nationalism which was a 'spiritual attitude, a path of life (*lewensrigting*) which coloured every expression of life'. This was nationalism as a world-view (*lewensbeskouing*) which did not accommodate itself to the human being who has acquired it, but which directed and led such a human being and made a servant of him. The new nationalism worked in people like a form-giving (*gestaltende*), compelling power. The individual or man as a single entity was an abstraction which did not exist. Outside of society and the communal life, the human being would never realize himself. Man was specifically called to be a member of the nation. Of all human groupings, the nation was the highest, the most all-inclusive, the most total. Without membership of a nation, the human being could never fully be himself. It was not our love for our fellow human beings which made of us a nation, he continued, but it was our love for our nation which formed our love for, our interest in and our responsibility for our fellow human beings of the same descent as we were. This was because we recognized in them people who were bearers, or should have been bearers, of the same national values and principles as ourselves.[25]

There was a clear indication in Diederichs' essay of the *Überbau* which would, in time, arise from this basic concept of the nation.

The highest, ideal order, that nation-transcending territory where nations meet each other in a complementary way, cannot be seen in any other than a religious light. In religion every human life, every nation, discovers its grounding and meaning. Without a religious point of relationship and an ultimate object, the universe, the nation, and the individual would be incomprehensible, senseless and purposeless ... On every particular nation especially there rests this special task to accept its providential role as a nation, and by realizing it to play its part in the ultimate attainment of the godly purpose of the universe ...[26]

... The nation contains the essence of being human. It is the form of the individual's spiritual realization and perfection ...[27]

Love of nation is not in the first place love of people, territories or states, but rather love of the ever-prevailing values, on which the nation is based.[28]

Very clearly therefore, nationalism is a passion for the *idea* of the nation, for the special abstraction of freedom which it represents. '... nationalism finds its final justification and anchoring in the religious belief that the very ground of the being of a nation is in the will and love of God; that my love for my nation is a part of my loving duty towards God.'[29]

Both Hertzog and Smuts knew nothing of these new profundities which Afrikaner nationalism was being given. Even if they had been fully aware of Diederichs' treatise and realized what impact he was making on young, group-orientated Afrikaner students at the time, it is doubtful whether they could have understood its full significance. Time would show that among these very students, studying at Pretoria, Potchefstroom, Bloemfontein and especially Stellenbosch, there were many future major participants in the growth and triumph of what the leading political commentator of the Afrikaans press, as late as February 1972, described as: 'a party of vision, of reform, of broad and far-reaching plans for South Africa', possessed of a 'central and dynamic idea'. He elaborated his description as follows: '... the party with a sense of direction, the party with a philosophy and a plan, not enquiring whether some or other voter is comfortable, or not, but the party which by high-minded leadership causes the people to fall in behind it, for the sake of South Africa.'[30]

All this was still completely foreign to the experience of both Hertzog and Smuts. As we have shown, this was largely because they were essentially from the 'Age of the Generals'. Their whole political temperament was different to that of the rising Afrikaner *burgerstand*, struggling against those who ruled in the Anglo-Saxon cities, and increasingly becoming imbued with the urge to restore the Afrikaner to power. But not nakedly so; only in terms of a 'central dynamic idea', dedicated to a 'philosophy'. What was slowly gathering form and strength was a new kind of plan. Afrikaner society, led by a devoted 'band of brothers' meeting mainly at night, was ardently concerned with what it increasingly regarded as its special vocation: the radical reconstruction of a world which had become alien and intolerable. It was the logical development of the process of internalization, following the trend which had been created by the Peace of Vereeniging. In short, it embodied the true Puritan approach.

The pointer, of course, to what was happening within the ranks of nationalist Afrikanerdom was the symbolic Ox-Wagon Trek on the occasion of the laying of the foundation stone of the new Voortrekker Monument in Pretoria. Hertzog had been invited to perform the ceremony. He had accepted the invitation, but on condition that it would be generally acceptable. However, when certain political leaders objected to his presence, he refused the invitation.

The opening then took place without the man who had done more than anybody else of the quarter of a million present to promote the cause of the Afrikaner *eie*. Smuts had not even been considered. The event was, in fact, a massive demonstration of the new thought among Afrikaners. Diederichs' book had by that time been out for almost two years. He, and many others like him, had been expressing his thoughts from many platforms. For Smuts especially, it was still a far-off, unreal and esoteric language.

There had been a time in South Africa when the redemptive idea had been that of the all-inclusive Empire. Rhodes had confessed that 'God's ideal type, his own Anglo-Saxon race' was destined to 'help on God's work and fulfil his purpose in the world . . . and so bring nearer the reign of justice, liberty and peace.'[31] His was the authentic voice of Empire. Smuts, who had been sensitive to such claims during the life-time of Rhodes, in time embraced the system. The Empire became the Commonwealth. This (thought Smuts) was a vindication of his position. Here was a group of sovereign states, freely associated, bound by a common loyalty to the crown and to the values which had emanated from the Mother of Parliaments, all in one unsurpassable tradition. Here, thought Smuts, was the embodiment of holism. He never had any doubt that the well-being of South Africa and all its peoples, including his own people, the Afrikaners, lay within this great, free association of nations. It was a scintillating vision, so eminently worthwhile that he, Smuts, could never hesitate to pursue it, knowing exactly where his country's duty lay. Here was such a shining cause that Smuts, very much like his old comrade-in-arms and later in politics, Hertzog, was unable to discern in the political activity around him something essentially like the old British messianic role. Here, too, politically radical man believed that he had a special vocation in the world.

Victorian imperialism, which was essentially a militant and messianic capitalism, was a case of the original Puritan mind taking the 'triumph of the economic virtues' to its logical conclusions. The Afrikaners, too, in the predictable development of their own idea of redemption, would also experience the rise of capitalism out of the same protestant ethic. This was not for some mystical reason, but simply because in the struggle for power which lies at the heart of all man's political gospelling, money sooner or later presents itself as the alternative certitude, the alternative (man-made) redemption.

If the socio-political ideal, as it had first been formulated in Puritan America, had served as a model for all radical politics in subsequent societies, even those far removed from the original protestant ethic, the history and circumstances of the Afrikaners of Southern Africa specially favoured it.

From the start the position in the two hemispheres had much in common. There was the similar Teutonic background. After a period of persecution, each group undertook a long voyage over an unmapped ocean towards a new freedom: the Anglo-Saxons under the Tudors and Stuarts; and those who later became the Afrikaners, under Philip of Spain, Catherine de Medici and Louis XIV.

In the new countries they were faced with much the same kind of challenge. The forbidding frost-bound wilderness of New England, 'rolling its snow-clad leagues towards the grave',[32] found its equivalent in the sun-smitten veld, stretching away into infinite blueness. This is the kind of landscape in which man, restored to the fundamentals of his faith, finds himself particularly stimulated. It was, as Tawney says of early New England, a wilderness 'to be subdued with aching limbs beneath solitary stars'.

The protagonists were the New England frontiersman in his deerskins, becoming in time of crisis a Minuteman; and the Trekker in his corduroys, becoming in time of crisis the burgher on commando.

On their arrivals in the new country, a bewildering unknown confronted each group. Such humans as there were would have to be subdued as savages, whether they were the Red Indians of North America or the Bantu of Southern Africa. In both continents it became a Calvinist ethic impregnated with the pioneer spirit; and at the same time the pioneer spirit impregnated with the Calvinist ethic.

The emergent Afrikaners found themselves in a strange land, part of a dark continent. They were facing a vibrant landscape, charged with hidden threats. From the start, halfway through the seventeenth century, they were the spiritual kin of those Anglo-Saxons who were extending their Revolution along its messianic course in the Mother Country. They were also the spiritual relations of the early New Englanders, though they could hardly be aware of it.

Consider the parallels with the Puritans generally.

There was, for example, the use of the vernacular, the discovery of which is a well-known phenomenon in times of fundamental renewal. Luther's contribution to German language and literature was an achievement to be compared with his struggle for the renewal of Christendom. It was the dialect of the people which he regarded as the natural and proper medium to reach into the hearts of those who were thirsting for the Word. Calvin himself soon put his *Institutes* into French. The English Puritans, in revolt against 'the airy dews of effeminate Rhetorick' of the elegant Anglicans, insisted on 'plainness in the sermons of the spiritual preachers'.

In time a similar eloquence and passion for the vernacular (Afrikaans), in preference to the classic language of antiquity (High Dutch), would mark the emergence of the secular religion of the Afrikaners.

The Afrikaners of the 1930s, in giving birth to their own socio-political ideal, even produced their own John Milton. He was N. P. van Wyk Louw, who was to become the foremost figure of his time in Afrikaans literature. Like Milton, he would start his career as a questing young academic, deeply concerned with the thoughts and feelings of those of his people who felt themselves to be strangers in a strange world.

> Simple people ...

he had written

> ... who perform
> true and singly bitter things
> and singly fall like grains of seed ...[33]

Also like Milton, he would progress in the course of some third-of-a-century from almost complete identification with the revolutionary idea, to a critical loyalty and thence finally to a transcendent view of his time, people and society. In the late thirties it was, as with Milton, still a case of the poet lending his gift of language to the ideal.

> Will never a mighty beauty come
> like hail-white thunderheads that bloom
> above your mountain's darkest stance
> and never a deed occur in you
> to echo over earth, and taunt
> Time with its impotence?[34]

It was mostly the Bible which provided the vernacular with its strength to become the language of the new revolutionary movement. The Authorized Version of 1611 was not so much to the credit of James I as to the long line of English churchmen who had laboured so diligently to put the Scriptures into the language of the people.

'They turned their learning and skill', Haller says, 'to the task of developing out of the familiar common speech an English appropriate to the lofty matter they had in hand ... The result was the marvellous idiom of the English Bible.'

The same can be said of the Bible in Afrikaans, which first became available in the early thirties, exactly at the time when the Afrikaner *burgerstand* was forming in the cities, a decade before guidelines for the Afrikaners' revolutionary thinking were being published everywhere.

The English Puritans, pouring forth 'hearty supplications to the Lord' as the spirit moved them, have a familiar ring about them to South African ears. So, too, do Cartwright and Owen, arguing for the construction of a Commonwealth with a truly Christian frame. Thomas Dekker also struck what was, for them, an agreeable note: 'Remember, O you rich men that your servants are your adopted children ...' Dod and Cleaver, insisting on the father being the strict and respected head of the house, were also in tune with their beliefs. The father was God's immediate officer in the home and therefore a kind of magistrate. The house itself was a little church and Commonwealth, within the greater church and Commonwealth. Women had their appointed places and their first duty was the care of their offspring. Thomas Cobbett required a respectful distance always to be maintained between parents and children: fondness and familiarity bred contempt. 'The idea of the family, like that of the state as a ship,' Walzer says, 'revealed once again the overbearing Puritan sense of purpose.' *Doelgerigtheid*, the Afrikaners of our day have called it.

The parallels are by no means confined to relationships within the family. Social disorder and the reaction to it provides the broadest base for comparison. The London of the Tudors and Stuarts was for a privileged few a city of wit, elegance and grace. For a great many more it was a case of 'suburbs' which were no other than 'dark dens for adulterers, thieves, murderers, and every kind of mischief worker'.

Thomas Hobbes' observation about the unchecked human leading a life which was 'solitary, nasty, brutish and short' might well have been the fruit of his observations in London.

Urban conditions in the late thirties, and especially the forties, in many parts of South Africa, resembled this state of affairs: the difference being that those who had been, as Haller says, 'deprived of village solidarity' and who had become disoriented in the growing mob, were now almost exclusively black people from the traditional African areas of the country. Nevertheless, the reaction of the Afrikaners, who were now in a position to reconstruct the world about them, was much like that of the English Saints resolving the social chaos of their time. There was a great rottenness in the state and it had to be repaired.

'Days of solemn prayer,' Walzer says of the English revolutionary period, 'were also the occasions for public and private "exercises" designed to stimulate religious zeal and political activity.' Before going to London for the meeting of the Short Parliament in 1640, Sir Robert Harley kept a day with his family, praying for guidance . . .

Years later, in 1649, when the monarchy went, the remaining parliamentarians (Harley not among them), the army officers and the king's judges were stimulated and sustained by days of 'public humiliation', fasts and frequent prayer meetings. All this was intended to reinforce devotion to the cause, 'to calm the consciences of men'.

Electioneering, the holding of public office and public administration have been characterized in Southern Africa by similar phenomena. A cabinet minister triumphs in his constituency at the polls. He solemnly publishes a notice in the newspaper ascribing his victory to God and thanking him for Grace extended. Assemblies of all kinds – from political gatherings and writers' conferences to meetings of school committees – are opened with prayer. Public prayer is a public duty. To this end, the radio system lends its unstinted support.

Days of humiliation are also standard practice when natural disasters threaten. And religious exercises in the form of broadcast home devotions, Pentecostal periods of deep, emotional revival, faithful church-going and powerful sermonizing have also been part of the Reformed tradition in South Africa.

*   *   *

Smuts, the Field-Marshal, Prime Minister, and *Oubaas*, leader of his country in war, was approaching the climax of a remarkable life. He probably knew neither Diederichs nor van Wyk Louw, except as names he might have casually heard or read about. Nor did he know any of the other intellectuals who were helping to form the new redemptive idea of nationalist Afrikanerdom. The true significance of the *Broederbond* was far to the right of his pale-blue line of sight. Like Hertzog, he saw the *Bond* only as a secret, potentially subversive organization, the members of which were, at least, not to be trusted with the running of the state. Therefore, he later took measures to prohibit all civil servants from belonging to it.

Far greater issues claimed his attention. What was happening in the *laager* of nationalist Afrikanerdom had become irrelevant. The world was moving towards a new era; and he, Smuts, would play his part in it.

The different factions of opposition under Malan and van Rensburg were scrapping with each other. In any event, Afrikaners in their tens of thousands were helping in the war effort. The United Party, supported by the Empire-minded Dominionites, the Labourites and the 'Native Representatives', was more firmly in power than any other government in the history of the Union had been. Smuts, had he studied Diederichs or listened attentively, might well have experienced an instinctive rejection of both style and sentiment. The real significance of what Diederichs was saying would, however, have escaped him. This would have been even more true if the speaker had been the weighty P. J. Meyer, addressing a group of enthusiastic Nationalist students.

'What especially comes to decisive and determining utterance in the religion of the Afrikaners,' Meyer wrote,

is the subjection to the ordinations of God as the Almighty and All-knowing Disposer over the lives and destinies of the individual and the *volk* even to the smallest details ... Subjection to the Ordinations of God as He has revealed it in His Word, and acceptance of the individual and national task as divine calling which should be honoured in His name, is then the directing channel in which the essence of Afrikaner *volkskap* (being as a nation) is unfolded, and in which the Afrikaans order of values, as it has been given in the Christian faith, is realized.

The Gospel is not directed to the human being as an absolutely autonomous and isolated entity, but to the human being as creature and therefore as a member of a specific nation...[35]

Not only the individual, but also the nation, as part of Creation, has been called by God...

The Afrikaner accepts his national task as a divine task, in which his individual life-task, and his personal service to God has been absorbed in a wider, organic context...[36]

This, like the undulating eloquence of Diederichs,* struck a new, abstract note in the world of Afrikanerdom. It was, however, not a new note in the world of man. Its style, as we have seen, had appeared in many places at many times. It was the language of political messianism, radical politics, an emerging socio-political ideal and the developing Afrikaner revolution. It was also the language of self-motivated man.

Meyer was very much in demand as an orator during the early forties, addressing a great variety of meetings with his brand of effective rhetoric. In 1942, when speaking to the students during a national conference, he reached conclusions which expressed the feelings of an ever more radical and inward-growing circle of Afrikanerdom:

To Afrikanerdom belong only those who by virtue of blood, soil, culture, tradition, belief, calling form an organic unitary society.[37]

This nation (*volk*) is by nature an organic wearer of authority (*gesagskleding*) with the patriarchal leader as the chief bearer of authority of the nation, and with the members of the nation as active and co-operative workers.

The national Afrikaner state of the future is therefore the political embodiment and ordering of the whole of Afrikanerdom as an organic articulation of authority, and is in this sense also a medium of Afrikanerdom to protect and promote its own fulfilment of calling (*roepingsvervulling*).

The Afrikaner national movement as bearer of the future national state of the Afrikaners is thus at the same time a people's institution by means of which a natural national leadership will be formed, the

---

* He has since become a benign Minister of Finance who amusingly quotes Shakespeare, Confucius and others, at budget speeches.

inwardly directed organic interaction of the nation can be assured and individually the national members (*volkslede*) can be disciplined by constructive service to the nation (*volksdiens*) as an organic whole.

In the future Afrikaner national state (*volkstaat*) the undivided power granted by God rests with the Afrikaner state authority. This undivided state power, is limited in its exercise by the sovereignty in a particular sphere (*soewereiniteit in eie kring*) ordained by God in original creation; in the organic human entities such as the Church, the individual, the family, and the nation. Furthermore, power shall only be exercised in accordance with the principles of law contained in the Word of God, and the natural legal ordinations (*regsgegewenhede*) as consistently revealed in history.

The positive and God-given rights of the individual, the family, the nation, and the Church, are then protected and promoted by the Afrikaner nation in the sense of mutual duties to society which may not be shirked.

The future Afrikaner national state will be a leadership state, an authoritative state, and a corporative state.[38]

Dr G. Cronjé also talked to the students, providing much food for thought for the many groups among the nationalist-minded Afrikaners discussing the past, present and especially the future, in terms of the new nationalism. For a number of years he had been developing his own total view of things. He finally published it in 1945. He called the book *'n Tuiste vir die Nageslag (A Home for Posterity)*.[39] It was closely aligned to what Diederichs, Meyer and some others had also written. But it was more than that. In its own way, it was a remarkable piece of preliminary draughtsmanship for the coming system. Essentially, everything which was to be part of an 'unfolding' of the redemptive idea of 'Apartheid' or 'Separate Development' was contained in these pages.

'The racial policy which we as Afrikaners should promote,' Cronjé stated at the outset of his book, 'must be directed to the preservation of racial and cultural variety. This is because it is according to the Will of God, and also because with the knowledge at our disposal it can be justified on practical grounds.'[40]

God's creation was one great whole with sense and meaning. Every part of this variety of creation (*skeppingsverskeidenheid*) within that whole had its own task and function. Every race could only honour its own task and function according to its own nature and potential, when it had the necessary *separate* opportunities to do this.

'Indeed,' he said,

the Boer people have themselves gone through the crucible of imperialist and capitalist domination and exploitation. They still show the wounds and bruises of it all. Their national life and culture have been disrupted. As a nation they almost perished because they served the interests of other people. They know what it means to see the *eie* destroyed, but they also know what it means to promote through their own efforts a national revival and restoration ... The Boer nation can therefore fully understand the sufferings of the Bantu. It is that same imperialism and capitalism, having them believe that the foreign is better than what is their own, which seeks to destroy their tribal life ...[41]

With a view to the future and to an enduring solution of South Africa's racial problems (and therefore also those of Africa as a whole, according to Cronjé) it was not only desirable but also necessary that Southern Africa, at least, follow a common policy of racial apartheid. In the long run, according to the Afrikaners' own view of Christian nationalism, the black race, under the tutelage of the Whites, but also by their own efforts and in accordance with their own disposition and potential, would develop their own system of values, culture, morality, world-view and spiritual aristocracy. This, too, would be 'Christian-nationalist' by nature. It would represent their own particular contribution to the culture of humanity, of which they formed a separate part. This would require complete separation of the races. Only in this way could the white race make certain of the purity of their blood and assure a home for their posterity. To this end and the solution of this great problem, the Boer nation had a task and vocation.[42]

Meyer,[*]expressing the same belief with a deep appeal to history, had written: 'In the vow at Danskraal ...' (just before the battle of Blood River), '... the Boer people entered into a Covenant with God so as to maintain themselves as God's people;

---

[*]Later to become Chairman of the Board of Control of the South African Broadcasting Corporation.

to honour their separate calling as God's ordination (*Godsbestemming*), to fulfil it to the glory of God.'[43] It was a Covenant, Meyer said, entered into on behalf of all posterity.

Cronjé worked out most assiduously the details of his suggested all-inclusive policy of 'Apartheid' or 'Separate Development'.[44] *Mutatis mutandis*, the same policy would apply to all the races in Southern Africa, even where, as in the case of the Coloureds, there was no separate territory. But a separate fatherland would have to be given to them, and their achievement would have to be their emergence into nationhood through their own strength, with their own world-view and culture.[45] There would have to be a Coloured Council to look after the interests of the coloured people. The Council would be made up of representatives from seven to ten regional areas. Presumably this was an interim measure.

Because the 'responsible guardian' could not escape his responsibility, which was also his calling, he should not only be guided by the wishes of those of whom he was in charge. He should have the courage to decide what was in the highest interests of the Whites as well as the non-Whites.[46] Power for the Whites was necessary. The white man was determined to retain supremacy in South Africa, because should he lose it, that would be the end of the white race on the continent of Africa.

The policy of apartheid was designed to ensure the survival of the white race. Justice towards 'posterity' (*nageslag*) was at the heart of it, but also justice towards the Bantu, whose survival as a separate race with their own culture, and whose development towards higher levels, would be ensured by it.[47] Of course, the implementation of the policy would cost a great deal. There was, however, no other final and permanent solution. The Afrikaners had to say: 'It shall be done, whatever the cost.' This was not something which could be measured in monetary terms.[48]

This was, indeed, a radical solution. But the shortest way to the overcoming of South Africa's problems was to implement racial apartheid in the most radical possible way.[49] This was required of the Afrikaners as their Christian duty.

Cronjé did not leave it at a mere discussion of the theory.

Vocation, justice, Christian duty, ethnic and cultural distinctiveness, the need for drastic measures... The detailed exposition of these qualities soon indicated that the high cost of the policy would include more than money. Generally, the social chaos still prevailing in the country would have to be overcome. Many white people had become victims of these social conditions, and on the whole South Africa was a hodge-podge (*mengelmoes*) society. In view of the still-existing poverty among many Whites (he was obviously thinking of the immigrant Afrikaners gathered in the fringe-areas of the cities), a condition brought about by imperialism and capitalism, far-reaching measures were required.[50] To this end, local racial segregation was immediately necessary, with an eye to racial purity and the prevention of miscegenation. This would be an interim measure and would not only mean residential but also political separation.[51] It is apparent from the context that Cronjé had in mind especially the Coloureds living in certain areas among the Whites.

The whole labour pattern would have to be altered. There were existing conditions (mixed unions, etc.) which threatened the survival of the Whites. Cronjé's clear indication was that legislation would be necessary so as to revise labour patterns which could not be reconciled with the basic concept.[52] There was a great danger of 'white' Coloureds trying to pass for white. There was great danger also of an infiltration (*insypeling*) of non-white blood into white in this manner.

The obvious conclusion to be drawn from Cronjé's detailed examination of this threat was that legislative action would have to be taken so as to be able to distinguish between Whites and 'white' Coloureds: establishing, perhaps, a population register.[53] Further legislation would be necessary to combat the threat of miscegenation: 'We can be of one mind that the more radical racial segregation is applied, the better it will be,' Cronjé declared.

The more consistently the policy of apartheid could be applied, the greater would be the security for the purity of our blood and the surer our unadulterated European racial survival ... total racial separation ... is the most consistent application of the Afrikaner idea of racial apartheid.[54]

For the securing of the future ('The Creation of a New Future'), an interim period of about one generation would be necessary: 'about 25 years'.[55] Presumably this would enable the relevant authority to implement the idea in all its practical details as suggested by Cronjé. By that time, the ideal of a re-ordering of the country in terms of the concept would have taken place. An assured future for the white race, and justice for all, would be the result.

This generation, Cronjé insisted, would have to attempt the total and final solution.[56] It was essentially a task for the white race.[57] That he was, however, thinking primarily of the Afrikaners is clear from his consistent reference to the 'policy of apartheid of the Boer people'.[58] In fact, a chapter-heading epitomizes it all as the 'Task of the Boer People'.[59]

Cronjé's concept was that of total separation, also territorially. Basically his total view was a remarkably correct forecast of what was to be attempted. The order which was ultimately to arise on the coming to power of the Afrikaners was not prepared to accept the demand for complete territorial separation. But almost every other detail of Cronjé's vision would become a part of the socio-political ideal of apartheid. Even his alternative use of the term 'Separate Development' was, in a sense, prophetic.

The book formed the subject of intense discussion within the *Broederbond*. In the cells (*afdelings*) Cronjé's facts, figures and arguments were thoroughly dissected, critically weighed and basically accepted. What strikes the objective viewer after more than a generation is the assumption and unquestionable belief, in the writings and speeches of Meyer, Cronjé and the other members of the new intellectual élite, that a new order would arise in which the Afrikaners would be able to implement the whole new concept of a reconstructed South Africa. On a par with this is their faith that this order would last for so long that the future could, in terms of the new vision, be finally secured.

The same enormous confidence had been apparent at the time of the draft constitution of the coming Republic. It was not affected by the brilliant success of Smuts's wartime leadership, nor the growing ascendancy of the anti-war groups – the

Herenigde Party under Malan, the *Ossewabrandwag* under van Rensburg and the New Order under Pirow. Everywhere in the country study groups were meeting, talking and planning, all on the assumption that the Republic and the reconstructed South Africa, containing the triumph of the Afrikaners, was only a matter of time.

The deep musings on the nature and content of the coming new order were not only the work of the more academic intellectuals. This was apparent from the work done by the *Suid-Afrikaanse Bond vir Rassestudie*, of which M. C. de Wet Nel, later to become one of the most dedicated exponents in politics of the idea, was at one time the secretary. From 1935 the group had already busied itself with the concept of 'Apartheid'. The word itself had become fairly current among both academic and political intellectuals. In 1943, D. F. Malan had already included the word in his political vocabulary.[60] In September 1944, a *Volkskongres* at Bloemfontein had decided:

That it is in the interests of the white and non-white populations of South Africa that a policy of apartheid be followed, so that each of the non-white population groups will find the opportunity to develop according to its own characteristics (*aard*), in its own area, so as to acquire eventually full control over their own affairs ... That it is the Christian duty of the whites to act as guardians over the non-white races until such time as they have reached that level where they can look after their own affairs ...[61]

In 1945, 'Apartheid' as a concept, without attention to the *minutiae*, was declared the official policy of the *Herenigde* Party. Two years later, a commission was appointed to work out all the details. No doubt Cronjé's book, which by this time had been discussed by study groups in many parts of the country, was immensely important in the translation into political terms of the concept of the nation, with its full implications for the multi-national situation in South Africa: and also in the formulation of the new socio-political ideal as 'practical politics'. Cronjé had published his second book in 1947, with two eminent theologians of the Dutch Reformed Church contributing chapters. Its title was an indication of its predominant thought and sentiment: *Regverdige Rasse-apartheid* (*A Just Racial*

Separation). It was generally an affirmation of what he had said in his first statement of the new vision. It was, however, more succinctly presented, and it had the advantage of the whole-hearted support of two respected church-figures.

The crux of the whole matter regarding guardianship, Cronjé declared, was to be found in the implementation of all the details of the policy. 'It amounts to intervention in the existing reality with a view to effecting such changes that the desired ideal will gradually be approached.'[62] 'Apart-making,' he went on to say, 'is a giant task. To hesitate before this would be a grave error. If there is no racial separation, racial mixture will follow. There is no middle way.'[63]

Remarkable, too, was Cronjé's formulation of the basic dilemma, albeit unconsciously. Those prepared to undertake the task, he said, would have to do justice towards themselves. Racial apartness was the only way out of this dilemma.[64] The implementation of the policy would require more daring and courage than the Whites of this country had ever been able to muster.[65] Should economic welfare stand in the way of this ideal, such then would have to be their sacrifice. Rather poorer and white, he said in effect, than richer and tan-coloured.[66]

When God had willed (ordained) separation, Prof. E. P. Groenewald emphasized in his own contribution to the book, then He wished this separation to be complete.[67] The fact that God had given the various nations their separate existences, implied that they should remain separate. Israel itself was the proof of how God had willed national separateness.[68] Scripture itself provided full support for this.

There was Deuteronomy 32:8.

When the Most High gave the nations their inheritance
when he divided the sons of man
he fixed their bounds according to the numbers of the sons of God . . .

There was also Acts 17:26.

From one single stock he not only created the whole
human race so that they could occupy the entire earth,
but he decreed how long each nation should flourish
and what the boundaries of its territory should be.

221

Above all, there was Genesis 11. Building the Tower of Babel, men attempted, sinfully, to preserve the unity and homogeneity of the human race. God intervened, however, and upset the plans of the builders by a confusion of tongues. He then ordained the division and distribution of nations over all the earth ...[69]

At a *Volkskongres* on race relations in Bloemfontein in July 1947, under the auspices of the Dutch Reformed Church, it was decided that, should there be sufficient Scriptural grounds for the policy, there was no need to concede to any argument from opponents.

Dr William Nicol, one of the influential Scottish line within the Dutch Reformed Church, emphasized the need for survival, in his contributions to the book. 'We can be good Christians,' he declared, 'and at the same time watch over the survival of our race with a holy gravity.' Justice, however, had as always to prevail. The Afrikaners, being true to their 'traditional policy', had a grandiose – *grootse* – calling.[70]

What did Smuts know or understand about all this? He had completed the most successful part of his whole career. His contribution to the Allied victory and his leadership, not only in South Africa but in the world generally, was beyond dispute. He had been an inspiration to the Allied cause in many spheres. The world that Atlas was carrying was far bigger than that of South Africa. That was his strength, but also his weakness.

The atomic bombs were dropped over Hiroshima and Nagasaki. The Third Reich had been destroyed; and now it was the turn of Japan. Out of the holocaust a new world would arise – and Jan Christiaan Smuts, the Boer General, the British Field-Marshal and Prime Minister of the Union of South Africa, would again play a leading rôle. He had been the mind behind the Covenant of the League of Nations. At Lake Success, he would again be called upon to advise and formulate. The preamble of the Charter of the United Nations was his work. 'He filled his roles as soldier, statesman, philosopher, and prophet with distinction. When he spoke the world listened. In Britain and the United States he was highly esteemed and he was repeatedly showered with honours.'[71] For Smuts, in the light of the tremendous things which had taken place on the world-stage, the bickerings and theorizings at home must have seemed much like Klee's twittering birds: unreal little bodies chirping away into balmy nothingness. Had his ear been closer to the ground, perhaps, instead of tuned to the cosmic music from greater, more splendid fields, he might well have discerned deeper notes at home which would have given him cause for alarm. He might even have recognized the sounds as being the same as those which, for the past two centuries, had constantly been heard in the Christian West.

The twittering of the birds, in fact, foreshadowed the dawn. It was, however, a threatening dawn rising broodingly, silently, in a murky sky – the upcoming Afrikaner Revolution.

The United Party, barely conscious of the many war-time irritations, was even less conscious of the fact that the Afrikaner soldiers who had gone out to fight the Italians and the Germans were still basically Afrikaners. They were members of the newly arisen *burgerstand*, still largely *platteland* strangers in Anglo-Saxon cities but now afforded a new sophistication by the very fact of their participation in the war. If there had still been a great many 'Poor-Whites' in 1938, the war finally put an end to both the term and the mass. The middle class had triumphed.

This was the situation in 1947, with the nationalist Afrikaners meeting in the *Broederbond* and elsewhere, talking into the small hours and cogitating on the new vision of a policy which would finally put an end to the inchoate state of the country. A massive black proletariat was building up in the ghettoes of the cities, posing a threat to the survival of the white race and especially to the Afrikaner nation, as lately conceived and described.

Even if Smuts did not properly understand what was taking place in the mind of nationalist Afrikanerdom, he might well have sensed that the maintenance of the political entity of the Commonwealth was, with the return of peace, no foregone conclusion. South Africa most certainly, especially the Afrikaners, needed to be reminded of the excellent company in which they had the fortune to be: part of a free association of kindred nations with the power to ensure the peace of the world.

The Puritans in Africa

To this end, King George VI and Queen Elizabeth and their two daughters, Princess Elizabeth and Princess Margaret, were invited to undertake a royal tour through South Africa.

It became a procession like a Roman triumph, with Smuts in the lead: an extended pageant of Commonwealth loyalty, Commonwealth membership and British sentiment. On the whole the Afrikaners took it with mixed feelings. In the cities they were inclined to be aloof, with H. F. Verwoerd, as editor of *Die Transvaler*, refusing to notice the presence of the royal company at all. On the *platteland*, Afrikaners still rooted to another kind of tradition received the visitors with rustic hospitality and not without humour. The King, Queen and the Princesses enjoyed it all: they were being taken around by the best guide in the country, Jan Christiaan Smuts. In a sense, he *was* the land.

At the start of the tour, Smuts was formally presented by the King with the Order of Merit. It seemed to be the crowning honour in his career. When the Royal Family eventually returned to Britain, Smuts and those around him were warmly confident that South Africa had been secured for a larger cause than the parochial politics of the nationalist Afrikaners. This indicated exactly Smuts's loss of contemporary sense.

About a year later, he was out of power. With almost nothing to raise expectations that the Government was in danger, the country went to the polls in May 1948. The rhetorical confidence which had been a feature of the planning of intellectuals like Diederichs, Meyer, Cronjé and others suddenly, astoundingly, proved to be of substance. The *Herenigde* Party under D. F. Malan, with 70 seats, supported by the Afrikaner Party, under N. C. Havenga, with 9, had a majority of 5 over the United Party, under Smuts, with 65, the Labour Party, under Madeley, with 6, and the 3 'Native representatives'.

Atlas had stumbled, because he could no longer watch the ground under his feet. What he had been supporting for so long now lay in ruins about him.

The country Smuts had served so long and well had suddenly, almost without warning, rejected him. The soldiers who had come back from the war and whose support he had taken for granted had turned against him. The machine of government, which had grown so ungainly and bureaucratic during the war, suddenly faltered and stalled. The cities had not, as expected, led to a loss of identity among the immigrant Afrikaners. Dr William Nicol had once said that the lack of Afrikaans-medium schools on the Rand in the early forties had caused a whole generation of young Afrikaners to be lost to Afrikanerdom. Somehow, this had not taken place. In the cities, with all their forces of disintegration, Afrikaners had naturally gathered in certain areas. Communities had arisen and they were now asserting themselves as the new *burgerstand*. It made no difference whether their way of life was not that of the *platteland* any more. They had become urbanized and had accepted the ways of the cities. Yet, superimposed on everything, was a new, resentful nationalism. Its inner force was derived from two sources: the experience of being foreign in areas of predominantly Anglo-Saxon culture; and the newly-apprehended threat of a black proletariat which, since the war, had become a daily experience. Everywhere black workers went streaming to their jobs by day and back to their smoky, formless places of abode by night. The more affluent English in the better suburbs were not as exposed to this threat as the Afrikaners, who were the recent arrivals. Even if the life-style of the *platteland* had been left behind, there were more ways than one of expressing group loyalty, or of expressing group-dread of submersion. Blood still walked where it could not creep. The demobbed soldiers had added immensely to the depth of this feeling.

Did Smuts ever think of it in this way? Did he ever, in the relative inaction of opposition after May 1948, discover the true reason for his defeat? It is doubtful. It is more likely that in the many pensive hours between May 1948 and September 1950, when he died at Doornkloof, he thought simply, but with a certain anguish, of the great rift which had grown through the years between himself and so many of his own people. He and Hertzog had been political opponents, yet they had remained friends. The same could be said of Havenga, who had fought with Hertzog. It could also be said of the other stalwarts of the Anglo-Boer War who still remained. Their numbers now were few. He, Smuts, did not understand these new Afrikaners with their involved and sweeping oratory.

The present author remembers meeting Smuts immediately after he had been given the Order of Merit by King George VI at Government House in Cape Town. That was in early 1947. Smuts was then at the pinnacle of everything: famous, revered, secure, and utterly confident. He spoke and acted accordingly. A year later the present author met him again, this time at the famous Kirstenbosch Botanical Gardens, at the foot of Skeleton Gorge, on the east side of Table Mountain. It was a Sunday afternoon. He was clad in khaki shirt and trousers, with the one sleeve of the shirt hanging loose. There was a stave in his hand, and on his head a white panama hat. He had spent the day on his beloved mountain. Coming down the pathway in the gorge, he would stop every now and again, to chat to those who recognized him and paid their respects. His pale-blue eyes seemed constantly to be searching the view over the Cape Flats to the surf-fringed sea and the distant mountains.

What was he thinking about? In that far-probing mind there would still have been a rich variety of memories gathered in the course of a long journey: remembrances of reading Kant's *Critique of Pure Reason* in the veld, while on commando; condemning Colyn to die for treachery to his fellow Boers; sunlit family days at Doornkloof where the grasslands of the highveld swept up to the homestead; discussing Hegel and holism and the incomparable flora of the Western Cape with Rudolph Marloth at three in the morning; botanizing through Southern Africa with Hutchinson of Kew; glorious days on his beloved Table Mountain; with, as might have seemed, all the land before his feet. He might even have recalled the surprise registered when during the war he had arrived in Johannesburg from Cairo, producing from the Dakota Queen Frederika of Greece as an unexpected visitor ...

In May 1950 Smuts suffered a slight coronary thrombosis and was confined to bed. His wife, and the rest of the family, were unanimous that he should not be sent to hospital, but should remain in bed at Doornkloof.

At first he insisted on keeping to an old, rusty, iron bedstead with a coir mattress, on a small enclosed *stoep* adjoining his study. After much persuasion, he agreed to take to his bed in the tiny bedroom near his study.

From everywhere in the world, inquiries and good wishes started pouring in to Doornkloof. From everywhere advice and a variety of medicaments were sent.

'Never did he speak any words of criticism or bitterness of his political foes,' his physician recounted. '...The only slight tone of disappointment I ever noted during my conversations was against those of his fellow-Afrikaners who, he thought, did not regard him as one of them because he thought wider than the South African scene.'[72]

What moved him deeply was to be taken on trips into the beautiful highveld country. On 4 September, being somewhat better, he was even allowed to be driven to his beloved bushveld. After this last day in the veld, which had been such a vital element in the personality which was Smuts, he died after a sudden collapse, in the presence of all his family.

The chronicler of these last days tells how he went to Doornkloof and met Mrs Smuts, standing alone under a dim electric light. Together they went to the room where the *Oubaas* – the Old Master – was lying.

'He lay in his military uniform, and quietly she said: "*Dag, Pappa, slaap gerus. Totsiens!*"* And as she turned to leave the room: "He is with Japie now." – Japie being her eldest son, who had died some years before.'

He was buried on 15 September. The funeral procession moved from Irene to Pretoria, and from there by train to Johannesburg.

At each station on the way ... the speed was slackened to permit the standing crowds on the platforms to pay their last respects. Crowds of all races ... were on the station.

At Irene Station, near his home, an African children's choir stood to sing the train through the platform lined with flowers. At Olifantsfontein, Africans lined the fences along the rail track, heads bowed, hands folded. A quarry edge was lined with silent watchers ...[73]

---

* 'Good-bye, Papa. Sleep well. Till we see each other again!'

Policemen and ex-servicemen of the Second World War lined the streets, some grim, some weeping, but all at attention. *Oudstryders* – veterans – of the Anglo-Boer War were there, too. They were the last of a generation. The Age of the Generals had finally, irretrievably, sunk into history.

At the same time it was the confirmation that a new era had arrived: the Revolutionary Age of a Band of Brothers.

The growth of an intellectual élite out of the new *burgerstand* was the true power behind the revolutionary idea of the forties. The broad basis was a great variety of 'separatist' cultural societies and organizations, all under the aegis of the *Broederbond*: but with relatively few in the know and ostensibly linked by a strictly culturally concerned co-ordinating organization.[1]

By the late forties, the Party had appointed a Commission to formulate the new thought for party purposes, with a view to the coming general election of May 1948. The belief that the term 'apartheid' was here for the first time put into currency is only true insofar as it then became part of the political issues of the day. As we have already seen, Cronjé, especially, had made full use of the term, also its alternative – separate development – in his book *'n Tuiste vir die Nageslag*. With great thoroughness he had also examined all the logicalities of the new concept.

Chairman of the Commission was P. O. Sauer, son of J. W. Sauer, who with John X. Merriman and James Rose-Innes had served in the Rhodes cabinet in the early nineties. With much of the Cape tradition of moderation in him, he seems to have acted as a catalyst. In the Commission there was also E. G. Jansen who was to be Minister of Native Affairs in the new Nationalist Government, and in 1950 also the first Afrikaner to become Governor-General of the Union of South Africa. He had been writing and speaking on the new political fundamentalism almost at the same time as Cronjé, but in a more selective field.

'We as Whites,' he had once stated,

have been instrumental in the disruption of the tribal life of tens of thousands of Natives. We have robbed them of the opportunity of undergoing their own development. We have tried to make white men of them which they can never be. We allow all sorts of strange ideas to be propagated amongst them, so that the authorities and all whites are increasingly discredited in their eyes.[2]

What the Commission ultimately produced was in the nature of a party manifesto, as well as a confession of faith. All the Afrikaans newspapers supporting the National Party (as the *Herenigde* Party was now generally referred to) published the findings prominently.[3]

The policy of apartheid, the Commission decided, was based on the Christian principle of right and justice. In contrast to democratic rights for all, withholding it from nobody on the basis of race or colour, a system was preferred which would not only maintain and protect the white race as a distinctive group, but would also provide the same guarantee for all national groups as separate communities. 'In their own areas' such groups would be able to live and develop their full capacities as national entities. All groups would not only discover a new self-respect and national pride, but also mutual respect. No one race would any longer threaten the future of any other. To this end, it was fundamentally necessary for the white race to be protected and maintained in its position (of guardianship). Any policy, *lewens-en-wêreldsbeskouing* – world-view – or political belief which denied or threatened this would need to be resisted. There was no question, the Commission emphasized most gravely, of suppressing or exploiting the non-Whites. The ideal of separation between the races would take place on a 'natural basis'. The various national groups would be rooted in their national soils. Such Bantu as had become de-tribalized would be stabilized by a strict system of influx control. They would live in separate areas and not be regarded as permanent residents. They were 'visitors', having come to the white areas to offer their services, while still being attached to their traditional homelands. As such they would not be entitled to share in the social and political rights of the Whites. In this way the 'white character' of the cities would be protected.

Labour organization and education would also become part of the white guardian's responsibility. Bantu trade unions would not be allowed and labour control would be instituted. The state itself would see to the welfare of Bantu labourers. Bantu education would have to be aligned to the special needs and level of development of the Bantu. It would use the vernaculars and take full cognizance of the national characteristics of the people it had to serve. It would, in fact, be both Christian and national.

In the House of Assembly and the Cape Provincial Council, representation would cease. The seven special senators would remain, but would have restricted voting rights. Local government in the various Bantu reserves would be instituted; and, in the cities, urban councils would be purely advisory.

For the Coloureds, a Representative Council would be established with the right of electing three white representatives each to the Cape Provincial Division and the House of Assembly. Local councils to see to the special interests of the coloured people would also be instituted.

The half-a-million Indians in the country would have no representation whatsoever in the law-making processes. They were a foreign element and would, like the Coloureds and the Bantu, be settled in separate areas. The activities of the many Indian traders outside their own areas would also be drastically cut. The proper policy for the Indians was one of repatriation to their country of origin. To this end, the co-operation of India would be sought.

Essentially, there was a clear consensus between Cronjé's exposition of the 'permanent solution for our race problems' and what was contained in the Report. What Cronjé's design had included but which the Report lacked would, in some form or other, become part of the legislative programme the new government of Malan was to embark upon during the early fifties with reforming zeal.

The Report could be seen as a statement of the new theologized nationalism with all its corollaries and its conclusive crystallization after its growth of a decade or more. The students whom Diederichs, Meyer and Cronjé had addressed so stirringly in the late thirties, had by this time reached political maturity and were already impatiently hammering at the portals of politics. Among them was B. J. Vorster, who had been active in the *Ossewabrandwag* during the war, and had been interned by

Smuts for his pains. As a student at Stellenbosch and a leading figure in student politics, he had listened attentively to the speeches by Diederichs, Meyer and Cronjé. Now the time seemed to be arriving to put away all differences between the National Party, the *Ossewabrandwag* and the Afrikaner Party, and unite as Afrikanerdom. This was the dream of Malan, and the dream was being fulfilled. Vorster, too, would later become Prime Minister.

Die Burger's summary was not the formal manifesto, which was to follow later. It contained the heart of the Sauer report. Again it emphasized the fundamental principles of the new approach: in every possible sphere of the national life there would be separation between the races. This would be both to prevent race friction and to give each ethnic group the opportunity to develop to its full extent 'within its own area'. The Whites would engineer and administer the dispensation as a matter of trust, vocation and guardianship. The alternative was *gelykstelling* – equality – and that would mean the end of Western civilization.

The formal declaration by the National Party of its race policy was also confirmation that the politics of Afrikanerdom had finally been accepted as more than just a working programme for the running of the country. It was now the logical expression of a *volk in beweging* – a people's movement. The goal towards which they were now striving with such disarming confidence, *doelgerigtheid* – dedication to an ideal – and energy, was that of the 'permanent solution'. This meant the final securing of the future and the definitive vindication of all that the Afrikaners in their 300 years of history on the continent of Africa had worked, hoped, prayed and suffered for. They were a people who had articulated for themselves a political theology and secular creed, with a view to establishing their identity and survival.

When exclusive Afrikaner power came like some heavenly herald announcing the end of *vreemdelingskap* – the effect of being strangers in their own country – and also the promise of the future, it was the occasion for bewildered joy. The pervading mood was much like Wordsworth's at the time of the French Revolution

> Bliss was it in that dawn to be alive
> But to be young was very heaven. . .

For many, the hand of Providence was once more unmistakably in evidence – as it had been at Vegkop, Blood River and Majuba . . . It demanded deep reverence, humble thankfulness and renewed dedication to the ideal of a justly separated and therefore revivified society. It required from the Afrikaners a *geloofsdaad* – an act of faith. The act would be the all-inclusive unfolding of the redemptive idea. The faith would be, albeit unknowingly, the secular one of revolutionary Afrikanerdom.

A decade or so after the National Party's accession to power in 1948, a theologian of the Dutch Reformed Church wrote at the end of an exhaustive justification of the policy of accommodation of the Calvinist ethic to the new vision:

> Should the non-Whites then cruelly murder us and cut us into shreds, then that barbarism will triumph which was so wondrously checked at Blood River. But this, precisely, is for us a matter of faith: we believe that God in any case has made merciful provision for our people. But in any case, our choice remains that of rather perishing on the way of obedience than to melt into the non-Whites, to forfeit our identity and our sacred calling.[4]

The distinguishing mark of any of the 'revolutions of the saints', or their revivals in some or other form at various points in history, is a collective sense of vocation.

Growing in any grace is the exercise of that grace, Perry Miller noted in his analysis of the Puritan mind. All human institutions, as de Tocqueville said of the New England radicals, become malleable, capable of being shaped and combined at will. And Reinhold Niebuhr observed of Puritan America generally that its citizens believed that they were a separate nation, called by God to create a new humanity.

When the Afrikaners suddenly found themselves in power in 1948, it was the real start for them of 'growing in grace by the exercise of that grace'. They were going to construct a moral world in which everything would become malleable, capable of being shaped and combined at will. They would start to behave as a separate nation called by God to create a new humanity.

The great figure in this attempt to reconstruct the world in terms of a new socio-political ideal, towering over all his contemporaries, was not the man who, that day in May 1948, found himself Prime Minister of South Africa. It was not D. F. Malan, nor his immediate successor, J. G. Strijdom. It was H. F. Verwoerd, who, as editor of *Die Transvaler*, had become the most articulate intellectual in the new dispensation.

Kruger, Hertzog and Smuts, as we have seen, were men of tragic dimensions in the style of Atlas. Verwoerd, too, was to attain tragic stature, because of the manner of his death. As such, he would be the epitome of the Promethean Afrikaner.

The myth of Prometheus concerns the Titan, friend and benefactor of mankind, who steals the fire of heaven from the gods by holding a fennel-stalk close to the sun. As a result he then becomes the fire-bearer to mankind, whose survival in a cold and cheerless world is at stake. In the second and only remaining part of the Aeschylean trilogy, Prometheus' 'love for human kind' is described as that of a 'god not fearing the wrath of the gods', because he has 'given to mortal men honours beyond their due.'⁵ In the play, Power and Force, with the aid of Hephaestus, bind the miscreant to a rock in a Scythian gorge. According to the myth an eagle then devours his liver which is continually renewed. In the play this is hardly relevant, for it is Prometheus' heroic defiance which is the heart of the matter. Of tyrannous Zeus, father of the gods, Prometheus dares to say: 'Yet not care was in his heart for miserable men, and he was fain to blot out the whole race ... I only dared; I rescued mankind from the heavy blow that was to cast them into Hades.'

This man, declares the leader of the Chorus, is 'fashioned of rock'. He will concede nothing. It is not through pride and insolence that he defies the power set against him. It is rather because he alone listened to the 'sad story of mankind, who like children lived until I gave them understanding and a portion of reason.'

> Let tempests beat on the earth
> Till her rooted foundations tremble ...
> Yet all he shall not destroy me!

Neither D. F. Malan nor his successor, J. G. Strijdom, would become either another Atlas or the first (Afrikaner) Prometheus. Both were transitional figures. The process of internalization of Afrikaner politics, its adoption of a theological perspective and the formulations of a distinctive Afrikaner world-view, which the new intellectuals had so assiduously wrought, had only obliquely affected them. D. F. Malan, whose political roots were still in the soil prepared by Hertzog, had as a controlling urge the unification of uprooted and fragmented Afrikanerdom. In this he succeeded outstandingly, but it became such an overriding passion that he was relatively impervious to the new socio-political ideal which was slowly but surely being hammered out in the many intense discussions of the inner circles.

Malan's view of apartheid – or, as Cronjé had already preferred to call it, 'separate development' – was relatively simplistic. God had ordained the nations to be as they were, he would declare. This he accepted with restful assurance. God had decreed *verskeidenheid* – variety; and so it had to be accepted. Nature itself was the evidence of this. Why, in the animal world, too, there was a natural and distinct separation between the species. Anybody who knew the habits of the sea-birds on the coastal islands of the Cape could testify to this. The penguins and the Cape gannet never mixed. Neither did the zebras and the wildebeest where they grazed together in their natural habitats. The political kingdom was something different to the Kingdom of God, which was not of this world. Above all, the Afrikaners in power had to be large-hearted towards those entrusted to them . . .[6]

There is no evidence that Malan ever involved himself deeply with the kind of grand design which Cronjé had propounded with the support of theologians and which intellectuals within his party had been working on in various fields. The restoration of the alienated Afrikaners – who had now more or less established themselves in the cities – was of such importance that the matter of race relations generally received only secondary attention. Nothing indicates this better than Malan's autobiography. The very title indicates its theme: *Afrikaner Volkseenheid en my Ervarings op die Pad daarheen (Afrikaner National*

Unity and My Experiences on the Way to it.) In the whole book – which, within its limits, is valuable enough – there is hardly a reference to the greater issues of colour facing not only Afrikanerdom, but South Africa generally.

Almost the whole of Malan as a political leader, as the first Prime Minister of a completely Afrikaner government, could be summed up in his own two mottoes, which he never tired of emphasizing. The first was: 'Bring together all who, from inner conviction, belong together.' The second was: 'My God, my people, my country!'

J. G. Strijdom, who succeeded Malan when he retired in 1954, was a similar figure. He was a charismatic man of much forcefulness but he, too, seldom indulged in the full theory of the new socio-political ideal. God, people, country, for those who belonged together because of 'inner conviction', was sufficient for him, also. The inner conviction of Strijdom – and here he made other emphases than Malan had done – was firstly the coming Republic. It would be a white Republic, because white supremacy was indispensable for the good of all. The Afrikaners, especially, had the inescapable duty to govern well for the good of all. They should never shirk this responsibility, nor should they be afraid to govern. On the whole, as in the case of Malan, his political philosophy was etched in broad strokes without too many subtleties; and in the Transvaal especially it had great appeal.

D. F. Malan was already in his middle seventies when the mantle of the premiership fell upon him. It was in the eve of his life and the six-and-a-half years he held office was more in the nature of an elder statesman enjoying the fruits of years of unswerving faith in, and service towards, the cause of his people. The younger men who had grown up politically under his guidance had developed and refined their thought in the various commissions, study groups, executives and inner circles in which they were active. So they soon became the true, dynamic force within the new government. This was especially true of Verwoerd whose single-minded drive and intelligence were apparent from the start. The 'torrent of legislation' which followed during the fifties constantly bore the stamp of his

intellectual approval. Via the *Broederbond* there were other
dedicated minds, all helping to translate the *apartheidsgedagte* –
the concept of separation – into positively negative and negatively
positive law-making. They were determined to see to the logical,
consistent 'unfolding' of the idea. Most important among these
was still P. J. Meyer. This was perfectly understandable: it was,
after all, not just a party having its run of office, merely being
concerned with the transient matters of the day. It was literally
a *volk in beweging* – a people's movement.

Verwoerd had been defeated in the election of 1948, but had
entered Parliament as a senator. In 1950, he became Minister
for Native Affairs. In the determined stride of the revolution
there was primarily the massive effort to deal with the shapeless
black proletariat of the Rand; to make them fit into the general
design. In the vast, rationalized operation against the inchoate,
this was the obvious starting-point.

Verwoerd was soon at the centre of things. He had the vision.
He had been writing burningly, at length, about apartheid in
his newspaper for nearly a decade-and-a-half. He was utterly
devoted to the ideal. This he epitomized in a speech to the
Senate in September 1948: 'In every field of life one has to fix
one's eyes on the stars, to see how close one can come to
achieving the very best, to achieving perfection.'[7]

The content and style of that first major speech was already
unmistakably that of a man who believed that he was guided by
the hand of destiny.

'What is the situation as it exists?' he asked.

Europeans and non-Europeans travelling mixed in the trams and in
the trains; Europeans and non-Europeans mixing are already in hotels
and places where meals are served; engaged more and more in taking
possession of the theatres and the streets; engaged in devastating the
reserves; engaged in seeking learning which they do not use in the
service of their own people, but which they use to cross the border line
of European life, to become traitors to their own people . . .[8]

And the man speaking in the Senate on that September day
left no doubt about how he planned to correct this *mengelmoes*,
this mixture, of a society.

I want to state here unequivocally now the attitude of this side of the House, that South Africa is a white man's country and that he must remain the master here. In the reserves we are prepared to allow the Native to be the masters; we are not masters there. But within the European areas, we, the white people in South Africa, are and shall remain the masters . . .[9]

The various tribal groups would find national homes where their own 'brains and intelligence' would find expression. In the urban areas, which he regarded as the 'white man's country', they would have 'local rights' and local councils. The Fagan Report of 1948, which had declared that the urban Bantu had to be accepted as a permanent part of the urban scene, was summarily rejected. Those Bantu who came to the cities were like the Italian workers going to France. They were merely visitors.

For the purposes of preventing race friction, there would be separation on every possible level. The concomitant of this was full and worthy development of the reserves.

Where we are prepared to accord to non-Europeans the right to their own opportunities of development, where we bring it about not by means of the sword, but through the benevolent hand of the Europeans who are in the country, then we do not arouse the suspicion of the world outside . . . that there is oppression, but show them there is a policy which seeks right and justice towards all.[10]

Pelzer remarks that the speech, made on an Opposition motion of 'no confidence', was a 'revelation'. What it revealed was not only a man utterly devoted to the ideal of a South African society in terms of the basic concept of the nation as the pre-eminent entity and to the full restoration of each race to its own, but also a man with leadership qualities, equalled by no-one else in the country. Here was no ordinary politician or even statesman. Here was a man of unusual intelligence, integrity and courage. He spoke without notes and with great clarity, logic, conviction and at great length. He was never bitter, ruffled, or at a loss. He knew exactly what he wanted to say and how to say it. He had the dominant presence of a man called to a task.

For the next eighteen years, Verwoerd would variously enlarge upon the themes of his speech to the Senate of September 1948. Certain emphases would shift and refinements would take place. These would include an enlargement of the concept of the nation so as to accentuate whiteness rather than Afrikaner cultural affinity. It would also include the positive pronouncement that the Bantu homelands would be free to develop towards complete, sovereign independence. This, however, would by no means be new to the *apartheidsgedagte*. It would, in fact, be fully in accordance with Cronjé's plea in 1945 that the Bantu undergo their own 'Christian-national development'[11] and have their 'own fatherland in which they can enjoy national self-determination, and where social justice can be accorded them . . .'[12] On the whole, however, Verwoerd would not deviate in the slightest degree from the concept he had analysed, and the design he had sketched in his first major speech as a parliamentarian. He would revise nothing.

In 1950, as already noted, he became Minister for Native Affairs. In 1958 he succeeded J. G. Strijdom, who died in office after serving for only three years after the retirement of D. F. Malan in 1954.

In 1960, after a series of African riots in the outskirts of towns and cities during the previous year, there was the emergency of Sharpeville. The Pan African Congress had encouraged Africans to refuse to carry passes and to go to police stations and invite arrest. A large number of these protestors, near the police station at Sharpeville, were fired upon and sixty-nine were killed. In Cape Town, 39,000 Africans moved in an amazing procession upon the city, after riots had also broken out in the nearby African townships. A few weeks later, an attempt was made on the life of Verwoerd by a white man, Pratt. Although critically wounded, he miraculously survived and made a complete recovery.

The country was in a state of emergency. But, by August, peace had been restored. In October of the same year, a referendum decided in favour of a republic, possibly within the Commonwealth. It was as much a logical outcome of the concept of separate white nationhood as the abolition by Acts of Parliament in 1957 of the Union Jack as a South African flag, and of *God Save the Queen* as a South African anthem.

With both the African National Congress and the Pan African Congress prohibited by special legislation, Verwoerd proceeded in March 1961 to London in an atmosphere of restored but uncertain tranquillity, in order to attend the Commonwealth Premiers' Conference. The object was to give formal notice that South Africa intended changing its form of government to become a republic. Sharply critical attitudes towards apartheid on the part of the other members of the Commonwealth, strengthened by the troublous events of the recent past, forced the issue. With expectant silence at home, Verwoerd took the decision. South Africa would leave the Commonwealth and henceforth go it alone – as a republic. It was the culminating moment in the 'triumph of Afrikaner nationalism'.[13] It was also the fulfilment, for the while, of the Afrikaner dream, and a triumph for a man who, though himself not a born Afrikaner, had become Afrikanerdom's most articulate and vital exponent. It was not merely the culmination of his work as Premier since 1958, but the climax to his quarter-of-a-century-long devotion to an ideal, first as a newspaper editor, then as Minister for Native Affairs, and lastly as Prime Minister. He believed unquestionably in the ability of those with the right temperament, ideas, faith and sufficient vitality to organize the impossibly involved South African complex into an enduring system, providing identity, peace, security and happiness for all.

From September 1948, when he first addressed the Senate on the great issues before the country, to 31 May 1961, when the Republic of South Africa was at last formally inaugurated, it was the presence of Verwoerd which remained the dominant element. Even when he deferred with great respect towards D. F. Malan or J. G. Strijdom, the sensitive observer would have had no doubt which personality was the truly dynamic and constructive one. '. . . he impressed both his supporters and opponents with his intellect, his dedication and his strong will. More than anyone else he was the architect of and driving force behind the policy of apartheid . . .'[14]

How precisely had the idea 'unfolded' during the fifties and early sixties?

Never in history have so few legislated so programmatically, thoroughly and religiously, in such a short time, for so many divergent groups, cultures and traditions, than the nationalist Afrikaners of the second half of the twentieth century. Never has such a small minority of all those affected done so with such a high sense of purpose, vocation and idealism. Never have so few drawn such sharply critical attention from a wondering world. Never has such a volume of criticism been so wide of the mark.

For almost all of it was directed against the 'harsh, oppressive policies' of the Nationalist Government; against the 'tyranny of apartheid'. *It was ineffective because it did not understand that the manifest harshnesses, the patent injustices, were all the oblique but necessary results of a most rational, most passionate, most radical will to restructure the world according to a vision of justice; all with a view to lasting peace, progress and prosperity.* As such it was true to the peculiar life-style of Western Puritan man, which had expressed itself in a variety of movements from both the radical Left as well as the Right: not merely in their countries of origin, but everywhere where their influence triumphed.

There are two dicta of H. F. Verwoerd which are crucial in this regard. They express the true power, but also the true weakness, of the peculiar redemptive idea to emerge from the *burgerstand* which Afrikanerdom, too, had become.

They first formed the heart of Verwoerd's *Message to the People of South Africa* on 3 September 1958, ten days after the death of J. G. Strijdom, when Verwoerd had been elected by the Party caucus to the Premiership. 'The policy of separate development,' Verwoerd said in his broadcast to the nation, 'is designed for happiness, security and the stability provided by their home language and administration for the Bantu as well as the Whites.' The heart of what has been said here is: designed for happiness.

The second dictum was in the nature of a slogan which Verwoerd had coined to indicate the purpose of the system. '*Skep self u eie toekoms!*' he declared. 'Create your own future!'

In a circular on 9 September 1966, mourning the tragic death of H. F. Verwoerd, Prime Minister of the Republic of South Africa, the executive of the South African Bureau of Racial Affairs – Sabra – declared: 'With this slogan he planned and gave form to the policy of autogenous development by virtue of which a right to exist will not only be guaranteed to the Whites, but also to the non-white ethnic groups in South Africa.'

The dicta can be combined into a single sentence: create your own future by a design for the happiness of all.

The law-making of the fifties was predominantly negative in character: attempting to separate the 'scattered and mixed' conditions Verwoerd had referred to in his Senate speech of September 1948. The 'cornerstone of positive apartheid', as T. E. Dönges was to refer to it,[15] thereby became the *Group Areas Act* (1950) in which clearly demarcated residential areas were devised for all the various racial groups. Dönges, who was second only to Verwoerd in his intellectual approach to the idea of apartheid, his rational planning of its implementation and competence, fully realized that this would, in the course of the next decade or more, mean a gigantic reorganization of communities. Whole populations would have to be shifted, many from areas where they had lived for generations.

A special board was instituted to start investigations prior to marking out all such areas in and around towns and cities where White, Coloured, African and Indian would henceforth have to live. In almost all cases this meant the removal of the 'non-Whites', because the great majority of the Whites had more or less firmly established themselves in the better areas.

Closely akin to the *Group Areas Act* was the *Resettlement of Natives Act* (1954), by which the Government empowered itself to remove some 100,000 Africans from the squatter camps and slums in the western areas of Johannesburg and to re-settle them in hygienic and well-ordered conditions in Meadowlands. It was nevertheless the occasion for Trevor Huddleston's world-ringing cry of protest that a living community (Sophiatown) had been cruelly disrupted.[16]

For the new system to work it was patently necessary to stabilize the racial groups and, as far as possible, also to know exactly to what group a person belonged. Any crossing of racial lines (although there had never been very much) was made even more difficult. Among the first of the measures to be taken by the new government was the *Prohibition of Mixed Marriages Act* (1949). The following year, its complement was adopted in the form of the *Immorality Amendment Act* (1950) which prohibited sexual intercourse between Whites and *all* non-Whites. Where it was often virtually impossible to distinguish between darker-skinned Whites and lighter-skinned Coloureds a *Population Registration Act* (1950) (for the compilation of a racially-classi-fied national register) was obviously necessary. A *Reservation of Separate Amenities Act* (1953), which kept the races apart in their daily 'mixing' in public places, was also necessary. '... what had previously been custom had now become written law.'[17] The various race groups would henceforth be compelled to make use of the separate public amenities (on buses, trains, in theatres and so on); and it would be no defence to plead in-equality in the provision of such amenities.

For the purpose of controlling the movements of individual Africans in the country, an *Abolition of Passes and Co-ordination of Documents Act* (1952) was passed, rationalizing existent pass laws, streamlining them and providing now for a 'reference book' to be carried by all African men. The *Bantu Education Act* (1953) was meant to reorganize African education more or less on the lines of the recommendations in the Sauer Report. The *Extension of University Education Act* (1959), following somewhat later, was a logical development of the principle of ethnic self-sufficiency, closing the 'white' universities (except by way of special permit) to all Africans, Coloureds and Indians, who would henceforth have to attend their own institutions of higher learning.

Of cardinal importance in the implementation of the *apart-heidsgedagte* was the *political* separation of the races. The *Bantu Authorities Act* (1951) established rudimentary structures for African self-government in the various homelands. The act was elaborated to more sophisticated levels by the *Promotion of Bantu Self-Government Act* (1959). The *Urban Councils Act* (1961) provided for local advisory bodies in the cities, intended primarily to provide ethnic links with the tribal areas to which the urban Africans, within the framework of apartheid, were essentially bound.

Meanwhile, almost from the start of the new administration, there was a tougher nut to crack: that of the political representation of the Coloured people, for whom no separate homeland existed and who somehow had to be fitted into the design. Various attempts were made by legislation to remove the Coloured people from the common roll and to provide separate political institutions for them. The Opposition, basing their resistance on the requirements of the *South Africa Act* (1910) for a two-thirds majority, took the matter to court. When the Appeal Court decided against the Government in March 1952, recourse was taken to an act establishing Parliament itself as the ultimate High Court in constitutional matters. This, too, was declared invalid. It was in the time of the premiership of J. G. Strijdom that the struggle was finally resolved by appointing sufficient additional government senators to attain the necessary two-thirds majority, at the same time by increasing the quorum of judges in the Appeal Court in constitutional matters to eleven, and appointing the additional judges accordingly. In this way, the coloured people were also politically separated from the Whites.

Social, educational and political separation . . .

A crucial matter was 'non-white' industrial labour, on which the expanding post-war South African economy was becoming increasingly dependent. The *Industrial Conciliation Act* (1956) (as amended) empowered the formation of separate trade unions for different races. It also provided machinery for determinations, reserving particular work for specific race groups.

Obviously such stringent measures needed special powers to combat political activity at least as radical as that of the nationally-conscious Afrikaners embarked on their reforming task. The *Suppression of Communism Act* (1950), the *Criminal Law Amendment Act* and the *Unlawful Organizations Act* (1960), provided drastic powers, with severe penalties for political activity 'deemed' to be advancing the objects of Communism. Communism itself became a statutory offence and included far more than confession to Marxist-Leninist beliefs. By a process of 'naming', individuals were officially listed as Communists, thereby entailing certain disabilities. In 1962 sabotage, which likewise was now statutorily defined, became a capital offence. Amendments in 1963 and 1964 made provision for summary trial, house arrest and capital punishment, where saboteurs had received training outside the country. Solitary detention for up to ninety days had been empowered by the *General Law Amendment Act* (1964). The *Criminal Act* of the following year sanctioned detention of witnesses up to 180 days in cases involving security.

By the middle sixties, it had all become a vast superstructure inhabited by a growing multitude of functionaries to keep it working. Everything was based on the fundamental concept of the nation.

What Diederichs had written in 1936 was as relevant as ever. What its full implications were in the particular context of multi-national, multi-racial and multi-cultural South Africa had only now become apparent. And the man who was making it apparent, not only for all his own country to see but also for the world to contemplate and wonder at, was H. F. Verwoerd.

The point needs re-emphasizing. Here was a Promethean figure, who deeply, sincerely and passionately believed that he had a saviour's gift, not only for his own people but for everyone. He resembled Prometheus because he was prepared to accept the full anger of the divinities: to defy them if need be, for the sake of a needful humanity.

Let us now look deeper into the heart of this man who was so fully the expression of revolutionary Afrikanerdom. More than anything else, his speeches tell of his vision.

We believe that it can be done sensibly: not by wild theories; not by sudden changes; not by unwise actions, which bring with them bad social and economic consequences. By looking far ahead and planning wisely, one can achieve the preservation of European civilization and yet develop South Africa in such a way that both Europeans and non-Europeans can live in a manner which is satisfactory and in which no racial group becomes a threat to any other . . .[18]

. . . care for the tree of separate development which has been planted so faithfully with all your powers so that more and more fruit may be plucked every season . . .[19]

I do not know why when one tries to organize anything carefully and well so that that object one envisages can be achieved, the hon. member should regard it as wrongly inflicting a system upon people. Do we not all try to be systematic in our everyday activities? . . .[20]

As a young nation we are like a young couple with many children who see far into the future, how their children and children's children carry on that for the sake of which they have laboured, and to whom it is worthwhile leaving something. We are a young nation with great possibilities and for that reason we are a happy people. We have a great future and high ideals to live up to and which we can live up to . . .[21]

. . . we say like the Voortrekker of yore, 'we can still struggle' . . .

We shall keep on fighting for the survival of the white man at the southern tip of Africa and the religion which has been given to him to spread here. And we shall do it just as they did! Man, woman and child. We shall fight for our existence and the world must know it . . . We are not fighting for money or possessions. We are fighting for the life of our people . . .[22]

Hence we send this message to the outside world and say to them once again that there is but one way of saving the white races of the world. And that is for the White and non-White in Africa each to exercise his rights within his own areas . . .

We are trying to dig down through the clay to the gravel and bed-rock so that the nation of South Africa may exist to remote times in the future.[23]

Perhaps it was intended that we should have been planted here at the southern point within the crisis area so that from this resistance might emanate the victory whereby all that has been built up since the days of Christ may be maintained for the good of all mankind. May you have the strength, people of South Africa, to serve the purpose for which you have been placed here! . . .[24]

Our attitude is that matters have now reached the stage where we can proceed to the next stage in our positive plan of development. . . . For a change they could also have tried to have a great vision. But South Africa . . . places its faith in the governing party alone.[25]

And if with admiration we look back at the way the forefathers by the purity of their lives left us a white nation, then we have to realize that it is our task also by a pure and decorous life to maintain a white nation here. Great is the pain and suffering of any family and any friend when this highest law has been infringed. But greater still

is the pain and the damage to a nation when some of its children have
sinned against its blood . . .[26]

The different nations from which we are descended have each had a
golden age, a period in which they reigned supreme among the other
nations in world history. We here in South Africa have not yet had our
golden age. We are as yet but the builders of a nation. But our nation
will also be led to a zenith and in that climax of that golden age we
shall also **be** of great significance to the world, still greater than now.
We are already a nation, small in numbers but yet great in our deeds
. . . We have been planted here, we believe, with a destiny – destiny
not for the sake of the selfishness of a nation, but for the sake of the
service of a nation to the world of which it forms a part, and the service
of a nation to the Deity in which it believes . . .[27]

I have earnestly asked myself whether the advocates of total unity
of the different races can bring justice and fairness to everybody.
I am absolutely convinced that integration in a country like South
Africa cannot possibly succeed . . . I am seeking justice for all the
groups and not justice for only one group at the cost of the other
three . . .[28]

If meddlesome people keep their hands off us, we shall in a just way
such as behoves a Christian nation, work out solutions in the finest
detail and carry them out. We shall provide all our races with happiness and prosperity.[29]

A superstructure of functionaries becomes necessary if this kind
of social and political idealism is to work properly. Theologized
politics, aiming to re-structure the world in the finest detail, not
only needs these functionaries, but also 'think tanks'. This is
modern jargon for the intellectuals, political and academic, who
have themselves become institutionalized. In effect this means
that new intellectual institutions will be founded. It also means
that existing institutions (e.g. the Church) will be drawn into
the whole structure to play their parts as spiritual advisors.

Early in 1950, with the new Afrikaner administration dedicated
to its ideal, the South African Bureau of Racial Affairs – Sabra –
was founded. 'By a policy of free and separate development,' it
declared in an early statement of belief, 'we must understand the
territorial separation of European and Bantu, and the provision
of areas which must serve as national and political homes for the
different Bantu communities and as permanent residential areas
for the Bantu population or the major portion of it.'[30] Summing

it all up, Sabra believed that a policy of separation was practicable; that it was the only policy which could be regarded as just and fair; and that it could be put into practice without creating insuperable economic problems.[31] The granting of political rights to the Bantu, it believed, of the kind which would satisfy their political aspirations was altogether impossible in a mixed community, since such a step would endanger the present position and survival of the European population. If this danger was to be avoided, and at the same time the Europeans were not to violate their own conscience and moral standards, a policy of separate development would prove the only alternative.[32]

Academics of the University of Stellenbosch formed the core of Sabra. Two things, especially, were apparent from these early pronouncements by them. The first was the closeness of their thinking to what Cronjé had already asked for in 1946: complete, or nearly complete, separation between Whites and Africans. The emphasis on the necessity for 'national and political homes for the different Bantu communities' would also serve as a powerful stimulant to the development of Verwoerd's own thinking.

It was generally known during the late fifties and early sixties that a measure of tension existed at one time between Verwoerd and the Sabra academics at Stellenbosch. Sabra itself had logically concluded that separate development meant fully independent Bantustans, a conclusion Verwoerd himself would reach in the early sixties. Before this could happen, however, a crisis developed in Sabra, and the executive – nearly all of them founding Stellenbosch members – resigned and made way for more conservative elements. By this time, however, Verwoerd had shifted the emphasis in his approach to the matter of separate development. On 23 January 1962, it finally came to expression in the form of an announcement in the House of Assembly that the Government had decided to grant the Transkei self-government. The way was thereby opened for all African reserves (homelands) to follow the same course.

Apart from great and detailed attention to the full implementation of the theory, the unfolding of the idea, Sabra, especially as reconstituted, also served as a kind of spiritual clearing house, in which the concept of apartheid could constantly be restated in clear philosophical and theological terms. This was for the benefit of all who needed at regular intervals to be reminded of its metaphysical rightness and moral correctness.

'The political leaders, who formulated the policy of separate development in the past', one philosopher wrote,

left us in no doubt: in the policy of separate development it should be fundamental that we grant unto others what we claim for ourselves. This is playing practical politics, but the moral grounds and the deepest justification for it is that all other people, *in casu* the non-Whites, are our fellow human beings, that they bear in themselves the image of God; with an own intrinsic worth and dignity which is not to be assailed, and which we should always respect. Moreover, it is a fact that in our particular ethnic situation separate development offers the only true potential for the non-Whites to come to self-realization as human beings . . .[33]

One of the basic values therefore which lends meaning to the concept of 'apartheid', is the value of national binding (*volksverband*). National binding has for us a very deep and real meaning and value. Just like the individual, the nation has an intrinsic worth and dignity. The worth of the nation is even higher than the worth of the individual: therefore we may with justice and good conscience demand from the individual that he bring the greatest sacrifice to the nation, e.g., in time of war.[34]

Colour is for us important because it is indicative of national and cultural binding . . . if we say that it turns on cultural and not on colour or racial difference, should we then not be prepared to integrate with westernized non-Whites?

. . . But it is not just a matter of the individual. Every individual is a member of a nation and therefore every individual is like the spout of a funnel – the individual we accept is an opening through which a whole nation and a whole culture can flow . . . Integration with the Coloureds therefore means, ultimately, integration with all others.

. . . But above all we are Christians who stand under the command of the Master that we should love our neighbour as ourselves . . . It is therefore essential to the meaning of apartheid, that together with the separation between nations (*volke*) and cultures, the Whites also accept the responsibility for the well-being and development of the non-Whites.[35]

This is but a fragment of an enormous volume of philosophical, theological, anthropological, sociological and, at the same time, socio-political writing to appear in quarterlies, newspapers, books, official reports and so on during the fifties and sixties. The collected material would constitute a fair-sized municipal library. Probably never in history have so few written so much. They spoke eloquently and argued forcibly and sincerely about the validity of their secular faith – as the Afrikaners of the second half of the twentieth century. What had started in 1936 with Diederichs had been a trickle. Within a generation this trickle had become a flood. It is an impossible task to absorb it all. Neither is it necessary.

The essential elements were once again set out by M. C. de Wet Nel at the eleventh Annual Conference of Sabra at Stellenbosch in April 1960. His opening speech,[36] in his capacity as Minister of Bantu Administration and Development, was also in the nature of a review of progress made in the realization of the socio-political ideal. Apartheid, he gravely insisted, was basically different to segregation, which had been the name for the racial discrimination which existed prior to the coming to power of the Nationalist Government. Apartheid, he assured his audience, was the broadly conceived, fundamentally sound, formula for the regulation of colour relations, accepted by the South African nation and consistently put into practice. The extensive legislation since 1948 had all been designed for the eventual self-determination of the Bantu. The urge of the established white population to find a *permanent* and ethically just solution cumulatively produced the policy of apartheid as a *fait accompli.*

It was necessary again to restate the basic principles of this policy. The first was that every nation, irrespective of race or colour, was called by God to a divine task which no-one could destroy or frustrate. The second was that every nation, of whatever race or colour, had, like any individual, the inherent right to exist and maintain itself. The third was that personal national ideals and the ideals of every national group were best realized within their own national sphere (*volkskring*). The corollary was that there should be maximum separation between the races in all the necessary strata of human relationships by means of a 'balanced process of separate, autogenous development'. It was wrong to say that the old Republics had merely been a stage in the evolution of apartheid. General Hertzog, too, had formulated segregation, but never apartheid.

Their past tradition helped the Afrikaners face the great task of the future. The miracles in the history of the Afrikaner people strengthened the faith and trust in the justice of their task and calling. As long as the Christian conscience remained the lodestar of action, there was no cause for fear. 'I am convinced in my soul,' said de Wet Nel with measured emphasis, 'that our policy of apartheid will yet serve the world as a model by which good racial relations can be created.[37]

Our becoming was surely not merely a caprice of Providence. If we understand and accept it, then we know that our own existence and that of the Bantu national groups, cannot be lamely surrendered, but must be conserved and defended as a priceless heritage for the generations to come. This we can only do with a policy of apartheid – honest and robust (*gespierde*) apartheid.[38]

Tangible proof of what had been effected in the twelve years of Nationalist government, it was argued, was the fact that black slums in and around the cities had been entirely cleared; that there had been a great increase in the numbers of black teachers, nurses, shopkeepers, construction workers, and so on; and that the rate of literacy among the Bantu was already higher than that of any other state in Africa, or that of India.

As necessary for the *apartheidsgedagte*, as for the idea of democracy or even national socialism, was the full support of the spiritual Establishment: the Church serving a particular province. *Vox populi est vox Dei* as a claim has had its variants. In the history of the Puritans in Africa, it became a case of *vox Dei est vox Separationis*. Cronjé, preparatory to the crucial change in government in 1948, fully realized this. Therefore in his book *Regverdige Rasse-apartheid* (*A Just Racial Separation*) he had added the special contributions by two eminent church leaders. The party itself had been sensitive to this when it had appointed G. B. A. Gerdener, Professor of Theology at the Theological Seminary at Stellenbosch, to serve on the Sauer Commission.

From April 1950 to December 1960, the Dutch Reformed Churches as variously constituted were almost constantly busy trying to interpret, formulate, justify, reconcile and pronounce on the matter of apartheid and the Scriptures. It was an intellectual effort second only to that of the statesmen and politicians who had laboured with such dedication for the formulation of the new socio-political ideal.[39] In a series of conferences, reports and statements – at times in anguish – various church bodies during the fifties came to the conclusion that the policy of separate development could be accepted as a healthy basis for the happy co-existence of Whites and Bantu.[40] God had ordained a multiplicity of languages and nations (Genesis 11:6, 9 – the Tower of Babel – and Acts 17:26 were once again relied upon), and Christ had sanctified these different spheres of authority (*gesagskringe*), which God had ordained.[41] A number of ministers of the *Nederduits Gereformeerde* Church, after the racial disturbances of 1960, declared that they could accept the policy of independent, autogenous development if it were applied in 'a just and honourable way'. To this they added riders that the policy, especially in its initial stages, would necessarily entail a measure of 'personal discomfort and privation'. Furthermore, it was urgently necessary that non-Whites should always be treated in a way consistent with human dignity. Here they quoted Micah 6:8:

... and what doth the Lord require of thee, but to do justly, and to love mercy, and to walk humbly with thy God?[42]

After a decade of spiritual and moral support by the Dutch Reformed Churches, it came as a considerable shock to Verwoerd in April 1961, when discussion between the World Council of Churches and the eight member churches in South Africa – including the largest part of the most powerful of the Dutch Reformed Churches, the N. G. Churches of the Cape Province and the Transvaal, meeting at Cottesloe in Johannesburg – came to conclusions which seemed to be a complete rejection of everything the Afrikaans churches had previously sanctioned as being in accordance with Scripture. At the same time, it seemed to be a rejection of the socio-political ideal of apartheid.

All racial groups, the meeting decided, which were permanently resident in the country, were part of its total population and should therefore be regarded as indigenous. The Church had a particular responsibility to witness fearlessly within a society. No-one should be excluded from any church on the grounds of race or colour. There were no Scriptural grounds for a ban on mixed marriages. Migratory labour excluded the possibility of social stability for the Bantu. From a Christian point of view, the integrity of the family needed to be safe-guarded. Wages for the great majority of non-Whites were below the accepted standards for a healthy life. Job reservation had to make way for a fairer dispensation. In the Bantu areas, opportunities had to be provided in accordance with human dignity. Where a person was domiciled, he should also have the right to own land and to participate in the government of his country. Nationalism was in order as an expression of self-realization, but there was a danger of its striving after its objects at the expense of others. There was no objection to the direct representation of the Coloureds by Coloureds in Parliament. Regarding imprisonment without trial, except where absolutely necessary, Christian law, justice and freedom required that nobody be punished without a proper trial in public. Regarding Asians in South Africa, they, too, should be remembered in the general requirements of justice towards the various racial groups. Where 'non-Whites' were resident in white areas and could only reach the churches in their own areas with difficulty, the authorities should provide them with places of worship in the white areas. Whites should also make their own buildings available for this purpose. Any legislation which inhibited the preaching of the Gospel to all people in all circumstances was unacceptable. With appreciation for what had already been done by the authorities regarding the housing of Bantu and other 'non-Whites', it was also urgently necessary to provide owner-ship and to plan residential areas with a view to the economic and cultural level of the inhabitants . . .[43]

The N. G. Churches of the Cape Province and the Transvaal declared in an addendum that the resolutions taken were not irre-concilable with a policy of 'differentiation' on a Christian basis. Furthermore, the Bantu who should qualify for participation in government were those domiciled in the white areas, with no other homeland.

In a more detailed addendum, they declared that the Church very definitely had the responsibility to act as the conscience of the state. Furthermore, such Bantu as had no other permanent home, could not, in due course, with a Christian conscience be excluded from rights, including political rights. The Coloureds had the right to participate in the 'highest word' spoken on their behalf; and that was in Parliament. Regarding mixed marriages, legal, social and cultural factors should also be taken into account. Nobody was to be excluded from any church on the grounds of race or colour, but account had to be taken of good order. Like the Cape church, the Transvaal church, too, affirmed its belief that a policy of differentiation was to be reconciled with the resolutions taken during the discussions. [44]

The effect on Verwoerd of the Cottesloe conference and the participation and agreement by an important part of the Afrikaans churches was electric. Moreover, with *Die Burger* giving the startling impression that it was in agreement with the decisions taken at Cottesloe, Verwoerd immediately made known his deep disapproval of the whole sorry business. Obviously, the entire *apartheidsgedagte* had suddenly been threatened from a most unexpected quarter. Should the moral rightness and metaphysical soundness of the idea be seriously questioned and should it lose the full support of the Church, it could not possibly hope to retain the enthusiasm and loyalty of Afrikanerdom. Magisterially, Verwoerd, in effect, called the Dutch Reformed theologians to order. They had been unduly influenced by the World Council of Churches, in the end submitting to their liberal views. What, had they discounted everything the Dutch Reformed Churches had been saying in meeting after meeting, in conclusion after conclusion, for ten years or more? Theologians, too, had to keep a single mind, remembering the high purpose of apartheid, never doubting the Afrikaners' potential to discover for themselves the way to the stars. Neither would he allow this group of leading churchmen to confuse the nation. They would have to recant.

And recant they did: enough of them, and in sufficient

measure, to undo everything that had taken place at Cottesloe. Soon professors of theology were explaining as best they could how it had all come about. The most obvious explanation was that everything had happened in the shadow of Sharpeville, on 21 March 1960.

And yet, the ghost of Cottesloe would return to haunt the Afrikaners' wayward theologizing. There was evidence that, in spite of the silencing, recantation, bowing of heads and deep cogitation, something remained. The Church could never quite be the same again.

Three months after Cottesloe, a little more than a year after Sharpeville, one of its outstanding personalities, a man who had been a commanding figure as Moderator, had occasion to express himself on the prophetic task of the Church in a time of crisis.[45]

'Are we,' he asked,

in these times of crisis prepared to listen again whether God, perhaps, has something to say to us? Or do we run the risk of our informing God that the route we are following is, in every detail beyond question, also His way for us? ... Our church should be on its guard not to create the impression that national existence, as such, has already become an end in itself ...

I cannot avoid the impression that a large part of our people do not yet fully realize what great sacrifices will yet be required from us to preserve our racial integrity in a manner which will assure justice, to all parties, and will enable us to qualify for the blessing of Heaven.

Within the N. G. Church itself, there was soon a strong counter movement. Prominent among them was the editor of the N.G. Church weekly *Die Kerkbode*, Dr A. P. Treurnicht. In a series of leaders from 1961–4, he restated the case for a church policy closely aligned to the theologized, mystic concept of the nation. Once more, the well-tried passages of Scripture were involved: Genesis 11, Deuteronomy 32:8, Acts 17:26.

But now, through Treurnicht, a new emphasis had emerged. He stressed the idea of ordination, of the nation as one of many autonomous spheres of existence – *soewereiniteit binne eie kring* – existing in themselves as entities, as organisms and endowed by their Creator with their own inner structures, each with its own particular 'law of life', to which absolute obedience was owed. [46] Such a 'law of life' was as much part of the inner structure of things created as the law of gravity or other natural laws.

In the time of the Third Reich, the Lutheran Church had a massive theology of this concept. It came to be known as the *Ordnungstheologie*. Within this Theology of Ordination, particular life-spheres were initially the nation, state, and fatherland. But elements like race and blood were soon added. A minister of the N. G. Church was later to comment critically,

> God had ordained this German nation and had its particular history to emerge from His providential ruling. God had ordained the constitution of 1933 (the unpopular Weimar Republic which had preceded Hitler, God, of course, had not ordained!) God had caused me to be born in this territory, within these boundaries, with this Aryan blood in my veins. These were ordinances of the Creator. They were Ordinances of Creation.
>
> And now the ethical responsibility towards these things could not be divorced from them. Therefore one had to honour these decrees, keep them pure, and extend them . . .
>
> So a completely new concept of sin originated in the theology of ordination. Because the ordinations were revealed truths to which obedience was due, sin became, in the first place, disloyalty towards these things.
>
> Because the ordinances of creation extended directly and unblemished from the hand of God to the human being, they contain divine authority. Together with the unblemished conscience of the human being, they form the moral and norm of ethics. [47]

The German *Ordnungstheologie*, and the so-called *Deutsche Christen* who professed it, led to the reaction of the Confessional Church of the thirties. In this the Swiss Reformed theologian, Karl Barth, played an important role, strongly resisting the new development in the Lutheran Church.

Treurnicht's pieces in *Die Kerkbode* (in support of the concept of separate development) spoke on behalf of the Church. But he had not taken his cue from the German theology of ordination. Neither had he found support for this concept of the nation in

Calvin. It was rather in neo-Calvinism, especially in the writings of the Dutch theologian, Abraham Kuyper, who also became Prime Minister of the Netherlands, that the whole concept of *soewereiniteit in eie kring* – autonomy within a particular sphere – had originated.

Soevereiniteit in eigen kring was the Dutch title of an address at the inauguration of the *Vrije Universiteit* of Amsterdam in 1880.

The principle, of which this title speaks, was used by Kuyper to found a university which, under the legal guardianship of the state, would yet be free of both state and church. In the principle of sovereignty in a particular sphere Kuyper was, in fact, dealing with the old problem of freedom and authority. [48]

True to the Reformed tradition, he was, in fact, simply making a plea for a division of authority and for particular 'civil liberties', as the concept, with far less theorizing, became known in the Anglo-Saxon world. How, from this relatively simple beginning, the idea of sovereignty within a particular sphere came to be built up into a neo-Calvinist 'life-system' (as Kuyper described it) of its own would require a treatise of its own. For the present purposes it is enough to say that both Kuyper and the Dutch philosopher, Dooyeweerd (author of *A New Critique of Theoretical Thought*) were responsible for this remarkable growth.

In the South African context, in the struggle to reconcile the idea of separate development with the Christian Gospel, the Kuyper–Dooyeweerd theology, as it grew and was stated and restated, became of the utmost importance. It was, in fact, a *deus ex machina* by which the basic concept of the nation as an ordained, sacred entity, to be safeguarded at all costs as part of our Christian responsibility, could be vindicated.

In his *Stone Foundation Lectures*, Kuyper himself gives a clear indication how the idea of sovereignty within a particular sphere took hold of him and carried him along with it to a point where it became neo-Calvinism in its definitive form.

' ... all life has first been in the thoughts of God,' he said,

before it came to be realized in Creation. Hence all life necessarily bears in itself a law for its existence instituted by God himself.

There is no life outside us in Nature, without such divine ordinances – ordinances which are called the laws of nature – a term which we are willing to accept, provided we understand thereby not laws originating from Nature, but laws imposed upon Nature . . . [49]

There is a 'second sovereignty', implanted by God in the social sphere (of existence) 'in accordance with the ordinances of creation'. The fundamental idea here is that the sovereignty of God, in its descent upon men, separates itself into two spheres. On the one hand is the mechanical sphere of State authority, and on the other, the organic sphere of the authority of the social circles. And in both these spheres the inherent authority is sovereign, that is to say, it has above itself nothing but God.[50]

Next to the mechanical sovereignty of the State there are the organic sovereignties of the various social spheres ('family, business, science, art, and so forth'). 'In this independent character a special higher authority is of necessity involved and this highest authority we intentionally call – sovereignty in the individual social spheres . . .' These have 'nothing above themselves but God'. 'As you feel at once,' Kuyper intriguingly informed his American audience, 'this is the deeply interesting question of civil liberties.'[51]

But Kuyper relies on the story of Babel (Genesis 11), explaining the origin of peoples and nations. This is a view which would be drawn on heavily by theologians of the Dutch Reformed Churches in South Africa to justify the inclusion of the nation in the very 'individual social spheres', the organic entities, ordained by God as such. 'For God,' he says elsewhere in his Stone Foundation lecture on *Calvinism and Politics*,

created nations. They exist for Him. They are His own.

And therefore all these nations, and in them humanity, must exist for His glory and consequently after His ordinances, in order that in the well-being, when they walk after His ordinances, His divine wisdom may shine forth.[52]

It is a relatively simple matter to see how Kuyper's 'sovereignty in the individual social spheres', as fully extended to a 'life-system' by Dooyeweerd and others came to be used as the most powerful of the neo-Calvinist supports for the secular faith of the Revolutionary Afrikaners.

Treurnicht's writings in *Die Kerkbode*, as later published in an anthology, have as their predominant theme the idea of the nation as the ordination of God, with its own inner structure and 'law of life', which had to be honoured and obeyed.[53]

'We believe,' Treurnicht stated in a piece, epitomizing the credo, not only of the writer, but of all who rejected the conclusions of Cottesloe,

> that justice is best attained by way of differentiation or separate development. When we say this, we do not mean justice as a kind of impartiality in which the parties cannot be separated, but precisely a holy partiality for the promotion and securing of the characteristically own (*karaktereie*) of each; for their striving, in harmony with each other. Justice is therefore no cowardly surrender of one's own strivings, rights, and claims. Justice is obedience. Justice is to live according to the rule or law of the Creator. [*Note here the* Wetsidee, *the 'Idea of Law'*] To act according to the law for your own life, is to express your own pure character and identity. Your own particular character (*eiesoortige karakter*) is therefore your 'law of life', and the obedience to it is justice. Therefore we say that autogenous development is the best exercise of justice. Justice is plurality.[54]
>
> Whoever deserts his own post and endangers his future, who by virtue of a misconception of love or justice, undertakes to fulfil the task of someone else, is not exercising justice, but is disloyal to his own calling and law of life . . .[55]
>
> We are honestly but hopefully convinced that a political formula or policy is to be found by which justice as set out above, can be afforded to all.[56]

It was the clearest, most generous support for the Afrikaner revolution in the whole history of the Dutch Reformed Churches. It reflected a great deal of similar thinking within the Church. Those 'liberal' elements which had high hopes at the time of Cottesloe now fell silent and retired more or less gracefully into the background. Some even revised their views completely. But one, who had once been Moderator of the N. G. Church in Transvaal, the Rev. Beyers Naudé, resigned his position as Moderator and as minister to become director of a new ecumenical organization, the Christian Institute, which rejected apartheid as a 'false gospel'. This cost him his status as a *dominee*: a minister.

So the idea of apartheid or separate development, as it had grown under the forceful leadership of H. F. Verwoerd, was fully ascendant once more. He had suffered no digressions and had triumphed once again.

It was all reflected in 1966 in the *Report of the Committee on Current Affairs of the General Synod of the Nederduits Gereformeerde Kerk*.[57] Everything that had been said about race relations and attendant matters at Cottesloe had now officially been re-formulated. The themes as stressed by Treurnicht, representing the upsurge of neo-Calvinism (in a sense, even neo-Kuyperism), were at last formulated with great thoroughness. The report contained them all. Once again, reliance was placed on the happenings at Babel as recounted in the eleventh chapter of the Book of Genesis.[58] The idea of ordination was stressed. So was the organic existence of the nation as a 'curious individual'.[59] Once again the philosophy of 'sovereignty of each in its own sphere' was respected. The nation had its own 'law of life'...[60]

Essentially, the views of Treurnicht had been accepted by the Commission. For the *apartheidsgedagte*, it was all of the highest importance.

'The Church regards the nation as a distinctive human community,' the Report said,

with a common origin, history, language, customs, culture, living area and destiny. A diversity of such national groupings is in agreement with the revealed will of God ...[61]

The rights and freedoms of a nation are founded in this distinctiveness and distinctive character, as it emerges from history from the work and will of God and His leadership. Its own nature and character is its law of life.[62]

An infinity of words ...

It is a difficult task to keep track of even a fraction of them. Most soon fell away into the abyss of history. Some, however, remained. The human tragi-comedy is always enacted anew by those who stand at the centre of these heroic but absurd attempts 'to create (their) own future' and ultimately rationalize human existence.

It is in this light that we must see H. F. Verwoerd. He made a magnificent effort to impose on the world his own Promethean vision of life. He experienced the dark days of Sharpeville; the horror of the attempt on his life; the deep economic slump which followed in the early sixties; the shock of Cottesloe; and the critical voices raised by writers and academics, even at times by *Die Burger*. But it seemed as if the day of true fulfilment was about to dawn.

By the mid-sixties, public affairs were once more on an even keel. In fact, the ship of state was ploughing strongly ahead through sunny seas. The militant left which, round about the turn of the decade, had been a serious threat, had been brought to heel by the tireless efforts of B. J. Vorster, Minister of Justice in Verwoerd's cabinet, commanding the security police. An economic boom seemed to be developing. Confidence was rising like an African summer.

Even the literary and academic critics were more contained.

Verwoerd had even gone so far as to reprimand obliquely but unmistakably Afrikaans literature's pre-eminent figure, N. P. van Wyk Louw. Like Milton in old age, and reflecting the disturbing, naked verse of his later period, shorn of all embellishments,[63] van Wyk Louw had in a festival play[64] looked critically and revealingly at Afrikaner heroes and at current values recommended to the *Volk*. The occasion for Verwoerd was the quinquennial celebration of the Republic. Before a multitude of people he exclaimed:

Oh, if it could also be granted us as it was granted in the past to great nations in their hour of fame that those would come forward [the literary artists] who do not ask hesitatingly 'what is a nation', but who will cry out: 'This is my nation, my nation is like *this*, thus they can do wonders, *thus* it can create its own future.'[65]

Van Wyk Louw, a few days later, was moved to reply to Verwoerd's veiled attack on him and rejected with some emotion the innuendo that he was no good Afrikaner. The two men, it was obvious, had little to say to each other. Verwoerd's world was a sealed, rationalized one to which the revelation of the poet was a distinct and serious threat.

The aura of the socio-political ideal is often of such an intensity, that matters closer at hand become blurred. In fact, impaired vision itself is the inevitable result of fixing one's gaze on Utopia. It shines so brightly on the distant horizon that the eyes – especially the inner eye – is affected. While there may still be a dim consciousness that something is happening in close proximity to the viewer which *prima facie* could hardly be accepted as moral, reassurance is found by keeping one's gaze fixed on the distant light. In its limpid purity all perspectives will, in the end, be restored. Everything done, however hard or inhuman, will be discovered to have been fully justified. Faith, hard work and the willingness to make sacrifices, all in the name of the ideal, are the guarantees of moral rectitude.

For all radicals of Puritan lineage, of whatever time or place, matters of morality are decided by the knowledge that God himself has approved. God's appointed or elect have been called upon to perform a specific task. This task is automatically right, as God is in his heaven, and is on the side of the ordained (the saints). All hesitancy should be abandoned; and the way to the stars lies clearly ahead.

To this the revolutionary idealism, the secular creed of the Afrikaners of the second half of the twentieth century, has proved to be no exception. For the sharp and unabated criticism which the policy of apartheid or separate development has drawn upon itself, the total rejection of it by a large part of the world, the rejection at the same time of the architects of the system, the Afrikaners, has been exactly because of the endless sequence of hard things done to powerless peoples. It is not merely the ideal which sanctions these measures, but also God, towards Whom the doer has a special messianic relationship. But 'God' is an interchangeable term. In the case of the Jacobins, it finally became the 'Supreme Being', as evidenced by the festival of 8 June 1794. In the case of Marxism, it became 'History'. Vaguely, it also becomes that most indefinable of revolutionary terms, 'Destiny', which has found its equivalent in the Afrikaans language as *lotsbestemming*.

'Destiny' and 'calling', like 'God' and 'History', are, in the systems of radical politics, standardized equipment. Afrikaners themselves, significantly of deep Calvinist convictions, have consistently been the most penetrating critics of the socio-political ideal of the Revolutionary Afrikaners, on this very score. They have severely criticized the ways in which the ideal end has engendered dehumanizing and intolerable means.

Writing in *Die Burger* on 30 October 1967, Dr A. M. Hugo, at the time Lecturer in Classics at the University of Stellenbosch, examined what had been done to congregations of the Dutch Reformed Mission Church in and around the Cape Peninsula by the energetic and consistent implementation of the 'cornerstone of positive apartheid', the *Group Areas Act*.

The letter was in essence an appeal to readers of *Die Burger* to help relieve the 'serious financial straits' in which the N. G. Mission Church had found itself. This financial crisis, Hugo pointed out, was to a large extent the direct result of the 'present government policy of "resettlement" of Coloured communities'. Hugo quoted the Rev. W. J. van der Vywer, a white minister of the (coloured) N. G. Mission Church, who had previously written in *Die Kerkbode*:

Because of these resettlements a number of church buildings in white residential areas will soon fall into disuse and will have to be sold. From a business point of view most of these buildings are, however, almost useless, so that *great* losses will be incurred, especially when one takes into account that new church buildings will have to be erected elsewhere.

The N. G. Mission Church Synod, Hugo said, had, in a special report, dealt with the deep hurts and hardships of members of the Mission Church, who had been forced to leave District Six in the heart of Cape Town.

'The Church itself will suffer great financial loss,' the report had stated. In spite of the Department of Community Development's accommodating spirit in determining values of affected property, the replacement of church property would cost more than R1½ million.

Congregations that have already freed themselves of debt after many years of struggle, will have to start all over again. Due to the mass removals of church members, with all the financial implications for them personally, their ability to contribute has been adversely affected . . .

Proclamations have already declared the church buildings of more than fifty congregations to be affected property. These buildings are mostly of great historical value. There is e.g. the *S.A. Gestig* in Long Street, Cape Town, which is the equivalent to the Mission Church of the Groote Kerk.* There is also the *Sionskerk* at Paarl, the Rhenish Church at Stellenbosch, the churches at Worcester, Beaufort West, George, Upington, and many others. The Coloured People simply have to abandon these, and bid farewell. This is suffering almost too deep to understand. The Church shares this pain with its members. Their heritage is no longer theirs.

Hugo, in *Die Burger*, also referred to the white Moderator of the Mission Church, the Rev. J. A. J. Steenkamp, who had also written to the same paper (21 March 1967) on the effects of the group area removals. Masses of Coloureds, Steenkamp had said, who had known a closely-knit church community in their old homes, had been thrown together by the proclamations of group areas into

large new Coloured townships where there are no church facilities for them, or where they are still hopelessly inadequate ... N. G. Mission congregations like Goodwood, Woodstock, Ebenezer (District Six and surroundings), the *S.A. Gestig* in the city centre, Wynberg, Retreat, and others, have been affected to such an extent by the removals that the church buildings will remain, but the members live in areas where they can no longer visit their churches. Neither can the church reach them. In short, we have churches without members, and members without churches!

The inevitable result, Steenkamp had concluded, was a return to heathenism.

The Rev. D. P. Botha, the white Actuary of the Mission Church, had, on 23 October 1967, also written to *Die Burger* and had shown that of the old congregations which had existed before 1900 no less than thirty-five had been affected.

'In the Peninsula alone,' Botha had stated,

eleven church buildings have been affected. Those of us who witnessed the pain and suffering with which devoted members of congregations took leave of the three church buildings which have already been lost to them, shudder at the thought at what may happen when the doors

*Most historic of the Dutch Reformed church buildings in South Africa.

of all the affected church buildings are closed for the last time ...
For the sake of steady community development the Coloured People
may not be cut loose from their historic roots.

Hugo, quoting these statements by fellow Afrikaners in the
service of the N. G. Mission Church, added:

One would like to express the serious hope that publication of these
facts (for which we thank *Die Burger*) will cause more than one to place
a serious question mark over the whole policy of group areas, of mass
removals, of human dislocation and uprooting, of the whole process
euphemistically termed 'community development'.

A question mark, he went on to say, should be put over a
policy which required the disruption of congregations of the
Church of Christ and which sought to destroy the patient
spiritual labour of generations with a single stroke of the pen.
Likewise, there was a question mark over the incomprehensible
silence of a *Moederkerk* – Mother Church – which, as far as he,
Hugo, knew, had never yet used her powerful influence with the
Government of the country to intercede on behalf of a Daughter
who had been treated in this way. There was, finally, also a question mark over the white members of the N. G. Church who had
never yet been informed by official sources of these matters.
To this Hugo added a plea that, at least, those who had been
uprooted in this way should be fully compensated, taking into
consideration what they would still need to pay for new buildings,
after the old ones had been sold.

There was a further, particularly bitter, aspect about the whole
matter. There had been some concern about the demolition of
the church of the *S. A. Gestig* in Long Street, Cape Town, as it
was an historic building. There were, however, many other such
historic church buildings in District Six, at Simonstown, Kalk
Bay, Stellenbosch and Somerset West. These buildings, which
were also threatened, had caused no concern to the white public.

'The heart-break and the despair of tens of thousands of
people have quietly escaped us,' Hugo concluded:

But now, when a historic monument is threatened, we all take up
the pen! ...

A civilized people cares reverently for its monuments of the past.
But a civilized people, and certainly a Christian people, see to it

that its government finds in itself 'to do justly and to show mercy' (Micah 6), towards all who live within its boundaries.

The removals of people 'disqualified' from living in a particular area, with resulting hardships, often of a nature beyond compensation or repair, were epitomized in the forced dispersal of the N. G. Mission Church congregations in the Western Cape. In rare instances, Whites were also displaced and re-settled in terms of the *Group Areas Act* in new areas. But these were only the exceptions proving the consistent implementation of the policy. Everywhere in the country, the brunt of this 'social engineering' and the burden of trying to fit life into an abstraction of freedom was borne by the less privileged, almost powerless, 'non-Whites'. Officials were often at great pains to make it all acceptable.

It was quite true, one such person declared before the Synod of the N. G. Mission Church in 1966, that Coloureds have had to make the most sacrifices. But the Coloureds should not be sentimental and should remember that they would be re-settled in new, healthy communities with all their socio-cultural amenities.[66]

The question of District Six was raised, where the Coloureds had through generations built up a natural 'group area'. This was a part of Cape Town beloved by artists for its true Cape character, its immense vitality and the fact that it was a living Cape community.

The new social engineers saw only the slums, the petty crime and the poverty. Above all, they saw only the ideal of a South African society engineered to a 'master plan'. District Six had to go, it was decided. Protests – amongst the strongest of them from Afrikaners – sounded everywhere. Why could District Six not be restored? Why could the slums not be removed, and so much which was truly of the Cape be renewed – for those who had been living there for so long? For those who had struck such deep 'sentimental' roots in the place? Why did tens of thousands of these people have to be uprooted at enormous cost and sent to the distant and characterless Cape Flats, from whence they had to commute arduously and expensively to their city jobs? Why had those who had, in fact, been removed only been compensated at values which represented less than half of what the new stands – which the bulldozers had opened up – were worth to affluent Whites who would move in?

To buy up the properties needed for re-planning, the visiting government official at the Mission Church Synod declared, would cost at least R30 million. Development would cost an additional R20 million. District Six should therefore become white, because it would be beyond the means of the Coloureds to live there. The rejoinder to this was that re-settling from 60–70,000 people in a distant, sandy wilderness, where everything had to be started from the veld, to provide them with the amenities they had enjoyed in District Six, would be no cheaper. In addition, the extra daily travelling expenses would in the course of a decade run into many millions. And this would have to be paid by those affected themselves. District Six would in any event be demolished and re-built . . .

There were many other areas where the striving after the great ideal, the determination to erect the edifice of apartheid at all costs, had led to inhumanities. Basic, too, to the concept of separate development was the rigid classification of the population into racial categories. The Act[67] defined White, Coloured, Native (or Bantu); later, by proclamation, 'Coloured' was subdivided into Cape Coloured, Cape Malay, Griqua, Indian, Chinese, 'other Asiatic' and 'other Coloured'. Amendments to the Act took place in 1962, 1964, 1967, 1969 and 1970. The effect of the 1967 amendment was to make descent, and not 'appearance' or 'general acceptance', the determining factor in cases where there was doubt as to what group a person belonged to. The amending act of 1969 put the onus of proof on any person claiming to belong to any racial or ethnic group.

If the *Group Areas Act* had caused 'suffering too deep to understand', as the Report of the N. G. Mission Church had said, the massive attempt to organize finally all people within the South African state into racial categories, once and for all, did no less. Inevitably, a considerable number of people were discovered living in the twilight between White and Coloured. Also, inevitably, race classifications, made in terms of the Act (as amended) by 'officials' (as defined) soon led to a persistent series of cruel situations. Families suddenly found that they had been divided by an act of state: one set of brothers and sisters being classified as Coloured, the other as White. A white mother could even discover herself to be the parent of a non-white child.

The situation, which has repeated itself on a number of reported occasions, and on an innumerable number of unreported ones, was dramatized by the case of Sandra Laing in October 1967. Sandra, born in 1956 at Amersfoort in a hospital for Whites, from well-known, well-established and indisputably white parents, was registered after birth as White, and in due course baptized in the white N.G. Church at Amsterdam, Transvaal. She had always been rather dark-skinned, with crinkly hair, but for the first eight years of her life it made no difference. Sandra was accepted by her playmates, in her school, as white.

At Piet Retief, where she first attended school, she was a boarder and shared dormitories, tables, swimming bath and so on with all the other children. According to her parents, Mr and Mrs Abram Laing, no unkind word had ever been spoken to her. In June 1964, however, the Laings were approached by the Administrator of the Transvaal, Mr Van Niekerk, together with the local member of the Provincial Council, Mr Martins. Then, for the first time, they heard with shock that there were objections to the presence of their daughter in the Piet Retief Primary School. This was the beginning of a lengthy and involved correspondence with the provincial authorities, also with the Secretary for the Interior. The parents told an Afrikaans Sunday paper[68] that, when they had first heard of the objections to Sandra, they had thought death had come upon them. They realized, however, that for her sake they should keep on fighting. A son of the Laings, also dark-skinned, with black, curly hair, was with Sandra at Piet Retief.

In February 1966, the Secretary for the Interior applied in terms of the Act for a re-classification of Sandra Laing as 'Coloured'. The application was granted. Then the real trouble started. Where Sandra had previously, in spite of her appearance, gone to school happily at Piet Retief, things changed abruptly as soon as she had been re-classified. Her parents duly received a letter from the principal of the Piet Retief Primary School in which they were asked to remove their daughter in terms of a request by the Transvaal Department of Education. Mr Laing, in turn, notified the principal that he would not remove Sandra. Seven days later, she was brought home by the police.

At great expense, trouble and spiritual turmoil, Sandra's father took the matter to court. His effort met with some success. His daughter was again duly classified as white. Sandra, who had spent some eighteen months at home after her removal from the Piet Retief Primary School, was thereupon assigned to the white school at Sheepmore, which was nearest to where she was living. The damage, however, had already been done. Many local Afrikaners, who felt great sympathy for the little girl in her predicament, agreed that, in view of the wide publicity the matter had attained, it would be cruel to have Sandra in any white school in the neighbourhood. A local farmer said: 'The children – any children at a white school – would torment the child and make her life a misery.'[69] He was probably right. In fact, the only hope for Sandra in this dim, fearful world she had been led into, was in some private institution or other, away from the area where everything had taken place. This is exactly what happened. Sandra Laing was eventually accepted as a pupil in a private school in Johannesburg.

In the regular reportage of strange excesses, especially by the Sunday newspapers, both those supporting, or those critical of, the Government, other similar cases came to the notice of the public.

The case of Sandra Laing faded into the background and in the public conscience.* And yet, there was sufficient evidence that Afrikaners who had perhaps once shared the vision of a South Africa reconstructed to the design of apartheid, were now shaken by the frequency with which cases like that of Sandra Laing somehow had to be dealt with.

'I refer to the tragedies which took place in the case of the

---

*Since these words were written she has married an African and is living simply but happily in the Transvaal.

little Laing girl,' an Afrikaner said in a letter to the Sunday newspaper which had carried the original story,

... also in the cases of the Mullers of Barkley West, of the Crags School at Knysna. Towards these things the great majority of our ostensibly Christian Afrikaner people have maintained a deathly silence. We watch the sufferings of parents, but especially that of children, allowing it all to pass without protest.

Where, Christian Afrikaner, is your justice? Is this coldness which you exhibit your answer to the command that you should 'love your neighbour as yourself'?[70]

In some strange way the human hardships in trying to fit life and reform society into an abstraction of freedom, seemed to bear more heavily on the Coloureds – those who were the fellow Westerners of the Whites – than on the Africans. The reason for this, perhaps, was because the very proximity of these mahogany, tan-coloured, light brown, off-white and almost white people, sharing territory, religions, languages and culture generally, sharing also in many respects a common ancestry with the Whites,[71] presented a greater threat than that of the Africans. For the Africans, there were at least sizable and fertile areas of South Africa which could be developed regionally, holding out the promise of independence as Verwoerd had finally envisaged at the beginning of the sixties. For the Coloureds, there was no prospect of an independent homeland.

The *Group Areas Act*, racial classification, the provision of public amenities on a basis of separation and the *Immorality Amendment Act* (1950) seemed to hit them particularly badly. The latter extended the prohibition of sexual intercourse, which since 1927 had only applied to the relationships between Whites and Africans, to Whites and all who were non-White.

The new measures against 'Immorality' became the subject of a penetrating study by J. J. F. C. Heydenrych on the social implications of the application of Article 16 of the *Consolidating Act* of 1957.[72] The effect of the article was a further broadening of the definition of 'immorality', so as to include any kind of sexual activity between Whites and non-Whites and not necessarily intercourse. As such, it was a general sharpening of the efforts to prevent all sexual contact between Whites and the members of the various other population groups. Significantly, there was no attempt to see the voluntary contact between these latter peoples themselves as constituting immorality. As such, it was purely a measure designed to 'protect' the Whites, as part of the policy of apartheid.

Investigating the results of Article 16 up to the mid-sixties, Heydenrych came to the conclusion that white men were the main transgressors. In spite of what was believed to be a water-tight definition of 'immorality' in 1957, an unusually high per-centage of those prosecuted were not convicted. This was probably because public prosecutors, acting on the instructions of Attorneys-General, declined to prosecute, probably motivated by the knowledge of the 'enormously disrupting effect' of the application of Article 16 on an ever growing circle of people: children, descendants, relations and whole communities.[73]

From the end of the fifties to the mid-sixties, there was an enormously disturbing record of suicides, attempted suicides, murder, culpable homicide, 'other dangerous behaviour' and flight from the country, as regularly reported in the daily press.[74] There were also the cases where white men declared before court that they loved the coloured girls they had been accused of having criminal sexual relations with, and wished to marry them. There was one occasion when the sister of the co-accused (the coloured girl) had already legally been married to a white man.[75]

The reaction by the largest part of the South African press to the dismal record of charges under the Immorality Act was epito-mized by the *Star* on 5 February 1962. The Act, the *Star* said, had blown up to 'something monstrous and horrifying what would otherwise have passed as a peccadillo'. 'The Immorality Act ought to be abolished ... It is itself an immoral act – per-haps more immoral than the thing it seeks to prevent.'

The Afrikaans press, notably *Die Burger*, on occasions ex-pressed itself in similar terms. On 22 February 1962, it referred to the 'nameless anguish caused to innocent women and children by the trials and sentences as a result of the Act ...' It also referred to the 'other evil results, less concrete but no less real, such as tension and suspicion in the ordinary human relation-ships between the races'. Finally, *Die Burger* deplored the 'unforeseen by-products ... [of the act] ... which has not done honour to our public life, and the name of South Africa'.

In his comment on the public reaction to the application of the Act, Heydenrych concluded that the Immorality Act had, indeed, been 'the cause of a substantial proportion of the unexplained suicides of white men'. The public, in its reaction to the Act, was probably 'caught in a moral and ideological conflict'. While the object of the Act was supported, the effects of prosecution and sentence were looked at sceptically. The consequences of prosecution under the Act, said Heydenrych, were so destructive that its effects were completely out of proportion to the nature of the offence. In spite of relatively heavy sentences, there was a tendency on the part of magistrates and judges to be sympathetic towards people accused under the Act. An aspect of the prevailing thought on 'immorality' was the potential it contained for 'the most dangerous form of blackmail or intimidation': the kind which made it impossible for the victim to claim the protection of the state as a citizen.[76]

Future generations, Heydenrych prophesied in the conclusion of his study, would refuse to believe that the Immorality Act was either morally, culturally or politically justified as a measure 'to protect the weak from themselves'. Neither the methods used, nor the punishments meted out, nor the measure itself, would be regarded as having been justified. The assurance for this conclusion was the writer's belief that a new social order and a new way of thinking was already developing. This would not be reconciled to the further pursuance of the provisions of the Act.

Closely akin to the 'Immorality' legislation was that prohibiting mixed marriages. The *Prohibition of Mixed Marriages Amendment Act* (1968) extended the existing legislation so as to include South African citizens living abroad, who had contracted a 'mixed marriage' in terms of the principal Act. Such marriage, the amending Act now declared, would henceforth be void and of no effect in the Republic. Moreover, the partners, should they venture to return to South Africa, could be prosecuted under the Immorality Act.

It was a very real issue at the time. Breyten Breytenbach, most eminent of the younger Afrikaans poets, had married a Vietnam-ese wife and was living in Paris. Now he was prevented from returning to his native land. There were bitter reactions from Afrikaans poets and writers. For some time, the matter was debated in an atmosphere of intense feeling. The authorities were adamant. The policy would be honoured. Breytenbach and his Vietnamese wife, however charming, would not be allowed to live in the country as man and wife.*

It was all grossly absurd; but it was policy. It was also the dictate of a radical dream, an utopian ideal. Common sense or other human considerations had nothing to do with it. Certain theologians supporting the policy would have described it as all part of the 'law of life' of this particular nation. There was nothing more to be done about it.

Group areas, population classification, sexual contact between Whites and non-Whites ... The enormous attempt at radical reconstruction of South African society had led to changed conditions in several areas disturbing to the white conscience, including public amenities, entertainment and sport.

During the fifties and sixties, separation of sporting bodies was uncompromisingly insisted upon, being a logical outcome of the policy. Early in 1963, the then Minister for the Interior announced that *white* internationals only represented *white* South Africa. Likewise, *non-white* internationals would represent *non-white* South Africa. Beyond the country's boundaries, however, this would not be allowed, irrespective of the skills of the participants. For the purposes of the Olympic Games, Whites and non-Whites would choose their own repre-sentatives. The white sporting authorities (S.A. Olympic and National Games Association) would then, after liaising with 'non-white' leaders, decide on the Olympic contingent. All this was academic, because South Africa was, in fact, excluded from participation in the 1968 Olympic Games in Mexico City. During the previous three to four years, she had also been ex-cluded from a number of other international sporting events.

* Early in 1972, Breytenbach and his wife were brought to South Africa by the Nationalist mass-circulation Sunday newspaper *Rapport*, successor to *Die Beeld*. In spite of highly critical statements, Breytenbach was generally fêted, especially by younger Afrikaner writers.

Verwoerd had said at Loskop in the Transvaal in 1965 that visiting teams, like the New Zealand Rugby Team (the 'All Blacks'), would not be allowed to bring 'non-white' (Maori) players on a tour to South Africa. However, B. J. Vorster, who succeeded Verwoerd, revised this in 1967.

In 1968, the whole matter of trying to fit the life of the country into the framework of separate development was again dramatized. Again, the central figure was coloured.

Basil d'Oliveira, who had previously left South Africa because there was no prospect for him as an unusually talented cricketer of ever playing for his own country, was chosen as a member of the British M.C.C. touring team to South Africa. His inclusion, however, was seen as a political move; and the M.C.C. was informed that d'Oliveira was not acceptable. Thereupon, the M.C.C. cancelled the tour. In 1970, they announced that no further cricket test matches would take place between England and South Africa, until cricket in the Republic was played on a multi-racial basis and teams were selected purely on merit. Soon afterwards, South Africa was suspended from a number of other international sporting bodies.

Early in 1972, d'Oliveira re-visited the country of his birth, coaching coloured cricket teams. Just before his return to England, an attempt was made to arrange a special match between white and coloured players as a token of honour and appreciation towards a man who had, against great odds, reached the highest pinnacle in this sport. Permission to play the match on a field near Cape Town, however, was refused.

An Afrikaner, describing himself as a Nationalist born and bred, wrote as follows to *Die Burger*:

There are limits to the long-suffering tolerance of us all. Although I have been full to bursting for some time now, I have always pinned my hopes on realities, and kept myself from this present kind of utterance. Now my cup spills over its brim . . .

Is there a clearer case for merit, on international level too, than precisely this, where it concerns one of our country's own sons: a man who has already achieved world-wide recognition for his proficiency as a sportsman, also for his spirit? Was this not a golden opportunity to demonstrate to our critics that we are prepared to live here in good fellowship with those of another colour? What harm would this concession have done to our policy, or anything else dear to us? Or is the policy itself so vulnerable, that even a gesture of goodwill or humanity should be regarded as a threat? ...

And now I ask myself: are we really busy maintaining and extending a civilization, or are we ... busy demolishing and destroying, with heart and soul, our Christian sense of neighbourly love ...[77]

An example of apartheid in the public amenities was provided by the great new Nico Malan theatre-complex in Cape Town. This was built at a cost of R12 million, towards which the labour, skills and taxes of Whites and Coloureds through the years had contributed. It was now, however, strictly reserved for Whites only, while the amenities it provided were in no way to be duplicated elsewhere.[78]

There was also the racial zoning of beaches. Inevitably, the best places with the best amenities were accorded to the group in power. The vast preponderance of worthwhile beaches on the often magnificent South African coast was reserved for Whites. This was to be expected. In March 1969, the then Administrator of the Cape, Dr J. Nico Malan, had said that white selfishness was frustrating all attempts to provide decent beach amenities for coloured people. This selfishness, he also declared, had to be seen to be believed.[79]

The year 1965 saw H. F. Verwoerd at the height of his power as Premier. The government was more firmly entrenched than any other in the history of South Africa. The economy of the country was set for a boom. The threat from the militant left was almost eliminated. There was no sign of slackening in the drive towards the ideal of a radical, rationally reconstructed society, or the faith in the ultimate validity of the *apartheids-gedagte*. But there were, nevertheless, a spate of measures which would deeply have puzzled a newly arrived, but objective, observer.

It was the year in which Breyten Breytenbach had been refused permission to bring his Vietnamese wife to South Africa to meet his parents. A proposed visit to Cape Town of the United States aircraft-carrier *Independence* was cancelled after the South African authorities insisted that its pilots who landed in the country should be white. It was the year in which a white taximan, fearful of deviating from policy, said that he could not accept a blind white girl, accompanied by her coloured maid, as passengers. White and non-White, he said, could not travel together in the same car. White and coloured children were not allowed to take part together in a Red Cross pageant at Maynardville. Coloured music-lovers were compelled if they wished to attend the symphony concerts in Cape Town City Hall, to use separate entrances, ticket offices and toilets. At the same time, their seats in the auditorium were strictly roped off at the back of the hall. It was the year of the provision of separate reading tables in the central principal library in Cape Town, though White and non-White used the same books. It was . . .

It was the year after the refusal of Cabinet ministers to attend diplomatic functions, or other receptions, where Blacks and Coloureds were present as guests. It was the year after 'non-Whites' were prohibited membership of white scientific societies. It was . . . But the list is a dreary one. It is also, in a sense, inexhaustible.

What it demonstrates is the way of radical, puritan man, in his relentless search for happiness, pursuing his impossible ideal at almost any cost. It is both the Thirstlander on the highveld of Southern Africa, and Ahab, the New Englander, on the oceans of the world.

The end is tragi-comic. Whether, in a given context, we call it tragedy or comedy is a matter of where the emphasis lies.

In the case of H. F. Verwoerd, the most forceful, intelligent and dedicated exponent of apartheid, it was tragedy.

What happened on that fateful day of 6 September 1966? There had been a general election. Riding the wave of unprecedented success, Verwoerd had unexpectedly gone to the country for a mandate to pursue his vision in what promised to be its decisive stages. The step was perfectly timed. In the election the Nationalist Party had achieved a majority of almost three to one over the combined opposition. The mandate was now complete: the country had gratefully accepted the gift of enduring national and ethnic security from Verwoerd. He had said that its people should 'create their own future'. He had set the example. They were inspired by his faith and his dedication to the ideal. The great majority followed him thankfully. He had, like Prometheus, brought to them fire, promising life and happiness. Like Prometheus he could say of a purblind Zeus, the tyrannous force opposing man in his search for happiness:

> Yet no care was in his heart for miserable men, and he was fain to blot out the whole race and in their stead create another. None save me opposed his purpose; I only dared; I rescued mankind from the heavy blow that was to cast them into Hades . . .

Others before him had discerned the fire and described it. He, Verwoerd, had brought it to men themselves, bearing it carefully in a fennel-stalk to all who had need of it. It was a tireless, selfless and courageous act. For that very reason, it was also incipiently tragic.

The rumour had spread that in the speech he was to make in the House of Assembly at the start of the afternoon sitting, Verwoerd would give an exposition of the final stages in the unfolding of the idea of separate development. At the same time, it would be a re-affirmation of the socio-political ideal and of the faith with which he had inspired his people. A few days previously, at Pretoria, he had for the first time met and conferred with the head of a free, black Southern African state, Chief Leabua Jonathan of Lesotho.

Verwoerd never used notes. Neither did he have any that afternoon. Nobody had any details of what he was going to say. The whole country sat waiting tensely to hear his speech. It promised to be the most important he had ever made.

The country was peaceful. The operation against those who had threatened or attempted sabotage or insurrection had entirely succeeded. Vorster, as Minister of Justice, working closely with an efficient force of security police, had seen to this. There had been considerable protest against measures like house arrest, incarceration without trial, uncompromising methods of investigation and so on. The protests had lasted for some time; and had then seemed to die down. There was no doubt about it: the country was at peace, and Vorster and the security police deserved a great deal of credit for it. During the early, troubled sixties things could very easily have got out of hand. At Rivonia and other places, the revolutionary opposition had been struck severely...

In the House of Assembly itself where, in accordance with general policy, only white messengers could work, there had been some difficulty in obtaining suitable staff. In fact, when a man called Dimitrio Tsafendas knocked at a side-door one day to inquire whether there was an opening, the Chief Messenger was only too pleased to invite him inside. Whites generally had grown out of these kind of jobs.

Tsafendas was accepted. In spite of the fact that he seemed to be a maverick, rather introverted and not always satisfactory in his work, he remained on the staff as a messenger.

No attempt had been made, either by the parliamentary staff or the security police, to check on the past of this man who had been engaged in this most casual way. Had they done so, they would have discovered an important fact. He had been engaged as a White, but was, in fact, a Coloured. Neither was he born in South Africa. He had come to the Republic from Mozambique in a rather doubtful way. He was of mixed Greek and Mulatto descent.

Verwoerd had already taken his place in the Prime Minister's seat in the House of Assembly. There was an air of great expectancy over the House. On the member's benches, in the press gallery and public galleries, everybody was tensely waiting for an epoch-making restatement of policy, with perhaps new emphases and visions.

A messenger was suddenly seen to cross the floor of the House. In an odd way, he seemed to be out of place. He seemed to be in a hurry. And his clothes were disarranged.

He *was* out of place and in a hurry. His clothes were indeed disarranged. For the next moment, having reached the bench of the Prime Minister, he suddenly drew a dagger from under his jacket and lunged with it at Verwoerd. The blade entered Verwoerd's heart.

There was confusion. Members grappled with the assassin

and struck him down. But on the floor, in front of the Prime Minister's bench, Verwoerd himself was lying outstretched. He was already dead.

In this strange, gothic way, a man of indubitable stature came to his end. He had dreamt mightily, worked unceasingly and talked tirelessly. He had been struck down by the hand he himself had introduced into the inner sanctuary.

It was yet another tragedy in the history of a country, of a people, who had already known an unusual amount of it.

The essence of it was irony.

11 The Rise of Afrikaner Capitalism

On 17 February 1938, a centenary festival was held at Blaauw-krantz, on an upper tributary of the Tugela. A hundred years earlier the area, like that between the nearby headwaters of the Bushman's, another part of the Tugela system, had been the scene of massacres following the death by violence of Retief and his men at Mgungundlovu. The main speaker was the old *veldprediker* – field-chaplain – of the Boer forces in the Second War of Independence, J. D. Kestell. Now he was a man of 84, addressed by all as *Vader* Kestell, probably the only one ever to have been accorded this title as a spiritual leader of the Afrikaner people.

Like all such festivals, it was an occasion for oratory. Mostly, speakers had urged those gathered together to re-discover the values which had enabled the Voortrekkers to pioneer a 'wild and dangerous territory'. This time, however, there was a difference. Those gathered at Blaauwkrantz and other places to celebrate the Day of the Covenant were doing so at a time when the Afrikaners were in flux, uncomfortably out of place in their new urban surroundings, conscious of their being strangers in an Anglo-Saxon world, and were taking stock of their true position. True enough, they had consistently taken the political lead in the country. Every Prime Minister since Union had been an Afri-kaner. Nationalism, as expounded by Diederichs, Meyer, Cronjé and others, had been given a new dynamic. Nevertheless there was a growing yearning for real Afrikaner power: to estab-lish an order in which the oldest part of the white population would no longer feel itself foreign in their own country. Over all lay the shadow of the third-of-a million of rural poor, who in the early thirties had been the subject of a broad, intense investiga-tion by the Carnegie Commission.

The problem, in fact, was already being solved by the very process of urbanization. The newly urbanized Afrikaners had already progressed from menial to skilled work, from blue-collar to white-collar jobs. The professional class had also been extended. In business, an executive class was already embryonically there.

The Afrikaners themselves, however, hardly understood this. What held their attention was the recent memory of the report by the Carnegie Commission, and the still too-obvious fact that the money in the country was in the hands of 'foreign elements'.

My Nasie in Nood – 'My Nation in Peril' – was the theme of Kestell's Blaauwkrantz address. Before an intensely attentive crowd, he deplored the fact that so many descendants of the Voortrekkers and even earlier pioneers had forfeited their Afrikaner consciousness. 'Before us,' he declared, 'there arises a multitude of unhappy ones who, in spite of themselves have been cast into misery ... There are 300,000 of our own flesh and blood who have sunk into penury: materially but also spiritually ... A *reddingsdaad* – an act of redemption – must be extended towards them.'

The recurring line *my nasie in nood* was taken up by Afrikaner-conscious cultural and political leaders everywhere. It led to the first Economic Congress of the People, a month or so after the outbreak of World War II, the lead being taken by precisely the political and academic intellectuals who had come to the fore in the new urban culture of the Afrikaners. Among them were men like P. J. Meyer, N. Diederichs, T. E. Dönges and H. F. Verwoerd. This meant that the *Broederbond*, the workshop in which the new Afrikaner nationalism was being shaped, was alive to the necessity of an advance on both the political and economic fronts. In the mid-thirties, the organization had been directly responsible for the founding of key financial institutions.

It was the saintly *Vader* Kestell who summed it all up at the *Volkskongres* of 1939. 'We must look after each other,' he said, 'because we are blood of each other's blood. We belong to each other – we, the small Boer nation, here in South Africa. This drives us to rush to the aid of those of our brothers and sisters who are in need; to help them to help themselves. We do this in the firm belief that we as a people should save ourselves . . .'[1]

The theme *'n Volk red homself* – 'a nation saves itself' – would in time be more assertively expressed by H. F. Verwoerd as: *Skep u eie toekoms* – 'create your own future'.

Kestell, steeped in the Reformed tradition of his people, may well have sensed that the plea without qualification would be misunderstood, for he added: 'Deeper still is the conviction in our innermost being that we can effect nothing without God. We acknowledge that He in His sovereign power rules all our destiny.'[2]

What Kestell seemed to be intuitively apprehensive of was the positive, programmatic construction of the future to an all-providing design. His vision of Afrikanerdom placed on a sound basis of economic independence was nearer to the views of the Potchefstroom academic, L. J. du Plessis, who in the old tradition of Hertzogite, socialist nationalism, pleaded at the *Volkskongres* for capital to be used in the co-operative way. Mere money power built on sand could not be the object of the Afrikaners' economic efforts, he said. This was foreign and had foreign connections. It was not the way of the Afrikaners.[3]

Du Plessis was not openly opposed at the meeting. He was simply, in all charity, by-passed. In fact, he himself realized soon enough that what was happening could hardly take place within another kind of economic structure than had hitherto existed in the country. The very manifesto issued by the *Reddingsdaadbond* – fully established by the Congress – was one of extensive programmatic action within a capitalist framework. There were socialist elements in it, including the monthly contributions of members towards the economic advancement of their fellow Afrikaners as a whole, some attention to agricultural co-operatives and consumer organizations, and communal participation in facilities for recreation and insurance. But the heart of the manifesto and, in fact, the only part of the whole scheme for economic rehabilitation to show true vitality, was that of 'organizing the capital power of the Afrikaners'. This would be centred around an investment company with an initial capital of £30,000.

Kestell died two years after the *Volkskongres*, still happy in the thought that his Blaauwkrantz plea had shown such quick and positive results. Had he been a younger man, or had he had more experience of the way in which capitalism through the centuries had grown out of the 'protestant ethic', he might well have had misgivings. After all, the whole of Kestell's motivation had been that of a massive act of economic redemption, a huge helping hand extended to the 300,000 poor.

At the *Volkskongres*, however, T. E. Dönges delivered a paper on *The Mobilizing of the Capital Savings of the Afrikaner* and M. S. Louw spoke on the *Employment of Afrikaner Capital*. Already prominent, too, were: F. Meyer (Iscor), H. J. van Eck (Industrial Development Corporation), M. S. Louw, C. R. Louw, C. G. W. Schumann and A. D. Wassenaar, all men who were to become pillars of Afrikaner capitalism. This was no mere band of Afrikaner socialist-nationalists bent on distributing alms to needy fellow-Afrikaners. This was – as was the case, too, in the wider context of the socio-political ideal – consistently a band of brothers: still warily feeling their way into the capitalist society of the twentieth century, deeply determined to prove that there was nothing done by Anglo-Saxon or Jewish South Africa in the field of business which they, the Afrikaners, could not improve on. These were days of relative economic innocence. The collective interests of Afrikanerdom were still the dominant element. It was another lane added to the freeway to the stars. That the lane would, in time, branch off to become an alternative route to happiness, nobody could foresee.

There was particular pleasure at the *Volkskongres* at the founding of the central investment organization.[4] There was also pleasure at the founding of an Afrikaans Chamber of Commerce and Industries, and an Economic Institute.

The early forties, as we have seen, was the low-water mark in Afrikaner nationalism after Hertzog. Smuts was leading the country in politics and war, and the nation-conscious Afrikaners were in disarray. The attempts now to broaden the field of positive Afrikaner activity, trying to penetrate the world of business and industry, were, for largely the same reasons, often disastrous. Numerous companies, appealing to sentiment by use

of the prefix *volks* – a leftover from the days of socialist-national-
ism – lasted for a short time, then succumbed ignominiously.
Nevertheless, loyal Afrikaners contributed liberally to such
companies – farmers, schoolteachers, academics, doctors, lawyers and so on. Shares were mostly bought, not because of the
sound investment offered, but because it was the Afrikaner thing
to do: one supported the *eie*, including the economic *eie*, even
if it cost you money. That it so often proved to be without
substance or hopelessly mismanaged was, on the whole, accepted
philosophically. By the mid-forties, there was enough worthless
scrip in deceased estates around the country to paper the houses
of a great many widows and orphans; or to file or frame later,
as interesting pieces of Africana.

Two things were happening which Kestell had in no way
envisaged. In the fast expanding post-war industrial economy
of South Africa, the term 'Poor-White' was becoming increasingly rare. In its place, the *burgerstand* had arisen. At the same
time, Afrikaner businessmen had learnt a great deal from the
mistakes of the early forties. Sounder undertakings with better
management and a deeper grasp of the workings of capitalist
society were now consistently being launched.

Slightly more than a decade after the first *volkskongres*, a
second was held. It was both a stock-taking and a re-affirmation
of the Afrikaners' determination to establish themselves, not only
politically, but also economically.

'The meaning of this congress cannot be overestimated,' D. F.
Malan, who had meanwhile become Prime Minister of South
Africa, stressed at the time.

Eleven years have passed since the first *volkskongres* of this kind
took place, also here in Bloemfontein. That was after the Great
Awakening which the rolling wheels of the symbolic Ox-Wagon Trek
had brought about. It had happened under the inspiring leadership
of that unforgettable Man of God, and Man of the People, *Vader*
Kestell. The enormous upsurge in the emotions of our people should
not be allowed to evanesce like the morning dew. The mighty stream
of reborn love for the nation, the feeling of unity must not be allowed
to disappear unused in desert sands. It *must* ever be converted to
permanent, self-perpetuating values; and the necessary machinery

must be created. The trek must continue. The course has been fixed, unchangeably. The potential and ultimate end is without limits . . .

For all who wish to look back on the road travelled by the Afrikaner people, one thing should be clear, and that is that this economic forward movement was born out of crisis. The Afrikaners had to resist the growing rate of disintegration. Relying on their own inner strength, they had to rise, or perish . . .[5]

Nothing indicates the true nature of the Afrikaners' economic *risorgimento* better than these words of D. F. Malan. Nothing indicates more clearly how, also in the case of the Puritans in Africa, capitalism in this part of the world of Western Protestant man also assumed its particular shape by virtue of a socio-political ideal, a secular creed; in short, radical politics.

The deepest-lying motive in man's self-sufficient efforts ('create your own future', 'relying on their own inner strength') is power. But naked power, as we have seen, is not possible for Western Christian man, especially of Calvinist-Puritan leanings. All who in the early days of Calvinism had been gathered in its great net and who had resisted the absolutism of the Church of Rome, had not done so solely for reasons of true Christian belief or authentic faith. Many had militantly opposed the church, seeking to answer power with power. These had formed the true dynamic in Puritanism. They were the saintly revolutionaries who wished to reform the world and establish justice. What they needed above all was power, but it had to be power acceptable also in Christian terms. Therefore, it became couched in terms of a socio-political ideal. This very ideal, however, tends to engender, sooner or later, the spirit of capitalism. For money presents itself as *the* alternative certitude for those who have already acquired political dominance. This means, in the final resort, man setting up for himself, 'relying on his own inner strength' and 'creating his own future'. And the more man claims divine approval for this attitude, the more he relies on his own rational efforts. Man distrusts the true plenitude of grace in the garden of the world. Man seeks to have knowledge of good and evil by stealing the fruit from the Tree in the middle of the Garden. The happiness which was sought has been turned into banishment.

Or it is man and the Tower which he will build, so that it

reaches unto heaven. Relying on his own unity and inner strength, he undertakes this heroic task to create his own future. The Tower grows, and its top loses all contact with the earth; so too the builders. One day, God looks down in surprise and wishes to know what in heaven's name is going on. The end, again, is confusion. In the world of increasing abstractions, words have lost their meaning. Mysteriously, heaven has proved to be hell.

It would have been predictable, if there had been observers with the full knowledge of what had happened in history not once, but many times. But man always re-learns his lessons, and then forgets them again. Man in a situation of being a stranger – as the *platteland* Afrikaners, who came to the Anglo-Saxon cities, were – needs to answer power with power. He sees in this the only hope for his future. Here lies the true answer. Puritan man, however, cannot do this in an open bid for supremacy, only in terms of a great ideal; in terms of what is, in a sense, basic to man's spiritual life, that is to say, freedom. It is a self-created idea, however, and so it becomes an abstraction of freedom. What it wills is a programmatic re-structuring of the world in terms of this abstraction.

It is rationalism, applying equally well to the socio-political ideal as to the spirit of capitalism. The latter, R. H. Tawney has described as the 'deliberate and systematic adjustment of economic means to the attainment of the objective of pecuniary profit'. Tawney argued that Calvin, understanding and accepting the tenor of the age with its new money economy, prepared the way for what in Puritanism became the triumph of the economic virtues. Calvin, we have seen, did enforce a certain rigorous discipline at Geneva; but as Biéler has so exhaustively shown, his concern for exploited man, suffering at the hands of the economically more powerful, was an authentic Christian concern. Anthropologically, Calvin and Marx, we need to remind ourselves again, would have understood each other. It was the Puritan ethic, arising out of primitive Calvinism, which gave birth to both the socio-political ideal *and* the spirit of capitalism.

'What in Calvin had been a qualified concession to practical exigencies,' Tawney says, appeared in some of his later followers as a frank idealization of the life of the trader, as the service of God and the training ground of the soul . . . Puritanism in its later phases added a halo of ethical sanctification to the appeal of economic expediency, and offered a moral creed, in which the duties of religion and the calls of business ended their long estrangement in an unanticipated reconciliation.[6]

It was the Puritan spirit, in fact, which, especially after the Industrial Revolution, finally set up the money-changers and traders in the temple. The Puritan qualities and the admiration of them remained, says Tawney, when the religious reference and the restraints which it imposed had weakened or disappeared. It is in this sense that both Britain's Victorian Empire, and the equally staggering dimensions of modern American philanthropy, should also be seen.

Weber's examination of the connection between religious radicalism and economic progress, the growth of a worldly asceticism, stressed the 'systematic, rational ordering of moral life as a whole'[7] and stressed the way in which Puritan man was bent on subjecting his fellow man to the 'supremacy of a purposeful will'.[8] This is rationalism, because it is the utter reliance on Organized Man, as Henry Luce once put it.[9] Moreover, formal acknowledgement may still be made to Providence in a variety of ways, ranging from Weber's 'worldly asceticism', to its emotional counterpart, Pietism.

The heart of the matter is power. Here is the true and abiding motive. And pre-eminently those within the Calvinist-Puritan ethic, who secretly yearn for power, find it impossible to do so openly, nakedly and unashamedly. It is the concept of their particular system of idealism which justifies, for them, their search for survival, identity, fulfilment and happiness, which power represents. The Puritan mind is exceedingly tough; but its conscience is correspondingly tender.

As to what comes first, there can be no question: it is the socio-political ideal. History has demonstrated this time and again. It has also been so in the case of the Puritans in Africa. Therefore, it would be correct to qualify the theses of both Tawney and Weber by saying that the spirit of capitalism rises not out of authentic, but out of secular, religion. The socio-political ideal immediately precedes the capitalist spirit. This is not a rule, but a trend.

Economic independence in the life of any community or people is a legitimate concern. The real wealth of man, however, as Ruskin said, is life itself. It can be taken that when Kestell made his appeal at Blaauwkrantz for the economic rehabilitation of Afrikanerdom, remembering especially the 300,000 of the Carnegie Commission, this was the predominant mood behind his thinking.

It was also the predominant mood of the *volkskongres* of 1939. In this light D. F. Malan, opening the congress of 1950, also saw the economic progress of his people.

An indication of how things had developed according to classic capitalist forms is afforded by the case of L. J. du Plessis, who had made the plea at the first *volkskongres* in 1939 that the Afrikaners' economic independence should be sought on predominantly co-operative, that is to say, socialist-nationalist, lines. Now, eleven years later, du Plessis himself admitted that the *Reddingsdaadfonds*, to which thousands of Afrikaners had contributed their small monthly amounts, intended as a central fund for general Afrikaner economic revival, had not come up to expectations. The result of all their labours had been only £100,000. In the intervening years, du Plessis added, a 'change of emphasis' had taken place. The *reddingsidee* – the idea of economic redemption – had now made way for the idea of 'development and consolidation'. To this he added, most significantly: 'And the co-operative method has slowly been converted into the mobilization of capital.'[10] Isolation, too, as far as business was concerned, had come to an end. There was now greater contact with 'other elements in the population'. What he was saying, in effect, was that the forward-going Afrikaner businessmen and industrialists had discovered that capitalism, too, was one and indivisible. There could be no real growth with the nation-conscious Afrikaners taking in each others' washing. The economic potential of South Africa as a whole had been left largely untapped by many generations of Afrikaners, outside of agriculture. It had been almost totally neglected by the oldest part of the white population, and was now to be fully exploited.

The academic from Potchefstroom was, in fact, announcing that Afrikaner capitalism would move strongly ahead, especially now that the new nationalists had come to power. At the same time it was a last, gentle word of farewell to the socialist tendencies which had been a characteristic of Afrikaner politics since the time of the Pact Government in the twenties. It was also the definitive charter for a new generation of Afrikaner capitalists. Within the next two decades they would go 'from strength to strength'. Simultaneously, all the typical phenomena of consumer capitalist society would begin asserting themselves.

The story of the rise of Afrikaner capitalism is, as J. L. Sadie, an acute observer of the scene, has described it, the story of the rise of the New Men. In effect this means the rise of the new kind of Afrikaner, different to the semi-feudal, soil-rooted *plattelanders*, living in serene self-sufficiency on their ancestral lands. He was also different to the *volksmanne* – men of the people – who had represented Afrikanerdom in parliament during the Age of the Generals and to the general *burgerstand* which had developed in the fringe-areas of the cities between the wars. He was also different to the intellectual élite which had extruded out of this middle class and had largely constructed the new socio-political ideal and to the political leaders who had appeared as part of the same process. He was different to the professional class which had for a long time formed the upper layer of the *burgerstand*; different, too, to the combination of many of these elements, professional man, politician, intellectual and *volksman*, devoted to the notion of a nation redeeming itself. These were the New Men.

'This indigenous factor was the New Men who answered the appeal to action to rescue a people at that time still burdened by some 300,000 members degenerating in the vicious circle of impoverishment,' Sadie has stated.

It was a call to the social conscience . . . of the Afrikaner. While initially a certain amount of mass action and sentiment was not without its usefulness, in the longer run it was the qualities and activities of the relatively few which proved to be of lasting significance. Men of bold imagination and energy appeared on the economic horizon from within the community itself. Imbued with a spirit of enterprise which they wished to apply in the economic field, they were innovators who graduated out of traditional society. That their innovations consisted of no more than an adaptation of economic processes already well-known among the more developed English-speaking community did not make them rank lower in inventiveness or creativeness. The essential point is that their economic actions were different from those preceding them in the same society . . .[11]

It is a premise of the business leaders that the large, financially powerful, concern is the most effective means of increasing the share of the Afrikaner as employer in the economy. Another premise is that they appeal to the Afrikaans consumer only by way of the quality of their product and service and not by invoking sentiment. These enterprises and those established by the government, offered the necessary opportunities for the training of managers and other executives who can continue the work of the old guard who lacked this background and had to learn by doing . . .[12]

Success bred further success in a cumulative upward progression. The Afrikaans *Handelsinstituut* – the Economic Institute – which had been one of the positive results of the first *volkskongres* had been urging its members for many years not to rely on the sentimental appeal. The essence of their message was that real economic progress had always been the work of successful *entrepreneurs*. These were the few, endowed with the necessary talent for organization and requisite vision and drive. In this respect, the Afrikaners were no different to the peoples in their countries of origin.

A leader in the new Afrikaner business field of the time described the requirements for the true *entrepreneur*.[13] He should be a creator, he said, whose creative deeds are in the service of the community. He had to be so absorbed in his task, and find such expression in its performance, that consideration of personal gain would find no place. Neither should he set a commercial value on his services. He should rather apply his talents so that by means of increased opportunities for employment his fellow Afrikaners would find a meaningful place for themselves in their own country. In all, enterprises should be strictly built on sound economic principles, but consistently provide increased opportunities for eager young Afrikaners to enter the world of business. The Puritan tone of these sentiments are obvious. They are representative of the view of the leaders of Afrikaner business in the two decades following the end of World War II. They are sentiments also reminiscent of the Henry Fords *et alii* in the classically public-minded mood of American money.

M. S. Louw in insurance, Sadie evaluated, C. R. Louw in newspapers were two originals of the New Men ... In the same tradition was A. D. Wassenaar, whom he declared was 'the great exponent of the idea that the Finance House and other financial institutions are the key to Afrikaner progress in the business world'. So too, C. H. Brink, the first official of the *Federale Volksbeleggings Ltd (F.V.B.)*, the central investment company which had been a feature of the original manifesto of the *Reddingsdaad-idee* in 1939, the only element in the scheme to show true vitality. So, too, H. B. Coetzer who was the 'moving spirit in *Federale Mynbou*', the first Afrikaner Mining House, established by *Federale Volksbeleggings*.

He engineered the link-up between *F.V.B.* and Anglo-American, which led to the assumption of control by the former General Mining and Finance Corporation, an old established Mining House whose numerous interests encompass investments worth R250 million. T. F. Muller, a former technical director of *Federale Mynbou*, and director of some forty companies, became managing director of General Mining.[14]

In a nutshell, this was a description of the whole profound change in life-style of a people who up to World War II had been almost completely devoid of business acumen. Their predominant figure of caricature was still Hoggenheimer – the Anglo-Semitic figure of vulgar and ostentatious wealth, meant to symbolize the *geldmag* – money power – as it had come down in memory since the *Goudoorlog* – Gold War – the Anglo-Boer War, as it was still sometimes referred to.

Now, here in the sixties, only two and a bit generations removed from the Second War of Independence, the New Afrikaners and the *geldmag*, in the form of the mammoth Anglo-American Corporation, had discovered each other. It was enough to make Kruger turn in his grave. He would certainly have regarded it strangely. In only a slightly lesser degree, it was foreign to the originator of the slogan *'n Volk Red Homself* –

Vader Kestell. Had he lived long enough, he would most certainly have said that this was not quite what he had intended.

There was no deflecting the New Men from their course, however, once they were on their way. Two sons of the *platteland* epitomize even more impressively the metamorphosis which overtook the Puritans in Africa. They were both born and raised on the Karroo, the vast inland plateau of the central Cape Province. They had only the background of Karroo farm-life and small-town citizenry and no experience of business or industry. But they were to become *entrepreneurs* of an entirely new order in the economic history of South Africa. Compared to them, the 'innovator *par excellence*', M. S. Louw, would soon seem old-fashioned.

Jan S. Marais came from Fraserburg, a hamlet lost in an infinity of plain and distant flat-topped mountains, melting into another infinity of steely-blue sky. Serving an apprenticeship during the forties with the *Federale* Group, he set off on his own venture in 1955, after touring the world and looking closely at the way things were done in economically progressive countries like the U.S.A. 'Starting from scratch . . .' Sadie relates,

the assets of this company exclusive of hidden reserves, grew by leaps and bounds to touch the R300 million mark by the end of 1965. Full of ideas and very much alive to the most modern business methods, Jan S. Marais developed this creation of *F.V.B.* with hire-purchase and personal loan transactions as its principal activity, into a 'one-stop Bank' catering to all or most of the financial needs of the public, including commercial bank services.[15]

Diversifying in a great many ways, as the sixties progressed, the name of Trust Bank became synonymous with dynamic aggression, putting swing into the business style of the Afrikaners as few would have thought remotely possible, even at the time of the second *Volkskongres* in 1950. On the whole, they gave a big boost to the image of the *verburgerlikte* – bourgeois Afrikaners. Afrikaner undertakings were long past the stage of steady conservatism and settled growth. Now, in ventures like Trust Bank, the broad layer of suburban Afrikaners were given the opportunity to share vicariously in the adage, attributed to Archimedes: 'Give me where to stand and I will lever the world.' This stance, more and more were discovering, had no essential need of a political shape.

This, in a sense, was even more the case with the other son of the Karroo, A. E. Rupert. Across the north-eastern horizon from Fraserburg lay the historic town of Graaff-Reinet, the scene of the first responses of an awakening Afrikanerdom to the double challenge of conquering British and invading Xhosa at the end of the eighteenth century. From the summits of these surrealistic hills, the Karroo infinity seemed to be even more infinite.

'Anton E. Rupert,' Sadie records,

dynamic spirit of this world-wide empire of the Rembrandt Tobacco Group, is in a class of his own. Renouncing a university lectureship, he started off in a humble manner, but as a practical idealist with a talent for forceful marketing. New ideas on product promotion are his forte. Putting his creed of 'industrial partnership' into practice, according to which the participation of local interests is a prerequisite, he joined forces with overseas tobacco companies until today the cigarettes manufactured by his group in twenty-six factories, situated in fifteen countries, are sold in 160 countries on five continents. Believing in remaining ahead of competitors and the anti-tobacco campaign through research, his group established world-leadership in the production and marketing of the king-size cigarette, the king-size filter cigarette, the menthol-filter cigarette, and the king-size cigarettes with a 'multi-filter', the super-porous 'multivent' paper, and the ultra-modern gold band filter. His latest tie-up with a company in Germany will boost the turnover of the world-group from R600 million to some R870 million. His new venture is the establishment of a liquor empire in South Africa, Oude Meester Cellars, which links up with Whitbreads of Britain and Heinekens of the Netherlands.[16]

In the late thirties, Rupert had been a leader of the very nationally-minded Afrikaner students who had sat at the feet of Diederichs, Cronjé and Meyer. He had shared their sentiments deeply, and his own little tobacco venture had started as a direct result of the appeal of Kestell and others that a nation should save itself. Within a generation, he was addressing audiences around the world on a great variety of subjects. His speeches were duly published in a special series. Before a group of Afrikaner businessmen in a leading country town of the Western Cape, he had occasion to say: 'I am a man with a Christian conscience, child of Christian civilization. I am Afrikaner-born. I am a South African. I belong to the Western world. I am a world citizen.'[17]

There was no question about the speaker's deep commitment to his ideal.

His organization was built up to its world-wide proportions in little more than a decade-and-a-half. What was more, the organization soon built up philanthropic activities on an equally impressive and world-wide scale. The arts especially benefited handsomely from the patronage of Rembrandt. So, too, did the old Cape Houses in Stellenbosch, Graaff-Reinet (Rupert's home-town), and other places, many of which were restored to their pristine beauty, all due to the magnanimous interest shown by the Rupert Organization. So, too, did nature conservation.

In fact, nothing the Americans had ever done in the all-encompassing good works of Protestant capitalism could be said to have surpassed this amazing and sudden flowering of Afrikaner business efficiency and public spirit. On the contrary, the Americans could well have benefited by a careful study of the method, as it had evolved in the white Protestant South of the African continent.

'The West faces the temptation of wealth,' Rupert said in nicely measured tones when addressing Canadian businessmen.

Every sage, every saint and every philosopher of history has warned against the consequences of accepting without thought or heart-searching the privilege of wealth ... That is how Knossos, the rich and civilized capital of ancient Crete, fell in a night to the invading Mycenaeans. That is how Rome fell to the Barbarians. Can you afford the uncomfortable expenditure to ensure the safety of your luxurious way of life?[18]

The shades of Weber and Tawney would, perhaps, have joined that of Kruger. They would have experienced common amazement that this fragment of reformed humanity – the Afrikaners – had, so soon after their 'Age of the Generals', provided such striking evidence of the essential correctness of their insight.

Wherever capitalism has arisen on the firm foundation of a secular religion, high-minded puritanism has inevitably clashed with the growth of a culture of banality.

Early in the seventies, the spirit of the age for an expanding cadre of the *burgerstand* – living either in the cities or formally still on the *platteland* – has been epitomized by the ultimate status symbol of the 'Golden Bath', complete with its golden taps and constituting the centre of a bathroom suite, costing what most would pay for a four- or five-roomed house. By the beginning of the seventies, it had become sought-after by as motley a company as one could imagine: from ranchers owning huge estates in the outer Sandveld to the new instant millionaires of the overspilling cities.

This ultimate trend in religion and the rise of capitalism among the Afrikaners of Southern Africa is contained in the personal history of one of the most remarkable of modern Afrikaans poets. This is the captivating story of a *platteland* boy, also from the Karroo, emerging from an often hard, bitter, but nevertheless appealing landscape, to a time of mean and sometimes desperate struggle in the city; finally to material triumph and splendour, but also deep disillusion.

> I shall not lead the reapers now,
> my blood's a cooling ember;
> but when you stride across the field
> your right hand will remember . . .

So he once wrote of his childhood days in the Sneeuberg country at harvest time.

> . . . By two the heaven and the earth
> are one white molten flood,
> and every clod an ash-blue coal,
> the corn as red as blood . . .[19]

The life of G. A. Watermeyer (b. 1917) would be a fitting subject for a great narrative. When, most remarkably and strangely, his very gifts of poetry had been turned to the use of 'hidden persuasion', to the art of advertising, as nobody before him in the country had done, so that he eventually became a director of the company and a man of considerable means, he still remembered, with deep poignancy, the *platteland*. A fine house in an exclusive suburb, a collection of rare antiques and books and a number of highveld farms could not quite restore wholeness to the boy from the Sneeubergs who had once written such splendid lines on the unspoilt landscape of his youth.

In a poem called *Kronieke van 'n Reklameman*, which might be translated as *Chronicles of a Hidden Persuader*, he was later to confess:

>   Five days without shine or interlude of laurels
>   without breast-plate or back-shield
>   against the thin whips of the marketeers
>   I weigh and I am weighed
>   I make and I am made
>   according to the changing silhouettes
>   in the panorama of purpled products ...
>
>   ... And when the drive is at an end
>   and all is ruin and done with
>   and all is dead and done with
>   I lead four stallions from my broken horizons ...

He died in June 1972, at the age of 55.[20]

Had he lived, Watermeyer might well have written a poem with the title: *Homage to the Golden Bath*. For this ultimate symbol of vulgarity represents what Arnold Toynbee has described as the 'banalization of art and morals' which attacks a society when it has become lost to abstractions of fulfilment, in other words, the ephemeral self which is idolized in the form of a group, an institution or money, leading to a schism in the soul.

In the gurgling waters being emitted through the hole in the golden bath, one may dimly discern the stirring sounds of *La Marseillaise* or *The Red Flag*.

With the death of H. F. Verwoerd as its climactic act the time for tragedy had come to an end, at least for a while. Comedy had taken its place. Black comedy, some would say, played by white people.

Part Four: A Tragi-Comic Eye

Part Four: A Tragi-Comic Eye

12 The Irony of Afrikaner History

The range of comedy is as extensive as that of tragedy. It may present itself in the lightest, even the most fanciful, of moods. But it may also present itself in the grimmest, even the blackest, of humours. Like tragedy, its effect is cathartic. The difference is that the cleansing or redemptive action of tragedy necessarily entails the sacrifice of the protagonist. In comedy, there is an even chance that he may participate in the cleansing process of laughter. If he could only gain perspective so as to see and evaluate the charade in which he has been the principal player, humility would be restored and life could start afresh. The Rueful Countenance of the Knight of La Mancha appears through history in the oddest places and at the strangest times.

Dürrenmatt, Beckett, Weiss, Pinter, Ionesco and others recognized its reappearance in the West after the Second World War. Inevitably, the coming of the *burgerstand*, the rise of Afrikaner capitalism, with money providing an alternative basic value to that of the radical political order, provided the opportunity.

Soon the new-style pursuers of happiness in the bourgeois context were making their appearance. The *burgerstand* indulged in trite trivialities in pleasant suburban fields, while the more enterprising of them in the new fields of business achieved the longed-for status of 'millionaire', like *kakiebos* at the end of a long Cape summer. Ambitious, clever politicians climbed the party pyramid, because power means office and office means privilege. Calculating, dedicated functionaries were devoted to the construction of a machine of perpetual motion; while young intellectuals solemnly dissected the state of the nation in an array of 'discussion groups'.

It was the start of the Vorster era. Another who had sat at the foot of Diederichs, Cronjé and Meyer in the late thirties and early forties now, at last, accepted the mantle of Verwoerd. He had been the forceful and energetic Minister of Justice who had been largely responsible for the taming of the militant left. Now, as Prime Minister, with his own style of often sardonic humour, he became the advocate for a policy of relinquishing isolation. There was to be no compromise on principle, he insisted. The ideal of separate development would be as sacrosanct as ever. But the Afrikaner would emerge from his isolation, would seek contact and conversation with other groups, especially with the English-speaking South Africans. The process would not stop there, however. The Afrikaners – South Africa – should move outwards into the world. And the world should be convinced of the basic rightness and goodness of the policy of separate development.

This was adding a political dimension to what had already happened in the growing world of Afrikaner business. Towards the late sixties, the river, formed by rivulets, now showed signs of bursting its banks. Everywhere the business schools were being attended by more and more eager young Afrikaners, alive to the possibilities of what seemed to be the expanding South African universe. From the business schools, by way of graduation within the growing Afrikaner concerns themselves, by recruitment from the traditional occupations of teaching, medicine, the law, even the ministry, the ranks of the New Men were being swelled from day to day. Integrated into the managerial grid, they were soon operating in the efficient way peculiar to the 'protestant ethic'. Clubs and restaurants began to see increasing numbers of Afrikaner executives, clad in dark suits, ordering their food and wines with discrimination and entertaining business contacts from overseas. More and more were seen relaxing on golf courses. The Prime Minister, a personal friend of Gary Player, himself became the model. His image at times was predominantly a golfing one. Nor did his ministers lag behind. Half the cabinet, however meagre their sporting talents, seemed to develop a taste for this most distinctive preoccupation of the affluent society.

Flitting around the globe on a great variety of missions, the New Men, operating on expense accounts, soon acquired international manners. Afrikaner business moved outwards into the world, long before politics thought of doing likewise. What the young executives had to sell, however, was no abstraction promising a secure and meaningful future. What they bought or sold was what all others like them in the capitalist society of the West (and those who had accepted the West) had always been buying and selling.

The general run of Afrikaners soon took up this cue. 'Growth' became the watchword. Growth, they soon discovered, meant acquiring the right kind of shares and selling them shrewdly. The Johannesburg Stock Exchange, never a familiar field for Afrikaners, suddenly saw their advent. They arrived, they bought, they sold. It soon became a fever, reaching its climax in 1969. Fortunes were easily made and lost, the important point being that Afrikaner capitalism, too, became a mass concern.

The prime interest of thousands whose daily reading priorities had formerly been sport and politics now became stock-market prices. In the old days shares had been bought carefully and discriminatingly in the few established Afrikaner institutions; except where sentiment, which had always been a consideration, exceeded its normal bounds and where all good judgement had been forfeited, such as had happened in the early forties. Now shares – any kind of shares – became the potential, if not for the best investment, then for the most stimulating gamble. Academics, farmers, school teachers and typists all joined in. The Afrikaners were newly discovering what they had previously been missing out on.

The philanthropic exercises of the Rembrandt Organization were, to a lesser degree, a preoccupation of other New Men in the world of Afrikaner business. There was a trend towards quicker, more effective methods. It was an onward march such as the *Volk* had never known. Inevitably, it began to incur the methods which once produced the Great American Fortunes, as chronicled by Gustavus Myers. Power in the political field has always guaranteed adventurous free enterprise. Sophisticated business transactions are best manipulated when one has the ear of the establishment. There is an inestimable value in knowing the official mind, of sharing in its prior knowledge and of receiving its commissions, sanctions, concessions and blessings. The art of making money shrewdly, but in full accordance with approved business methods and within the requirements of the law, became an essential part of the economic life of the Afrikaners. *Vader* Kestell's vision of a nation saving itself had long since ceased to have any meaning. Afrikaner business could only be successfully conducted in the way that had always obtained in any capitalist society, including Anglo-Saxon/Jewish South Africa. Millions of others had made money in this way and had been assisted towards it by their sharing in the fruits of power. Why not the Afrikaners?

The sprouting millionaires, appearing in the strangest places, were the truest evidence of this. Under-thirties and under-forties, dealing in land, houses, mutual-funds, entertainment, fertilizer, film-making, sex and so on, strove to emulate giants of business and industry who had already proven themselves elsewhere, notably in the U.S.A. The Afrikaners in business had acquired a self-confidence which exceeded that of their political brethren. Sometimes the roles were combined, making it even more effective.

A fair number came to early grief, plunging friends, supporters and shareholders into financial embarrassment. But they soon bounced back again. When husbands could no longer trade, due to the restrictions of the Insolvency Act, willing wives were there to take their places. When flourishing companies, which had been paying out golden dividends, suddenly collapsed (the leading spirits having meanwhile sold their interests in their own companies), those left to carry the (empty) cans were seldom very much the wiser.

The style of living followed those of the sociological pattern which caused Vance Packard to record the story of the Hidden Persuaders, the Status Seekers, the Pyramid Climbers and the Wastemakers: giving valuable evidence to Herbert Marcuse in writing his analysis of 'one-dimensional man'.

Very soon, within the space of a generation after the start of the Second World War, the *plattelanders* congregating in the suburbs had acquired most of the graces, disgraces, thought-patterns, attitudes, styles and myths of capitalist/industrial man anywhere in the modern world, but at its most expressive in white, Western, Protestant communities. This happened especially in the fast-growing industrial complex of the Pretoria, Witwatersrand and Vereeniging triangle.

There was a new accent on formal success, beginning already at school level. A petit-bourgeois class of white-collar employees quickly emerged and was cast into the mould of a new hier-archy. Subtly, the predominant ethic became concerned with getting on in companies which had become little or larger cogs in the wheel of an expanding money-economy. This was true as well of the public service. With top management becoming increasingly remote, there was a corresponding growth of 'thing-mindedness'. Humans were becoming 'tidy packaged men', part of the bureaucratic whole, providing poets of the modern theatre with fertile material. This was the new moneyed class, isolated, pressurized and conditioned by a thousand subtle hidden influences in their daily routines, from suburb to office, factory, classroom, drive-in, the seaside and back again to their homes ... Money counted; and without any special legislation (as had been necessary in the political field of race relations) new social stratifications set in.

In the community of functionaries, those of relatively humble origin were determined to rise to the top. In the expanding metropolis, there was no opportunity any more for the unself-conscious enjoyment of the things of the earth. The *platteland* became a pallid memory. Lakes, beaches and game-reserves were now the means of escaping the rigours, tensions and in-creasing pressures of the times.

People were always conscious of the forward-thrusting exe-cutives, who had made it to the top. Independence of mind became a most difficult thing to achieve. Daily intake from the media became like food, drink, and stimulants to more intensive living. Where men mass together, opportunities exist for con-ditioning, manipulation and packaging. Work becomes a mech-anical memory; and both the creative joy of a bountiful earth, and the humbling, cleansing experience of disaster, belong remotely to a half-forgotten *platteland*. Necessarily in the money-economy into which the Afrikaners had so easily and quickly been integrated, they, too, became fair game in the play of fashioning a perennial order of 'superb consumers', to supply not only the body but also the mind. The gathering places for spiritual discourse were no longer just the new, tidy, suburban churches, with their excellent *burgerstand*, leading blameless if colourless lives. They were also the new Afrikaner service organizations, like the *Rapportryers* (an offshoot of the *Broederbond*), the counterpart of Rotary, the Lions and so on. There was for love-starved wives and lonely widows the moral instruction – the secular cant – of interminable 'stories' on the commercial radio. Glossily bright new periodicals with resplendent advertising and heavy Sunday newspapers offered titillation of various kinds to the new suburban sensitivities.* When the suburban congregations of the Dutch Reformed churches tended to become too uncomfortably middle-middle and upper-middle class, there were exciting emotional experiences to be sampled, offered by the proletarian evangelists, including the sects and newly established churches of 'apostolic' leanings. There were even the resplendent assemblies of the supermarkets, where the selling-message of the secondary producers was highly successful. Meanwhile, and by the same token, the Afrikaners joined in the great throng of polluters, congesters, frenetic developers and beauty-destroyers, while hardly knowing it.

The poet as prophet, interpreting the new society of Afrikanerdom, appeared in the person of D. J. Opperman. With an even deeper insight than that of his contemporary, van Wyk Louw, into the nature of the new industrialized world of the Afrikaners, he wrote, using as a motto the lines of a finely attuned Calvinist poet of the older order, Totius: *The farmers' paradisal state is now a moleheap, grey and great*:

> From tunnels of the night I stare
> on smoke and fog; carried in iron rails
> into the circles of the city there.

* The cry had once been against anglicization. Now the 'American Way' had intruded in myriad ways. In the new national enthusiasm there was still complete innocence of this. Irony for them who had sacrificed all for the *eie*.

Chimneys and rooftops under sunlight lie
Like corrugated iron and broken glass
left on the bottom of a dam run dry ...

Then, catching the poignant mood of it all:

... Eyes sprout from every knot in noonday light
and after midnight I can see my days –
a bunch of loquats that a bat grips tight

One day I felt my throat grow tight:
There in the coal yard stood
a pear-tree blossoming white.[1]

There was, too, ordinary mundane resistance to the great
commercial embrace of Mammon. Youth, like youth anywhere
where money has triumphed, clumsily but sincerely objected by
discarding what they sensed to be spurious by a return to the
primitive in music, dress and life-styles. True enough, many
remained respectfully conformist within the suburban framework: far more so than their English-speaking contemporaries.
But this was merely because their own industrialized business
community still retained certain disciplines which the others
had never found necessary. By the early seventies, however, the
language of this province of the 'Counter-Culture' of the sixties
had become Afrikaans as well.

Sex was almost on a par with golf as a barometer of the new
society and of the changed attitudes of urbanized Afrikaners
operating within the 'unbreakable economic equation'. Relevant
here are the observations by Packard about the problems of an
executive preserving his dignity against all conditions of the
outer world. Sooner or later, there would be a deep-seated urge
to take off his clothes with his dignity. At conventions or on
other business assignments, he could happily take time off to
associate with a call-girl. There was a psychological need to do
this.

In the old days of the pioneer Afrikaners, their love-life had
known an obvious and healthy lustiness. Families were generally
large. This robustness was, however, combined with a steadfast
loyalty to marriage partners. The cases on the various treks and

305

in the life of farms and villages, where this strict moral code had been transgressed, were negligible.

In the consumer society of the modern industrial city, as Lewis Mumford has shown, sex undergoes its own permutations.[2] The great variety of sexual experience which became part of the life of the *burgerstand* resembled that of all other groups which had shared similar situations in the modern world. The variations were infinite, both in heterosexual and homosexual terms. The appetite became compelling, the style both promiscuous and extravagant.

When the home scene became too familiar, there were always the new, splendidly luxurious spas in the neighbouring black states. These provided adventurous week-enders from the Republic, both from the cities and from the *platteland*, with all the permissive entertainment they lacked at home because of restrictive legislation. Not that things were not progressing locally. For example, at Randburg, in the early seventies, at the extending frontier of suburban expansion in the Transvaal, a band of 'selected Afrikaner businessmen' – there with their wives – joyously participated in a jet-style strip-tease show to the point of full frontal nudity, while chosen males massaged the oleaginous breasts of the performer. When this fellow Afrikaner of the cities – if that is the word – had 'done her thing', she was given a standing ovation. The wives sat silent or only clapped politely. Thereupon a male member of the audience, inspired by the spectacle, did a strip-tease of his own.[3]

Man's vision is not only impaired by the bright light of the political ideal. It is also impaired by present confusion, by the huge involvement of the consumer world he has to meet. The result is an inability to see things in their entirety or in a perspective of universal validity. This accords with Kierkegaard's famous extremes of despair: that of being utterly concerned with infinity, with no feeling for the present: and that of being utterly concerned with the present, with no feeling for infinity.

The Afrikaners, approaching the last quarter of the twentieth century, were now faced with a double dimension of the internalized challenge facing the newly arisen *burgerstand*. The socio-political ideal operated now within the New Capitalism of our times, that of mass participation – of the *Volk*, too – through the trade in shares, in money, take-over mergers, multinational corporations and, more than ever, the self-perpetuating power of the managers, working towards a dictatorship of business.

After the death of H. F. Verwoerd, at a time when the Afrikaner *entrepreneurs* were really getting into their stride and assiduously defining the great alternative of money – 'Industrial Partnership', A. E. Rupert called it – the socio-political system of the revolutionary and radical Afrikaners was assuming staggering proportions.

In the near quarter-of-a-century from 1948 to 1971, the superstructure on the basic concept of the nation had grown enormously. No less than 231 separate measures were adopted in this time: proclamations, regulations, administrative measures on specific issues and Acts of Parliament. The Acts alone numbered some 173.[4] From 1962 to 1967, the public service necessary to keep all this operating had increased by forty-two per cent. Serving in no less than forty government departments, twenty per cent of all Whites actively employed were here, in the early seventies, in some way or other, servants of the state.[5]

As an exercise in political logic, it was enormous. Has any body of legislators of comparable size, anywhere, at any time, ever undertaken the re-structuring of time and society more painstakingly and determinedly? Nothing seems to have escaped the attention of those set on building the new order in the vision of a finally radicalized and rationalized South African society.

There were measures dealing with population registration, citizenship and immorality. There were also measures dealing with representation of coloured people on central governing bodies. This was the cause of crisis after crisis in the fifties until, by enlarging the Senate and quorum of judges in the Appeal Court, the coloured people were eventually removed (Act 30, 1956) from the common roll of voters they had formerly shared with the Whites. Subsequent measures also related to political representation of the coloured people, providing for separate bodies for the coloured and Indian communities. Early in the fifties, provision had already been made for separate representative bodies for Africans. In this a climax was reached in the *Transkei Constitution Act* (1963), providing the territory with its own legislative assembly. Complementary measures provided for local government of Africans in the urban areas and also for local management committees in coloured and Asian group areas. Far-reaching administrative measures provided for territorial and residential separation and occupation of land and premises, mainly with respect to Africans.

This was the so-called 'Eiselen line'. Dr W. M. Eiselen, a man dedicated to the socio-political ideal, was then Secretary for Native Affairs. There was extensive legislation in this particular field, of which the *Natives' Resettlement Act* (1954) and the *Group Areas Act* (1950 and 1957, as amended) were the main structures. Many amending acts were added to the *Community Development Act* (1966) and the *Consolidating Group Areas Act* (1966). Acts dealing with urban African affairs imposed restrictions on the presence of Africans in certain areas and on their right to seek employment. Other measures regulated the presence of Africans in rural areas. Machinery was established for the proper functioning and development of the Bantu homelands. A host of measures dealt with the racial zoning of towns, the establishment of a Bantu Development Corporation, Border industries, Transkeian trading and the promotion of economic development generally in the homelands. Then there were measures dealing with the immigration and employment of foreign Africans. Some measures dealt with separation in employment, the heart of which were the *Industrial Conciliation Amendment Acts* (1956 and 1959), in which further restrictions were placed on the operation of mixed trade unions and further provision was also made for 'job reservation'. Others provided for separation in education, the substance being provided by the *Bantu Education Act* (1953) with the intention of completely re-structuring African education.

In the same category were various measures establishing separate systems of education for Coloureds and Indians and a series of separate universities, providing higher education for each separate ethnic group. Further measures dealt with housing, separate amenities, entertainment and sport.

Last but not least, there was massive legislation dealing with the control of activities deemed to be undesirable. Bedrock of this was the *Suppression of Communism Act* (1950). In all, forty-two different acts were passed in the course of these twenty-three years dealing with public safety and the security of the state alone.

Remarkable, however, was the fact that by far the greatest number of transgressors did not fall foul of the *Suppression of Communism Act*, or the acts dealing with terrorism, sabotage or sanctions for detention without trial. Rather, they failed to comply with the various restrictions on the presence of Africans in certain areas, and on their right to seek employment. For example, the Commissioner of the S.A. Police reported that for the year 1968–9 a *daily* average of 1732 people had been sent for trial (mostly to special courts) for infringements falling within this category. This added up to a total for the year of 632,077, representing 26.5% of the total number of prosecutions of people of all races, for all offences.[6]

The administration of such an enormous body of special legislation would obviously bring about what a student of public administration in South Africa referred to as 'institutional proliferation'. 'This phenomenon,' a commentator sympathetic to the establishment remarked,

refers to the constant multiplication of new institutions at various levels of government and in various spheres of public affairs as part of the price of having 'big government'. Though South Africa has a population of just over twenty million, it has about forty separate government departments and over a hundred statutory boards, councils, commissions and corporations. This unwieldy structure inevitably creates a tremendous problem of co-ordination ...[7]

The classically comic assessment of the phenomenon was, of course, that of Professor Parkinson, containing his hilarious insight into the folly of humans trying to organize their world to final rationality – only to create a total lack of reason. To this, Dr Peter has added the further insight of observing that proliferating functionaries in such societies tend to be promoted to their levels of incompetence.[8]

What has all this heroic striving of the Afrikaners, by far the largest part of it in the high days of H. F. Verwoerd, ultimately produced? The answer, inherent in the tragi-comic perspective, lies in the irony of history. The irony of Afrikaner history is no less moving than the irony of American history,[9] or that of any other group which at some time or other has considered itself to have been called to a messianic task.

In the Vorster era, the late sixties and early seventies, an ingenious argument was advanced and widely used to vindicate the socio-political ideal of separate development.[10]

Separate development, it was said, should be seen as a great edifice arising from the earth. It was essentially a sound and noble structure, accommodating a great variety of peoples, providing everybody with the necessary living space, containing every possible amenity for the various groups, offering to everyone goods according to their needs, while demanding contributions from everyone according to their abilities. Essentially, it was a living monument to the utilitarian idea of 'the greatest happiness of the greatest number', which was important also to the New England pragmatists.[11]

But the edifice could only be erected, it was further argued, by the use of proven methods. Much scaffolding would have to be used, which would encompass the whole building and hide its true aesthetic value. The scaffolding (all the hard, uncompromising measures) was ugly but necessary. It was a *sine qua non*, for only in this way would the edifice arise to become, in the fullness of time, the great accommodating system in which everyone could find a meaningful future. The scaffolding would be taken down at the completion of the building; and then it would be seen in its proper perspective. The true beauty would at last be revealed.[12]

This is intended as a parable. And as a parable it should further be explored.

The great edifice, one first has to realize, can only be erected when the architects have spent many months, even years, at their drawing boards. When eventually the builders start, the plans can no longer be changed in their essentials. Only smaller details can be altered, but always strictly 'within the framework' of the blueprint. To start questioning or rejecting the basic elements would upset everything. There must be, in the abstract, a definite goal and equally definite plans of how to realize it. The blueprint is indispensable, however much it is denied in public.

The edifice grows. The structure rises above the excavation into bedrock. It becomes the *Überbau* resting on the broad foundation of the collective – nation, state, people, proletariat and so on. The builders go to work with great ingenuity and devotion, and often astounding energy. The ideal of the completed task spurs them on. In the finished building, everyone will be accommodated. It becomes a variation on the theme of: *In my Father's house are many mansions.* And they plan to provide the greatest happiness for the greatest number.

The work continues, steadily and tirelessly. In fact, this is not just a building: it is a kind of a city, a *civitas terrena*. Nevertheless, its top may reach unto heaven. Then it will most certainly, too, become a *civitas Dei*.

The city grows and grows. The architects and owner-builders are devoted, hard-working and dedicated. This is because they believe themselves ordained to their tasks. When everything is complete, they will at the same time have demonstrated their particular fitness for the task. Obviously, not everyone can be entrusted with the building – only the architects and owner-builders, those specially called.

Then something strange happens. This deep belief in special vocation requires a corresponding growth and consolidation of power. How else can such a heroic task be performed? How else can the edifice reach its proper proportions, providing accommodation, happiness and a guaranteed future for everyone? Power is necessary and, as the edifice grows, more power will be needed.

This means functionaries, both of an administrative and political kind. The proliferating functionaries now become increasingly conscious of their extended power. By the same token they lose sight of the inherent frailty which is man, and therefore of themselves. Frailty in power means its abuse. The fruits of power become overwhelmingly the privilege of those who wield it. This is the origin of the saying that power corrupts; and absolute power corrupts absolutely. The great bodies of functionaries start competing among themselves. They accept that even the city they have built does not guarantee happiness. Happiness also means looking after your own special interests.

The originators, architects and owner–builders, who have worked so assiduously on their edifice, soon take possession of the roomiest, most comfortable part of the structure, with the finest views and best amenities. They are not fully aware of giving top priority to their own interests. On the contrary, there is articulate insistence that the edifice provides for every-body. It is, in fact, a kind of Providence. This is because the architects and owner–builders, whatever their formal piety, have an infinite confidence in their own ability to carry the whole project through to a successful conclusion. In a sense, it is intended as an end to history.

The intentions of the architects and owner–builders remain noble and varied. A further strangeness, however, is that in providing for their own accommodation in the edifice, which will have the best views and the most excellent amenities, they also provide all entrances, with the most elaborate steel-doors. Windows, too, are guarded with heavy bars. There is no chance of anyone getting in unnoticed. Nor is there much chance of getting out unnoticed. What people discern from afar after a time is that the whole edifice has become like a fort.

In part, this is the fault of wrong planning: a miscalculation by the architects and owner–builders. Apart from spoiling the view, they discover that some of the various groups which should have been accommodated have, in a rather puzzling way, been overlooked. Temporary accommodation has been found for them in the basement or the back part of the building. The intention is to shift them to their own quarters some day; but this is difficult for these have become more populated than expected. In any event, the edifice is such an enormous and heroic structure that these 'others' who are only temporarily among the architects and owner–builders are, in actual fact, indispensable to the smooth running of the edifice as a going concern.

One day, a most dismaying discovery is made. It resembles in a sense that once made by a child watching a royal procession in which the king imagined himself to be dressed in the finest of royal robes. The child, deaf to the praises ringing around him, remarked stupidly but truly that the king had no clothes on. In fact, the king had exposed himself.

The discovery in the case of the edifice comes from writers, poets, philosophers and theologians living within the structure. Look, they begin pointing out with disturbing insistency, the scaffolding which was so ugly has now, most mysteriously, grown into the edifice itself. To remove it might be dangerous. The whole, in fact, will collapse, should it be done. What's more, the barred windows and fortified doors have compounded the ingrown scaffolding, which has become a fixture. The hope that once existed that the scaffolding may be removed is a forlorn one. The ugliness still remains.

Man loves not evil, but himself – to excess. *Amour-propre*, as La Rochefoucauld said, is his special torment. This inwardly-turned passion makes of man an idolator and the tyrant over all others, should fortune but provide him with the means. This is, of course, essentially what St Augustine, Calvin, Hobbes (in his way) and many others always insisted on. Man turning inwards on himself is defensive man, because he is anxious and faithless – however sincerely religious he may be. Not everyone who says: 'Lord, Lord!' will enter into the kingdom. Faithless man is man without God and therefore he has no alternative but to be in excess of himself: to be like a god. *Oordaad is sonde* – 'excess is sin' – the *platteland* Afrikaners used to say in their young and humorous days. This is man out of place, who strangely refuses his own identity exactly because he so desperately seeks to assure himself of it. Man out of place is man imprisoned by himself and, by this inward-turning defensiveness, covered by a tragi-comic outward show of strength or excellence.

The heroic but absurd structure of power he erects must necessarily become a fort, a *laager* of the spirit. This is the cosmic joke man plays upon himself: wanting to be like a god and, in the attempt, reducing himself to bondage. The bondage becomes absolute when the power-structure is embellished by the socio-political ideal.

Man out of place, man in excess, is inordinate man, as St Augustine would have said. This is sinful man. His sin becomes most apparent in the form of social injustice or tyranny or else an entrenched mediocrity and privilege.

All true power, for the reasons stated, is exclusive in nature. The fact that it is collectively expressed in no way mitigates it. The collective is the greater self. The love for the collective, as class, race, people, nation, state and so on, to the point of idolization is the greater *amour-propre*, causing the greater torment. The basic dilemma of Western Christian man, dreading the loss of power and, at the same time, dreading being judged the perpetrator of injustice, is here exposed. This is also the special dilemma of the Afrikaners. Dilemma is the intimation of irony. We need to remind ourselves again that in Western Christian history there is no Shaka who, on hearing of the death of his mother, Nandi, ordered a general wailing of the tribe for a night and a day. He then ordered a general massacre of all those whom he thought were not displaying sufficient grief, all pregnant women and their husbands to be killed during the following year, all cultivation to be stopped and all cows' milk to be spilled . . . Neither is there a figure like Mzilikazi, of whom his only friend, Robert Moffat, after the punitive Voortrekker commando had sacked the Great Place of Mosega, said that the evils now coming on the Ndebele were only what he had expected: Mzilikazi had ruled on the highveld with an iron sceptre. His warriors had shed the blood of thousands, often unprovoked.

No doubt, if one goes back far enough in Western history, such figures will be found. But once the Christian West became more or less established, it was no longer possible.

Not that the 'demands of conscience' were sufficient to change the true nature of power. *Plus ça change plus c'est la même chose* is a platitude, but still true. The chances are that there was more hope for Shaka or Mzilikazi than for Robespierre encouraging the Terror in the name of not only *liberté, égalité, fraternité* but also the Supreme Being; or Adolf Hitler, as part of the task which 'Providence has set us all', preserving the identity of the nation by the mass extermination of the Jews; or Lenin writing to G. Zinoviev on 26 June 1918 'that the workers in Petrograd wished to react to the assassination of Voladarsky by mass terror and that you . . . stopped them. I decisively protest . . . This is impossible!'[13] Impossible in the name of the great concept of man which seeks to restore the worker to humanity, from the alienation he suffers at the hands of the exploiters. But, quoting Lenin, the 'horrors, savagery, absurdities, and infamies of capitalist exploitation' were indeed put out of mind by the opiate of pharisaic religion. And when the Falangists shot Spain's greatest poet of the day, Garcia Lorca, who was never a member of any political party, that, too, was done in the name of a great ideal and a fine sentiment: the Spanish nationalist vision of a restored society.

One could continue in this way in various keys. There are many examples: the Puritans of Old England who executed Charles I; the Puritans of New England who hanged the Quakers; the Inquisition which burned the heretics; the Dutch (V.O.C.) who mass-slaughtered the Chinese in Batavia in 1740; the British who massacred the natives at Amritsar in 1919; and the Afrikaners in power who now have not only Sharpeville as part of their history, but also District Six and the break-up of many established congregations of their own Dutch Reformed Mission (Daughter) Church in the Cape Peninsula. This is in addition to the inhumanities of much race-classification, group area apportionment, 'immorality' and so on.

Hegel was only partly correct when he declared that absolute and abstract freedom was the source of tyranny.[14] The source is man's lack of faith, his love of himself, his consequent most passionate and determined pursuit of happiness and will to power. The abstractions of freedom are Western man's peculiar apology for this. They are his substitute for faith and therefore his secular religion and justification of power.

The two modes of power peculiar to the West are Caesar and Mammon. Even if the age is a permissive one, and even when getting undressed in public seems to be *à la mode*, neither of these two figures can be seen without their clothes on. The open mind of a child may again notice and remark on it. Great comic writing always needs the eye of a child. In fact, the cult of nudity among those who are anti-Establishment – hippies and so on – may well be more profound than we imagine. It might be a taunt, an invitation to see man as he is, without his plumes.

The various 'revolutions of the saints' which arose out of the Calvinist-Puritan ethic and the tremendous attempts to re-structure society were Western Christian man's attempts to live with his newly sensitized conscience, after Calvin. More than ever before, power had to be acceptable to both God and Man.

As we have seen, it was no longer good enough to claim, as did James I of England, that kings could justly be called gods 'for they exercise a manner of resemblance of Divine power on earth'; nor as Louis XIV did when he announced himself to be the state; nor as Napoleon Bonaparte did when he summoned the Pontiff of Rome to attend his crowning of himself; nor as Wilhelm II of Germany did when he confessed: 'Considering myself as an instrument of the Lord, I go my way'; nor even as Hendrik Witbooi did when hearing the Lord speak to him in the mountain pass of Khani-gukha ('It has come to pass! The road lies open! I lay on you a heavy burden!'), believing himself henceforth to be the Scourge of God in South-West Africa. Since Calvin, let it be said again, such divine injunctions, sanctioning the struggle for power by a gifted individual, have no longer been enough. To be really effective, to serve its purpose as justification, as inspiration for attaining the ideal, it has had to be part of something greater: a vision of a brave new world, a restored society, the coming Kingdom of Man.

The first of the socio-political ideals, we have said, was contained in the Declaration of Independence. The sorcerer's apprentice set in motion here the only-too-willing spirits.

The line, as has been shown, runs straight from the Declaration of Independence, through the Declaration of the Rights of Man by the French National Assembly in August 1789, to the Jacobins. A witness of this was Mirabeau, leader of the revolutionary National Assembly, who wrote of the 'sublime manifesto of the United States of America'. So, too, was Lafayette, who helped prepare the French Declaration of the Rights of Man. The revolutionary spirit engendered by the Declaration of Independence has penetrated nearly all the world: not only France of the Jacobins, but also Communist Russia, Maoist China, the many revisionist movements of our time, pre-eminent being the revolutionary 'Counter-Culture' of the sixties in the U.S.A., also the Afrikaners of the radical Right in Southern Africa. And, out of these secular religions with their deepest roots in Puritan history, there arose, too, the looming figure of Mammon. Here, as power, was ever the best alternative. So then, the Protestant ethic or religion which, in the views of Max Weber and R. H. Tawney, gave rise to capitalism, was not an authentic faith. It was rather Western man's secular creed, his tremendous attempt to sanctify his struggle and attain power by containing it all in the context of a socio-political ideal.

The basic dilemma of Western man is how to reconcile power with justice. It is therefore, too, that of the Afrikaners – and, because they are in power in South Africa, the basic dilemma of the Whites generally. The problem for us can be stated alternatively as how to reconcile self-salvation and the Christian faith of which the core is: *For anyone who wants to save his life will lose it; but anyone who loses his life for my sake will find it.* The horns of the dilemma are still those of surrendering power and suffering moral condemnation. The thought of a loss of power causes us to shudder. The thought of being counted among the unbelievers causes us to shudder even more. The way out for us, we conclude, is that of retaining power and at the same time retaining faith. Faith, however, we re-define for ourselves as being faithful to our calling and to the noble task ordained to us, that of redeeming the world. To this end, power is necessary; but because it is part of the work of ordination, there is also peace within our souls. We affirm we are re-structuring the world; but this logical, positive action is God's will. When we have discarded God and put in his place the Supreme Being, or History, or Destiny, the position is no different.

This exercise demands all our spiritual forces. We were faced with a choice between two evils and we have made of it an acceptance of two self-manufactured goods.

What confounds us in the end are not our enemies but the imponderables. These include the mysterious way in which the roles are upset, where things do not work out as envisaged and where logic is refuted.

For anyone who wants to save his life ...

In the case of the Puritans in Africa, the particular ironies which history has produced have already partly been indicated in our further exploration of the parable of the edifice and its scaffolding. In order to implement the idea, greater power has been sought, claiming at last that no other group could possibly be entrusted with the future. Meanwhile, of necessity, the operators and functionaries proliferate. It is *they* who come to govern. Here, too, the mighty, rational attempt to weaken our enemies and strengthen ourselves has only resulted in our strengthening our enemies and weakening ourselves. For the simple fact of a superfluity of power has caused those who do not share in it but feel it, to resist. They resent the vast overgrowth of things, the easy acceptance of privilege. The older power gradually becomes senile and reactionary; the younger, irreverent and militant.

How deeply ironic it is that the Afrikaners, who through all their history faced the future with open minds, accepting in their own true, Reformed tradition the works of Providence, now like all other radical systematizers have found it necessary to structure the future to exactly the type of blue-print which vast edifices require. In the same way as the freedom of the people promised by *vox populi*, by *liberté, égalité, fraternité*, by the dictatorship of the proletariat, by a myriad of modern revisionist restatements of the Marxist-Leninist confession; in the same way as the freedom of the corporate state or nation as promised by the Fascist Right between the wars – so the freedoms of various nations within the same geographical context as promised by separate development, has proved to be, in no less measure, a radical attempt to establish by *rational* means the ultimate certitude.

It is likewise ironic that the very accusation which theologians among the Afrikaners have been levelling for years at their opponents – that of humanism and of making the Christian faith nothing more than a social gospel – proves to be precisely the weakness of their own vision. Here, too, the concept of the edifice arising out of the earth, accommodating all, clearly shows how recourse has been taken to purely human means in the attempt to ensure identity, fulfilment, survival and happiness. Was it not a brilliant international lawyer, a man who pleaded the case for South Africa with such exceptional advocacy at the International Court at the Hague during the sixties, was it not he who also wrote that the many hard measures found necessary in the implementation of separate development were merely the by-products of 'successive South African governments . . . serving the greatest good of the greatest number'[15]? Did he not also say that the policy of separate development was essentially pragmatic? Was he not accepting here the very tenets of modern humanism with its utter dependence on the human mind, on human knowledge, of what is good and evil? Ironies, in the case of the Afrikaners, too, crowd the scene as the play develops.

A people who in their heroic age were the victims of a succession of imperial onslaughts on their life, might now suddenly discover themselves to be not only the new social gospellers, not merely the new humanists, but also the new imperialists. How strange, how contradictory it all is. For the spectacle of emergent Bantustans, each being presided over by a Commissioner-General, brings back moving memories of the days when the Afrikaners were presided over by an equally resplendent British Governor-General. Or there is even something of an imperium of antiquity to be distinguished in the spectacle of the Minister for Bantu Administration and Development dutifully and concernedly touring through the various Bantu homelands, almost like a Roman proconsul journeying through the provinces.

Suddenly the arch-enemy, Communism, may be discerned alarmingly close. It slipped in, so to speak, by the back door, because extremes have an affinity for each other. Not only does this pertain to stringent control over the arts, detention without trial, or the naming of buildings, schools, and other public institutions after minor, serving politicians. There is also a profound affinity between the notion of the state withering away when the great edifice of the classless society has finally been completed; and the notion of the ugly scaffolding being taken down when once the great edifice of the regulated multi-national society has been finally brought about.

By far the most disturbing of the ironies to be seen, however, lie exactly in the areas where Caesar and Mammon have embraced each other. For with the rise of capitalism, and with the *burgerstand* increasingly sharing in all its affluent comforts, white South Africans since the Second World War have become prominent among the groups in the world with high standards of living. This is very largely because of the massive economic integration of those who are non-White into the South African economy. By 1970, almost 4 million African, coloured and Indian industrial workers had already been fully absorbed, compared with some million-and-a-quarter Whites. In the services, mining and quarrying, the construction industry, the many branches of manufacturing and agriculture, the dependence of white South Africans on the skills of black and brown workers had become absolute. Job reservation scarcely existed any more, simply because there was no possible way to keep the economy of the country running, maintaining the tremendously privileged life of Whites themselves, other than by accepting this integration as an 'irreducible and stubborn fact'. Seventy-two per cent of the nation's workers were now black or brown.[16] The very privilege which the structure of separate development had afforded the Whites had brought about the massive integration of Africans, Coloureds and Indians to a point of no return.

The radical socio-political ideal has not only given rise to apartheid and separate development. It has also given rise to the new capitalism to which the émigrés from the *platteland* have, within a generation, fully aligned themselves. Last, but not least, the secular faith has, precisely because of this burgeoning prosperity, drawn into the pyramid the very people the socio-political ideal had intended to separate.

If this is true of the Africans, with Soweto, the black twin of Johannesburg, having become the sub-continent's biggest all-black city, it is even truer of the Coloureds. Their population is almost as large as that of the white Afrikaners. They share fully in the white cultures, the white 'homeland', they have about thirty per cent white blood in their veins and they have contributed to white South Africa, both Afrikaans and English-speaking, some seven per cent of their own blood. For them there is not even the remote possibility of a 'separate homeland' where they could establish their own separate freedom.

The irony of Afrikaner history is also closely bound up with that very concept of Afrikaner 'nation-consciousness', which had been stressed with such incessant eloquence since the mid-thirties, when Diederichs had for the first time formulated Afrikaner nationalism in fundamental terms. Here was the *sine qua non* for redress of a condition of the Afrikaners being estranged in their own country: of suffering under the rejection, the coldness and remoteness of the Anglo-Saxon cities. Now, in spite of – some would say because of – the policy of separate development, a similar kind of nation-consciousness had arisen. It, too, had been motivated by a feeling of deep resentment; a deep-seated urge for the redress of past wrongs; a conviction that the nation was the real answer; that only by closing ranks and asserting the national self in every possible way, could justice be re-established, human dignity restored, future happiness ensured. This new consciousness was black.

Early in 1972, a particularly articulate voice would express all this in terms which to Afrikaners, regarding it objectively, even with some humorous detachment, would recognize immediately, both as regards style and content.

'A philosophy of liberation,' this voice would declare,

requires a reappraisal of the policies and institutions of the Black Community. We must re-evaluate everything we are doing and saying.

321

We must rise now to the level of conceiving of the black interest as a universal interest. Too many people think blackness means withdrawing and tightening the circle.

On the contrary, blackness means expanding, and widening the circle, absorbing and integrating instead of being absorbed and integrated. And from that perspective it is easy to see that a philosophy of liberation requires black people to cast their light not over one thing but over everything. We must rise now to the level of black hegemony, the idea that blacks must establish moral and cultural authority over the whole.[17]

Increasingly, it seems, black consciousness in South Africa will express itself in this way. And the Afrikaners, whose recent history deals specifically with this kind of thing, will know all about it. Whether their attempts to outflank this challenge as they once did that of the British by means of a mass inland immigration – outflank it now by heading it off in the direction of separate geographical entities for the various black polities – whether this will succeed is beyond calculation. There is, at the time of writing, only the indication that the problem will deepen.

Lastly, among the most excruciating ironies to which the modern Afrikaners became subject, was the fact that perhaps the most articulate voice to take up the cause of black nationalism was that of Abraham Fischer, scion of one of the oldest and most respected Afrikaner, Orange Free State families. His grandfather was Prime Minister of the Orange River Colony; and his father, a judge of the Supreme Court of South Africa in the Orange Free State. In 1964 Fischer, who had had a most distinguished career at the Johannesburg Bar, was charged under the Suppression of Communism Act. After a trial in 1965 which caused world-wide interest, and having made a remarkable speech from the dock, pleading the cause of the black peoples of his country, comparing their cause with that of the Afrikaners at the time of the high tide of British imperialism (especially 1899–1902), Fischer was sentenced to life imprisonment.

$$\star \qquad \star \qquad \star$$

Contemporary attitudes among the Afrikaners are allegorically expressed in two closely related but nevertheless fundamentally different pioneer movements in their history.

The Great Trek of 1836 represents the first of these, and can be seen, if one prefers, as the true response to the challenge of the environment, new ground and a series of blows, pressures and penalizations. These were offered by the advent of the British at the end of the eighteenth century, and by the movements of black Africa claiming the same pasturage for their herds. The Thirstland Trek of the 1870s represents the second of these attitudes and can be seen as the idolization of a particular institut-tion, leading to increasing estrangement from both the world as it is, and from the true self. As such it becomes a 'schism in the soul'. In this particular case its modes of avoiding the challenge become that of both archaism and futurism: moving at the same time onwards towards a non-attainable future and backwards into a dead past.[18]

The Retief Manifesto, whatever its limitations, is the authentic voice of the Great Trek.

We are resolved, wherever we go, that we will uphold the just principles of liberty ... We will not molest any people, nor deprive them of the smallest property, but if attacked, we shall consider our-selves fully justified in defending our persons and effects ... We make known that when we shall have framed a code of laws for our future guidance, copies shall be forwarded to the colony for general informa-tion ... We purpose in the course of our journey, and on arriving at the country in which we shall permanently reside, to make known to the native tribes our intentions, and our desire to live in peace and friendly intercourse with them ... We are now quitting the fruitful land of our birth, in which we have suffered enormous losses and continual vexation, and are entering a wild and dangerous territory; but we go with a firm reliance on an all-seeing, just, and merciful Being, Whom it will be our endeavour to fear and humbly to obey.

What distinguishes the Great Trek from the Thirstland Trek is precisely the way in which an ephemeral human institution was kept within its limits. This is epitomized in the institution of the *laager*.

In the case of the Great Trek, the *laager* was a movable thing which served its purpose admirably as the most practical way in which to set up camp and at the same time maintain a system of military defence. The important thing about the *laager* of the Great Trek was that it served its purpose when, and as long as, it was necessary. When it was no longer necessary, with a view to the real physical situation, the *laager* was broken up and the Trek moved on. Basically, it was a case here of a sensitive regard for the realities of life.

Where there was error – such as the unseemly conflict between hard-headed leaders, the questionable practice of taking child apprentices when commandos had gone off on punitive expeditions, the unhappy 'trial' and execution of Dambuza and Kombazana by Andries Pretorius – it was the kind of error which could be adjusted by reasonable consideration and a renewal of attitudes and faith. It was not a fugue, a wandering with a loss of contact with reality. It was not a pursuance of a vision on the far distant horizon, to be striven after whatever the present cost.

The objectives of the Great Trek were concrete, immediate and limited. The goals were of the kind which had previously been reasonably investigated and accepted. There was little talk in the Great Trek of a world-view. There was much talk of definite areas and lands which could be acquired by purchase, treaty or occupation, where the land was desolate; of requiting force with force; and of dispensing summary justice.

The Thirstland Trek was different. It was a dramatization of the process of internalization and of the way in which an ideal becomes an obsessive abstraction of freedom. The *laager* was also a central institution here, but it soon became an institution to which an absolute value was attached. It no longer consisted of the practical arrangement of men, animals, wagons and household goods. It had rather become a fixture of the mind, which for that very reason contained the threat of derangement.

The story of the Thirstlanders and their passionate search for an ultimate Calvinist Utopia, for final self-sufficiency in isolation, is the story of a significant part of Afrikanerdom pursuing its impossible ideal, whatever the cost. At the same time, it is the story of any radical group anywhere carried away by its messianic, chiliastic task to reach a state of human happiness for which no measures at the present time are too grim, no sacrifice too great. It is the dramatization of utopian thinking. The end, in all cases, proves mysteriously to be the very antithesis of what has been so valiantly, but absurdly, striven for. This, in the final resort, is what the irony of history means.

The *laager* in the case of the Thirstlanders ceased to be a movable object, a practical measure for the purposes of human habitation in a still wild and dangerous territory and for human self-defence. The *laager* was internalized and became the Trek itself. Now it was a permanent preoccupation with the *eie*. It was a spurious *eie*, however, which only pretended to exist; which, because it had lost all contact with reality, was no longer the *eie*. The *laager* of the Thirstlanders was an institution of final sanctity. In this fatal isolation, mesmerized by a sense of calling, the Thirstlander ultimately trekked to the very denial of his own strivings. In history, the Thirstlanders never reached Beulah, Land of Rest. It was meant to have been the fulfilment of a Calvinist dream. It turned out to be the disenchantment of a Catholic reality.

The model of the progression of radical politics, which has been suggested, can now be taken a few steps further.

As the revolution grows older, as functionaries increase (because power requires more and more of them), as the *Überbau* becomes a self-defeating overgrowth, breakdown threatens. Man's ultimate design always becomes the model for his defeat: a tragic defeat when the progenitor discovers too late how he has wandered; a comic defeat, which for that very reason opens the way to redemption, when he can view it all betimes from a universal vantage point and discover in it the occasion for laughter. Man trying to wrest power from his opponent and redeem the world offers the classic situation. The new order gradually accepts the very attitudes it once despised. It becomes its own denial, the very thing it once intended to destroy for ever. This is how the Commonwealth of Saints becomes both the Commonwealth of Imperialist Saints and the Commonwealth of Capitalist Saints. This is true even where capitalism and imperialism do not present themselves to the world with easily recognizable features, such as is the case in Soviet Russia.

Man is never really upset by his enemies, but rather by the changing of the roles in a way beyond human understanding.

13 Reality and Renewal

In what kind of world does modern radical Afrikanerdom in the seventies find itself? It is important that this be known, for the prospects of returning to reality and encouraging renewal could only properly be considered if the particular modern ethic of this dominant group in Southern Africa is seen in a contemporary context.

Since the end of the Second World War, the predominant spirit of the age has again been revolutionary. The great classic revolutions of the saints have seen a modern proliferation of style and mode, while retaining the essential motive of reforming society into a basic abstraction of freedom. The Maoists in China and the Latin American revolutionaries have been prominent cases in point. Like almost all other modern pursuers of the revolutionary idea since the Second World War, they have been of the left. Only in the case of the Puritans in Africa – the Revolutionary Afrikaners – has radical politics expressed fully itself as a movement of the right.

Revolt is resistance as such to any kind of power-structure which by reason of its enjoying the fruits of power and office has undergone a subtle process of spiritual disintegration. Revolt is not concerned with structured 'alternatives'. Its true function is simply the engendering of creative unrest. Renewal may arise from this new questioning, rejection and turbulence. 'Do not suppose that I have come to bring peace to the earth; it is not peace I have come to bring, but a sword.'[1] But he who said this also insisted: 'Do not imagine that I have come to abolish the Law and the Prophets. I have come not to abolish but to complete them.'[2] These two passages from the book of Matthew epitomize authentic resistance.

Earth, unlike the Moon, knows no Sea of Tranquillity. In this respect at least, Hegel was right. Struggle is the condition of renewal, character is shaped in the turbulence of the world and the human being only realizes himself in the pain and anguish of existence. For Hegel, however, this was not the corollary of man's freedom, but the necessary movement of history, as a struggle of opposites, united in a cosmic love-hate relationship. There is no escaping the deadly rhythm in which revolution follows revolution, striving towards its final expression in the Absolute. Happy will be the genius who finally puts the apexstone to stand in its appointed place, so that the universal arch of history closes at last.

Marx, we should remember, was critical of Hegel on a number of scores, especially regarding the acceptance of the Divine Plan. He himself, however, believed in the inevitability of History, the true leader being merely a kind of cosmic midwife. Hegel was very much the mentor of Marx, as he has also been of Herbert Marcuse. Like those who in Calvinist-Puritan theology believe in the doctrine of the elect (that man is capable of nothing constructive, but does all that is positive and creative by virtue of Grace), yet set about things in an unbelievably energetic, positive way, Marx and classical Communism generally believe in the activist revolutionary changing the world. God has elected the Puritan and he is out to prove it. History has elected the Communist and he is out to prove it. It was exactly the revolution of the proletariat – which Marx saw as finally engineering the keystone of the Worker's Paradise – which in time became the fulfilment of the Russian Imperial Dream as no Czar ever dreamt of it. This is strange when one reflects that imperialism was exactly one of, if not the most important, expressions of the antithesis to which the thesis of the struggling proletariat was opposed.[3]

This remarkable twist of irony finds its counterpart in the capitalist world in the phenomenon of massive affluence, leading not to the amelioration of man's existence but to the paralysing congestions of modern living, or to the steady destruction of the human environment by the products of modern technology. All this is sufficient evidence that history is not merely the ceaseless struggle of opposites. History is also the absurd play of the

Heavenly Joker. In Hegel's heroic system there is no room for either comedy or tragedy. All is rational.

What are the causes which brought about the phenomenon of Marcuse, a German expatriate settled in California, who became in the sixties the most effective critic of the Abundant Society? What has made him the prophet of the 'Great Refusal' of the sixties, elevated to that position by the very young who had been raised and cosseted in Abraham's bosom? Like all revolutionary ideas, Marcusian theory can be explained in terms of the inability of the Welfare State, which is the abundant society, to realize its early promise. Again, just because a system of human rationality must here be answered by a more adequate rationality which in the end never lives up to its promise, it must fail. This is because whatever its messianic faith in its own powers it proves strangely to be unreasonable.

Reason, or our free intelligence, is not the same as rationality. Rationality, by its very attempt to usurp the work of Providence, is the abuse of reason. Reason in real Christian terms is 'present where it is', and may in time prepare us for revelation. Rationality, on the other hand, is a vision, conjured up in anxiety of a coming security which is also a coming final order, and therefore happiness, consciously engineered by the frailty which is man. When faith is lacking and the threat of the future looms up large before us, there is in the usual run of things no alternative but to push our human freedom beyond its limits.

All human systems in time fall apart. Other systems take over. But the sickness of the thesis is precisely also the sickness of the antithesis. This is our dread of being.

There is no faith on the part of those for whom power is a final end. There is only the desperate identification with what must take the place of faith: the new idea which will shatter the old, bringing to all the reconstructed world. There is no faith, and therefore no patience. God will only help those who help themselves. Man has travelled through space, and God was not there. Man must necessarily construct his own Heaven. This is as much the attitude of the existing power-structure, as of those who oppose it. The old order must be spurned, razed to the ground, so that the real, lasting order can arise. Power must be answered by power, ideology by ideology. There are no half-measures. There is only the tearing down of the old structure so that a true abode for man may be erected in its place.

The Old Right becomes the New Left, and the Old Left could quite easily become a New Right. Extremes meet because in the final resort they are alike.

Mammon in modern dress is an advanced stage of the Old Right, and the New Left singles it out for attack for having become either rich and clumsy, or slick and sophisticated. It represents the most vulnerable area.

In the society of ever increasing abundance, it is the modern corporation of the 'new industrial state'⁴ which is the organism requiring utter loyalty. Its ethic is a wasteful consumer welfare. Accompanying everything is a planned spoliation of earth, air and water, and all that live in them. Nature, inevitably, becomes grossly abused. Creative man is once more in chains: but unlike Marx's workers, he now has more than his chains to lose. The revolutionaries of the 'Counter-Culture' were not they who laboured for their capitalist masters, but the young and eager intelligences, the sons and daughters of the privileged. Willingly they refused their own affluence because they had sadly discovered that in the enormous framework of American 'corporate structure' into which they had been born, they had to forfeit their autonomy to the dictatorship of business. The workers themselves were no good for the true revolution because they had long since sold themselves for high wages and congenial benefits. No longer were they capable of shaking the conscience of the world. They were, in fact, firmly part of the corporative power. Political awareness, which is equated with human awareness, had to come from another quarter. The appeal was to the students and school children. It was a kind of latter-day Children's Crusade, conquering the earth and reforming it: if not for Christianity, then for the wider concept of making the world a better place to live in. It was neither Jesus nor Marx, as Jean-François Revel has explained. It was the transcendent revolution.

And, most significantly, America is the true home of the Puritan Mind, which is the mainspring of all attempts to reform the age. Essentially, it remains Marcuse's message of release from 'one-dimensionality'. The great, affluent and abundant society has been a massive confidence trick. In its pretence of grand tolerance, of freedom for all, man has nevertheless become the slave of massive, if subtle, authority.

His very standard of living had become the prime source of corruption. His consciousness was expertly moulded by the highly efficient methods of a society primarily concerned with promoting its own image. The problem has not been to strike a compromise between freedom and the demands of corporate business. The problem has been to create a new society in which man is not the slave of institutions which hold him captive. Marcuse saw the new society as an order in which the national product could be achieved with a minimum of heavy labour and injustice. Increasing automation would dispose of the biblical command to labour by the sweat of one's brow. Eden would have been restored, and man would at long last have arrived at his true home.

It was not so much this utopian vision which identified Marcuse's concept as yet another socio-political ideal. It was primarily his conclusions regarding the methods to be employed by those who rebelled against the system. 'I believe that oppressed and subjugated minorities have a natural right to resistance,' Marcuse declared, 'they have a right to employ illegal means if legal means have proved inadequate.'[5]

That this was no mere idle talk we know from contemporary history. A tremendous sense of urgency took hold of youth all over the world. Believing that they were reaching towards full humanity at last, the rallying calls rang out across the globe. 'Freedom!' in 1950 become 'Power!' in 1964 and, logically, 'Revolution!' in 1968. Here was the high identification with, and action on behalf of, all the alienated young of the world. Marcuse pointed the way to an increase in violence, should the need arise. These were the New Activists. Their doctrinal stand differed only in style, not content. With them there were distinct overtones of the Far East, with faint echoes of Christianity.

The phenomenon of the New Activists and the New Pacifists, damning the system, is classically epitomized in Hamlet's most famous soliloquy. The choice lies between a positivist resistance to the iniquities of the world, its rottenness, or a passive rejection and escape from it. Both attitudes meet at the point of rebellion.

For the New Pacifists, the aid of body- and mind-expanding techniques is sought, in sex and drugs. The New Activists most courageously take up arms against a sea of troubles. The New Pacifists, in a manner of speaking, suffer the slings and arrows of outrageous fortune, contracting out.

It would be superficial to believe that the society of our time could well have done without these manifestations. In the key of untempered power, however, with an arrogant authority pursuing its dream of happiness, the Hegelian dialectic becomes inevitable. When the old order has reached the stage of complete control over the lives of others, and there is never a sign of resistance from within, power will answer power, either by way of assertive or passive refusal.

What we now need to consider is whether this, indeed, could bring about the 'greening'[6] of a society. It would then answer the question whether a counter-power or a counter-culture holds out prospects, too, for the Afrikaners and South Africa.

Man, cast into a fathomless universe, lives in dread. Such is his natural condition. This, as Paul Tillich said in *The Courage to Be*, is not fear, which might be nothing else than a normal and healthy physical reaction; this is our dread of the Abyss, expressing itself as the will to power.

The revolutionary idea we construct is the guarantee of our security, but only in illusion. It necessarily contains the idea of exclusion, however much we may venture outwards. The point is, we go out armed, still determined to convince those we meet on life's way that we have found the answer. We must necessarily become defensive.

The hall-mark of radical politics is its final belief that the socio-political ideal is so right, that any methods to realize it are permissible. Everything will be justified by the justice which comes in the end. Inhuman means are then rationalized in the name of a more human order. The result is obvious: we suffer from the schism within. We are divided inside. We want to change the world and only change ourselves. The last laugh is with the devil. His tyranny has now established himself inside of us. We have engineered his victory.

Irony remains an ever-present theme where power follows its course. What we have already discerned in the case history of the Afrikaners of Southern Africa is a universal phenomenon. It is not only that of power engendering power, it is the more subtle undermining of intentions in a way which escapes the notice of all but the tragi-comic eye.

The case of the Soviet Union has already been mentioned. In the iron embrace of Mother Russia more peoples, cultures, lands and races are contained than in any other empire in history. But in the United States, where increasing Abundance was designed to lead to what the late Henry Luce called 'the Fabulous Future', the billion dollar science and industry of hygiene has led to a defilement which can no more be calculated. The ingenious manufacture of more and more labour-saving machines has not made life easier, but immensely more complicated. The vast speeding-up of traffic by means of super-freeways has only speeded things up for destruction. Roads, like the air-lanes, have already become hopelessly congested. How refreshing to see at least some New York policemen going about their business on horse-back.

In South Africa, too, as we have seen, revolutionary Afrikanerdom's most noble intentions are being undermined in a way which still escapes their notice. African colonialism in the form of British imperialism was first questioned and finally undermined by the still feudal Afrikaners. But in the new hierarchy which has evolved, and with the ideal of distinctive freedoms for each separate ethnic group before us, they witness the revival of colonialism – exactly by those who less than a generation ago so unequivocally rejected it.

The meaning of this for the Afrikaner radicals of our time who have striven to establish a definitive South African order is that the great ambitions of visionary man are in the final resort undermined by what is incalculable. History negates man's intentions and dreams, pointing to a mystery beyond human equations. This is the dominant theme of the Gospels. It is also that of great literature.

The myth of the Fall, the myth of the Tower, are the abiding cyphers for all great comic or tragic writing. They represent man trying to become his own Providence.

Seen through the temperament of the artist, the attempt is both comic and tragic. Man overreaches himself, because *hubris* is the substitute for faith. The perceptive telling of the human story needs to be constantly re-told, to reveal to ourselves the extent of our error. Attempting to be our own Providence we wander after figments of the mind, defeating ourselves precisely because we wish to save ourselves.

When the artist reveals, with the sublimity of insight which Grace has afforded him, the fragile creature which is man, we may find it a cause of both laughter and fear. Failing this restoration of a true sense of proportion, we must learn by defeat. Intending to provide our particular heaven, we learn in horror that we have invited hell.

The present writer remembers a day in 1965 visiting on the New England coast at Mystic Seaport the original model of the ship of Captain Ahab, the *Pequod*. It was the *Charles W. Graham*, which had sailed over the oceans of the world and had brought back to Nantucket many millions of dollars worth of whale oil. Standing there in those cramped quarters between the stout beams of that little ship, he relived all the strange human and inhuman adventures of the man, Ahab, possessed by a vision of fulfilment. He remembers thinking that the equivalent in South African history of the *Pequod*, so primitive yet so adequate to its heroic but absurd purpose, was the ox-wagon: perhaps the wagon of the Thirstlander, like Ahab madly pursuing his dream of ultimate happiness in the capture of the Ideal; in the 'heartless immensities of the world'.

What now are the facts which they, who in the course of three centuries built so much – farms, towns, churches, schools, a language, a great variety of excellent public institutions, in fact a whole indigenous West European culture in Southern Africa – have to face, here in the middle of the seventies?

The dominant reality facing the Afrikaners and for that

reason South Africa as a whole is the prospect of new radical forces which will most certainly be stimulated by a refusal on the part of the White Protestant establishment to relinquish its position of almost exclusive power.

Those who now hold power gained it by opposing an older hegemony. Even when they have justified their position by the most lofty idealism, they now find the roles reversed. What cannot be hidden is that they, in turn, have become the established order.

But the nemesis of man-made things is also the ageing process. Here, too, it becomes the enormous structure of mediocre over-government which calls forth in the still young and militant the same responses and reactions which they who are still in power themselves so deeply experienced.

In the case of the Afrikaners, who only fully came to power in the post-Second World War world, it is not Anglo-Saxon South Africa – their old opponent – which comes into the picture, but those who remain alienated from the true body politic: a proletariat on the periphery.

Despite their present power, the Afrikaners' prospects may well be dismaying. This is ironic because they have worked so tirelessly and paid so much in blood and sweat for what they believe to be their proper due. Calm reflection should inform those who seek to lead, that a sudden confrontation with an enemy from across the borders of their country will, without the loyalty and co-operation of black/brown South Africa, cause an impossible situation.

How could a small, highly privileged minority in the long run see to inland security – guarding every farm, village and city – and at the same time man the far-flung borders of the country? A confrontation between a dominant minority and an enormous proletariat, *in* the body politic, but not *of* it, would arouse militant sympathies for the latter far exceeding anything previously experienced. The result would be almost complete isolation. For the first time, economic sanctions would be severely felt – when even old and trusted friends could no longer be relied upon. Economic chaos would mean political anarchy.

Neither is there much comfort in the technique of being clever rather than strong. Delaying actions, shifts, artifices, the doubtful art of semantic jugglery – saying not what you mean, and meaning not what you say, pretending that power is to be shared, while in actual fact it is not – will only serve to increase bitterness. Indications have already been given by the Coloured Representative Council that mere 'contact' with a still dominant white authority is not enough. To call an authority to order, the vote is indispensable. Should further representations on the part of these fellow Westerners – the Coloureds – meet with the same response, even the loyal supporters of the policy will have nothing more to say. The abstraction of freedom would then have finally disappeared. The rest would be silence.

In the youthful days of the Afrikaners' socio-political ideal, it was a favourite theme to speak of the many sacrifices which would be necessary to see the effective, logical unfolding of the idea to what was generally referred to as the *eindbestemming* – destiny or final end. Here, too, the ambiguities of history have had their say. For, indeed, sacrifice will be called for, but in a way and to an extent never in any way envisaged by those who were so assiduously planning the future, promising general happiness. For what has now become apparent is that the real sacrifice which history has come to demand from white South Africa, especially from the Afrikaners, is a voluntary relinquishment of hegemony. Proper government, in order to work, can never be the prerogative of the privileged few. It is *hubris* to believe that one people, one party, one church or one group alone can be entrusted with the future.

'Of course', many declare, 'but we can only move as fast as the electorate will allow. Ignoring the real fears of people will put us out of power. Then all is lost.' The answer to this, through the ages, has been leadership. For the measure of greatness here is exactly the ability to lead, not to be led by the highest common factor. Leading means taking the people along with you towards a renewal which to the faint-hearted once seemed to be dangerous. The faith, humanity and serenity of an inspired leader infuses his society, making the members of it share in his greatness.

One thing is certain: the old order changes, yielding place to the new. This is no less true of separate development. Here, in the mid-seventies, the socio-political ideal which promised so much has most strangely forfeited its conceptual wholeness and fallen into three parts.

Firstly, there is the very substantive and acceptable plan to develop certain traditionally African areas of the country so as to become autonomous states. Practical reason, as the writer Alan Paton has declared, makes this more or less generally acceptable, providing there is genuine progress towards full autonomy.

Secondly, there is the variation called parallel development, designed to meet the situation where the position of the Coloureds, for whom no separate homeland is available or possible, could no longer be accommodated within the all-inclusive design. Semantics come to the rescue. As far as the Coloureds are concerned, it is solemnly stated, things are 'not yet quite clear'; in politics there are no 'instant solutions'; one should not try to see 'the end of the road'; it is a matter of evolution, not revolution; life is not 'logical'; nobody can tell where the road ahead will lead to. Meanwhile there will be socio-economic advancement for the Coloureds, ethnic autonomy and so on.

The sound argument about the limits of politics would have been more than plausible, if it had not been for the fact that the very concept of separate development had been presented from the start as a way of redemption, as the radical, rational answer to the future. Words, said Thucydides, referring to his own troublous times – and he was thinking mainly of political words – so easily become fair phrases used to cover guilty ends.

Such is man. Such, too, are the Puritans in Africa – no better, no worse. The vision leads onwards to what we believe to be happiness. But, in pursuing it, we wander anew like the Thirst-landers.

Thirdly, and most destructively, the socio-political ideal has become a vast system of structured privilege.

> We have proclaimed ourselves the heirs
> To all the richest and most pleasant places
> In this productive land, all the best suburbs
> And suburban houses,

337

All the best farms, forests, and open spaces,
More and far better colleges and training centres,
More and far better schools and nursery crèches,
Best seats in train and bus, concert, cinema
And races.
Best camping spots for day and night *braaivleises*
And oh, most holy to us, all the best places
For fishing, surf or swimming.
Including all (or nearly all) the coast-line
that skirts the Fairest Cape
(Home, incidentally, of the Coloured people).[7]

In this condition, all who are white, also those who hate apartheid, have come to share. But it is the inventors – the Afrikaners – who take the rap.

'What a piece of work is a man,' Hamlet remarked. He might well have been commenting on himself as the supreme example in literature of a man with a mission: pursuing the ideal of justice at any price and discovering in conclusion a stage full of dead bodies. For the real struggle is that of power. And our setting right of the out-of-joint world to the measure of some concept of freedom must justify the ascendancy we seek.

How then could renewal come?

We have seen that, in the Hegelian way, power will oppose power and eventually take its place. There is, however, no evidence in history that succeeding power-structures synthesize towards the ultimate glory of the Absolute. On the contrary, new orders can be infinitely worse than those they have removed.

Remembering the story of this fragmentary but much written-about part of Western man, to imagine that all that the Afrikaners need is another system, preferably from the revisionist left, would be too easy to be true. If the socio-political ideal they have chased this past quarter-of-a-century proves in its inability to deal with the South African situation to be finally invalid, there is, in fact, only one true alternative. *That is to rediscover their own most genuine tradition. This would mean returning to the original Calvin, also in the matter of civil government.*

338

Marthinus Versfeld once said that he was no conservative, he was a conservationist. As a conservationist he had a deep respect for roots. Therefore he was also a 'radical'. They are real roots, however, and they are rooted in the true Christian heritage, which for him is best represented in St Augustine.

Versfeld writes as an Afrikaner who has become a leading Catholic. But much of the authentic Calvin is still to be discerned in him. This is simply because the authentic Calvin is also the authentic Augustine.

Remember again Calvin's quoting St Augustine in the *Institutes* on the essence of the Christian religion:

As the orator when asked, What is the first precept in eloquence? answered, Delivery; What is the second? Delivery: What is the third: Delivery: so if you ask me in regard to the precepts of the Christian Religion, I will answer, first, second and third, Humility.[8]

Man relying on his own final abilities commits the sin of idolatry. Let no man flatter himself. Left to his own designs, he is a devil. The happiness he needs is entirely from God.

Power as the short cut to survival, identity, fulfilment and happiness is therefore also against the truest tradition of the Afrikaners: the original Calvin.

But Calvin, of course, was only what he was because he was such an excellent Catholic. And the original Calvin is also part of the true Christian tradition in its entirety.

What does it mean in practical terms? It means, in the first place, finding a true synthesis by abandoning the idolatrous belief that political man can work out his own fundamental and eternal 'principles'. In this sense, every principle leads to the devil, as Nietzsche once said.

It means bringing politics back to its true dimensions, as the *société provisoire* of which Calvin wrote. As such, no temporary authority can pretend to be the architect and engineer of its own fundamentals. '*For the foundations, nobody can lay any other than the one that has already been laid, that is Jesus Christ.*'[9]

This means that politics, having no 'apostolic ministry' or message for the soul, should concern itself rather with the ordering of society in unity, equity and reason, preparing for what must yet transcend this imperfect order. (cf. p. 131).

When the Great Concept takes over, it becomes a tyranny. Then we soon find the finest people bowing down before it and trying, at the same time, to be good Christians. We need nothing more in statecraft, as in all things, than common sense, which is the substratum of faith, as good craftsmanship is the basis of art.

The *société provisoire*, Calvin insisted, for the sake of orderly administration needs authority. This is both the rule of law and of intelligent, enlightened administration. When things age, a synthesis can relatively easily be effected. A change in government is then no catastrophe, but brings the stimulating possibility of renewal.

The civil order, imperfect as it is, *needs* authority which, in turn, requires a measure of violence. But, said Calvin, this can never be an absolute order, an absolute authority. *The civil order is therefore enjoined never to exceed its bounds.* It does exactly that when it pretends to become its own Providence.

This is precisely why Calvin described religious nationalism as one of the destructive forces in society, as a substitute for the Christian religion. '... *de plus, elle est extrêmement ambigué et peut parfois recouvrir l'expression fidèle de la foi,*' says Biéler.[10]

Man has a free intelligence; and when the civil order has acted in a way which inhibits those living within its sphere of government with sufficient maturity to exercise this intelligence, it becomes seriously at fault. They should have real participation in the ordering of their own lives. Keeping these people in a state of subjection is to exceed the bounds of the civil order. This would be a betrayal of the true heritage of Calvinism.

Millions of words have been spoken and written since the early forties when the intellectual élite of the *burgerstand* began working out the redemptive socio-political ideal. Millions of words, it can also be said, have been spent in debate within Afrikanerdom, especially since Sharpeville, but increasingly as the sixties advanced. Academics everywhere – the under-forties, particularly, writers, poets, theologians and philosophers – feeling themselves captive in a system, have struggled to test the validity of the political order. In almost every movement of questioning or rejection, from the extreme left to the extreme right, but also, and far more significantly, among those who are beyond ideological good and evil, Afrikaners have taken the lead. The *Volk* has long since ceased to be the homogeneous whole it seemed to be in the early fifties. The dissident Afrikaner, the angry Afrikaner, the philosophically analytical Afrikaner, are all in the centre of a kind of national anguish.

In this spiritual turbulence, expressing itself in debate, there is probably as much potential for a substantial renewal as was the case during the second half of the seventeenth century in Old England. Five outstanding figures of this English age serve here as a pointer as to how a true synthesis in the world of the Afrikaners could also come about.

Milton, Newton, Bunyan, Baxter, Locke ... Greatness is rare in any age. But times of stress and troubles may produce them when they are least expected. Radical Afrikanerdom, we have seen, has already known its own Milton in the person of N. P. van Wyk Louw, who towards the end of his life, like Milton, had little faith in the revolutionary idea. Increasingly he expressed what he had written towards the end of the fifties: political convictions could not be a *lewens–en wêreldbeskouing* – a world-view, simply because politics had essentially to do with the practical ordering of a society and was therefore strictly limited.[11]

Furthermore, the moment one started believing in the dominance of the single will, one was on the way to accepting totalitarian values.[12] The hard, naked poetry of his final years (*Tristia*) expressed both his disillusionment and renewal of faith in values which went far beyond the limits of politics.

Many other restless voices have sounded in poetry and prose this past decade.[13] Ingrid Jonker, who died by her own hand, epitomized much of it in a poem at the time of Sharpeville telling of the death of a child, struck by a policeman's bullet.

The child who only wished to play at Nyanga in the sun is everywhere
The child has become a man and travels through all Africa
The child has become a giant and travels through all the world.
Without a pass.[14]

The Church, too, in various ways, and in spite of tendencies towards institutional alignment with the political order, has also in our time known its prophetic voices, reminding their people of the true fundamentals of their Reformed faith. A figure like B. B. Keet will increase in stature, now that he is dead. A lifetime of witness to the true meaning of the Gospels is at the same time an affirmation of the best in the Reformed tradition. Apartheid, Keet conclusively reminded his church and people in the late sixties, finds its complete rejection in the history of Christ and the Samaritan woman at Jacob's well at the town called Sychar. Jew and untouchable Samaritan there reached over centuries of hate and rejection to each other, not by way of 'principle', but by way of love and acceptance . . .[15]

'Are we in these times of crisis prepared to listen again whether God, perhaps, has something to say to us? Or do we run the risk of our informing God that the route we are following is, in every detail beyond question, also His way for us?' So asked A. J. van der Merwe, shortly after Cottesloe. He was at the time Moderator of the N. G. Church of the Cape Province.

Some people in the Church went their independent ways, struggling with this very question, like Beyers Naudé who led the Christian Institute as an ecumenical movement. He too had once been Moderator of the N. G. Church, in the Transvaal.

Other, younger, theologians have remained within and form part of the Church's unremitting task of re-discovering its own heritage. One of them, J. J. F. Durand, has been at the centre of the tremendous involvement of the urban Africans within the framework of separate development. He has said rightly that whatever answers there are will be decided by nature of the motivations of those within the Reformed tradition.[16] At Potchefstroom, where probably more of the original Calvin has survived than anywhere else, the inner debate in Afrikanerdom has often been at its most meaningful. What is Christian nationalism? the men of *Woord en Daad* have asked. Has the political struggle of the Afrikaners always been carried by the unadulterated Reformed tradition? In what measure has the ideal of Christian nationalism become the ideal of Nationalist Christianity?[17] Where this has indeed happened, either because of ignorance or deliberately, the crying out of the name of Christ over immoral politicizing is the sin of blasphemy.[17]

Are there also among the Afrikaners the political philosophers and social scientists, who like Locke could bring their society back to a true respect for reason in the ordering of our socio-political lives?

J. J. Degenaar and other Afrikaner academics have been writing and speaking for a release of their own people from 'metaphysical tyranny', in other words from what happens when abstractions of freedom are pursued with relentless idealism. What is pre-eminently necessary is that people should appear who could help restore a tradition in which Bunyan, Newton, Baxter and Locke share as much as those of the modern day such as Denis de Rougemont, André Biéler and Karl Barth.

Barth especially would have relevance for the modern Afrikaners, as another figure from within the Church, Murray Janson, has shown in his treatment of the part Barth played in the rejection of the *Deutsche Christen* and the fatal theology of ordination in the time of the Third Reich. He also points to his historic leadership in the *Bekenntniskirche*.[18]

The potential within the Dutch Reformed Church as a whole is unmapped, but it is also unmistakable. When Tobie Muller, a brilliant young theologian, more than half-a-century before Vorster succeeded Verwoerd, and a few years before his untimely death, declared that 'a healthy nation dwells so little as any normal person on the day of his death', that 'gravestone patriots' are useless for society, and that a people who remain faithful to their own best traditions are for all practical purposes proof against destruction, he was speaking also for the present time, and on behalf of the present Church.[19]

This accords with what a number of others, writing from within the ethic of the original Calvin, have also said. In 1960, D. P. Botha, pleading for the necessity of accepting the Coloureds as full members of the Western society of Afrikanerdom – because they represent the rise of a Third Estate – closed his book by quoting the well-known words of D. F. Malan, but now in a new and relevant context: 'Bring together those that belong together.'[20]

The way of faith, Kierkegaard insisted, was the way of being oneself. When am I as a human being myself? When I restore my intelligence as a freely creative medium, not because I am autonomous, but because I am God's peculiarly endowed creature, entrusted with freedom. The death of that freedom is idolatry.

This is the heart, too, of Versfeld's writings. It is also the 'Socratic spirit': the 'faith of a free man accepting his dignity from the light of the divine obscurity and walking with others because he can stand on his own feet. All human certitudes are suspect.'[21]

Within a man-made conceptual framework, I am necessarily held captive, and can never therefore be myself. For intelligence, which expresses itself both as reason and sensitivity for what is revealed in a way which is beyond reason, life must be approached with a certain abandon: re-discovering the 'wisdom of insecurity'.[21] Authority in the civil order is necessary; but, as St Paul said of the law when writing to the Galatians, the law is merely a kind of tutor, but being a Christian requires more. It needs the faith which is active in love. Regarding Christian liberty, Calvin said, means also that the consciences of believers may rise above the law, cheerfully obeying the will of God.

If the law can be the kind of yoke which prevents us from being fully human, how much more will it not be the case where we have enclosed ourselves within the framework of a radical political system? For this, more than anything else as we have seen, becomes the tyranny, the all-pervasive presence, of a total idea.

The really great advances in history – in art, science and civil government in its various aspects – have appeared when man has emerged out of bondage and behaved like the free intelligence he was intended to be. The indications here have been the ability to transcend all human frameworks; to surpass – to use the language of modern business – the 'managerial grid as a key for mobilizing human effort'. But the grid of the New Industrial State, it should be remembered, is no different from the grid of the socio-political ideal. All-inclusive systems of any kind hold the mind in thrall.

Of course, man will continue to construct them because he will continue to yearn for power while preserving his conscience. His 'key managerial orientations in business' will reflect his style, too, in redemptive, radical politics. This is the risk of freedom. Man must choose.

The Afrikaners – the Puritans in Africa – will be no more exempt from it than any other part of the human family. As such, they, too, will need to rise above it, to survive as a culture and people.

When Jesus came in sight of the city, St Luke tells us, he wept over it and said: 'If only you had known on this great day, the way that leads to peace. But no, it is hidden from your sight. For a time will come upon you when your enemies ... will bring you to the ground ... because you did not recognize God's moment when it came.'

Knowledge of our true condition must be attained before it is too late, and no new synthesis can grow. This is very much the concern of the philosopher, theologian, statesman and creative artist. But for a lasting renewal to take place, wider sensibilities will be needed. Grace is no prerogative of the 'creative minority'. Their task is best fulfilled along the dusty roads of life, beside the wells and springs of a thirsty land, among the hungry people on a hillside in the veld.

To be immersed in the human situation is to assume without illusion, in the mood of playful irony, all that life requires from us. It means accepting, with the prospect of humour, conflict, struggle, disaster, death, never surrendering to depression or guilt, but rather to the knowledge of human frailty; to meet the world as it comes, knowing that life can and should be a shining experience.

Notes

2. *The Heroic Age: Trek*

1. Cf. F. A. van Jaarsveld, *Honderd basiese dokumente by die studie van die Suid-Afrikaanse geskiedenis*, Cape Town, 1971, p. 54.

2. Cf. Leo Marquard, *The Story of South Africa*, Faber & Faber, 1968, pp. 124–5.

3. Alexis de Tocqueville, *Democracy in America*, the Henry Reeve Text, as revised by Francis Bowen, further corrected and edited by Philips Bradley, New York, 1948, vol. 1, p. 31.

4. Cf. Albert Camus, *The Rebel*, Hamish Hamilton, 1953.

5. Cf. *500 Years, a History of South Africa*, edited by C. J. F. Muller, Cape Town, 1969, p. 99.

6. C. W. de Kiewiet, *A History of South Africa – Social and Economic*, Oxford University Press, 1957, chapter 2.

7. Cf. *500 Years*, op. cit., p. 130.

8. De Kiewiet, op. cit., chapter 11. The 'outflanking' can be interpreted as being relative to both the British and the Xhosa.

9. Cf. A. Biéler, *La Pensée Economique et Sociale de Calvin*, Geneva, 1961, pp. 174, 177.

10. Cf. Leonard Thompson, *The Oxford History of South Africa, Vol: 1: To 1870*, edited by Monica Wilson and Leonard Thompson, Oxford University Press, 1969, part 1, chapter 9, p. 391.

11. ibid., pp. 394–5.

12. ibid., pp. 404–5.

13. Cf. Edwin W. Smith, *The Life and Times of Daniel Lindley, 1801–1880*, Epworth, 1949, p. 107.

14. Thompson, op. cit., p. 359.

15. George McCall Theal, *The History of South Africa, 1505–1884*, vol. 6, p. 390. 'Star' edition: facsimile by C. Struik, Cape Town, 1964.

16. Thompson, op. cit., p. 362.

17. Theal, op. cit., p. 393.

18. ibid., p. 394.

19. Frances Ellen Colenso, *The Ruin of Zululand: An Account of British Doings in Zululand since the Invasion of 1879*, London, 1880.

20. Cf. Theal, op. cit., vol. 10, on the Zulu War, chapter 13.

21. From *Fallen Induna* by C. M. van den Heever, translated from the Afrikaans by William and Jean Branford.

3. *The Heroic Age: The Wars of Independence*

1. Marquard, op. cit., pp. 190–91.

2. A. M. Hugo, *The Cape Vernacular*, inaugural lecture as Professor of Classics, University of Cape Town, 11 May 1970, New Series no. 2, p. 18.

3. De Tocqueville, op. cit., vol. 1, p. 355. Generally on the American Indians, pp. 336, 350–5.

4. Cf. James Bryce, *Impressions of South Africa*, London, 1897.

5. Goethe, *Faust*, Act 2, lines 1335–6.

6. Cf. F. A. van Jaarsveld in *The Standard Encyclopaedia of Southern Africa*, vol. 2, p. 595: the essay on T. F. W. Burgers.

7. Theal, op. cit., vol. 10, p. 268.

8. R. H. Tawney, *Religion and the Rise of Capitalism*, Penguin edition, p. 270.

9. Cf. F. A. van Jaarsveld, *The Afrikaner's Interpretation of South African History*, Cape Town, 1964, p. 3.

10. The phrase is Tawney's.

11. De Kiewiet, op. cit., p. 135.

12. ibid.

13. ibid.

14. E. S. Walker, *A History of South Africa*, Longman, 1927, p. 463 et seq.

15. *Briewe uit Transvaal* (1896–99) by G. A. A. Middelberg, introduced by Dr E. J. du Toit Spies, in the *Hertzog-Annale* of the *Suid-Afrikaanse Akademie vir Wetenskap en Kuns*, July, 1953, p. 156. Translated from the Dutch.

16. ibid., p. 158.

17. ibid., p. 145.

18. ibid., p. 117.

19. *500 Years*, op. cit., p. 286.

20. *The Milner Papers* (*South Africa*) 1897–99, edited by Cecil Headlam, Cassell, 1931, vol. 1, p. 242.

21. N. J. van der Merwe, *Marthinus Theunis Steyn*, Cape Town, 1921, vol. 1, pp. 186–7. Translated from the Dutch.

22. ibid., p. 190.

23. De Kiewiet, op. cit., p. 138.

24. Cf. Uys Krige, *Olive Schreiner: A Selection*, Cape Town, 1968, p. 160.

25. The bust of Rhodes by Tweed is housed in the monument designed by Sir Herbert Baker and J. M. Swan, with sculpture – the original of *Energy* – by Watts. The Kruger sculpture is the miniature by Anton van Wouw.

26. Cf. Winston S. Churchill, *London to Ladysmith via Pretoria*, London, 1906.

27. Cf. the *Rand Daily Mail*, 6 January 1906.

28. Deneys Reitz, *Commando, a Boer Journal of the Boer War*, London, 1939, p. 290.

29. ibid., p. 294.

30. ibid., p. 296.

31. J. D. Kestell, *Met de Boeren-Commando's*, Amsterdam, 1903 p. 276.

32. From *Kruger's Statue* by Toon van den Heever, translated by William and Jean Branford.

4. *The Coming of the* Burgerstand

1. This is the well-known theme of Arnold Toynbee in *A Study of History*, Oxford University Press, 1935.

2. The concluding paragraph in D. W. Krüger's *The Age of the Generals*, Johannesburg, 1958.

3. Cf. Walker, op. cit., p. 507.

4. From *Winternag (Winter's Night)* by Eugene N. Marais. The poem was the true start of an upsurge in Afrikaans poetry.

5. Cf. G. W. T. Omand, *The Boers in Europe: A Sidelight on History*, London, 1903, p. 84.

6. ibid., p. 107.

7. Cf. *Selections from the Smuts Papers*, vol. IV, edited by W. K. Hancock and Jean van der Poel, Cambridge University Press, 1966, pp. 201, 209.

8. ibid., p. 288.

9. Walker, op. cit., p. 585.

10. C. M. van den Heever, *Generaal J. B. M. Hertzog*, Johannesburg, 1943, p. 447. All extracts translated from the Afrikaans.

11. Cf. David Welsh, *The Oxford History of South Africa, Vol. II*, edited by Leonard Thompson and Monica Wilson, Oxford University Press, 1971, pp. 262–4.

12. The cartoonist, the most famous in the history of the Afrikaans press, was D. C. Boonzaaier.

13. From a leading article in *Die Burger*, 31 January 1972. Translated from the Afrikaans.

14. Welsh, op. cit., p. 202.
15. Cf. *500 Years*, pp. 371–2.
16. Van den Heever, op. cit., p. 730.
17. ibid., p. 649.
18. ibid., p. 113.
19. ibid., p. 632.
20. ibid., p. 754.
21. ibid., p. 758.

5. *The Original Calvin*

1. Cf. John Calvin, *Institutes of the Christian Religion*, 2:2:11.
2. Biéler, op. cit.
3. Tawney, op. cit., pp. 126, 301.
4. Cf. K. R. Popper, *The Poverty of Historicism*, Routledge & Kegan Paul, 1957, chapter 21: 'Piecemeal versus Utopian Engineering'.
5. Biéler, op. cit., p. 131–2.
6. Calvin, op. cit., 4:20:32.
7. ibid., 4:20:7.
8. ibid., 4:12:7. On standards of Agreement: 4:20:1, 15, 16.
9. Tawney, op. cit., p. 127.
10. Calvin, op. cit., 4:20:1. Cf. also Biéler, op, cit., on the *double régime* in human affairs, p. 208 et seq.
11. Biéler, op. cit., p. 423.
12. ibid., pp. 302–4.
13. ibid., pp. 251–5.
14. ibid., p. 80.
15. ibid., pp. 307–10.
16. ibid., p. 311.
17. ibid., pp. 316–18.
18. ibid., pp. 327–8.
19. ibid., p. 340.
20. ibid., p. 358.
21. ibid., p. 342.
22. ibid., p. 346.
23. ibid., pp. 351, 353.
24. ibid., pp. 453–73.
25. ibid., p. 170.
26. ibid.
27. ibid., p. 178.
28. ibid., p. 397.
29. ibid., p. 400.

30. ibid., p. 401.

31. ibid., p. 420.

32. Tawney, op. cit., p. 127.

33. ibid., p. 135.

34. Cf. no. 54 of the *100 Aphorisms* in the Henry Beveridge translation of the *Institutes*. Also Calvin, op. cit., 3:19:4.

35. Cf. Max Weber, *The Protestant Ethic and the Spirit of Capitalism*, Allen & Unwin, 1967, part A, chapter IV; also notes 39, 41 and 65 to chapter IV.

36. Michael Walzer, *The Revolutions of the Saints – A Study in the Origins of Radical Politics*, Cambridge, Massachusetts, 1963.

6. *Rebels not Revolutionaries*

1. Biéler, op. cit., pp. 104–6.

7. *Revolution and the Puritan Spirit*

1. William Haller, *The Rise of Puritanism*, Oxford University Press, 1938, p. 18.

2. ibid., p. 8.

3. Tawney, op. cit. p. 202.

4. Haller, op. cit., p. 51.

5. Denis de Rougemont, *La Part du Diable*, Gallimond, 1946, chapter 29, part III. Translated from the French.

6. Haller, op. cit., p. 330.

7. Biéler, op. cit., pp. 184, 400.

8. Cf. note 34 of *The Original Calvin*. Also Calvin, op. cit. 3:19:4.

9. Perry Miller, *The New England Mind: The Seventeenth Century*, New York, 1939, p. 470.

10. 1 Peter 2: 9, 10.

11. Calvin, op. cit., 3:24:12.

12. ibid., 3:7.

13. ibid., 3:19:4.

14. ibid., 3:23:14.

15. Cf. note 35 of *The Original Calvin*.

16. Herbert W. Schneider, *The Puritan Mind*, Ann Arbor, 1958, pp. 70–71, also chapter III.

17. Miller, op. cit., p. 49.

18. Schneider, op. cit., p. 99.

19. Miller, op. cit., pp. 393–4.

20. ibid., p. 395.

21. Schneider, op. cit., p. 86–7.

22. ibid., p. 97.

23. ibid., pp. 97–8.

24. ibid., p. 98.

25. ibid., p. 97.

26. ibid., pp. 125–6.

27. ibid., p. 155.

28. De Tocqueville, op. cit., vol. 1, p. 43.

29. As described by Gustavus Myers in *The History of the Great American Fortunes*, Modern Library edition, New York, 1936.

30. De Tocqueville, op. cit., vol. 1, p. 31.

31. ibid., pp. 31–2.

32. ibid., p. 43.

33. Cf. Reinhold Niebuhr, *The Irony of American History*, New York 1952, p. 24.

34. De Tocqueville, op. cit., vol. 1, p. 58.

35. Alain Clément, in *The United States*, Life World Library, New York, 1968, p. 50.

36. In the article referred to.

37. Niebuhr, op. cit., p. 140.

38. ibid., p. 142.

39. ibid., p. 149.

8. *The Socio-Political Ideal*

1. Cf. A. N. Whitehead, *Science and the Modern World*, Cambridge University Press, 1936, chapter 1.

2. Cf. Lewis Mumford, *The Condition of Man*, Secker & Warburg, 1962, chapter 10.

3. The reference is to the book by Frantz Fanon.

4. Marthinus Versfeld, *Dialogue between Christians and Marxists*, University of Cape Town Summer School Lecture, 1968.

5. Ezekiel 24: 9, 10, 11 (Jerusalem Bible).

6. Biéler, op. cit., p. 454.

7. ibid.

8. ibid., p. 392.

9. ibid., p. 412.

10. ibid., p. 413.

11. ibid., p. 420.

12. ibid., p. 433.

13. ibid., pp. 436, 437, 440.

14. ibid., p. 253 et seq.

15. Popper, op. cit., chapter 11, section 17.
16. Cf. Fritz Stern, *The Politics of Cultural Despair; A Study in the Rise of Germanic Ideology*, Anchor edition, New York, 1965.
17. Stern, op, cit., p. 169.
18. Schneider, op. cit., p. 142.
19. ibid., p. 154.
20. Stern, op. cit., p. 190.
21. ibid., p. 178.
22. ibid., p. 382. The title of a poem by Moeller van den Bruck.
23. ibid., p. 354.
24. ibid., p. 143.
25. ibid., p. 349.
26. ibid., p. 358.
27. Walzer, op. cit., pp. 317 et seq.

9. *A Band of Brothers*

1. F. A. van Jaarsveld, *Van van Riebeeck tot Verwoerd*, Johannesburg, 1971, p. 247. Translated from the Afrikaans.
2. Marquard, op. cit., p. 238.
3. Van Jaarsveld, op. cit., p. 250.
4. A. N. Pelzer (editor), *Verwoerd Speaks*, Johannesburg, 1966, p. 13.
5. ibid., p. 168.
6. ibid., pp. xiii, xiv.
7. Van Jaarsveld, op. cit., p. 250.
8. Published in London, Cape Town, New York, 1947.
9. After the Malan-Hertzog *hereniging* the name of the party was changed to the cumbersome *Herenigde Nasionale Party of Volksparty*. Only in 1951 was the old name of *Nasionale Party* restored.
10. Cf. Roberts and Trollip, *The South African Opposition*, Cape Town, 1947, p. 112.
11. Cf. E. Roux, *Time longer than Rope*, Gollancz, 1948.
12. Cf. Muriel Horrell, *Legislation and Race Relations* revised edition 1971, Johannesburg, p. 3.
13. ibid., p. 4.
14. ibid., p. 5.
15. ibid., p. 7.
16. ibid., p. 7.
17. ibid., p. 8.
18. ibid., p. 110.
19. David Welsh, *The Roots of Segregation, Native Policy in Colonial Natal 1845–1910*, Oxford University Press, 1972.

20. Horrell, op. cit., p. 1.

21. ibid., p. 4.

22. N. Diederichs, *Nasionalisme en sy Verhouding tot Internasionalisme*, Bloemfontein, 1936. Translated from the Afrikaans.

23. ibid.

24. Dr Abraham Kuyper, *Calvinism, Six Stone Lectures*, Grand Rapids, 1943, p. 27.

25. Diederichs, op. cit., pp. 11, 17, 24–5, 44.

26. ibid., p. 37.

27. ibid., pp. 52–3.

28. ibid., p. 63.

29. ibid., p. 64.

30. 'Dawie', political columnist of *Die Burger* on 26 February 1972.

31. Cf. van Jaarsveld, *The Afrikaner's Interpretation of South African History*, op. cit., p. 3.

32. The phrase is R. H. Tawney's.

33. From *Die Dieper Reg* by N. P. van Wyk Louw, translated by Guy Butler.

34. ibid.

35. P. J. Meyer, *Die Afrikaner*, Cape Town, 1940, pp. 32–3. Translated from the Afrikaans.

36. ibid., p. 33.

37. P. J. Meyer, *Demokrasie of Volkstaat*, A. N. S. and A. N. J. Brochure, Stellenbosch, 1942, p. 29. Translated from the Afrikaans.

38. ibid., p. 29.

39. Published at Stellenbosch, 1945. Translated from the Afrikaans.

40. ibid., p. 11.

41. ibid., p. 24.

42. ibid., pp. 32, 134–5.

43. Meyer, *Dir Afrikaner*, op. cit., p. 92.

44. Cronjé, *'n Tuiste vir die Nageslag* (*A Home for Posterity*), Cape Town, 1945, pp. 110, 149.

45. ibid., p. 167.

46. ibid., p. 102.

47. ibid., p. 40–1.

48. ibid., p. 202.

49. ibid., pp. 88, 181, 183.

50. ibid., p. 55.

51. ibid., p. 81

52. ibid, pp. 59–60.

53. ibid., p. 137.

54. ibid., p. 79.

55. ibid., p. 127.

56. ibid., p. 167.

57. ibid., p. 226.

58. ibid., pp. 37, 41.

59. ibid., p. 23.

60. Cf. E. Kohl, *Die Rassenfrage Südafrikas und die Haltung der Kirche*, (unpublished dissertation for Ph.D., Kiel, 1964), p. 44.

61. G. Cronjé, *Regverdige Rasse-apartheid*, Stellenbosch, 1947, p. 41. Translated from the Afrikaans.

62. ibid., p. 198.

63. ibid., p. 207.

64. ibid.

65. ibid., p. 161.

66. ibid., pp. 168 et seq.

67. ibid., p. 49.

68. ibid., p. 50.

69. ibid., pp. 40 et seq.

70. ibid., p. 22.

71. Cf. *500 Years of History*, op. cit., p. 382.

72. The *Cape Argus*, 8 June 1963.

73. ibid.

10. *The Promethean Afrikaner*

1. Cf. Welsh, *The Oxford History II*, op. cit., p. 406.

2. Cf. *Inspan*, October 1944, p. 18.

3. Cf. *Die Burger*, 29–30 March 1948.

4. A. B. du Preez, *Eiesoortige Ontwikkeling tot Volksdiens*, Cape Town, Pretoria, 1939, p. 226. Translated from the Afrikaans.

5. This, and the following extracts, from the translation by Paul Elmer More.

6. Personally noted.

7. Pelzer, op. cit., p. 1.

8. ibid., p. 14.

9. ibid., p. 16.

10. ibid., p. 16.

11. Cronjé, *'n Tuiste vir die Nageslag*, op. cit., p. 111.

12. ibid., p. 95.

13. *500 Years*, op. cit., p. 392.

14. ibid., p. 384.

15. Cf. Welsh, *The Oxford History II*, op. cit., p. 410.

16. Cf. Trevor Huddleston, *Naught for Your Comfort*, Collins, 1956.

17. *500 Years*, op. cit., p. 385.

18. Pelzer, op. cit., p. 55.

19. ibid., p. 158.

20. ibid., p. 167.

21. ibid., p. 192.

22. ibid., p. 210.

23. ibid., p. 210.

24. ibid., p. 211.

25. ibid., p. 224.

26. ibid., p. 317.

27. ibid., p. 494.

28. ibid., p. 645.

29. ibid., p. 728.

30. *Integration or Separate Development*, issued by the S.A. Bureau of Racial Affairs, Stellenbosch, 1959, p. 18.

31. ibid., p. 28.

32. ibid., p. 34.

33. 'Die Filosofiese Grondslag van die Beleid von Afsonderlike Ontwikkeling', *The Journal of Racial Affairs*, October 1971, pp. 148–9. Translated from the Afrikaans.

34. ibid., p. 150.

35. ibid., p. 152.

36. Cf. *Journal of Racial Affairs*, July 1960, pp. 167–86.

37. De Wet Nel., op. cit., p. 185. Translated from the Afrikaans.

38. ibid.

39. Cf. *Die N. G. Kerk in Suid-Afrika en Rasseverhoudings:* a summary of the most important conclusions reached on racial affairs from April 1950 to December 1960, Cape Town, 1961.

40. ibid., p. 7.

41. ibid., p. 17.

42. ibid., pp. 20, 21.

43. ibid., pp. 25 et seq.

44. ibid., pp. 30–5.

45. *Die Burger*, 23 March 1951. Translated from the Afrikaans.

46. Cf. A. P. Treurnicht, *Op die Keper*, Cpae Town, 1965, passim.

47. Murray Janson, *Die Kerk en die Ideologie*, Potchefstroom, 1967, pp. 32–6. The writer discusses the destructive effect of a theology of ordination, referring to the church in the Third Reich as a case in point. Translated from the Afrikaans.

48. Cf. J. Stellingwerf. *Gezag en vrijheid in het licht van Gods Woord* (*In Truth and Reality*), Johannesburg, 1971, p. 83. The author poses the question whether the idea of sovereignty in a particular sphere could be used to validate the idea of separate development, concluding that it cannot.

49. Kuyper, op. cit., p. 70.

50. ibid., p. 94.

51. ibid., p. 92.

52. ibid., p. 81.

53. Treurnicht, op. cit., pp. 19–21, 31, 38, 40, 44, 46, 50, 68–71, 76, 78, 82, 83, 95, 135–4.

54. ibid., pp. 19–20. Translated from the Afrikaans.

55. ibid., p. 20. Translated from the Afrikaans.

56. ibid., p. 21. Translated from the Afrikaans.

57. Cf. *Human Relations in South Africa*, report adopted by the General Synod of the Nederduitse Gereformeerde Kerk, Cape Town, 1966.

58. ibid., p. 3.

59. ibid., p. 42.

60. ibid., p. 42.

61. ibid., p. 54.

62. ibid., pp. 42–3.

63. As in *Tristia*.

64. *Die Pluimsaad waai ver*.

65. Pelzer, op. cit., p. 723.

66. Dr A. G. Kellerman, as reported in *Die Burger*, 3 November 1966.

67. The *Population Registration Act* (1950).

68. *Die Beeld* (then Sunday stablemate of *Die Burger*) where the story was reported as set out here.

69. Mr Carel Steenkamp in *Die Beeld* report during March 1966. Translated from the Afrikaans.

70. Letter by S. van Rensburg in *Die Beeld* during March 1966. Translated from the Afrikaans.

71. Dr J.A. Heese, a genealogist, also once an N.G. Church archivist, after the most extensive survey to date, found the ethnic spectrum of the Afrikaners to be: 34.8% German, 33.7% Dutch, 13.2% French, 5.2% British, 2.7% 'other European nations', 6.9% 'non-White' – mainly from early times via slave women from the East Indies – 3.5% unknown. Cf. J. A. Heese, *Die Herkoms van die Afrikaners*, Cape-town, 1972. The percentage of 'non-white' blood was later confirmed independently by the immunologist, Dr M. C. Botha.

72. J. J. F. C. Heydenrych, *Die Maatskaplike Implikasies by die Toepassing van Artikel 16 van Wet 23 van 1957:* dissertation for the degree of Ph.D., University of Stellenbosch, 1968. (Unpublished.)

73. ibid., pp. 133–4.

74. ibid., pp. 135–40.

75. ibid., p. 142.

76. ibid., pp. 153–61.

77. Willem J. van Heerden in a letter to *Die Burger*, 7 February 1972.

78. 'Madness', wrote columnist Schalk Pienaar, in *Rapport*, 10 December 1972. In January 1975 it was opened to all races.

79. Cf. the leading article in the *Cape Times*, 10 March 1969.

11. *The Rise of Afrikaner capitalism*

1. E. P. du Plessis, *'n Volk staan op*, Cape Town, 1964, p. 93. Translated from the Afrikaans.

2. ibid.

3. ibid.

4. *Federale Volksbeleggings Ltd.*

5. Du Plessis, op. cit., p. 168.

6. Tawney, op. cit., p. 238.

7. Weber, op. cit., p. 126.

8. ibid., p. 119.

9. Cf. Luce, *The Fabulous Future*, Time Inc., New York, 1955.

10. Du Plessis, op. cit., p. 183.

11. J. L. Sadie, *The Afrikaner in the South African Economy* (*Memorandum for the Canadian Royal Commission on Bilingualism and Biculturalism*), unpublished, p. 85.

12. ibid., p. 86.

13. M. S. Louw in *Tegniek*, June 1965.

14. Sadie, op. cit., p. 63 et seq.

15. ibid., p. 64.

16. ibid.

17. Address before the *Afrikaanse Sakekamer*, Worcester, 1959. (Published as a pamphlet, Stellenbosch, 1959).

18. Address to the Canadian/South African Businessmen's Association. (*The Challenge Before Us*), Stellenbosch, 1960, p. 7.

19. From *Harvest*, translated by Guy Butler.

20. Translated by the present author.

12. *The Irony of Afrikaner History*

1. From *Slag-heap Ballad*, translated by William and Jean Branford.

2. Cf. Mumford, op. cit., chapter 10.

3. As reported in *Rapport*, 19 November 1972.

4. Calculated from Muriel Horrell's compilation: *Legislation and Race Relations*, op. cit., revised edition, 1971.

5. According to figures from the Department of Statistics in December 1972.

6. Horrel, op. cit., p. 46.

7. Prof. Ben Vosloo in *New Nation*, April 1972, p. 3 (*Ben Roux: In Memoriam*).

8. C. Northcote Parkinson's *Parkinson's Law or the Pursuit of Progress*, and Dr Lawrence J. Peter's *The Peter Principle: Why Things Always Go Wrong*, represent the redemptive value of humour at its most relevant level.

9. The reference is to Reinhold Niebuhr's book of that name.

10. The regular feature *Current Affairs* of the South African Broadcasting Corporation used the image on 28 March 1972. At the same time it denied that the policy of separate development was in any way bound to a blue-print. But man-made edifices of heroic proportion cannot arise any other way. No blue-print, no edifice.

11. Cf. David de Villiers, *The Case for South Africa*, Tom Stacey, 1970, pp. 52, 89.

12. ibid., pp. 89–90, where the 'hardships which may be involved' are seen as 'transitional by-products'.

13. V. I. Lenin, *The State and Revolution*, 1917, p. 94.

14. Cf. Camus, op. cit., Penguin edition, p. 103.

15. Cf. de Villiers, op. cit., p. 89.

16. Cf. a special article in the *Sunday Times*, 31 January 1971.

17. Cf. *South African Outlook*, June/July 1972.

18. This is Toynbean. Cf. Note 1, *The Coming of the* Burgerstand.

13. *Reality and Renewal*

1. Matthew, 10, 34.

2. Matthew, 5, 17.

3. Cf. Lenin's *Imperialism: The Highest Stage of Capitalism*, 1916.

4. As J. K. Galbraith has seen it in *The New Industrial State*, Hamish Hamilton, 1967.

5. Cf. Herbert Marcuse, *One Dimensional Man*, Routledge & Kegan Paul, 1964.

6. The reference is to Charles W. Reich's *The Greening of America*, Allen Lane, 1971.

7. From *The Anatomy of Apartheid*, by Pattie Price (1967).

8. Calvin, op. cit., 2:2:11.

9. I Cor. 3, 11.

10. Biéler, op. cit., p. 105.

11. N. P. van Wyk Louw, *Liberale Nasionalisme*, Cape Town, 1958, p. 20.

12. ibid., p. 91.

13. During the sixties, the dissident voices in Afrikaans literature among the younger generation expressed themselves in the *Sestiger* movement, combining eccentricity in styles with questionings on the Afrikaner ethic. Outstanding among them were Ingrid Jonker, Breyten Breytenbach (living in Paris with his Vietnamese wife as an expatriate), André Brink, Hennie Aucomp and Etienne le Roux.

14. The translation is the present author's, from the poem *Die Kind* (*The Child*).

15. Professor Keet's rejection of apartheid as a system in terms of the Reformed tradition is best represented by his book *Whither South Africa*, Cape Town, 1956. There is also his pamphlet *Die Etiek van Apartheid*, 1957, to be noted. The reference here is to the article 'Skeiding Tussen die Rasse' in *Die Kerkbode*, 24 July 1968.

16. J. J. F. Durand, *Swartman Stad en Toekoms*, Cape Town, 1970, p. 164.

17. Cf. *Woord en Daad*, April 1972, p. 6.

18. Degenaar's writings include *Op Weg na 'n nuwe politieke Lewenshouding*, Cape Town, 1963, and *Sekularisasie*, Cape Town, 1967. Social scientists, like S. P. Cilliers, (*An Appeal to Reason*, 1971), H. W. van der Merwe *et al*. have also played a significant role in the attempt to restore reason to Afrikaner politics.

19. The Moderator of the Reformed Church in the Netherlands, Dr A. Kouiswijk, attending the fourth four-yearly General Synod of the N.G. Church in Cape Town during October 1974, and referring to decisions taken by the synod on a report by a special commission (Chairman, W. A. Cardman) on race matters, saw the position in South Africa changing so rapidly, that he felt the synod should meet again within a year for the purposes of review. (Cf. the *Cape Times*, 27 October 1974). The meeting, still treading warily regarding issues like mixed marriages, immorality between the races, nevertheless adopted most of the Cardman commission's recommendations. The

spirit of this was best epitomized by paragraph 3.3.2. of the report (p. 245). The unity of the church is a oneness in Christ, it said. It is in community of faith, which transcends all differences; which at the same time should be experienced and practised in the concrete reality of the church's existence.

20. D. P. Botha, *Die Opkoms van ons Derde Stand*, Cape Town, 1960, p. 173.

21. Versfeld's often brilliant writings include *The Perennial Order*, Society of St Paul, London, 1954, *Rondom die Middeleeue*, Cape Town, 1962 and *Persons*, Cape Town, 1972. He has been a potent influence among Afrikaans writers in both literature and philosophy.

Index

363

More about Penguins and Pelicans

Penguinews, which appears every month, contains details of all the new books issued by Penguins as they are published. From time to time it is supplemented by *Penguins in Print*, which is our complete list of almost 5,000 titles.

A specimen copy of *Penguinews* will be sent to you free on request. Please write to Dept EP, Penguin Books Ltd, Harmondsworth, Middlesex, for your copy.

In the U.S.A.: For a complete list of books available from Penguin in the United States write to Dept CS, Penguin Books, 625 Madison Avenue, New York, New York 10022.

In Canada: For a complete list of books available from Penguin in Canada write to Penguin Books Canada Ltd, 41 Steelcase Road West, Markham, Ontario.

Which Way Africa?

THE SEARCH FOR A NEW SOCIETY

Basil Davidson

A man would have to be very brave or very foolhardy to try to forecast precisely the pattern of Africa's future. Where events outrun the printing-presses, discretion is the better part of omniscience.

In *Which Way Africa?* Basil Davidson, the well-known writer on African affairs, has steered clear of political ju-ju. Instead – and definitely more to the purpose – he has made what is the only up-to-date and comprehensive analysis in English – and probably in any language – of the social, economic, and political motives, myths, ideas, and beliefs which underlie modern African nationalism.

Events in almost every corner of the continent have shown the world an Africa poised on the threshold of new ventures, an Africa in flux. Only such an analysis as the author has successfully achieved in this volume can help to delineate the kind of societies which will now tend to emerge there.

Mozambique: Memoirs of a Revolution

Rev. John Paul

'Here is the character of Portuguese colonial rule drawn not in statutes and statistics or in the propaganda of apology or denunciation, but in the lives of its various victims, white and black . . . Here is recorded the rise of the Frelimo movement; alongside the decline of a régime whose moral nonsense made it rely increasingly on terror to survive, and whose increasing reliance on terror only nourished the challenge to its survival' – Ronald Segal

Penguin African Library

Rhodesia

WHITE RACISM AND IMPERIAL RESPONSE

Martin Loney

The late 1950s and early 1960s saw the rapid and, in most cases, peaceful decolonization of Africa. But today Rhodesia remains colonized, no longer controlled by the imperial power, but still governed by white settlers. Martin Loney describes the history of the colony and of the continuous African opposition to the invaders.

Central to his theme is the development of the power of the intransigent white rulers; in his words, 'this book is about the historical development of that power, the systematic use which has been made of it to build a prosperous white society in Africa, and the consequent impoverishment of the African population. It is also about the complicity of the British governments, Labour and Conservative, in this process.'

In its assessment of the British sell-out and of the growing sense of national identity on the part of the African population, this is a book which will upset many of the comfortable ideas held about Rhodesia in this country.

Southern Africa: The New Politics of Revolution

Basil Davidson, Joe Slovo and Anthony R. Wilkinson

Visiting Somalia in 1964, Chou En-lai remarked that 'revolutionary prospects throughout the African continent are excellent'. With the collapse of Portuguese rule in Angola and Mozambique, the capacity of Rhodesia and South Africa to resist the demands of black revolutionary nationalism was greatly reduced, and the future of white supremacy looks shakier today than ever before.

The three contributors to this volume, although differing in outlook, do much to illuminate the situation in Southern Africa after the Portuguese withdrawal. Basil Davidson describes the war against Portugal, showing how, during a hard-fought guerrilla campaign against an occupying power, the nationalist organizations were able to lay the foundations of a new society by involving the people themselves in their own struggle. Joe Slovo analyses the changes in South African policy that occurred in an attempt to meet the new challenge, laying stress on their concern for military security at a time when the liberation movement has turned to armed struggle to achieve its inevitable aims. Finally, Anthony R. Wilkinson discusses the increasingly untenable position of Rhodesia, surrounded on almost all sides by African states hostile to white supremacy and willing hosts to the nationalist guerrilla formations.